T0329912

The
Sport Business
Handbook

Insights From 100+ Leaders Who Shaped 50 Years of the Industry

Rick Horrow, JD
Horrow Sports Ventures
Editor

with

Rick Burton, MBA
Syracuse University

Myles Schrag, MS

HUMAN KINETICS

Library of Congress Cataloging-in-Publication Data

Names: Horrow, Richard B., editor. | Burton, Rick, editor.
Title: The sport business handbook : insights from 100+ leaders who shaped 50 years of the industry / edited by Rick Horrow with Rick Burton, Myles Schrag.
Description: Champaign, IL : Human Kinetics, [2020] | Includes bibliographical references and index.
Identifiers: LCCN 2018042572 (print) | LCCN 2018060826 (ebook) | ISBN 9781492587439 (epub) | ISBN 9781492543114 (PDF) | ISBN 9781492543107 (print)
Subjects: LCSH: Sports--Economic aspects. | Sports administration.
Classification: LCC GV716 (ebook) | LCC GV716 .S5854 2020 (print) | DDC 796.06/94--dc23a
LC record available at https://lccn.loc.gov/2018042572

ISBN: 978-1-4925-4310-7 (print)

The web addresses cited in this text were current as of January 2019, unless otherwise noted.

Acquisitions Editor: Andrew L. Tyler; **Managing Editor:** Amanda S. Ewing; **Copyeditor:** Joyce Sexton; **Indexer:** Nan N. Badgett; **Permissions Manager:** Martha Gullo; **Senior Graphic Designer:** Joe Buck; **Graphic Designer:** Whitney Milburn; **Cover Designer:** Keri Evans; **Cover Design Associate:** Susan Rothermel Allen; **Photograph (cover):** ithinksky/E+/Getty Images; **Photo Asset Manager:** Laura Fitch; **Photo Production Coordinator:** Jason Allen; **Printer:** Sheridan Books

Human Kinetics books are available at special discounts for bulk purchase. For details, contact the Special Sales Manager at Human Kinetics.

Printed in the United States of America   10 9 8 7 6 5 4 3 2 1

The paper in this book is certified under a sustainable forestry program.

Human Kinetics
P.O. Box 5076
Champaign, IL 61825-5076
Website: www.HumanKinetics.com

In the United States, email info@hkusa.com or call 800-747-4457.
In Canada, email info@hkcanada.com.
In the United Kingdom/Europe, email hk@hkeurope.com.

For information about Human Kinetics' coverage in other areas of the world, please visit our website: **www.HumanKinetics.com**

E6918

To my dad, who was taken too early, who gave me strength, perspective, and vision that still guides me today.
—Rick Horrow

Contents

Foreword

Mike Krzyzewski

Duke University Head Men's Basketball Coach

This book, while not exclusively about leadership, is a tangible reminder of how much there is to be learned from innovative and committed people such as my good friend Jerry Colangelo, the author of chapter 16. To be clear, he has been an integral part of my professional life and valuable in my lifelong pursuit of learning.

I often reflect on when Jerry asked me to lead USA Basketball in 2005. I've told the media this in the past, but it is worth repeating here in the context of this book written by a collection of leaders and reflecting their leadership skills.

He and I felt we were going to build this environment, this good culture, in USA Basketball. But everyone had to have ownership. It wasn't the players adapting to us. It was everyone adapting to each other. You take the best practices of everyone, and you incorporate that into what you're doing, under the core principles of humility, hard work, trust, and the understanding that we were playing for something bigger than ourselves.

As proud as Jerry and I are about winning the last five major competitions (three Olympics and two World Cups), which had never been done in the history of basketball, I'm proud of the way we've done it. There were never any incidents. The players were great ambassadors for our game worldwide and great ambassadors for our country. They got it. They were proud of it. They acted as though they were part of the game of basketball, and not bigger than the game of basketball individually. That's the message that has been sent by Chris Paul and Jason Kidd and LeBron James and Kobe Bryant and Kevin Durant, just to name a few. And it's a powerful message.

I tell the players I coach that two is greater than one, but only if two can act as one. That's what we were able to do, to naturally act as one.

I have learned a lot from Jerry about organization, how he treats people, how he reacts to partners. People don't even realize the money he's raised for USA Basketball. It's not even in the same universe as what had been done before. He's the real story of USA Basketball. It's about his love of the game and embracing great standards. He'll go down as good as anybody who's been through the game, and the players know it.

He commands respect without demanding respect. I really love him, and I love the fact that he had confidence in me.

He is clearly a legend in the sport business world, and in this book, you will also read about many others with their own experiences and perspective on leadership. Of particular interest, look closely at how the leaders express their core values and how thinking big is embedded into their leading of teams.

As leaders, we all want to do our best work. We all want to have our personal values and professional philosophies come together and be something we can share with others. In turn, the people we influence hopefully then personalize it and build a career doing their best work.

This book provides insights to help you achieve those goals. It should help you think ethically and intelligently in the world of sport and help answer the question, "What kind of leader do I want to be?"

No matter what role you have in your organization, you can be a leader and make a difference in the team's success.

Follow your heart!

Preface

Imagine getting the most influential individuals in the history of sport business together in one room. Think of the biggest names you can imagine. Commissioners, owners, entrepreneurs, marketing gurus, brilliant investors, savvy negotiators, great business brains (that in some cases also sit atop outstanding athletic bodies), right there for your edification. You can ask any of them any question you want. Pour one executive a beer and ask him to tell you a story about the biggest mistake he ever made. Then go to the next table and ask her what she sees as the next big trend in the industry. Pick another's brain on how to manage a crisis or how to get buy-in for a revolutionary arena plan. Listen to how mammoth television deals are negotiated. Candid insights, hard-earned advice, and no-nonsense tips for success from more than four millennia of industry experience are at hand.

That, in a nutshell, is what *The Sport Business Handbook* contains: the greatest collection of sport business professionals ever assembled under one roof. And they are sitting in your conference room, ready for you to look to as needed. The sport industry has grown exponentially in the past 50 years, and this roster of authors I have asked to join us includes many who directly affected some part of that growth. This is a legacy project, a mastermind amalgam created by a generous group of more than 100 successful leaders who want to help you better navigate your place, discover your strengths, and develop your skills in the profession you have chosen—the dynamic, volatile business of sport.

I have had the good fortune of sharing significant face time with the people in this book. Why shouldn't you? They have willingly provided their knowledge to you with no compensation. Royalties are going to Special Olympics Maryland, not into contributors' pockets. They wanted to be part of this unparalleled collection in order to generously share their insights. Although these are perpetually busy people who are in demand, they were overwhelmingly gracious with their time and opinions. One of the unexpected joys of this process was the opportunity to explain the book's purpose with prospective contributors and pitch topics for them to cover that were challenging for them. We editors collaborated with them on content, each listening to the other's goals and passions related to sport business and how those aligned with this project. In every case, we found an excellent fit between chapter topic and contributor. In many cases, I believe chapters were made stronger because of these preliminary discussions with contributors. Their commitment to quality and completion, and a persistent curiosity, make it no wonder these folks have been so successful.

The result of pulling together these insights into one place is a win for readers like you, and for the industry as a whole. The chapters are grouped together into five parts, progressing from the personal assessment needed to launch your career (part I) to building your capabilities in the fundamental skills of selling and branding (part II), to technology and media awareness and activation (part III), and finally to deal making (part IV) and leadership skills (part V)—all these will be put to the test as you become an increasingly influential contributor to the industry.

In this book, we use "sport business" as a broad term to encompass all people and organizations that are involved in producing, facilitating, or promoting sport products. Sport products can include goods, services, activities, people, places, and ideas that focus on fitness, recreation, athletics, or leisure (Pedersen and Thibault 2019). The plural term "sports business" is sometimes used in the field as well, especially in a professional context.

Each of the 27 chapters tackles an essential topic that all those who want to be a force in sport business will face early and often in their career—and often when they least expect it. Through personal self-reflection and practical advice from people who have indelibly shaped the multibillion-dollar sport world that exists today, you will learn how to set yourself up for success. Learn how to network, honestly assess your strengths and weaknesses, and create a business philosophy. Discover how the experts handle important decisions and assess their surroundings to ensure they and their constituents act responsibly and decisively. Chapter contributors honestly acknowledge their failures and celebrate their successes as they outline the most substantial issues, trends, and challenges related to the chapter topic, with their suggestions, takeaway points, and solutions for navigating challenges along the way. They share tips that will help you achieve the goals you set for yourself and your organization.

Engaging sidebars provide insights from contributors who have left their indelible marks, often behind the scenes, on enhancing sport's production and power in the world. In the Game Changer sidebars, contributors share the life-changing moments in which their sport business career was irrevocably set on a new and rewarding path. In the 360 sidebars, contributors offer a different take on the chapter topic—a viewpoint that is sometimes contrary or counterintuitive. Readers are reminded through these sidebars that there are multiple paths to handling challenges. In this book, you will discover how and where to find the answers you need in the way that best suits your style and philosophy, straight from the voices who shaped your industry.

I have compiled clips of interviews that I've done on my media platforms with some of the subjects who contributed to this book. These clips are easily searchable online at www.thesportbusinesshandbook.com.

The book's 100-plus editors and contributors share these experiences to showcase the legacy of the past 50 years and how far the industry has come. Where will the next 50 years take us? The writers of this book will help you get there. The readers of this book—that includes *you*—will help us get there.

Rick Horrow
Miami, Florida
June 2018

INSTRUCTOR RESOURCE

An instructor guide is available for those who adopt this book for use in the classroom. See "Instructor's Note" that follows. The instructor guide is available at www.HumanKinetics.com/TheSportBusinessHandbook.

References

Pedersen, P.M., and Thibault, L. 2019. *Contemporary Sport Management*, 6th ed. Champaign, IL: Human Kinetics.

Instructor's Note

This book has been written so as to be a valuable reference book for sport professionals and an engaging read for anybody interested in listening to insiders in the sport industry discuss how they do what they do in the provocative, high-energy world of sport. We are aware that many instructors in secondary and higher education want to bring an applied approach to their sport management and sport business courses. If you are an instructor, you will find much in the pages of *The Sport Business Handbook* to help you prepare for your courses.

This book's package of skill building and industry knowledge to help readers on their way to a successful career is aided by an instructor guide prepared by Lee Igel and Elizabeth Haas Edersheim, both faculty at the prestigious Tisch Center for Hospitality, Tourism and Sports Management at New York University. They have curated a list of transcendental moments in sport business, with questions for instructors and students to consider when evaluating and assessing the moments' roles in sport history for classroom discussion or assignments. Some of these moments are well known; others will be news to many readers. All have left an impact. The intent of this collection of moments is to provide a historical context for the explosion of interest in sport economically, socially, and politically over the past 50 years. The book itself is driven by the stories and perspectives of major players in the industry. These breakthrough moments were captured for instructors who want to provide their students with a greater chronological understanding of the field, including how the moments played a role in future developments, what type of changes these moments helped spawn, and what sectors of sport business these moments were in. In addition, Harvard Business School Professor Emeritus Dr. Stephen Greyser has provided a commentary titled "Sport Business in the Classroom," which sets this book contextually within the academic history of sport business during roughly this same period of time. Dr. Greyser's perspective helps to show how this book can be used in applied sport management courses of various kinds, including capstones, courses that emphasize case studies, experiential learning opportunities, and internships. The instructor guide is available at www.HumanKinetics.com/TheSportBusinessHandbook.

Rick Horrow has compiled clips of interviews that he has done on his media platforms with some of the subjects who contributed to this book. These clips are easily searchable online at www.thesportbusinesshandbook.com. Whether in video or audio format, these clips are an outstanding opportunity to hear directly the voices of the authors whose words the students are reading. This brings to life the insights the authors are sharing, lending credibility to the applied course you are teaching. Discussion questions in the instructor guide provide you support in ensuring students will contribute to the classroom and consider the book's insights long after they use it in your course.

We are excited that the book can be used by readers for a variety of purposes. We hope that our instructor resources ensure you make the most out of our content to provide for the needs of your students.

Acknowledgments

First and foremost, I want to thank my dad, Ben Horrow, for giving me direction to be a pioneer even though he passed when I was only 11 years old. Thanks also to my family: Terri, Katie, Caroline, and Steve, as well as Oliver, Ethan, and Graham. And the Joneses, Hardens, Rendelmans, and Cunninghams, my extended family who provided support and understanding.

My staff and coworkers, including Karla Swatek, Betty Curbelo, Tanner Simkins, Jamie Swimmer, Jacob Aere, and (intern) David Cunningham, performed tireless work on this project and everything else going on at Horrow Sports Ventures.

I have been fortunate to have many people who, at various points in time, helped start, direct, and advocate for my journey in business and life: former U.S. Senator Bob Graham; former Oklahoma City Mayor Ron Norick; former Miami Mayor Maurice Ferre; Parker Thompson, Esq.; Larry Turner, Esq.; Nick Buoniconti, Esq.; Charles Mechem, Esq.; Phoenix sport legend Jerry Colangelo; baseball sport legend Larry Lucchino; agents extraordinaire Donald Dell and Bob Kain; NASCAR brain trust Brian France, Bryan Sperber, and Lesa France Kennedy; Dolphins owner Steve Ross; NHL Commissioner Gary Bettman; NFL Commissioners Paul Tagliabue and Roger Goodell; Philadelphia Eagles owner Jeff Lurie; Harvard Law professors Paul Weiler and Jim Vorenberg; Northwestern University debate coach David Zarefsky, and Group 1001 CEO Dan Towriss.

Other friends have provided strength and confidence through enduring friendship, including Mickey Saltman, Ted Killory, Scott Michel, Ted Abrams, Harry Klaff, Steve Lerner, and U.S. Supreme Court Chief Justice John Roberts.

Still other friends and mentors have provided real support in the public domain, media, and elsewhere: Bernie Rosen; Scott Ferrall; Dan Colarusso; Mark Lazarus; University of Oklahoma Athletics Director Joe Castiglione; John Terenzio; and Tom Reilly (who helped coin the moniker "The Sports Professor").

Friends and mentors who are no longer with us provide a reminder that life is precious and should not be taken for granted: baseball legend Gary Carter; entrepreneur and businessman Doug Wood; Miami Beach debate coach Ralph Carey; and radio legend Andrew Ashwood.

Mentors, peers, and friends who have achieved this level of success do so because they surround themselves with talented, excellent team players. For this book to become a reality, there were dozens of administrative assistants, public relations and communications specialists, advisors, legal counsels, executives, photographers, and illustrators who provided support for the contributors who joined our effort. We thank all of those who helped us stay on track toward publication.

Also a big thank-you to Brian Holding and Myles Schrag of Human Kinetics, who helped create the vision and make this book come alive; other HK staff who worked to publish this book you are now reading; and Rick Burton, whose writing and reviewing skills helped to ensure that the final product is everything it should be.

Part I

Launching Your Career in Sport Business

If you want to be part of the sport industry and ensure that its growth continues in a positive way—and even more to the point, that your organization or segment does the same—that goal starts with individuals like you. This first part lays the groundwork for the book by giving you the opportunity to consider what role you want to play, what your values are, and how you can set yourself up for success with standards that are important to you. Editor Rick Horrow opens by sharing his journey into the world of sport some 50 years ago and discusses how finding one's niche in that sphere always has required a bit of ingenuity, of being a craftsperson. His chapter ends with a challenge for you to self-assess. Using examples from the life of Roger Staubach, who has achieved success as an athlete, as a naval officer, as a businessman, and most importantly, as a husband, father, and grandfather, this section offers you the chance to navigate sport, business, and yourself in your own personal SWOT analysis.

Chapter 2 by Larry Lucchino is a commencement of sorts for you as you embark on your journey through this book and in the sport industry. Adapted from his own graduation address at Boston University when he was president of the Boston Red Sox, Lucchino offers essential lessons for the sport business professional. Lyn St. James closes out part I with her powerful story of relentlessly fostering meaningful business relationships by consistently being willing to relate to people and to "put herself out there." She provides a great reminder right from the outset that networking doesn't just come from going to a prestigious school or having influential family and friends. Rather, networking happens when you trust in yourself enough to open your mouth and share your story.

Horrow, Lucchino, and St. James address issues of integrity, core values, and developing your own personal philosophy. You will find that we return to these

foundations often throughout the book. In 27 chapters, the epilogue, and sidebars, it is hard not to notice how often these successful people return to those
concepts when making decisions and developing partnerships. It is hard—maybe
impossible—to be successful, to maintain and to be proud of that success, and
to make a positive difference in the world if you have not grounded yourself in
these ideas.

Rick Horrow

CHAPTER 1

Mastering the Craft of Sport Business

Rick Horrow

Editor Rick Horrow is CEO of Horrow Sports Ventures, host and executive producer of *Power of Sports* on FOX Sports, and host of the *Keeping Score* podcast on Thomson Reuters. He also serves as a sport business analyst for a number of other media outlets, including CNN, TNN, Yahoo! Finance, Bloomberg, NBC Sports Radio, and BBC World Service. His professionalism in creating relationships and effective partnerships in sport business and law over the past half century formed the impetus for more than 100 contributors to take part in this book.

One of my last memories of my father was of him buying four tickets (the face value of each, as I recall, was $5) for the family to see the season opener for the expansion Miami Dolphins of the American Football League. That was early in 1966, about eight months before the September 2 game at the Orange Bowl. Dad never did get to use his ticket. He was diagnosed with melanoma, which spread quickly and took him on March 11. I think of Dad often when Miami sports are on my mind, which is to say, I think of Dad often. Just four years later, in 1970, I distinctly remember sitting on a dock and looking across to downtown Miami from my home. I imagined an indoor arena there, like the Houston Astrodome or the Superdome being planned in New Orleans that had yet to break ground but sounded even bigger and better. I envisioned a home for pro baseball, basketball, and hockey teams to join the Dolphins in South Florida. Even though I was only a sophomore in high school, and even though there were virtually no collegiate academic tracks in sport law or sport business—certainly none that I had heard of—on some level I had already committed myself to transferring my passion for sport into a calling, a business.

In 1970, the average Major League Baseball salary was $29,303, a 30-second TV ad in the Super Bowl was $72,500, and virtually every NFL game was played on Sundays. Ground was broken on Schaefer Stadium (later named Foxboro Stadium) in Massachusetts, which would cost $7.1 million to build, using no public monies (Stadiums, "Foxboro" n.d.), while two of the infamous "cookie-cutter" stadiums were opened—Riverfront Stadium in Cincinnati, at a price tag of $50 million (Stadiums, "Riverfront" n.d.), and Three Rivers Stadium in Pittsburgh, for $55 million (Stadiums, "Three Rivers" n.d.). The New York Knicks' thrilling game 7 victory over the Los Angeles Lakers in the NBA Finals—famous for Willis Reed's stunning performance with a severely torn thigh muscle—was not seen live on broadcast TV in New York City because the local ABC affiliate blacked out the game.

Fast-forward to today, and the numbers could not be more staggeringly different (table 1.1). The average MLB salary for 2018 is $4.52 million, the Super Bowl fetches more than $5 million per 30-second spot, and $1 billion stadiums are de rigeur: US Bank Stadium opened in Minneapolis in 2016 for $1.1 billion (Stadiums, "US Bank" n.d.), and Mercedes-Benz Stadium in Atlanta opened in 2017 at a cost of $1.5 billion (Stadiums, "Mercedes-Benz" n.d.). Is it any wonder that mastering the craft of sport business is a much more complex goal today than it was when I was entering college? A craft is a special skill, like that of a mason or a silversmith. It's true that the world of sport, whether the high-stakes, competitiveness of professionals and elites or a local nonprofit or club looking to boost numbers, is simply a sector of the business world. But even before the hyperinterest in sport really took hold in the past 50 years, navigating the business of sport has always been fundamentally different. Many business principles apply, but to ignore the idiosyncrasies of sport today is to ask to be left behind. If you're going to be a craftsperson, it's best to have mentors to guide you. Reading this book, you will encounter some of the most successful mentors during a period in which sport has catapulted from a developing industry into a global force.

I first met some of these leaders when I was charting my path in the sport industry. I didn't know it then, but I was already following some of the advice that they present in these pages. I had a vision for where I wanted to go, and I charted a course (revising as necessary along the way). I sought out advice. I worked hard. I was learning a craft; mastery does not happen overnight.

FOUR CHARACTERISTICS OF THE SPORT BUSINESS

I also took chances. When I didn't see an opening, I chiseled my way through and created one. Not too many years after looking at the Miami skyline, after graduating from Northwestern and entering Harvard Law School, I had an inspiring and entrepreneurial law professor named Jim Vorenberg. After my first criminal law class with him in September 1976, I told him how I honestly felt. I already knew I was not interested in private law practice. But I had a proposition for him. I didn't play squash, but I had heard he was an avid player. I challenged

TABLE 1.1   Sport Industry, 1970 Versus 2018

Category	1970	2018
Price of a 30-second Super Bowl ad	$72,500[a]	$5,000,000+[a]
MLB average salary	$29,303[b]	$4,520,000[c]
MLB minimum salary	$12,000[b]	$545,555[b]
Super Bowl peak ticket price	$15 face value (adjusted to $91.52 with inflation today)[d]	$5,000[e]

[a]http://superbowl-ads.com/cost-of-super-bowl-advertising-breakdown-by-year

[b]www.baseball-reference.com/bullpen/Minimum_salary

[c]www.usatoday.com/story/sports/mlb/columnist/bob-nightengale/2018/03/28/mlb-salaries-2018-average-salary-payrolls/466592002

[d]http://bleacherreport.com/articles/1041324-ranking-the-average-ticket-price-of-every-super-bowl-since-1966#slide5

[e]https://sports.yahoo.com/face-value-super-bowl-lii-ticket-prices-revealed-seats-range-950-5000-012957369.html

Revenues and expenses: Back in the 1970s, ticket sales accounted for almost 60 percent of football's total revenue; today broadcast contracts account for about half of income (www.usnews.com/news/blogs/press-past/2013/02/01/us-news-questioned-pro-footballs-future-nearly-45-years-ago).

The average revenue of each NFL club in 1967 was $3.8 million ($23.8 million adjusted) (www.forbes.com/sites/forbespr/2016/09/14/forbes-announces-19th-annual-nfl-team-valuations).

The average expenses of each club were $3.2 million (www.forbes.com/sites/forbespr/2016/09/14/forbes-announces-19th-annual-nfl-team-valuations).

The Dallas Cowboys had $840 million in revenue in 2017. The Patriots came in second at $575 million in revenue followed by the Giants at $477 million (www.forbes.com/nfl-valuations/list). The average value of an NFL franchise increased by 8 percent over the previous year, according to the annual evaluation conducted by Forbes, coming in at $2.5 billion (www.usatoday.com/story/sports/nfl/2017/09/18/cowboys-again-lead-forbes-list-nfl-most-valuable-franchises/677935001).

him to a match. If I won, when it was time for me to write my thesis I would get to write on my topic of choice, the legal issues pertaining to fighting in hockey. If he won, I would take tort law, case law, and all the other staples of a Harvard Law education, and I would shut up about sports.

Vorenberg responded with an assertion and a rhetorical question: "There's no such thing as sport law and we don't teach it here. Second, what do I have to lose?"

I managed to defeat him, and if I forgot to tell you he was 81 years old at the time, in the name of honesty let me disclose that now. I don't recommend you take this approach with your professors today, but the result of that fateful proposal has propelled me forward ever since. It put me on a path to define the undefined for myself. I took the road less traveled to assist in defining a business that has grown to what some experts say is more than a trillion dollars annually (Medium 2017).

John Roberts coached me the next two years—in squash, not school—as I wrote and eventually defended my thesis. (Yes, that's right. Before Chief Justice

Roberts was managing the most exclusive and influential judicial body in the democratic world, he was just John, my fellow Harvard Law classmate, sentenced to rooming with me, my smelly socks, and my incessant trash talking. His skills in diplomacy and clearheadedness were put to the test early and often from 1977 to 1979, and the rest is history.)

There are four characteristics that mark the sport industry:

1. *It was the Wild West.* My friend Bob Ruxin wrote a seminal book in 1982, *An Athlete's Guide to Agents.* He quoted Bob Woolf, agent of hockey player Derek Sanderson, as saying, "The only qualification of being an agent is that you have an athlete who calls you an agent." No definitions, no terms, no requirements. I saw that as an opportunity, not an impediment. This characteristic is certainly nowhere near as much a part of the mix now as it was then. Regulations, professional education, higher education, and networking connections are far greater. But this is still a young industry.

2. *Every aspect of sport is scrutinized.* This characteristic is surely as prevalent as it ever was. We now have more studies and commentary about business and spreadsheets than Xs and Os. Off-field issues receive more ink and screen time than ever. Angles for sport coverage appear not just on the sports page, but also as political issues, marketing events, and news stories devoted to transgressions, cover-ups, and the like. There is an ongoing set of legal and business principles that are applied to the most visible facts and circumstances when the information deals with the million-dollar athlete and the billion-dollar owner. It's the court of law as much as the tennis or basketball court that interests people, and the emotional connection people feel for their teams and athletes is a business and community imperative for sport business professionals.

3. *The labels of sport business defy traditional analysis.* A corollary to item 2, how articles and sport-based courses are labeled still matters, but there is much more overlap of stories and classes now. For most big-dollar industries, public interest is segmented into only the most relevant information that affects people's lives, and it has been established for much longer than 50 years. In most fields, a set of parameters grows up around them, but it's all considered business. How we study and practice in this industry is accurately called *sport* business: sport business, politics and sport, sport psychology, sport administration, sporting endorsements, anthropology of sport, and a host of other disciplines around sport issues.

4. *The sport industry is defined by changing circumstances.* The business in many ways is defined most by changing circumstances. The world at large is of course influenced by social media, and business has become more global. In sport, this is writ large. The industry changes more regularly these days largely because it is so visible. Everyone wants to be in it, and that in turn spawns other business opportunities.

The Sport Business Handbook is a 50-year history of the evolution, the legacy, the overlapping, and the resilience of this burgeoning and booming industry, as well as collected advice on how to get into and excel in it from the visionaries, philanthropists, lawyers, marketers, technology experts, and communicators who made it so. They have their own defining entertaining moments and their own perspectives on what the future holds. They can't see everything on the horizon, but their experience is worthy of study.

In 1970, the AFL officially merged with the NFL, ABC first aired Monday Night Football, Muhammad Ali returned to boxing after being banned from the sport, and Curt Flood had just begun his challenge to baseball's reserve clause. The protests of the Mexico City Olympics were still swirling in the air, and along with expansion teams, rival leagues, and the ascent of television and more sophisticated marketing and storytelling techniques, seismic events in sport history were becoming increasingly common. From an academic perspective, the first sport administration program in the United States, at Ohio University, was just four years old. Modern sport business had arrived.

It's convenient to label the start of an era with certainty. We humans like nice round numbers, and as I've already stated, that was a formative time for me personally. Still, as the examples I have mentioned show, a new period of sport was unquestionably dawning at the start of the Me Decade. I'm not asking you to agree with me that modern sport business began in exactly 1970. I simply want to set the context for the rest of this book, which is a recognition of a half century of modern sport business and, I hope, a guide for the next half century. Give or take.

SOME GET IT . . . SOME DON'T

There are a number of people who are not in this book but are important, at least to me, for helping to define the issues in sport business.

- Bill Ford Jr., owner of the Detroit Lions, who made a strategic decision to bring the Lions back from Pontiac, Michigan, to Ford Field when the economics and political pressure were pushing the other way. The downtown renaissance of that singular American city followed.

- Edwin Pope, sports editor at the *Miami Herald* who pushed to get pro sports in South Florida when the notion was criticized as a venture in which first-generation transplants who already gave at the political office wouldn't contribute further. He was right; his critics were wrong.

- Former Richmond Mayor and current Virginia Senator Tim Kaine, who pushed to develop a comprehensive infrastructure plan for sport and entertainment economic development across Virginia.

- Chief Justice Roberts, my roommate who always encouraged me to follow my dreams and is passionate about the contribution of sport to providing a community good.

- On the other hand, Norman Braman, former owner of the Philadelphia Eagles, sold the team, and as a car dealer extraordinaire in Miami funded every referendum in South Florida that discouraged sport facility development.

A 50-YEAR FRONT-ROW SEAT

Ted Killory

Ted Killory joined Harvard Law School and sport business at around the same time as Rick Horrow, and he remembers the growth of the industry fondly. Killory practiced law for 30 years in the Washington, D.C., office of the international law firm WilmerHale. His practice has included working closely with technology and media companies, high-stakes litigation and regulatory matters, pro bono civil rights cases, and assisting colleagues on behalf of pro sport franchises. He now serves as general counsel to a privately held company with roots in the media business. To his chagrin, but not surprise, his playing tours in Europe and the Caribbean with the Harvard Classics basketball team were the peak, rather than the launching pad, of his athletic career.

Looking back 50 years, it seems almost quaint to recall the early days of the "business of sport." Other than the tech industry, perhaps no industry in our lifetime has undergone such a dramatic evolution. I have had the pleasure of witnessing that meteoric growth from multiple perspectives.

1. First and foremost, I have been a sports fan (hard not to be, growing up in Boston) and a lifelong student of the media.

2. Second, I had a window into the ground floor of the explosion of the sport business as a classmate and friend of Rick Horrow's at Harvard Law School, where he essentially invented sport law as a respectable academic discipline.

3. And finally, in my three decades as a lawyer at an elite Washington law firm, I have had the privilege of working with a host of talented colleagues who have gone on to serve as senior executives with NFL teams and other national sport enterprises, with my partner and now president of the Baltimore Ravens, Dick Cass, leading that dramatic professionalization of the business of sport.

To comprehend the enormity of that revolutionary change over the past 50 years, one need only reflect on the pre-1970s sport landscape. To paraphrase the late Tip O'Neill, almost all sports were local. My local pro football team—the then Boston Patriots—was owned by a local former sportswriter and PR guy who had pulled together the princely $25,000 AFL franchise fee. The players came from elsewhere but felt like locals because many worked at local insurance agencies or car dealerships in the off-season to make ends meet. And for a home stadium, those early Patriots bounced around among three local college fields that seated as few as 10,000 fans.

In those pre-cable, pre-Internet days of only three network channels, the sport universe beyond our local horizon consisted largely of the iconic ABC Saturday afternoon show that was must-see TV for my baby boomer cohort with a young Roone Arledge as producer. In a stroke of visionary branding it was ambitiously titled *Wide World of Sports*. In addition to a ragtag collection of log rolling competitions, curling, and demolition derby, it gave us the first televised (and usually abbreviated) glimpses of Wimbledon tennis, U.S. figure skating, World Cup skiing, British Open golf, and the NCAA Men's Basketball Tournament, for which the licensing fees presumably were minimal.

It is no surprise that when Rick Horrow told his late-1970s Harvard classmates that he intended to pursue "sport law and business," more than a few doubted his sanity. But over the ensuing decades—from my front-row seat at a law firm that was at the intersection of sport, law, and business—I have been privileged to see the explosive growth of the field that Rick helped grow. Bolstered by national and international media deals, stadium development projects, and even stadium naming rights deals that, standing alone, are worth many times the value of 1970 pro franchises, the sport business has become an enormous global enterprise that exceeds anything imagined 50 years ago.

While some may nostalgically yearn a bit for those "Wild West" days when pro franchises were available for the price of a nice suburban house, the reality is that the global business of sport now attracts sophisticated owners and a class of executives, professionals, and deal makers the equal of those at any top investment bank or Fortune 100 company. Rick Horrow, along with many of the contributors to this book, was one of the visionaries who helped create that sport revolution. Which is not to say that his many friends don't occasionally still question his sanity.

His mindset was if he couldn't get a new stadium in Philly, he was not going to allow one in Miami.

- Paul Finebaum, a sports radio and television personality in the Southeast, led a campaign against an Oklahoma City–type proposal in Birmingham, Alabama. As Ron Norick explains in chapter 18, the MAPS initiative was a tried-and-true way to develop community infrastructure. We now celebrate the new Mercedes-Benz Stadium in Atlanta. Birmingham was economically ahead of Atlanta 50 years ago but is far behind now. Such inward thinking is one reason why.

- Hank Goldberg, an ESPN pundit and advertising executive in South Florida, spoke against the value of sports there because he was shut out of advertising money.

- El Paso Mayor Oscar Leeser, who tried to undo the work of his predecessor, John Cook, in passing the most comprehensive public–private infrastructure bond issue for sports and entertainment development. Leeser did not believe in its implementation as it was done before he was elected. In fact, he is leading an effort trying to undo the commitment of building a multipurpose sports and entertainment arena in El Paso, which was part of the package that the voters approved in 2012.

You can probably see my personal bias in these specific examples, both in the geographic regions represented and in the emphasis on the importance of facilities. I see the development of sport facilities as akin to building a house: So many positive things can occur only once the structure is in place.

Whatever issue you can name in sport business, there are many examples of viewpoints and decisions made with either a clear understanding or misguided views of the big picture and the good of the community. You and I might argue about some of those choices, and we must acknowledge there is significant controversy about what roles sport does play, and should play, at all levels of society. The bottom line for me is that people in positions of power must overcome petty jealousies and disagreements. They should serve as visionaries who debate and cooperate with others to push initiatives forward. This is what leaders do.

WORKING TOGETHER

In contrast to other businesses, where executives compete in the board room, most of the sport industry is aligned with the common goal of rapid growth. Maybe because it is still young or maybe because the alignment of issues is clearer than in other industries, the people in it work together because they know their common enemy is complacency. That is why maximizing the fan experience and doing good work through sport are consistent themes throughout this book. We will pull together a number of other themes for you in the Epilogue.

Sport is a dynamic industry, an industry of best practices. This book is the most comprehensive collection of these ever assembled, which is good for you because here is the reality: Everybody is trying to get into sport. More than 1,000 sport studies and sport business–related higher education programs exist around the world under a large array of names: sport management, sport administration, sport marketing, leadership in sport, sport law, sport in society, global sport business, with corresponding courses in management, law, ethics, finance, marketing, media, communication, sales, negotiating, public relations, human resources, analytics, consumer behavior, organizational theory and behavior, advertising, and on and on.

Forty years ago, it took a squash game against a very old and accomplished man to persuade him to allow me to write a sport-centered thesis. Studying sport in universities today is much more codified, but entrepreneurial principles still apply and are presented here for people like you who want to get in, stay in, and get better, or, at the least, just read about a fascinating economic and cultural history of the modern era. As I said at the outset of the chapter, sport is thousands of times bigger than it was in 1970. The business of sport is now more than $1 trillion, compared to less than $100 million 50 years ago. If we take 1970 as our semiarbitrary starting point, how much bigger—and better—might the sport industry be when we craftsmen and craftswomen celebrate our 75th anniversary?

HARVARD LAW THESIS: A POSTSCRIPT

If our common enemy in sport business is indeed complacency, let my Harvard Law thesis serve as a reminder that putting your vision into motion can create ripples for you that extend far beyond your little pond. Once Dr. Vorenberg had sponsored my thesis on the legal aspects of hockey fighting and it was published by the law school, that exposure led me to become a key witness on a federal hearing on sport violence when I was just 25 years old. It seemed a dramatic event to me at the time. Even though the topic under debate—what constituted acceptable, that is, *aggressive* violence versus unacceptable, or *excessive,* violence—seemed overblown and didn't reflect my true position as a fan, it gave me an opportunity to get inside the sport tent.

Back in South Florida, I was hired by a law firm, which recruited me on the theory that I had solid training in commercial legislation. As the reader no doubt can deduce, I didn't last long. After five days, I decided to leave. I contacted Bob Graham, a Miami politician soon to be governor of Florida, whom I had met at a high school awards ceremony years earlier. I sought advice from him, and we both agreed that if we secured sport facilities in the city and state, pro teams would follow. That argument was validating to me. I asked if I could do free work for him, identifying how other communities pursued franchises. After half a year, I wrote a white paper that recommended the development of the South Florida/Miami Sports and Exhibition Authority, a governmental agency dedicated to building facilities and attracting franchises. I became its first executive director when it became an official entity under Governor Graham. Nick Buoniconti, who had just finished his hall of fame career with the Dolphins, had a similar vision for the region and gave me a job. I quickly realized that I had plenty of options to pursue my passion.

Pursuing it was not always easy, especially at first. Initially, I took my budding experience and sought out eight regional sport authorities, with 65 elected officials and 420 civic officials appointed to those groups serving as my bosses. In seven of those instances, those sport authorities were disbanded or defunded or passed to other jurisdictions only to be forgotten. In business, though, 1 for 8 is not a bad batting average so long as that one hit leads to something bigger. The lessons I took away from the early days of Horrow Sport Ventures were to be tenacious, to be comfortable with peaks and valleys, and to seek out people whose vision aligns with one's own. Whether being at the ground floor of a venture or helping a growing project gain traction because of your abilities, the sport business and communities benefit through competent and motivated individuals working on aspiring and ethical teams.

Soon after Horrow Sports Ventures was launched, I started coteaching a class in sport law at my alma mater. What a difference a decade makes. And as this book goes to press, my daughter Caroline's first year at Harvard Law School is under way. What a difference a half century makes.

SPORTS EVOKE OUR EMOTIONAL EXTREMES

Scott D. Michel

Scott D. Michel was shaped by sports as a child and an adult as much as his Northwestern University classmate, Rick Horrow. After graduating from the University of Virginia School of Law and clerking for a federal judge, Michel has practiced tax controversy law at Caplin & Drysdale in Washington and New York since 1981, including eight years as Caplin's managing member. He represents individuals and corporations in sensitive tax matters, and he is internationally recognized for his expertise in addressing unreported offshore accounts and assets. Michel is adjunct professor at the University of Miami School of Law and is a Fellow of the American College of Tax Counsel.

Rick Horrow outside the first office of the Dade County Sports Authority in November 1981, shortly after it opened for business.

Rick Horrow's magnetic enthusiasm for sports became a welcome addition to my life at Northwestern with him in the mid-'70s. We bonded over Smokie Links at Wrigley Field and beers at every available Chicago sport venue. Later I watched his career grow from a small office in the Dupont Plaza Hotel in Miami to now, as one of the most recognized and successful figures at the intersection of sport, law, business, and media.

Our nearly 50 years of friendship has caused me to reflect on the impact of sport. It entertains us, reveals incredible athletic skill and grace, conveys the value of hard work and discipline, and sometimes exposes tragic human flaws. But it is the emotional impact that is deepest and most intense, especially on our memories and personal history, and on our bonds with family and friends.

Most people can summon their earliest sport moments—for me, Roger Maris' 61st home run on a motel black and white TV. Then Browns versus Colts for the NFL Championship; I'm in bed with the mumps. Listening from Louisiana to Chick Hearn broadcasts ("In and out, heartbreak!"). A Summer Olympics opening ceremony, in living color! The Texas Longhorns (my parents' alma mater) winning the national championship, the tower then lit burnt orange with lights in the shape of the number 1. But in every one of these flashes, I see not just the TV screen. I see my parents, my siblings, and my friends.

More than anything recently (even realizing a dream—seeing Max Scherzer pitch a no-hitter for my beloved Washington Nationals), the Houston Astros' triumph in the 2017 World Series triggered these emotions. The Astros were like a member of my family when I was a kid. My father took me to Colts Stadium, where, in the humidity and amid the mosquitos, I came to love baseball. Summer nights meant Gene Elston on a radio under my pillow. (I kept score in Gene's special scorebook, which I ordered by mail, as did Rick.) I still see vividly my first view of the magnificent Astrodome, and also in the image is my dad driving the station wagon. I revered the home run scoreboard, celebrated my 10th birthday there with family, and attended both All-Star Games, the second one with Rick.

My mother was a huge fan, and our family suffered the Astros together. We mourned the devastating 1980 playoff loss while together in Houston for the funeral of a great aunt, who Mom just knew had laid a curse upon the team. I endured the 16-inning loss in Game 6 in 1986 in New York surrounded by Mets fans, then called Mom to commiserate. She and I were together with my brothers and sister for the last game in the Dome, their 1999 playoff loss. Each time, my mother would offer solace—"Y'all, they just got tired."

So as I watched game 7 in 2017, emotions stretched, texting family and friends, I just knew how ecstatic Blanche Michel would have been to see that final out. The 'Stros did not get tired. The tears I felt that night, and the emotions that stirred so deeply, are, as Rick knows, the best of what sport has to offer. It connects our memories, our loved ones, and one another, for all of time.

NAVIGATING SPORT, BUSINESS, AND SELF: YOUR PERSONAL SWOT ANALYSIS

You've heard some of my story. Now let's transition into your evolving story. I close this chapter by giving you the opportunity to reflect on what you want to get out of your investment of time and energy into our industry and, just as importantly, what you want to give back.

Sport business has its own peculiarities, and yet it goes without saying that it is part of a larger business ecosystem. Whether in North America or elsewhere around the globe, no matter what segment of business you might be involved in, a perpetual curiosity about yourself is important. Regular check-ins—as with a dentist or an oil change—are critical if you are to make the most of your career.

From afar, it seemed to me that one individual always exemplified success by consciously doing this: Roger Staubach. A Heisman Trophy–winning quarterback at the Naval Academy, Dallas Cowboys quarterback selected to six Pro Bowls, Super Bowl VI MVP, naval officer in the United States and Vietnam, executive chairman for the pioneering global real estate advisory firm of The Staubach Company, executive chairman of Jones Lang LaSalle Americas (JLL), husband, father, grandfather . . . Staubach is driven. He has shown himself to be a leader and a hard worker in every aspect of his life to get positive results.

He identified the following five values as anchor for The Holloway Staubach Company when it was created in 1977:

1. Balance
2. Teamwork
3. Respect
4. Integrity
5. Leadership

The sport business industry continues to grow annually, both in popularity and in the amount of revenue generated. New sports and variations of existing sports will be imagined in front of our eyes. Where were esports and 20/20 cricket a decade ago? Athletes engage with fans in previously unimagined ways. And the events and venues are places where our society's voices are heard. As this influence grows, there will undoubtedly be more and more individuals looking to find their role in the industry as they begin their professional careers and pursue their paths within it. Presumably you are part of this group since you are reading this book. This section is designed to assist you in assessing your strengths and weaknesses, while helping you to understand how you can achieve the level of success you desire and discover your place in the sport business.

SELF-EVALUATION

A self-assessment can help you gain an in-depth evaluation of yourself and your personal characteristics. Performing a self-assessment will force you to identify your most important values and highlight your greatest strengths. It needn't be a formal test, such as a personality assessment, though it certainly could be, along with reading books and articles, taking part in personal growth seminars and podcasts, and seeking out mentors who can provide guidance. A self-assessment might be as simple as taking the time to journal about where you see yourself in 1 year, 5 years, 10 years, and 20 years. Be as detailed and as ambitious as you choose, but be sure to date your entries. You will want to revisit and revise periodically—and you are not a static person. Priorities could change, as would your corresponding actions. A SWOT analysis, not unlike those that businesses devote significant resources to creating, is an incredibly simple and valuable tool if completed honestly. *SWOT* stands for strengths, weaknesses, opportunities, and threats. See figure 1.1 for an example to help you get started.

You can help yourself determine the type of position that is best suited to your personality, interests, and experiences. Alternatively, the analysis may help you see that you have some shortcomings that you must work on to achieve a goal that is very important to you. A mix of enthusiasm, honesty, and discovering your true passion can provide a road map for you. If a job or a skill is important to you, are you willing to take the steps necessary to overcome the weaknesses and threats you have identified? Maybe that will be the impetus for you to take the steps necessary to make that dream possible. And if you decide you aren't willing to do that, that is not wrong. Better to acknowledge that now and move on to what you truly do want. Such preparation may also help you better understand where your leadership skills lie—and that knowledge can pay short-term and long-term dividends for you.

By identifying your greatest strengths, you can determine how they may be best utilized. It is important to deeply consider your greatest characteristics and how you may be able to apply them moving forward in your professional career. Furthermore, performing an evaluation of yourself will allow you to recognize what you value most as a professional. Understanding your strongest personal values provides you with a tool for making career decisions. Every time you evaluate a situation, it is important to take a moment to reflect on your values and use them to consider how to best handle the situation while remaining true to what you believe in.

Using Staubach's five pillars is a great way to see how you can best place yourself for life success in any context.

BALANCE

While hard work and devotion to your profession are desired qualities, all employees should be encouraged to balance the responsibilities of their vocation with their faith, family, community, and self. Without balance on a personal level, any success is difficult to sustain. Just as importantly, balanced individuals allow for a consistently productive organization. Just as all of us seek healthy choices in the physical, emotional, spiritual, and communal aspects that make up our lives, organizations seek healthy choices in performance, finances, morale among stakeholders, and strategic planning. Whether you are part of a multimillion-dollar company charged with maximizing profits or a not-for-profit that works diligently for a cause, you will not achieve your goals if you ignore any of these categories. Balance is listed first because it is so rarely achieved in the modern world, and because when you feel clumsy or off center, it is an opportunity for improvement—not a reason to give up—so it's best to embrace the concept of balance today.

Recognizing imbalance in yourself or your organization can alert you to a weakness or, more accurately, an area in which you have room for growth. Every individual at any level of success has areas in which he needs to improve. What distinguishes the cream of the crop is one's ability to define those areas and turn them into strengths. Many people will choose to ignore or mask their weakest areas, perhaps even convincing themselves that those areas are irrelevant to their pursuit of success. However, by homing in on your shortcomings, you will develop a better understanding for how you can improve, both as an individual and as a professional. Furthermore, by recognizing an area in which you struggle, you can seize the opportunity to partner with someone who excels at it. We see examples of this in every industry, whether it be two coaches on the football field or two Fortune 500 executives. When Staubach first partnered with Robert Holloway to form The Holloway Staubach Company in 1977, both were cognizant

MY PERSONAL SWOT ANALYSIS

Name _____ Date _____

Strengths

1. _____

2. _____

3. _____

4. _____

Weaknesses

1. _____

2. _____

3. _____

4. _____

Opportunities

1. _____

2. _____

3. _____

4. _____

What kind of teammate are you? _____
_____

Threats

1. _____

2. _____

3. _____

4. _____

(continued)

Figure 1.1　SWOT analysis.

Looking Ahead

Where do you see yourself professionally one year from now?

_____

_____

_____

Where do you see yourself professionally five years from now?

_____

_____

_____

Where do you see yourself professionally 10 years from now?

_____

_____

_____

Where do you see yourself professionally 20 years from now?

_____

_____

_____

Figure 1.1   *(continued)*

From R. Horrow, *The Sport Business Handbook* (Champaign, IL: Human Kinetics, 2020).

of the areas in which they excelled, as well as the areas in which the other was better suited to handle business. By being aware of areas in which they lacked skill or experience as individuals, they were able to work together in a way that allowed them both to better utilize their strengths. This awareness and ability to work as a team was one of many reasons they were able to succeed.

TEAMWORK

Staubach has been a part of many different teams in his life, and so will you. Everything you achieve requires contributions of people surrounding you. It's incumbent on you to choose strong contributors, and they are responsible for fulfilling their role as best they can. Without the ability to successfully work as a member of a team, your success will always be limited by what you are able to achieve on your own. Regardless of what industry you work in, the collective efforts of varied specialists will always produce greater results than one person working alone.

When performing your self-assessment, think about some of the teams you have been a member of. What kind of teammate were you? Did you help those around you to reach their greatest potential, or were you more concerned with getting credit for the amount of work you completed on your own? Great teammates are not concerned with how their own contributions will be perceived. Rather, they are concerned with the results that the team will achieve as a collective group. The best teams have two common characteristics: consistency and chemistry. To successfully develop chemistry between teammates, there must first be a mutual respect among all members of the team.

RESPECT

Giving and receiving respect is a core ingredient of any positive relationship, including social and financial ones. Embrace the inclusion of diverse perspectives and cultural backgrounds. Inclusion builds a work environment that is positive for all regardless of race, age, gender, religion, or sexual orientation. To build a successful team, you must encourage and embrace the inclusion of diverse perspectives and cultural backgrounds. The most successful organizations are not filled entirely with like-minded individuals. In the business of sport, respect is vital. You ought to respect your opponent, respect your teammates, and respect your craft. By encouraging and allowing others to have a voice, you can find a common goal to shoot for and gain the trust of others. Our differences allow us to see unique perspectives that others may not be able to see, resulting in collaboration that allows us to accomplish more as a group than we could ever accomplish as individuals.

INTEGRITY

Integrity is a key ingredient in earning the respect of others. Without integrity, it is highly unlikely you will have the respect of your teammates, which will hurt your ability to be depended on as a leader. There will be times, both in business and in life, when you are faced with difficult decisions and potentially immoral actions. In these situations, it is up to you to remain true to yourself in your decision-making process. Staubach honored his commitment to the Naval Academy. He didn't request a stateside assignment when he graduated in 1965. He volunteered for a tour of duty in Vietnam. Whatever choice you are presented with, make a decision that you will have no regret looking back on it, knowing that it aligns with your core values and goals. Some people use shorthand to make the idea of integrity and decision making come to life: What would your grandmother think of the decision or action you are about to take? What would you think if you were watching a video recording of your action? If this action were on the front page of the newspaper, would you be proud or embarrassed? Integrity is achieved not in one singular action but by a constant commitment to be true to yourself and to reach your full potential. Always choose the harder right over the easier wrong.

LEADERSHIP

One myth to debunk is that people are born with the characteristics they possess. We are a complex chemistry of innate strengths, upbringing, and experiences that are constantly at play. We don't always achieve our goals as our respective games unfold, but we should be conscious of how we are playing. Are we acting with integrity, and do we know what objective we seek? Such questions are at the heart of leadership. All people can develop leadership qualities, regardless of their title within a company. The mind is a powerful tool and, if used properly, your greatest asset. People often confuse authority with leadership. The authority given to you is not what makes you a leader.

Leadership is one's ability to guide those around oneself and get them to act as a cohesive unit, capable of achieving more as a group than they would as individuals. Take a step back and evaluate yourself as an individual. Consistent and honest self-assessment is an important process that professionals from all industries should utilize, as well as an essential part of being a leader. Keep in mind that a personal SWOT analysis and any self-assessment process can do two things—identify your values and identify your goals. These are not the same. Goals are what you seek and values are what will guide you to reach them—or at least go after them—successfully. There are no shortcuts to achieving your goals, and often you don't take the path you thought would get you there. What is sure is that without adhering to your values, you likely won't get there at all.

TIMELESSNESS OF THE FIVE PILLARS

So how do *you* become a world championship–level leader? You must commit to *balance* in your own life and have *respect* for and from others. These values are built on *integrity* and earned through a commitment to *teamwork*. All of these traits build off one another cohesively, but you must possess them all to

GAME CHANGER

WRITE DOWN YOUR DREAM JOB

Richard Peddie

Richard Peddie suggests a tactic to make your goal tangible that he used when he was still imagining his career. After 19 years in consumer products, 4 years as president of SkyDome, and 2 years in broadcasting, Peddie became president of the Toronto Raptors. A year later the Maple Leafs purchased the Raptors, created Maple Leaf Sports & Entertainment, and made Peddie their president and CEO. Peddie had 14 busy years at MLSE building Air Canada Centre, BMO Field, and Maple Leaf Square, as well as launching Canada's first MLS team, Toronto FC.

In the 1960s, I hated watching Gail Goodrich torch the Michigan Wolverines for 42 points in the 1965 NCAA Championship game. I watched the University of Detroit's Spencer Haywood dominate my University of Windsor Lancers. And I was delighted when the Detroit Pistons drafted Dave Bing second in the 1966 draft. I really loved basketball. Unfortunately, I could not even make my high school team. When I was 20, I wrote in a journal that my dream was to lead a NBA team. Now, this is a crazy dream even today with 30 franchises in the league, but it was even crazier in 1967 when there were only 12. Little did I know at the time that when people have a clear inspiring dream they have a greater chance of realizing it. And that the odds increase even further when they write down their dream.

Upon university graduation in 1970, I started getting my ticket punched in all the areas that would ultimately prepare me for a senior leadership job in the NBA. I started a career in consumer products working for Colgate, General Foods (today Kraft Foods), and Pillsbury, where I learned about marketing and selling brands, market research, food and beverage manufacturing, finance, and leadership. During those years my dream never died, so when the president's role at the new retractable-roof SkyDome (today Rogers Centre) became available, I applied for it, knowing that an NBA president also had to know how to run a sport facility. During that time, I worked with current NBA Chairman Larry Tanenbaum to make an application for an expansion team in Toronto. While our bid failed, we did cause the NBA to bring the Raptors to the city. After SkyDome I moved on to be president of NetStar, which owned TSN, where I learned about broadcast rights deals, producing live sport broadcasts, and reporting on sport news. Then, 29 years after I wrote my dream down in my personal journal, I accepted the job as president and CEO of the Toronto Raptors.

As it turned out I followed *Chicken Soup for the Soul* author Jack Canfield's formula for success perfectly: "Decide what you want. Write it down. Review it constantly. And each day do something that moves you towards that goal."

In 1998, the Maple Leafs purchased the Toronto Raptors, created Maple Leaf Sports & Entertainment, and appointed me their first president and CEO. Over the next very busy 14 years, I used all of the learning and experiences I had gained from consumer products, facility management, and broadcast to help grow the organization into four pro franchises, three specialty sport television channels, and three venues. We grew enterprise value from approximately $300 million to $2 billion.

In January 2012, I retired knowing that I had successfully realized my dream job.

be a great *leader.* Missing just one of these values will mean your self-analysis is incomplete; your leadership will be diminished and likely will result in resistance from others. The five pillars are timeless. You will make mistakes, and sometimes fail to live up to the high ideals you set for yourself. Those pillars can hold you accountable and give you an ideal to strive for.

Every individual's self-assessment will be different from those of the people around them, and we must each learn to embrace the characteristics that make us unique. We must each learn to lead in our own way with our own greatest values guiding us through our journey. If every person were the same, organizations would be full of employees telling each other what to do while little to no work gets done. Comparing yourself to the people surrounding you places your focus on the wrong person. You must learn to focus on your own successes and compare yourself not to other people, but to the man or woman you were in the past. There is only one life and one career that you can control, and that is your own.

References

Medium. 2017. "How Big Is the Sports Industry?" https://medium.com/sportyfi/how-big-is-the-sports-industry-630fba219331.

Stadiums of Pro Football. n.d. "Foxboro Stadium." Accessed June 15, 2018. www.stadiumsofprofootball.com/stadiums/foxboro-stadium.

Stadiums of Pro Football. n.d. "Mercedes-Benz Stadium." Accessed June 15, 2018. www.stadiumsofprofootball.com/stadiums/mercedes-benz-stadium.

Stadiums of Pro Football. n.d. "Riverfront Stadium." Accessed June 15, 2018. www.stadiumsofprofootball.com/stadiums/riverfront-stadium.

Stadiums of Pro Football. n.d. "Three Rivers Stadium." Accessed June 15, 2018. www.stadiumsofprofootball.com/stadiums/three-rivers-stadium.

Stadiums of Pro Football. n.d. "US Bank Stadium." Accessed June 15, 2018. www.stadiumsofprofootball.com/stadiums/us-bank-stadium.

CHAPTER 2

Essential Lessons for the Sport Business Professional

Larry Lucchino

Larry Lucchino is president and CEO emeritus of the Boston Red Sox and currently serves as chairman of the Pawtucket Red Sox, Boston's Triple-A affiliate. He is also chairman of the Jimmy Fund, the philanthropic arm of the Dana-Farber Cancer Institute. A veteran of 39 years in Major League Baseball, Lucchino was formerly president and CEO of the Boston Red Sox, the Baltimore Orioles, and the San Diego Padres.

After revolutionizing ballpark ambiance and architecture by creating Oriole Park at Camden Yards, which fulfilled his pioneering vision of a traditional, intimate, old-fashioned downtown ballpark with modern amenities, Lucchino spearheaded the political and design efforts that created Petco Park in San Diego. More than a ballpark, Petco fulfilled its promise as a catalyst for redevelopment in downtown San Diego.

With the experience of Camden Yards and Petco Park, he was instrumental in conceiving and executing 10 years of major improvements to Fenway Park that preserved, protected, and enhanced "America's Most Beloved Ballpark."

Born in Pittsburgh, Lucchino graduated with honors from Princeton University and then graduated from Yale Law School. At Princeton, he was a member of two Ivy League championship basketball teams. The avid sportsman has the unique distinction of earning World Series rings (Orioles, '83; Red Sox, '04, '07, '13), a Super Bowl ring (Redskins, '83), and a Final Four watch (Princeton, '65).

Lucchino has been active in numerous civic and charitable efforts, particularly in the research and treatment of cancer. He is a board member and served as the cochair of the Dana-Farber Cancer Institute's $1 billion "Mission Possible" capital campaign, which reached its goal in 2009, and is on the board of Special Olympics International.

Editor's note: This chapter was adapted from a commencement address given by the author at Boston University in 2008 while serving as president and CEO of the Boston Red Sox. It has been amended, expanded, and updated for this publication.

I've been in the sport business for about 40 years, with the Washington Redskins, the Baltimore Orioles, the San Diego Padres, the Boston Red Sox, and now with the Triple-A Pawtucket, Rhode Island, PawSox. During that time, I've interviewed dozens and dozens of eager job applicants and many more who were entertaining the idea. I am no longer surprised at how many I've spoken to who have failed to make a critical distinction. There is a difference between professional sport and the *business* of professional sport. One is an athletic event typically played outdoors in front of thousands of people. The object is to outscore your opponent. The other is an enterprise enacted inside an office behind a desk. While a commitment to winning is paramount, its object is to make a profit and to establish a brand.

If your motivation to work in the business of sport is that you are an avid fan or that you like to bat the ball around on summer evenings, you'd be wise to reconsider. No one works in a butcher shop out of a love for a burger. The difference between eating a cow and carving one up is all the difference in the world.

I have been asked to share a few insights, perhaps offer a bit of advice to those of you who are trying to make your way in the business of sport. Some points aren't original with me; in fact, most are not. Sure as hell this baseball executive doesn't have many answers. But it's not outside the realm of possibility that I may have a suggestion or two that you may find useful somewhere along the line.

GILL'S RULES

Not long after law school, on the wall of my office, enlarged, framed, and prominently placed, I hung a quote I read in *The New Yorker* magazine. Young people starting out in their careers, Brendan Gill observed, were repeatedly counseled to awaken to the seriousness of life. To recognize that the breezy days of youth were over. One failed to heed this notification at one's peril.

This author disagreed. It seemed clear to him that the first rule of life was to have a good time. The second rule was to hurt as few people as possible in the course of doing so.

There was no third rule.

"No third rule" became my mantra early in my career. In time, however, I came to see how limited and even misleading that message really is. The author was wrong, and I was wrong for failing to question his presumption.

Through some successes and not a few failures, life corrected my callow belief in this clever message. A self-centered life is a meager life, I learned. A sterile life. A shabby life. A certain amount of selfishness is unavoidable—necessary one might argue—in order to fulfill our potential. Napoleon often failed to make it home for supper with the family. But if you take away nothing else from my spiel, it might behoove you to mull over this: While the business world is in some sense predicated upon selfishness, we nevertheless have an obligation to balance it with an altruistic responsibility to others and to the planet we live on.

Sermon over. Here's a list of some of the other lessons that life and the world of sport have tried their best to teach me.

GIVE A NOD OF THE HEAD TO MR. GILL'S RULES

Life ought also be fun and kindness is essential. His credo wasn't wrong, just incomplete.

BE BOLD

A line from a favorite movie goes something like this: "Fear is like a giant fog. It sits on your brain and blocks everything. Real feeling, true happiness, real joy, they can't get through that fog. But you lift it, and buddy, you're in for the ride of your life."

The lesson for me is take risks. Step out of your comfort zone. Though I can't always muster what it takes, I like myself best when I feel I have acted boldly. It was probably bold to assume we could move to Boston and acquire the Red Sox franchise in 2001. It was bold to disregard the consensus that Fenway Park could not and should not be saved. It was bold to believe we would eradicate the "Curse of the Bambino." It was bold to conclude that even a gifted 28-year-old could become a successful general manager.

In 1988, when I became president of the Baltimore Orioles, baseball "lifers" and the traditionalists stood by the unquestioned assumption that lifting weights made an athlete "muscle bound." Strength training was verboten. It hampered performance. As misguided as that notion seems today, when I proposed to install a fully equipped weight room to replace the rusting dumbbells strewn around a little-used stationary bike in the clubhouse, it was met with strenuous objections. You'd have thought I'd suggested players swing the bat by the barrel. "Weights? That's a football idea, Lucchino." To suggest such a thing was not only to fly in the face of accepted practice, it was to intrude into the clubhouse, once considered the exclusive province of baseball operations and as such, off-limits to the suits like me.

That wasn't my only intrusion into the sacrosanct clubhouse world. Professional athletes are thoroughbreds. As their employers, we had a compelling interest in their success. It made sense that their overall health and well-being should be a primary concern. Secretariat wasn't fed a diet of pizza and Coke. Yet the clubhouse, where during the season players spend 10, 12, as many as 15 hours a day, provided catered meals that sat congealing in chafing dishes for hours. Cold pizza. You could get soda, chips, candy, dogs, whatever. What you couldn't get was a nutritious meal prepared on the spot. The traditional "clubbies" ordered out. Most clubhouses around the Major Leagues were not equipped with kitchens, let alone with chefs.

In designing Petco Park, we included a fully equipped kitchen and hired a professional chef to run it. A player could still get a slice of pizza if that's what he wanted, but other, more nourishing options were available. The choice wasn't solely between pepperoni and sausage. In Boston, we retrofitted the Fenway clubhouse with a kitchen and hired a French-trained chef whose repertoire included Mexican, Japanese, Caribbean, French, you name it. He would prepare whatever a player wanted. The players were happier; and, as a result, I think they performed better.

Today the quality of clubhouse food has improved around the league. Just as weight rooms, once taboo, have become standard, so has the obligation to provide tasty, nutritious meals. I don't claim credit, but someone had to question the assumptions in order to get the ball rolling.

THE VALUE OF SHOWING UP

Joe Favorito

Being bold, as Larry Lucchino recommends, is important in the ambitious world of sport, but Joe Favorito (@Joefav) reminds us that the less exciting trait of persistence is also valuable. Favorito has more than 30 years of strategic communications and marketing experience as well as business development expertise in brand building, media training, crisis, and athletic administration. He has run strategic communications for the New York Knicks, Philadelphia 76ers, WTA Tour, and USTA. Since 2008, he has been an independent consultant on strategic communications, social media, brand marketing, and business development for clients ranging from Nickelodeon and Intel to MLB and NFL Media. Joe is on the faculty of Columbia University's Sports Management program and is cohost of the Columbia University Sports podcast *(The CUSP Show)* while maintaining a popular industry blog at joefavorito.com.

I've been lucky enough to meet great people at many different points in my career. Through everyone I meet, I glean just a tiny bit of information that I can carry with me moving forward. I try to instill that mindset into my students whenever I can.

How do you meet these people? How do these conversations happen in the first place? That's easy: Half the battle is just showing up.

Today, I emphasize the value of showing up to all of my students at Columbia University. In New York City, there are endless events and opportunities to attend every week. These events range from media to business and others, and are the perfect place for young professionals to figure out their career path. You never know who you're going to meet, and who is going to help you along the way. The secret you need to know is that you don't have to be in the greatest city in the world to adopt this mindset. Interesting people and events are everywhere, and sometimes where you least expect them. You decide whether or not you want to engage with them.

For some reason, we seem to have a fear of putting ourselves out into the world. Whether it's fear of rejection or a sense of complacency, realize that there is always a new experience waiting to be had. In the sport industry, people are willing to help. Everyone remembers what it was like to be young and unsure of what lies ahead. I'm always looking to connect with young professionals in need of guidance, and I'm not the only one.

Put yourself out there. Don't be afraid of uncertainty. Tackle it head-on and see what happens.

SMILE, LAUGH, AND BE PLEASANT

Sounds banal, perhaps naïve, but it's not. It's a profound occupational and personal advantage. There's a line from another old movie (my love of movies does not qualify me to succeed in Hollywood): "In this world you have a choice: You can be clever, or you can be pleasant. For years I tried clever. I recommend pleasant." I too have tried clever and have come to the same conclusion. My successor at the Red Sox, experienced, bright, analytical, and organized, also possesses a winning personality and exceptional people skills. He brings laughter and light to an ordinarily sober workplace. This special attribute is in no small part of why he got the job.

BE STRONG ENOUGH TO SAY "I DON'T KNOW"

When you don't know, say so. Don't guess. Don't fake it. To admit that you don't know is a start. People will respect your honesty and self-assurance, but in itself this is of little use. Now pay attention because I'm about to give you the magic incantation that will cause your stock to rise with your boss and with your colleagues, as well as with your clients, your friends, with just about everyone else in your life. "I don't know" is only a part of it and the lesser part at that. The full response to any question to which you don't know the answer is *"I don't know, but I'll find out."*

KNOW THAT LIFE IS TOO HARD TO BE LIVED ALONE

Find time for your family. You get only one. (Thank God, I can hear some of you saying.) Develop a talent for friendship. Friends fill a life; they represent perhaps the purest choices you'll ever make. And, if you work at it and are fortunate, the line between friend and family will eventually disappear. My two episodes with cancer were proof to me of that.

REMEMBER JACKIE ROBINSON

Be mindful of the catalytic effect one person can have on a community, on a neighborhood, on a nation, advancing a compelling cause or rectifying a horrific injustice. The Jackie Robinson Effect. Hold within yourself a capacity for outrage against iniquity. Be confident that if you fight long enough and hard enough, you too can make a difference. And like Jackie Robinson, know that you can do it with grit and dignity.

OPEN YOUR EYES

Your world is a rich, multicolored, multiethnic, multitextured, multicultural experience. Declaring that all groups are the same is a deceit; believing that some ethnic groups are better than others is a moral disgrace. Embrace and

GAME CHANGER

KEEP YOUR HEAD DOWN AND KEEP WORKING

Jay Bilas

Jay Bilas was able to be strong enough to tell his dad he didn't know if he could handle law school, which led his father to give him life-changing advice. Bilas was part of Duke University's heralded 1982 recruiting class and helped the Blue Devils reach the 1986 NCAA Championship game. He shot over 55 percent from the field for his college career, obtained a political science degree, and played professionally in Italy and Spain. After receiving his degree from the Duke School of Law in 1992, Bilas has been a color commentator and studio analyst for ESPN since 1995, and was twice nominated for an Emmy for Outstanding Performance by a Studio Analyst.

I wish I had some sage, profound advice on what it takes to be successful. I don't. Some people might say that there is no luck in success, that success is preparation meeting opportunity. While I'm sure there is some truth in that, I believe in luck.

When I was in my first year of law school, I felt completely out of place and close to overwhelmed. I had just finished playing three seasons of professional basketball overseas and had been offered a spot on Mike Krzyzewski's coaching staff at Duke, and I had been accepted to Duke Law School. I was surrounded by more capable and confident minds in classes and subjects I simply did not understand. Everyone around me seemed to have a solid grasp of the material, as if they came from a family of Supreme Court justices, and I felt like a foreigner in a strange land and I couldn't grasp the language.

The truth is, the people around me were smarter and more capable than I was. That is not some false humility, it was absolutely true. Just as I had competed against superior players and athletes, I was now competing with better minds.

After a difficult week, I called my parents to check in. After a conversation with my mother, she put my father on the phone to say hello. When he asked how I was doing, instead of my usual "Great Dad, how about you?" I told him that I was struggling. I wasn't sure I belonged in law school, or that I could hack it at this level.

After giving me a few ideas, my dad asked me a question. "How many lawyers do you know out there?" A lot, I told him in response. "And *you* are the one that can't do it? You don't get a prize for knowing it now, you get a diploma for knowing it at the end. Just keep your head down and keep working."

Just keep working. Simple, direct, and absolutely damn right. For my entire life to that point, everything had been laid out for me. I went from high school to college, I moved up as I aged up, and the steps were clear in front of me. I worked hard at the direction of those in charge of those clear steps. When I quit playing basketball to go to law school and work with Coach K, for the first time I was doing something I really didn't feel I had to do. I was doing something I had chosen to do. This path was my own, and I had not owned it yet. For the first time in my life, I had some real doubt.

After the conversation with my father, I did a great deal of thinking about what I wanted out of this. When I was a basketball player for Coach K at Duke, I played against far better athletes. But, that didn't mean that I couldn't win. I just had to work harder, to do more. After the talk with my father, I realized the game was the same in law school. Just because I wasn't among the smartest in the class didn't mean that I couldn't do it, and do it well. I decided to just buckle down and work. I had to be more prepared. I had to do more, and I did.

When I graduated, my father didn't really even remember the conversation that night when I had felt so close to quitting. To him, it was no big deal. To me, it was a life changer, and something I have thought about quite a bit ever since. In my law practice, I argued before federal courts and courts of appeal, and went up against so many superior lawyers, but I never felt as if I couldn't do it and win. I just had to keep my head down and keep working. Pretty simple.

Early in my law practice, I received an offer to do some radio broadcast work. It didn't pay much at all, just enough to cover my expenses. But, it was an offer to do something I really wanted to do, and if it didn't negatively impact my law practice, I wanted to try it. It was a really difficult balance, but I knew I could do it. I just kept my head down and kept working. I prepared my cases as my top priority, and then prepared for my games. When I was in each role, I concentrated fully on that role until I was finished, then I moved on to the next role and concentrated fully on that.

But, things haven't worked out well for me because I am so capable or so hardworking. I don't see myself differently in that regard from anyone else. I don't chalk up any success I have achieved as just due to what I have done. I am also extremely lucky, and I know it. I am lucky I was recruited to play for Coach K, and to learn from him for the last 35 years. I am lucky that my teammates at Duke said yes to Coach K just as I did, and that I have learned from them for 35 years. I am profoundly lucky that I was born to parents who showed me the way. My preparation and work have been of vital importance, sure. But the opportunity that my preparation met was driven in important part by very good fortune. By keeping my head down and working, perhaps I have been able to take my best advantage of that good fortune. That is all I can ask of myself. To me, that is the most important lesson I have ever learned.

celebrate the diversity that is the essence of American life, which is indeed the essence of all of life. We aren't all the same and shouldn't try to be. Revel in our differences. Immerse yourself in them. Exposure to the Other educates and illuminates. It encourages tolerance. It promotes understanding and harmony. It makes for a nourishing life.

SEEK BALANCE

A rich life is a balanced life. Don't focus too early or too hard on your sport career. Deviate a bit. Embrace change. Widen your gaze. If you have blinders on, take them off. The world is open and full of opportunity. In Freud's experience, mental health is a three-legged stool. It requires an aptitude for work, for love, and for play. You need all three. Unlike in baseball, in life even two for three doesn't hack it.

HELP SOME PEOPLE ALONG THE WAY

Find a cause you care about. Involve yourself. It's never too soon to start. For me, twice a cancer survivor, cancer research and patient treatment are at the top of my priorities. Life is not about warming yourself by the fire, it's about building the fire. And generosity is the match. To consider yourself—and to be considered—capable is good. To consider yourself—and to be considered—loving is even better. But to know yourself as generous is best of all.

There is a Chinese proverb (isn't there always?) that asserts that if you want happiness for an hour, take a nap, but if you want happiness for a lifetime, help somebody. Among our legal system's bedrock ideas—justice, due process, the right to representation—I include the notion of *pro bono publico,* the public good, and to work on its behalf is a noble aspiration. Stand for something greater than yourself. You do *not* work in the "toy department of life" if your sport organization and its heroes advance humaneness, compassion, and social justice.

LEARN TO CLARIFY AND SIMPLIFY

The greater intellectual challenge is not to unearth complexity and nuance; it is to translate them into clear and simple language, easily grasped. Einstein remarked that the definition of genius is to take the complex and make it simple. Sentences can be short. Expression can be plain. Divergent thinkers flaunt their intellectual virtuosity. Convergent thinkers make the points and win the battles. My boss and mentor, the great lawyer and sportsman, Edward Bennett Williams, an owner of both the Redskins and the Orioles and my great friend, once threatened one of our law partners with strangulation if, in discussing the case at hand, he offered up a another alternative, long-winded, impenetrable theory.

Simplicity and brevity are best. EBW was fond of saying, "Nothing is often a good thing to do and often a brilliant thing to say." I heard this repeated a hundred times. Like great athletes who perform with an economy of motion, great advocates profit from an economy of expression. There was an economy in the way Edward Bennett Williams tried cases that was not unlike the way Ted Williams hit a baseball or Joe DiMaggio patrolled center field. But a word of caution is in order here. As with all prescriptions, its efficacy is in its judicious application.

EXPAND YOUR REPERTOIRE

A good businessperson or lawyer has to have more than a fastball. You can't rely on just the one pitch. Early in my career, we represented the Redskins in an antitrust suit filed against the club and the NFL. By taking the lead in the case, the Redskins were accumulating major legal bills. On a cross-country trip to an NFL owners meeting, Ed Williams bellyached the entire way about us carrying both the burden of the work and the legal bills. I anticipated him giving his fellow owners hell at the meeting.

The next morning, a sweet, understated, almost meek Ed Williams politely requested the league's assistance in defending the suit, but only if the other clubs felt it fair and appropriate. If not, he said, we would understand and never raise the issue again.

From red-faced outrage one day to gentle supplication the next. He astounded me. When I asked what had happened to the fiery barrister I'd heard go off on the plane, EBW said, "Lucchino, if you are going to be a good lawyer, you better have several gears. You can't always operate in high—like some of our scorch-the-earth partners."

REMEMBER "IT'S THE PEOPLE, STUPID"

That is a paraphrase of James Carville's famous political maxim. The essence of leadership is not charisma or inspirational rhetoric; it is in assembling the best possible team. A gift for appraising people and their potential is paramount. So is an assessment of their ability to contribute and collaborate. "Putting the best possible band together" is a priority whether you are a GM needing to fill a slot at second base or the CEO looking to hire a marketing department. Recruiting talented people to staff your organization is crucial to success. And don't be afraid to search in unusual places.

RECOGNIZE IT ISN'T A FRATERNITY

All this about smiling and generosity and helping others is well and good. But I want to prepare you for a darker side of the world of sport. Because of the huge sums of money involved, the notoriety, the glamour, the proximity to these gifted athletes who, like movie stars and rock stars, are the aristocracy of our culture, the sport business has a darker side.

The number of qualified candidates for jobs in professional sport vastly exceeds the number of available openings. If it is your fortune to be hired, the competition becomes only more intense as people strive to get ahead. The utility infielder wants to start at second base. The guy drawing beers wants to manage the concession stand. Not everyone has your best interest at heart. They call it "palace intrigue." It's normal and natural, it's the way of things, but it isn't always pleasant. I don't want to give you the wrong impression. The front office isn't exactly a basket of eels all climbing over each another, but be forewarned. It's a business. It's not a fraternity.

GROW A THICK SKIN

Surgeons are never booed during an operation. An accountant is not second-guessed on talk radio. But a sport executive is fair game. Where sports are concerned, everyone's an expert. For a fan, it's part of the fun, and for a reporter it's her job. Professional sport has a symbiotic relationship with the press. We need them to keep us in the public eye as much as they need us to fill their pages and websites, but sometimes their agenda isn't congruent with ours. They want information it isn't always in our best interest to provide. For a reporter, accuracy is desirable but deadlines are pitiless. In the absence of all the facts, and out of time to uncover them, reporters resort to speculation. Notoriety is a double-edged sword. I've been praised in the press for things only some of which I've done. I've been vilified for things only some of which I've done. The point is that if you aspire to sit in the chair I once occupied, best not to be too thin-skinned.

EXERCISE YOUR BACKBONE

The players are not your friends. Their agents are definitely not your friends. This is not to say relationships cannot be amiable, even pleasant. Management and labor maintain a professional distance. It is obvious why this is so. Tens of millions of dollars are often on the table. Agents naturally want the best possible deal for the players they represent. The better the deal, the bigger their cut. Some are more scrupulous than others in justifying their demands. This is a diplomatic way of saying sometimes they lie. They withhold information about injuries. They inflate purported offers from other teams. Negotiations are not always contentious, but often enough they are. Your bullshit detector needs to be in good working order. To thrive in the world of sport, you need some backbone. You need some steel.

TRUST YOURSELF

Of the 108 billion people who have ever walked the earth—I looked that up on the Internet so it must be true—none, not one, not a single one has ever lived your life. No one in the history of humankind has ever had your exact set of abilities, your same attributes, your talents and tastes and urges; none occupy the identical point in time and space and so none can share your particular point of view. The road your life will take has never been traveled before. Columbus thought he was going to India. There are no maps. You have to draw your own.

Tell me then, who could possibly know better how best to live your own life or pursue your own career than you do yourself?

What I'm saying here is that when all is said and done, you've got to trust yourself. Not Einstein, not Freud, and certainly not Larry Lucchino.

10 PRINCIPLES FROM A "COLLECTOR" OF PHILOSOPHIES

Brandon Steiner

Like Larry Lucchino, Brandon Steiner has a list of principles that can be useful as you define your career path. Steiner is the founder and chairman of Steiner Sports Marketing and Memorabilia, the largest company of its kind in America. Considered a sport marketing guru, Brandon is a permanent fixture in the media as a regular on ESPN NY Radio 98.7 FM and as host of *The Hook-Up* with Brandon Steiner on YES Network. He has appeared frequently on CNBC, CNN, MSNBC, ESPN, and in newspapers including the *New York Times* and the *Wall Street Journal*. The author of *The Business Playbook: Leadership Lessons from the World of Sports* and *You Gotta Have Balls: How a Kid from Brooklyn Started From Scratch, Bought Yankee Stadium, and Created a Sports Empire,* Brandon lives in Scarsdale, New York, with his wife, Mara.

Courtesy of Steiner Sports.

Growing up in Brooklyn playing sports was step one in discovering a plan. As my life went on, I made countless plans and reworked them. I make my living in sport, but I've developed a business philosophy—one with a beginning, middle, and end.

Since my early days of playing sports, I've been privileged to have conversations about planning with some of the greatest figures in sport history: Joe Torre, Bob Knight, Larry Brown, Bill Walsh, Pat Riley, and Mike Krzyzewski, to name just a few. None of them ever said, "We won by the seat of our pants," or "We winged it." Playing without a plan is fine for the Brooklyn asphalt, but it won't lead to accomplishing any long-term goals or success.

The sport collectibles industry is not one that I created, but one that I helped improve and organize. To invent something is near impossible, but to improve something that already exists, to solve a problem, is the key to a winning strategy. Sports fans had been collecting autographs and prized sport items for more than

(continued)

100 years before Steiner Sports existed, but they lacked a sense of security and assurance that their attained autographs were real.

When we started, we had no formal partnerships with sport leagues, teams, and players. There was no authentication—no tamper-proof holograms you see industry-wide on autographs today. And, creativity was completely lacking from a product development perspective. Over the last 30 years, my goal has been to fix these problems, transforming the collector's experience and bringing fans closer to the games.

I'm a "collector" of success philosophies. I talk to coaches, contractors, corporate CEOs, managers, and manufacturers—you name them, and I've picked their brains and filed away their ideas about success.

I also like to hear the plans that athletes followed to successfully reach their goals. Athletes are good at what they do. We know them, or at least we think we do, because their feats are larger than life. Some people just look at the performances, but I see athletes themselves as unfolding stories—from childhood to college and from their professional careers well into their retirement. I like to trace the continuity and planning behind their greatest performances.

There are a number of core principles that transformed Steiner Sports from a $4,000 investment in the mid-1980s to a $50 million company. The endeavor began by trying to book athletes for appearances at various corporate events. I was a one-man shop with a phone, a Rolodex, a corner desk, and high hopes for success. Today Steiner Sports has 100 employees, is a bona fide leader in both the sport marketing and autographed collectibles industries, and has relationships with more than 2,000 athletes, along with some of the greatest sports teams and the leagues themselves.

The principles are not just about autographs or sports; they are applicable to any aspect of business, and there are 10 of them.

1. Start With a Road Map
2. Find Your Niche
3. Wake Up Nervous
4. Know Your Purpose
5. Go the Extra Mile
6. You Never Know
7. Get Focused
8. Nothing Changes If Nothing Changes
9. It's Not What Happens, It's What You Do With What Happens
10. See Success as a Habit

So, if there is one thing I have to offer you, it's this—just this: Be a light unto yourself. Seek advice, sure. Wise counsel is irreplaceable. Learn from an experienced mentor certainly. But trust yourself. At least then, when you make mistakes, and believe me, you will make mistakes, they'll be your own mistakes. You'll have no one else to blame. In short, you'll be accountable, which itself is a useful addition to anyone's portfolio of virtues.

A COMMENCEMENT

By reading this book, you are embarking on a journey through the golden age of sport business, sport law, and sport marketing. Chapters that follow come from some of the biggest names in the sport industry over the past half century, and their experiences will offer you entertaining and educational insights as you plan or continue your path in sport. Your upcoming hours spent reading this book seem to me an exercise in commencement, not unlike a college graduate's commencement to enter and contribute to the larger off-campus world. I was honored to deliver the 135th commencement address at Boston University's Nickerson Field, located a stone's throw away from our beloved Fenway Park. I hope that this chapter, adapted from that speech, provides some guidance for you as you seek your path in the exciting industry of sport.

The lessons I have conveyed here are those that life and the world of sport have tried their best to teach me. It is heavy on compassion and cooperation, and light on specifics. Later chapters will drill down to the traits and skills necessary to be successful in your working life. But I hope you will keep these "soft" skills at the forefront of your mind, even when you are fiercely negotiating a multimillion-dollar deal, explaining a key issue to a hard-headed rival, or mentoring a struggling young employee. Good luck.

CHAPTER 3

Fostering Meaningful Business Relationships

Lyn St. James

Lyn St. James has raced for more than 40 years, earned 1992 Indy 500 Rookie of the Year, is a seven-time Indy 500 driver, and has had victories at the Daytona 24 Hours, Sebring 12 Hours, Watkins Glen, and Elkhart Lake. She has set 21 national and international closed-course speed records of more than 225 mph, has raced internationally at the LeMans 24 Hours, Goodwood Festival of Speed/Revival, and 24 Hours of Nurburgring, and currently competes in vintage races and at the Bonneville Salt Flats. She has authored *Lyn St. James: An Incredible Journey, Oh By the Way,* and *Car Owner's Manual.*

Lyn is a former president of the Women's Sports Foundation and founded the Women in the Winner's Circle Project Podium Grant; she has made significant contributions to motorsports, both on and off the track. Her legacy is one of inspiration, encouragement, perseverance, and commitment to excellence.

As a motivational speaker, Lyn has presented to such companies as Bosch, Ford Motor Company, HSBC, Merrill Lynch, Nike, and GTE Financial, just to name a few. Her presentations are customized to the client's needs, ranging from teamwork to technology, performance, success, and finding and living your passion. She serves on the Kettering University Board of Trustees and serves as ambassador to the RPM Foundation.

I'd been funding my own racing for about five years and realized that if I was going to be able to be more competitive and move up the ladder into bigger and better race cars, I was going to have to find one or more sponsors. Sometimes necessity creates action, but it still requires "new information" and having a "business mindset" to create the action plan. For me, the "new information" was an article in *Car and Driver* magazine titled "Ford and Feminism," which focused on Ford Motor Company's interest in providing opportunities for women in the male-dominated automotive world. So due to necessity (needing financial support for my racing) and this "new information," I formed an action plan and began a letter-writing campaign to Ford Motor Company that lasted for almost three years. I wrote letters to the people quoted in the article telling them about my racing and saying that if they sponsored me I would help them sell cars to women and demonstrate their commitment to providing opportunities to women in nontraditional roles. They replied, "Thank you, but we're not into racing at this time," so I continued doing research on Ford and contacted anyone and everyone I could find at Ford Motor Company. I eventually had the opportunity to make a presentation, and in 1981, I was successful in getting Ford Motor Company as a sponsor. That ultimately turned my avocation into my vocation—professional race car driver!

Sport can mean many things to each of us: physical and mental exercise, competition, fun, challenge, leadership, teamwork, entertainment, socializing, learning new things, technology, and probably many more.

When I started driving race cars it was all about finding my passion—finally—and about learning the craft of racing and eventually winning! For the first five years, most of my racing was funded by my own dollars, but I soon realized if

Courtesy of Lyn St. James Racing LLC.

Lyn St. James celebrates after her historic 1985 victory at Watkins Glen.

I was going to be able to continue to race I was going to need to find outside funding, which meant finding sponsorship, which also meant racing in professional races. I knew that sponsorship was common in professional racing, so my goals took a new direction. I had to change my mindset to continue doing what I wanted to do. In other words, I had to accept—I had to embrace—the idea that sport means business. That was more than 30 years ago, and sport and business have only become more closely aligned during that time. With global sport sponsorships forecast to reach more than $62 billion in 2017, the business of sport is big business indeed.

DEVELOPING A BUSINESS MINDSET

I was fortunate because I was a small business owner (consumer electronics manufacturers rep and auto parts distributor), had been going to major trade shows like SEMA (Specialty Equipment Manufacturers Association) and the CES (Consumer Electronics Show), and had a good understanding of basic business principles. This gave me a huge advantage when it was time for me to approach my sport of auto racing not as an amateur, but as a professional. I was also fortunate that some of the biggest auto races in the country, the Daytona 500, the Daytona 24 Hours, the Sebring 12 Hours, and the Miami Grand Prix, took place in Florida, which is where I lived.

I quickly switched gears and developed what I call a business mindset, and not just for once in a while, but for all the time. My listening in all situations was influenced by a question going through my head: "Where was there an opportunity?" This included how I watched television (to see which, how, when, and where companies were spending dollars on advertising), how I read the newspaper (to see what was receiving attention and publicity and what print advertising was being sold), and what and who were people talking about in social settings. Over the years I've continued to do this and believe it's one of the reasons I've been able not only to find sponsors for my racing for 20-plus years, but also to help find support for important not-for-profits like the Women's Sports Foundation and the RPM Foundation, and to help mentor and generate support for other females in racing.

SEVEN RELATIONSHIP LESSONS

My experience has been that when you really take this concept to heart—looking at every interaction as a potential business relationship—the world seems to open wide for you. I want to be very clear here: I don't advocate diminishing other people, as though they are *only* a potential business relationship. If you or I take that approach, trust me, that relationship will be short-lived. The other party will move on as soon as possible—and who can blame someone for doing so if you don't seek an authentic connection? We are humans and deserve to work with others such that a reciprocal relationship can develop. With that in mind, I present to you seven relationship lessons that I try to live by and that I try to teach to others.

TAKE CHARGE TO HELP GIVE KIDS EQUAL OPPORTUNITIES

Shane Battier

Shane Battier used his influence and passion to create relationships in the nonprofit sphere that mimic the same traits that led Lyn St. James to pursue the career she desired. In both cases, they emphasized giving back. After a four-year college basketball career at Duke University, including a 2001 national championship and every major National Player of the Year award, Battier played 13 seasons in the NBA, culminating in back-to-back titles with the Miami Heat in 2012 and 2013. He is the only player to have ever won both the Naismith Prep Player of the Year Award (1997) and the Naismith College Player of the Year (2001). Visit takechargefoundation.org to learn more about his nonprofit work.

I believe that I would have been successful in life without basketball, but I don't know if I would have had the same opportunities if I had not had the sport. My parents did not have the means to fund my college education, but at the same time I would not have qualified for full financial aid. Thus, I was fortunate to have the game. As a former Duke University and NBA player I had the unparalleled opportunity to travel around the country and world. Whether it was Chicago or Los Angeles or somewhere in Asia or Europe, something that always stuck out to me was the unequal educational opportunity that was prevalent everywhere. Different cultures place different levels of importance on education, and I firmly believe that the best way to unlock one's potential is through education.

I would never have reached the top of the NBA without the help of others. Early along in my career I made a promise to myself that I would give back to those that helped me reach my goals. That is why I started the Shane Battier Take Charge Foundation. Focused on providing educational opportunities for kids that otherwise would not have them, the foundation is dedicated to providing resources for the development and education of underserved youth and teens.

I was very fortunate to grow up in a household that held a high premium on education. Ever since I was a kid my parents held me accountable in school. They sacrificed so much for me, and now I want to share that sacrifice by giving kids an educational experience similar to the one that I had.

Kids in underserved communities have so much potential, but their opportunities are often limited, and it shouldn't be like that; they deserve an equal shot. I would love for the Take Charge Foundation to be a beacon for people who want to impact their communities. We may not have all the solutions surrounding the lack of opportunities, but we do have passion and work ethic to create success. With hard-work ethic and passion, Newell Fleming, the foundation's executive director, my wife Heidi, and I have organically grown the foundation and are now active in three cities. Students in Detroit, Miami, and Houston are awarded scholarships annually, and we want to continue to expand, branch out, and reach more kids in more cities.

Not only athletes, but all people should find something to help make the community and world a better place. Leave something better than how you found it and make a difference—just do something. Donate your time, energy, or resources, donate something to make someone's life better. While it requires a lot of work and takes a lot of energy, the payoffs are amazing when you know you are part of a young person's journey.

Do well. Do good.

1. EXCHANGE = BUSINESS RELATIONSHIP

Realize that once there is an "exchange"—whether it's advice, product, cash, publicity, introductions—you're now in a business relationship. Honor that relationship and always look for ways to exceed the expectations of others.

2. CREATE AND MAINTAIN RELATIONSHIPS

My long-term relationship with Ford Motor Company far exceeded what I think both of us were aware of in the early years. What started out as a one-year race sponsorship agreement expanded into two annual contract agreements: one for race sponsorship and the other for personal appearances, test drive vehicles, or talent on corporate videos or consulting with vehicle engineers and media appearances.

3. LET YOUR GOALS BE YOUR GUIDE

Keep your goals as your focus in everything you do. I would always have short-term (annual) and long-term (three to five years) goals; write them down, and check them off as they were achieved and decide whether or not to move them to the next list. It helped me feel focused and often gave me a sense of achievement even when things at the moment may have not been going well.

4. WHAT CAN YOU GIVE? WHAT CAN YOU GET?

Look for what you can give as well as what you can get. Learn what the business objectives are of whoever you want to do or are doing business with. Another opportunity to exceed their expectations.

5. HONOR YOUR MISTAKES; LEARN FROM YOUR FAILURES

Racing has provided me with more failures than successes. But I would always search for the *why* so I could learn from it. I remember one early race where I crashed and couldn't figure out why; it drove me crazy. After hours of sitting alone and trying to figure it out (I had been driving the race car really well up until I lost it and crashed into a wall), I finally realized I had not adjusted well enough to the reduced weight of the car as it was using up fuel and just took the last corner as I had been every previous lap, which was too fast, and consequently crashed. I learned to be more aware of the changing weight over the course of the race, which made me a better racer, especially in long-distance races, which is where I ultimately garnered many of my later victories.

One of the biggest business challenges I experienced was at my rookie Indianapolis 500 in 1992. While it was an overwhelming success (finishing 11th and being awarded Rookie of the Year), I had to use a Chevrolet engine for the race even though I was under contract to Ford Motor Company. But at that time there wasn't a competitive Ford race engine available to me, so I got written approval from Ford Motor Company to race the Indy 500 in a Chevrolet. But while that approval was official and came from an executive at Ford, another executive at Ford was not at all happy with the situation. A few months later I was asked to come to that executive's office for a meeting; and it was clear to me to expect something other than congratulations and to remember that my contracts with Ford were annual. My concern was that I might be told that my contract would not be renewed. I was nervous and not sure what to expect. I did get a stern raking over the coals and while I tried to explain the circumstances (I was advised to be apologetic and humble and took that advice), I made sure this executive knew how much I appreciated the support Ford Motor Company had provided me over the years. but also shared with him how much more valuable I now was to the company since I had successfully raced in the largest single-day sporting event in the world to a worldwide audience with the Ford oval on my racing suit. Fortunately, this salvaged my relationship with Ford Motor Company, and my contract was renewed for another year.

6. ONCE YOU SEE THE OPPORTUNITY, SEIZE IT

My tenacity in pursuing Ford after reading the *Car and Driver* magazine article described in the opening section is a prime example of this. Another great example has been my experience with the Women's Sports Foundation, founded in 1974 by Billie Jean King. It is dedicated to creating leaders by providing girls access to sport. We don't use the word sponsorships, but instead refer to partnerships. Two examples are partnerships with Gatorade and Fox Networks, who support our Travel & Training Fund, and Chevrolet with their Goalkeepers campaign.

National Girls & Women in Sports Day (NGWSD) began in 1987 as a special day in our nation's capital to recognize women's sport and is now celebrated annually across all 50 states with community-based events, award ceremonies, and other celebratory activities. The Women's Sports Foundation was one of the founding members, and

I WANT TO BE PRESIDENT

Andy Dolich

Andy Dolich didn't let the on-court failure of his first professional team experience or his initial failure to grasp a colleague's career advice keep him from a rewarding life in high-level sport. Like Lyn St. James, he learned from mistakes. Dolich brings more than five decades of leadership in the sport industry including executive positions in the NFL, NBA, MLB, NHL, and pro soccer. The Ohio University Sports Management graduate was executive vice-president of the Oakland A's during their run of success in the 1980s and '90s, president of business operations for the Golden State Warriors and Memphis Grizzlies, and COO of the San Francisco 49ers. Dolich runs a sport business consulting practice in Northern California. Clients include TBT (The Basketball Tournament on ESPN), the Fan-Controlled Football League (FCFL), 3Ball USA, Stadium Links Golf, and virtual reality company Vhere. He is entrepreneur in residence at Menlo College.

My first job in sport was with the Philadelphia 76ers in 1971. At that time the team's General Manager Don DeJardin saw the value of the Ohio University Sports Management program. After discussions with Program Director James Mason he agreed to bring four interns to Philly with the guarantee that one of us would be hired as a full-time employee after our six-month internship.

I was the lucky Ohio U graduate to be selected as DeJardin's administrative assistant prior to the 1972 to 1973 season. It was my dream come true to be with an NBA franchise that had gone 68-13 in 1967 on the way to winning the championship led by the legendary Wilt Chamberlain. How was I to know what was coming?

During my first full season I was paid the princely sum of $5,200 as the 76ers went 9-73! Not a misprint, 9-73! For those who might not know, that's the worst record in NBA history, which stands to this day. How perfect that the Golden State Warriors, where I also worked as part of my career journey, went 73-9 in 2015 to 2016. The ultimate Outhouse–Penthouse example in the world of NBA basketball or any sport. What's harder to do, go 9-73 or 73-9?

To me it was a glorious time to be in the midst of chaos and disaster in that I was thrown headfirst into promotions, ticket sales, advertising, community relations, training camp, merchandise, and game operations. My year in "Hoops Hades" was the perfect laboratory to grow a working skill set and move up the career ladder multiple rungs at a time. In working with the NBA's losing-est franchise I was able to get comfortable about being uncomfortable in business areas that I could only dream about as a fresh-faced sport careerist.

Fast-forward to 1981 when I was hired by the Oakland A's after stops with the Maryland Arrows of the National Lacrosse League, NHL's Washington Capitals, and Washington Diplomats of the North American Soccer League.

I was confused as to how I might be considered for what might be the next adventure in my magical mystery tour and turned to a colleague, Jack Schrom, a successful executive with the Pittsburgh Pirates.

(continued)

I WANT TO BE PRESIDENT *(continued)*

> Me: *"Jack, how do I become president of a team?"*
>
> Jack: *"You can't be president until you are president."*
>
> Me: *"Huh? What is that supposed to mean?"*
>
> Jack: *"Grasshopper, you clearly aren't ready to comprehend the depth and complexity of what I have shared with you."*
>
> Me: *"You are correct, I have no idea what you are talking about."*
>
> Jack: *"Stay with me, nitwit. There are hundreds of candidates that are ridiculously multitalented. Some believe they are always the smartest person in every room, some hide their light under a basket, and some are completely delusional. You can only be president when the person on the other side of the desk believes you can be president. Do you read me now?"*
>
> Me: *"Hmmm."*

In working with my coauthors of our book *20 Secrets to Success for NCAA Student-Athletes Who Won't Go Pro,* I remembered the purported words of Michelangelo. When asked how he created the famous statue of David, he said "David was inside the stone. I just chipped away all the pieces that weren't David."

Want to succeed in the sport business? Get your chisel and start chipping.

---

during my years as a board member and president we would go to Washington, D.C. One of our activities was to visit congressional representatives to lobby on behalf of Title IX and usually included a "photo op." Rather than just smiling for the camera and taking a few moments to share small talk about being a race car driver, I was able to immediately turn the conversation into awareness about Title IX and how important it was to support and enforce Title IX. To me the situation was very similar when I would meet corporate executives while at the race track or in other social settings and seize the opportunity to discuss the specifics of my sport in hopes of being able to follow up with them for future support.

7. BE THE 3 Ps: PREPARED, PERSISTENT, PRESENT!

- *Being prepared* means being prepared at every level with regard to research, physical and mental fitness and preparation, technical, written, and visual materials, role playing in advance of a meeting—*everything!*

- *Being persistent* means never giving up! To me, *no* is *no* only from that person on that day!

- *Being present* means bringing your prepared self, being sure to listen, and not allowing any distractions to enter your sphere of awareness. Make notes after the event.

After getting the opportunity to test an IndyCar for the first time in 1988 at a track in Memphis, Tennessee (thanks to team owner Dick Simon), Dick said to me "*We* can do this"—not "*You* can do this"—with *we* as the operative word. I now had a successful test in the IndyCar and a team owner interested in having me as his driver, so the search for sponsorship started. I was under contract and racing for Ford Motor Company, but Ford was not into IndyCar racing, so I knew I was going to have to find sponsorship elsewhere. It was an ongoing mission and I was always researching, talking, asking people for introductions, and so on. After 150 rejections over a four-year period, the 151th company said yes; that company was J. C. Penney. How I was able to get in the door at J. C. Penney is an example of networking and persistence. A friend who had been writing most of my proposals introduced me to a friend of his, Sheila Plank, who introduced me to a friend of hers, Carrie Rozelle, who served on the United Way board and wrote to another United Way board member, W.R. Howell, then chairman of J. C. Penney, suggesting he take a look at my opportunity. He passed that information on to his executives, I was told to contact them, and after months of meetings in March of 1992 they agreed to provide some sponsorship for the 1992 Indianapolis 500. While it wasn't enough to complete the deal, Dick Simon agreed to get us started and said it was enough to complete rookie orientation and start practice, and he was confident that we would generate enough additional sponsorship to make it through the race, which is exactly what happened. My persistence, seizing an opportunity, and creating and maintaining relationships contributed to my success.

After my successful IndyCar test at Memphis in 1988, even though I wasn't having much success in securing sponsors (remember, 150 rejections) in 1991 I decided to spend the month of May in Indianapolis to better prepare for what it would be like if I did get to race there. Through the Women's Sports Foundation I had some friends who lived in Indianapolis, and they organized a Welcome to Indianapolis Breakfast for me in early May, which was wonderful but also a bit awkward since I was only visiting for the month and not racing yet. For me this was about preparation. I would go to the track every day (just as I would if I were racing) and I became comfortable with the fabric of the city and the track, including being on pit lane on race day! I'm so glad I did because when I *was* racing there the following year (1992), it did feel familiar. During the following years when I was racing in the Indianapolis 500 I would invite aspiring young female racers to work for me during the month or at least visit the garage and other "inside" areas of the track to see what it would be like if they ever made it to the Indianapolis 500. I had Danica Patrick, who I was mentoring at the time, as my guest and she was able to spend time in the garage and pits (even though she wasn't old enough to officially be there), and she rode with me in the prerace parade (along with her sister Brooke and my daughter Lindsay). Almost 10 years later (1995) she was awarded Indianapolis 500 Rookie of the Year!

GAME CHANGER

FIND DIRECTION WITH YOUR OWN MISSION STATEMENT

Marc Trestman

When Marc Trestman was struggling to determine his next professional step, he consciously envisioned where he wanted to be in the future, similar to Lyn St. James' spin at the Brickyard. Trestman is the head football coach for the Toronto Argonauts of the Canadian Football League. He has more than three decades of coaching experience in the CFL, NCAA, and NFL, including head coaching stints with the Argos, Chicago Bears, and Montreal Alouettes. In just six years in the CFL, he has hoisted the Grey Cup three times after leading the Argos to a record 17th championship in 2017. Marc has been recognized as the CFL's Coach of the Year twice and named a finalist for the award on two other occasions. In 2010, he wrote a book titled *Perseverance: Life Lessons on Leadership and Teamwork* that documents lessons learned throughout a life in football, including his unique people-first approach to coaching.

After losing my job at 50, I started doing some serious thinking about what I was doing and what direction I was going in. This began an introspection and transformation that has dramatically changed my personal and professional life. I was relentless in setting my path for the way I would live the rest of my life, so I started by asking the fundamental questions I had neglected over the years. "Why do I coach?" "Why do I coach the way I do?" "What does it feel like to be coached by me?" Answering these questions enabled me to develop a mission statement for my life's journey and a purpose behind my love for coaching football.

For most of my career up to that point I had thought of players as chess pieces, simply to get to the next first down, to get to the next coaching job, to make more money, and to receive the adulation of my peers. I realized I coached to get results for me, and at 50 I found it was not fulfilling. In my journey into self-discovery, assisted by a mentor, I began to understand that I wasn't in the football business, but I was in the ultimate "people business" of football.

I realized that players want their coaches to help them master their craft and I could help them get this done. But, my purpose was to grow leaders and to assist those on my journey to become better fathers, husbands, players, and teammates. I was going to use the toolbox of football to passionately pursue my purpose of teaching a leadership course on a daily basis.

I then needed a mission statement to guide me in my life daily, through the course of the season, and even on game day. I broke my mission statement into three parts:

1. To embrace the inevitability of adversity knowing that adversity opens many doors to finding out more about yourself and your team.

2. To stay humble during moments of success, always understanding we do not succeed alone, without the efforts of many others.

3. Finally—and this has really been my key to fulfillment—to have the daily passion to serve others, never asking or expecting anything in return.

Football is the ultimate "zero-sum" game. On every play, someone wins and someone loses.

Each and every week, someone wins and someone loses. What better environment is there to serve my purpose, work my mission statement, and test the limits of myself and those around me as we live and work together daily during the journey of a season?

How about you? What will your mission statement be? And where will you put it to the test?

MAKING THE MOST OF MY FIRST OPPORTUNITY

I feel fortunate that I found my passion (driving race cars) and was able to pursue it, first on my own, and then, with the help of sponsorship, able to do it professionally. I can honestly say that had I not gotten Ford Motor Company as a sponsor I very likely would have never been able to become a successful professional racing driver. Being named a factory racer gave me not only opportunity, but credibility, first within the industry, and second with the media and the fans. I had to prove my worthiness by delivering results (which I did), but without that opportunity I believe I would have continued to struggle race to race, year to year. Having a long-term relationship with Ford Motor Company not only enabled me to have a 10-plus year professional racing career in sports cars, but because I gained a high level of experience and success I was able to step into one of the highest levels of motorsports, the Indianapolis 500, and IndyCar racing, for another nine years. This opened me up to a much larger platform, which has not only helped me achieve many of my dreams and goals, but to also have a positive impact on others.

Part II

Building Your Branding and Selling Skill Sets

Branding and selling are vital to so many aspects of business, and sport business is no exception. In some very real ways, a modern sporting world crowded with options on how to spend one's time is even more dependent on smart branding and selling than other industries. The contributors to these six chapters have found success in a multitude of areas, as commissioners, owners, agents, entrepreneurs, and athletes, and collectively these six chapters express how wide-ranging your opportunities are when you build your knowledge and skill sets in branding and selling.

Stephen Ross advocates for the value of having a consistent process and vision when striving to reach your goals, something he first discovered in the real estate sector and transferred into myriad sport ventures later in his career. Bob Kain joined Mark McCormack's revolutionary International Management Group in its early years and helped shape a company that for decades was constantly finding industry needs to fulfill. Tom Ricketts' path to becoming a World Series champion owner with the Chicago Cubs was made possible in part by understanding the value of the historic brand that he and his family bought. His chapter on building a championship brand strips away the jargon and shows you how branding is at its core about connecting with your customers. Jack Nicklaus has embodied a mindset of authenticity over the course of a lifetime. As a golfer and businessman, he has repeatedly found success by ensuring that his businesses are authentic from stage one. National Hockey League Commissioner Gary Bettman explains how handling crises calmly and capably is vital to ensuring that your property, your brand, endures through difficult times. Crisis management is an important leadership skill; it's also, not surprisingly, an essential brand management skill. Finally, Major League Soccer (MLS) Commissioner Don Garber articulates how from the beginning MLS was dedicated to building a brand that reflected its core values—which was critical to finding its place within the crowded and established professional sport landscape it entered and has allowed it to grow in ways its leaders never even imagined at the outset.

Courtesy of the Miami Dolphins.

CHAPTER 4

Executing a Consistent Process and Vision

Stephen M. Ross

Stephen M. Ross, chairman and founder of Related Companies—an international real estate firm—assumed the responsibility of managing general partner of both the Dolphins and Hard Rock Stadium on January 20, 2009. He grew up in South Florida, and the Dolphins have been a lifetime passion for him. Ross reached a unique agreement with Miami-Dade County in June 2014 to modernize the home stadium of the Miami Dolphins. Phase I of the project was completed in time for the 2015 season and changed every seat in the stadium, rebuilt the concourses, and moved seats 25 feet closer to the field on the north and south sidelines. For the 2016 season, Hard Rock Stadium installed a state-of-the-art canopy and four giant high-definition video boards.

Ross is committed to supporting the community that supports the Dolphins. He strengthened the reach of the Miami Dolphins Foundation and used his platform to harness the unifying power of sport to advance race relations across the country through the establishment of the nonprofit organization Ross Initiative in Sports for Equality (RISE). The nonprofit was recognized in 2017 by ESPN Humanitarian Awards for the Stuart Scott ENSPIRE Award.

Ross graduated from the University of Michigan with a Bachelor of Business Administration degree and from Wayne State University Law School with a Juris Doctor degree. He later received a Master of Laws in Taxation from New York University School of Law. In 2004, the University of Michigan renamed its business school the Stephen M. Ross School of Business, and in 2011, the school awarded him an honorary Doctor of Laws degree at its commencement.

U.S. soccer fans have had increasingly more access to the world's greatest soccer leagues in recent years. No longer is the World Cup every fourth year the only time when the sport takes center stage. Major League Soccer's expansion has been impressive; the Premier League from the United Kingdom and Germany's Bundesliga can be seen on American television networks, and the Internet provides regular coverage of any teams that fans want to follow. But when I created the International Champions Cup in 2013, it was difficult to sell a soccer tournament on U.S. soil. I was confident that Americans wanted to see the best players on the planet, and most importantly, that they wanted to see them playing meaningful games. That's why we made it a tournament with teams from the top leagues, rather than a series of friendly matches. It caught on immediately. The first year, we had the largest crowd ever in the United States for a soccer game. A total of 110,000 people packed the famed Big House in Ann Arbor, Michigan—my alma mater at the University of Michigan. We've had sellouts everywhere from Columbus, Ohio, to Santa Clara, California; at the Rose Bowl in Pasadena, California, and MetLife Stadium in New Jersey. Our one dozen matches each year are all shown on international television to 800 million homes around the world. It has become a summer tradition in a short period of time. We correctly read how American soccer fans wanted to consume their sport.

I've been involved in sport business for only about a decade. What I learned about business really goes back about 40 years, as I built up Related Companies, the nation's largest private real estate company. This book includes contributors who have shaped the development and growth of sport in innovative and profound ways over that same length of time. My hat is off to them. When I bought the Miami Dolphins in 2008, I quickly found out that even though I had been a sports fan my entire life and a businessman my entire adult life, I did not know about the business of sport in great depth. As with any industry, there are all sorts of idiosyncrasies that I had to familiarize myself with, a steep learning curve to be sure. But I also had confidence in myself, because I knew to do my research ahead of time, and I knew that in many fundamental ways sport business is like any business. If I could transfer my commitment to executing a consistent process and vision from the world of real estate to the world of sport, I felt sure that I could make my own contribution.

WHY ARE YOU IN BUSINESS?

Can you answer that question? I know why I am in business. I like to look ahead and have the vision for something before anybody else. I don't want to follow what everyone else is doing. I like to assess a situation and take what others would consider a risk when I feel it is sure to work. That's how I built Related, which opened in 1972 and now has more than $50 billion in assets. I like to surround myself with bright, passionate, hardworking people. Those people are the secret to my success. Related now employs some 3,500 professionals. Equinox, which we acquired in 2006 to add a lifestyle element to our developments and value to that company through our real estate expertise, has around 15,000 employees. Add in those who work for the Dolphins and our other sport-related ventures (some of which are mentioned in this chapter), and we number nearly 20,000 employees. I feel a responsibility to these people, knowing that we will succeed if we all accept a common vision, face challenges, grow—and ultimately succeed—together. That is the case whether you are a small business or a major corporation, in or out of sport.

So again, why are you in business? That is the fundamental question if you are going to execute a consistent process for your vision in a world where your projects and deals are rarely of the cookie-cutter variety.

FINDING COMFORT IN RISK

Purchasing the Dolphins gave me entrée into the entertaining, challenging, and exceptionally fun sphere of sport, which has led me in some interesting directions that I otherwise would never have gone into. That exemplifies to me that when you take a risk, the rewards that result from doing so are never immediately evident. As a leader, you must provide consistency and be able to articulate a vision to your stakeholders. That may seem incongruent with the idea of risk taking. It is not. Showing a steady hand and doing the planning to make something happen may sound dull at first, but these actions are what allow you to take comfort in knowing that the risk you embark on is worth taking. You'll never fully take away the possibility of losing a lot of money or of an unforeseen incident altering your plans; they call it risk taking for a reason.

I honed my business skills and instincts over decades before I got to the NFL. By the time I bought the Dolphins for $1.1 billion, at that time the largest price ever for a North American sport franchise, I felt comfortable making gut-level decisions with high stakes on the line. The team is worth multiple times that today. In retrospect, the decision seems like a no-brainer. Make no mistake, when you have more than $1 billion on the line, there is no such thing as certainty. And in that case, I readily admit that I didn't negotiate well. I didn't have the leverage to do so. I bought at that price because that is what it cost. And I knew it was a unique opportunity. I let emotion get in my way, but I was fully aware of my reasons and what price I could justify. I took that leap with a clear mind about the numbers, and a plan in place to build a successful team just as I had built Related. I found the rules of the NFL to be very different than the rules of real estate and other business sectors. Everything is set up for parity. But that is fine with me. That is part of the challenge and is part of my continual education in the worlds I choose to work in.

I also found the complexity of the deal a pleasure. The more complex, the better, because it narrows the playing field and allows me to play a bigger game and be challenged by people who want to play a bigger game. I'm glad I did. Without purchasing the Dolphins, I wouldn't have been able to do the many other sport-related ventures that I now do, including the Champions Cup. Did you notice I opened the chapter with that more recent venture, a soccer tournament? I am constantly looking ahead. Get comfortable with risk by putting in your work ahead of time. Any way you look at it, whether regulations, taxes, or financing, deal making is much more complex today than it used to be. There is

GAME CHANGER

LEARNING TO BALANCE TRADITION AND INNOVATION

George Pyne

George Pyne accepted the task of expanding NASCAR's base of fans, a potentially risky business move. As Stephen Ross recommends, Pyne and NASCAR planned well and moved steadily forward. Pyne is CEO of Bruin Sports Capital, which he founded in January 2015. Backed by long-term capital from global private investors and WPP, the world's largest communications services group, Bruin specializes in developing high-growth, high-yield platform businesses in the technology, sport, media, live events, marketing, and entertainment sectors. Today, Bruin's reach spans five continents, and its companies are in business with virtually every top sport league, rights holder, governing body, blue-chip brand, and sporting event. Pyne is also non-executive chairman of Courtside Ventures, an early-stage fund launched in 2016 devoted to entrepreneurs transforming the intersection of sport, media, and technology. Courtside has backed 22 enterprises specializing in media, esports, virtual and augmented reality, data, AI, and live streaming, among others. Before Bruin, Pyne was president and board member of IMG Sports and Entertainment, and chief operating officer and board member of NASCAR. His leadership included significant advancements in on- and off-track operations and safety as well as an entirely new strategic approach to commercialization. All of this was the impetus behind the sport's growth from regional niche to national sensation.

I joined NASCAR in 1995 to help build and grow the sport. One of my primary objectives was to expand the sport from its Southern roots into a nationally recognized enterprise. I will always remember the advice that Bill France Jr., who was the president of the company at that time, gave me when I started. "Work hard, tell the truth and do not embarrass us," he said. Quite a task! He also said to be true to the product and fans that made NASCAR great.

When I arrived, our events were primarily in the Southeast. Many of our races were broadcast on The Nashville Network, our title sponsor was RJR Tobacco, and there were very few consumer-packaged goods companies investing in NASCAR. We worked hard to promote the sport to new brands and media partners and had tremendous success in taking it national. We tried many innovative approaches. Some would call them crazy, but they were always measured against respect for the product and respect for the values of the core fan, as Bill had told me on my first day.

One example is a partnership we fostered with The Coca-Cola Company while navigating Pepsi's long-standing relationship with NASCAR and International Speedway Corporation (ISC)—a public company controlled by the France family. In fact, Pepsi designed the NASCAR logo and owned stock in ISC at one time. Despite this lineage, I felt that Pepsi could be more aggressive promoting the sport.

I saw Coke as a potentially impactful partner for NASCAR, and a primary reason was that it had more resources than Pepsi. However, NASCAR had such loyalty to

Pepsi that approaching them was not allowed, and merely suggesting this was not appreciated.

The opportunity came when Coke dropped its NFL sponsorship. I told Brian France, Bill's son and the head of marketing at that time, that I wanted to approach the company. I sensed they would need a new partner and we were the right ones. Approaching them was blessed with a caveat to be careful. Brian said explicitly, "Be careful," and not much more. To me this was the great part about NASCAR. Brian had concern for the tradition but was open-minded about considering opportunities that could transform the sport.

The meeting turned into a long-standing agreement with The Coca-Cola Company that included the NASCAR racing family of drivers. Coke brought historic levels of marketing and promotional investment that over time played a significant role in the sport's transformation. The campaigns connected with hard-core and casual fans, authentically with the sport and with a genuine family feel. It was entirely in keeping with the best traditions of NASCAR. And, ironically, as a result of our agreement with Coke, Pepsi increased its spending and marketing of the sport behind Jeff Gordon to levels it never had before.

When I left NASCAR in 2006, we had a national racing footprint, our races were shown on NBC and Fox, our title sponsor was Nextel, and 100 of the Fortune 500 used NASCAR as a marketing platform. We also had more avid fans than at any other time in NASCAR's history.

While working with Bill and for NASCAR, I lived the values of honesty and integrity, along with a relentless focus on the core product and the fans who consumed the product. These values are so important for growing long-lasting, effective businesses, and Bill's advice lives on in me today.

---

lots to learn, but as you become experienced, you realize that you can get people on board to get the deal done. I always focus on the deal at hand, and figure that over the long haul if I do each deal as prepared and as dedicated as I can be, I'll do well. If you are in business, you are always taking risks. When people can trust you and your team to execute your process, from the due diligence and approvals to the financial package and government regulations, then it doesn't feel quite so risky.

BRINGING FORTH PASSION IN YOURSELF

When you are putting a consistent process into action, whether to purchase a team or a property, build a stadium, create a new event, or develop a product, you need to be honest with yourself. Beyond the preparation and the comfort with risk, do you have passion for your project? Is this where you want to devote your time and energy when you have a multitude of other options? This may not seem like an obvious or even critical step in executing your vision, but if you find that your own enthusiasm for the project is high, you will unlock it in other stakeholders. This is essential to getting deals done and projects completed with excellence. I'm not necessarily saying you have to write a fiery or poetic speech—though if that is what drives you and gets you results, go for it. Your passion could come from many places. In the case of the Dolphins, it was intensely personal for me. In the case of the Champions Cup, it was taking on the challenge of envisioning a new slant on an established sport. What business ventures and challenges get you excited? Nothing big ever gets accomplished unless the leader or leaders get behind it in an elemental way. It can't just be business. There is always another deal or project, and if you haven't determined whether it is important to you beyond the bottom line, when obstacles start to park themselves in front of you, you won't want to do battle with them. Those obstacles will chip away at you before you can take an ax to them.

FINDING PASSION IN OTHERS

Passion is everywhere in the world of sport . . . in the fans, the participants, the people throughout the organization and community who have devoted their lives to the games, and certainly those of us in the front office. Sport is entertainment. It arouses people's passions much like a concert; and more than with most forms of entertainment, you don't know the outcome. Producing a sport event is putting on a good show, where people can cheer or boo any team or any player. That is a unique experience in our lives. From that standpoint, it is not hard to instill your passion into your product when you are one of the leaders of a sport organization or event. However, spreading passion around your enterprise is not enough to be successful. To reach your goal, your passion is only part of the equation. When you combine that passion with extensive research, and find partners and collaborators who also believe in it and have skill sets and assets that complement yours, you are lined up to achieve your objective. When this happens, you can create something greater (see figure 4.1). I have found partners consistently who help make this work. There is value in knowing with some certainty what a partner brings to the table; but even if different projects require different partners, or old partners to play a different role, be clear in your mind about what you need and communicate it, so that the job gets done well and you are well positioned for the next time around.

A great way to illustrate how the passion of fans drives the production of sport is through today's rapid technological innovations. Sports fans want more analytics, more insights into the games they consume. We live in a knowledge-based environment, and they want to share that with their friends. I maintain that there is no saturation point in advancing technology in sport; you'll see more about the influence of technology in part III. One of the companies I bought since buying the Dolphins is FanVision, which provides devices that allow fans to get replays, statistics, and other analytics while they are at a game. One application with the technology that has really taken off is in NASCAR and IndyCar racing. With the device, fans can obtain radio feeds from their favorite drivers or watch

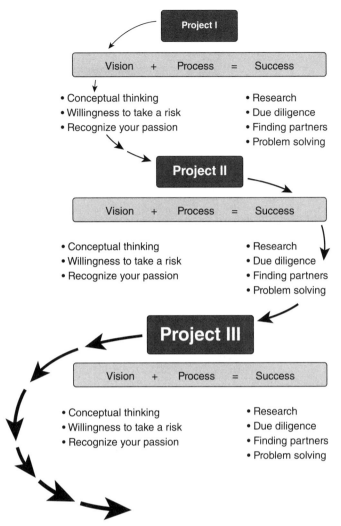

Figure 4.1 Success is a continual interplay of vision and process. Each success paves the way for even greater successes.

MAKE SURE YOUR MINOR LEAGUE IS MAJOR

David A. Andrews

David A. Andrews recognizes that success is achieved through expecting stellar personal and organizational performance and not taking shortcuts. Andrews is president and CEO of the American Hockey League, a position he has held since 1994. In that time, he has been one of the most influential executives in hockey and all of minor professional sport, guiding the AHL into unequaled times of prosperity with record levels of attendance and exposure, an impressive list of corporate partners, and an expanded league geography across North America. Andrews is an honored member of the Nova Scotia Sport Hall of Fame and the British Columbia Hockey Hall of Fame, and was a recipient of the Lester Patrick Award in 2010.

(continued)

I have been blessed to have enjoyed a 40-year management career in sport business, mainly in professional hockey but also in amateur sport and Olympic high-performance programming. What I have learned along the way is that pride in performance as an employee or as a leader is a difference maker.

Perhaps that is why I cringe at any reference to the American Hockey League as the "minors." No minor league should be comfortable with that designation.

David Andrews (right) presents the Calder Cup to the Grand Rapids Griffins after their 2017 AHL Championship.

"Minors" suggests "not as good," and we will never accept that.

With 82 years of proud history in our sport, everything that we do as an organization should be to the highest standard of performance, should set the bar for other professional teams and leagues, and should always deliver value equal to or greater than our competition. "Minor league" is not the objective!

Our brand equity at the AHL as a quality organization is a promise on which we must deliver, and we must deliver on it every day. All stakeholders regardless of their status should be able to trust our brand and our leadership.

Working with organizations at our level is the best training that anyone can get for a career in the sport industry: working typically within a small group of staff members where everyone must support each other, where 10 young people must do the equivalent work of 20 to succeed, where the bottom line really matters and every nickel counts, and where every committed employee will experience every facet of the sport business. In an environment like that, enthusiastic young people will learn and will have the opportunity to display their energy, talent, and leadership potential.

Paying your dues is not old-fashioned; it is the proven means to building a lasting career. Performing at a high level will be noticed, skills will be developed by trial and error, and these experiences will differentiate young people and qualify them over time for leadership and responsibility based upon actual substance rather than spin.

The alternative "shortcut" career approach of using strong interpersonal skills and networking to attain a position without having the experience to deliver on your personal promise is a recipe for failure for both the employee and for the organization.

Regardless of experience or job title, the path to success in sport business lies in demonstrating pride in performance, delivering on your promises, and bringing a smile to the workplace every day.

MAKING MONEY WITH THE MONEY YOU'VE MADE

Ric Edelman

Ric Edelman, a #1 *New York Times* bestselling author who has written nine books on personal finance, uses the example of a retiring athlete to explain how the process and vision needed for success in one part of your career can be completely wrong for another part of your career. Edelman is widely regarded as one of the nation's top financial advisors. He was ranked #11 on the Forbes 2017 list of Top Wealth Advisors,[1] and *Barron's* ranked him the nation's #1 Independent Financial Advisor three times.[2] RIABiz called him one of the "10 most influential figures" in the investment advisory field,[3] and he is an inductee of *Research* magazine's Financial Advisor Hall of Fame.[4] Edelman's financial planning and investment management firm, Edelman Financial Services, manages more than $21 billion for more than 36,000 clients in 43 offices nationwide.[5] Learn more at RicEdelman.com.

Congratulations! Your skill, talent, and hard work (with a bit o' luck tossed in) have led you to enjoy tremendous success in the sport industry. As a result, you've earned quite a bit of money, and you've been able to set aside some of it for the future.

How, then, should you be managing your investments?

Successful athletes, entrepreneurs, sales executives, and business owners often believe they should manage their investments the same way they've managed their careers and business activities. But that's a huge mistake. In fact, the very behavior that made you successful in your career will make you *unsuccessful* as an investor. In other words, when it comes to your investment strategy, do *the opposite* of what you do in your career.

Those in professional athletics (players, managers, and coaches) as well as businesspeople know the importance of agility. You must anticipate and respond to your opponent's (or competitor's) moves immediately. The emphasis on the short term is crucial—worry about this play, this game, this deal often without regard to long-term implications.

And we all know why the physical abilities of a linebacker differ so radically from those of, say, an outside hitter in volleyball. The skills and performance needed for success in each sport are different, so athletes focus intently on what's needed to maximize their success.

And yet, these two attributes of career and business success—great agility and intense concentration of effort—are disastrous for your investments. That's why successful people are often surprised by their failure as investors.

Successful investing is not about agility. Instead, the exact opposite is needed: a static, dull, boring, long-term buy-and-hold approach. Consider the S&P 500 stock index: Its average annual return for the five-year period ending December 31, 2017, was 13 percent, according to Morningstar. But if, during that five-year period, you had missed the 13 days when the index had made the most money, your return would have been zero. That's right: The entire profit of the S&P 500 occurred in just 13 days. Could you have picked the 13 days that mattered? Of course not. For proof, consider Dalbar's Quantitative Analysis of Investor Behavior. It shows that

(continued)

while the S&P 500 earned, on average, 10.7 percent per year over the past 30 years, the average stock fund investor earned only 4.66 percent per year. The reason? Poor timing by investors. They buy and sell at the wrong times, dramatically reducing their returns. This is why you need to be invested for the long term, paying attention to your goals, not what's happening now in the stock market, and taking no action based on what you think might happen next. Because you're almost certainly going to be wrong.

And instead of focusing on just stocks—in what would be a highly concentrated investment strategy—you instead need to diversify your investments broadly. From 2008 through 2017, a highly diversified portfolio of 16 major asset classes and market sectors—including real estate, bonds, oil and gas, foreign securities, precious metals, and more, as well as stocks—earned an average annual return of 7.2 percent. But if you had missed the best three asset classes each year, your average return would have been only 3.3 percent per year. It's virtually impossible to predict which 3, out of 16, will perform best from one year to the next—try picking which teams will be the top three this year!—so you're better off owning them all, all the time.

It's important that you develop and deploy the strategies necessary to win in your career. It's equally important that you develop and deploy the strategies you need to help you win with your investments. Don't assume that those strategies are the same, because they're not.

the race where the track is out of view. They can run apps from the device and access the Google Play store. I have invested money into a drone racing league, and have lots of plans for expanding technology in sport. With virtual reality and esports continuing to gain in popularity, the sky is the limit.

GUIDING PRINCIPLES

This is not a typical chapter on leadership, deal making, or project development. The secrets of those functions are about mindset and reads, like a quarterback reading a defense, more than they are about specific skills. Skills are important, don't get me wrong, but they are learned on the job as you get experience. You must first bring to your job an openness to get the work done and see what is coming in the future. I have written here about how to successfully shepherd projects through. I said at the outset of this chapter that I can't give you a cookie-cutter model for decision making in business because there isn't one. I do hope to have interested you in building the self-confidence, due diligence, and curiosity that leads to your questioning yourself whether what you are creating is worth it. If it is, then you can assemble a team, and together you will be able to consistently execute a vision through a process you trust.

I articulated five guiding principles when I founded Related. Those values help to guide me and my executives as we make business decisions. Becoming a pro sports team owner opened my world wider, giving me a chance to take what I knew in one area and applying it to another while simultaneously learning about that new area. The principles provide a compass in tough times, decision making, and moving projects forward. I've discovered, not surprisingly, that they are as important in sport business as they are to real estate business, or any other type of business you could name.

1. *Commitment to excellence:* We are committed to the highest standards of excellence and strive to always exceed customer expectations and be the best in our industry.

2. *Honesty and integrity:* Honesty and integrity are the foundation upon which we build all relationships. Above all, we stand by our word.

3. *Entrepreneurship and innovation:* Our entrepreneurial, change-driven environment challenges the status quo. We encourage creative thinking and are constantly searching for better ways to accomplish our goals.

4. *Employee opportunity:* Our employees are our greatest asset. We invest in them and challenge them to realize their professional potential, as well as our corporate goals.

5. *Accountability:* We are accountable to the company and to our customers, investors, partners, communities, and one another for the work we produce and the actions we take. We take ownership of our ideas, our projects, and our impacts.

In recent years, I have turned my attention to a $25 billion development in an industrial area on Manhattan's West Side known as Hudson Yards. When complete, it will be the largest private-sector commercial and residential development in U.S. history, a city within a city. For many years, I have kept a pair of boxing gloves and a head guard hanging near my desk. I now have those items at my current office at the Time Warner Center, and I expect to take them to Hudson Yards. Maybe I'm a little superstitious; since I've had success with them thus far, why not keep them around? But I also see them as a reminder of the link between my sporting and real estate lives, of how executing a consistent process and vision is about using the past to positively influence the future.

CHAPTER 5

Filling an Industry Need

Bob Kain

Bob Kain joined Mark McCormack's International Management Group in 1976 to be a tennis agent and proceeded to build IMG's tennis business into one of its most lucrative. IMG represented many of the biggest names in tennis over the past half century, as well as all four Grand Slam tournaments and the two other biggest tourneys in the world (Miami and Indian Wells). Kain created and built IMG's figure skating business, and along with Scott Hamilton, cocreated Stars on Ice, the most prestigious skating tour in the world. He also oversaw the building of IMG Fashion, the top model agency and fashion event promoter in the world, and became president and chief operating officer of IMG North and South America, prior to becoming president and co-CEO of IMG when McCormack passed away in 2003. When Kain retired from IMG in 2006, the company employed approximately 3,000 people in 61 offices in 30 countries, and represented more than 1,000 individuals and owned, operated, or represented more than 1,000 events annually. IMG was also the largest independent sports television company in the world, producing and distributing more than 10,000 hours of programming each year. Kain is currently on the USGA Executive Committee, and retains a plus-one handicap competing in senior amateur tournaments, including the U.S. Senior Amateur and British Senior Amateur Championships.

Billie Jean King was the most important athlete of the 20th century. There, I said it. With all due respect to a number of other legitimate candidates for that honor, I stand by that claim. She forever changed sport for women, and she did it not just through her skill as an athlete but by advocating for opportunities, creating events and infrastructure, changing perceptions, and understanding the business, marketing, and legal tactics needed to accomplish her goals. King was a key force behind Title IX as well as the public face in front of that legislation. She founded the Women's Sports Foundation and the Women's Tennis Association (WTA) Tour.

As an agent for International Management Group (IMG), I managed King in the late 1970s. IMG was already a well-known golf and television agency but only just beginning to be a major player in the tennis world. The WTA Tour had only begun in 1973. Its popularity was still on the rise in the United States and around the globe, but not everyone was a believer. Several of the U.S. events were start-ups that were struggling. King encouraged IMG to buy a couple of the existing events and create a couple more. We listened to her, and this became our first foray into owning and promoting tennis events. Virginia Slims was the first major domestic sponsor of the women's tour.

Fast-forward a few years. IMG was representing the men's Italian Open and German Open for sponsorships and television rights. Those tournament organizers did not want to run a women's championship because they felt these were money losers. Spurred on by King, we underwrote women's editions of the Italian and German Opens. Both remain successful today. Thanks to our client's urging, we became trailblazers in support of the first truly professional women's global sport and helped King make the WTA one of the most successful sport properties.

Sometimes, you won't originate an idea, as was the case with IMG and me in the example with Billie Jean King. But we were smart enough to recognize and trust a smart and visionary person and to partner with her to help make her vision a reality—and, I hope, to make that vision become a reality sooner and more successfully than if she had worked with someone else. She and we both had considerable strengths, and we respected one another, so we leveraged those strengths to fill an industry need. This is an important but often overlooked point: Having an idea alone doesn't fill an industry need. A need is filled when it becomes a reality, when it leaves a person's brain and exists in the world, and is received positively because it provides some value to some people.

Many times, you do originate the idea, and if you are serious about being in this business, I suspect you are brimming with ideas to share with the world. Good for you. This chapter is about being the catalyst who ensures that an industry need is met. I am going to start by sharing a counterintuitive reality that maybe I shouldn't admit. As an executive at arguably the sporting world's greatest need-filling organization in history, IMG, I probably shouldn't let you know that whether in or out of sport, the world doesn't really have that many needs that are critical to fill. We like to think that what we are interested in is the most important thing, and that everyone else should share our enthusiasm. But most of us get along just fine without every single desire being satisfied. The flip side of that reality is that there are plenty of ideas that, if brought to fruition, might make life easier, or more enjoyable, or help us connect with people more, or solve big problems. Innovation drives us to fill these needs—maybe we should call them wants. Often, when people have a transformative idea, no one else even knows it. The creators of that idea not only must bring their idea to life, they also must convince others that the need is there. Even if, as I said, most creations are not truly a need, when you create something that has value, you are improving lives of participants or fans. And the industry improves in turn. Filling a need is a series of wants and desires that become indispensable once in tangible form. There's no turning back—and if you were part of the development of that need, it's an incredible feeling.

ONE THING LEADS TO ANOTHER

IMG's origin story is a prime example of finding a need to fill. Its subsequent history is a series of decisions and actions that filled more and more needs as the sport industry exploded over the next half century. A brief explanation of the company Mark McCormack founded on a handshake will help you see the power of innovation and momentum. McCormack was a talented young golfer who played at William & Mary and competed against Arnold Palmer when the future legend played at Wake Forest. McCormack went to Yale Law School, and after graduating had job opportunities in Cleveland and his hometown of Chicago. He decided on the law firm of Arter and Hadden in Cleveland, which just so happened to be where Palmer was serving in the Coast Guard in the early 1950s and was still living when he won the 1954 U.S. Amateur title in Detroit. The two reconnected, and with Palmer's star on the rise, McCormack suggested he become Palmer's lawyer and agent—a highly unusual concept even for the most in-demand athletes of that time. They agreed with a handshake, and were bound together forever as one of the most influential partnerships in sport history.

McCormack was a visionary, able to translate knowledge from one industry to another in order to provide value to his clients and gain control over the new medium of television. One of his mentors was Lew Wasserman, chair of MCA and unofficial king of Hollywood. MCA represented the top talent in Hollywood in the 1950s and produced many blockbuster movies. Eventually, the Screen Actors Guild fought back against this dominance and brokered an agreement whereby producers could not manage talent, and talent agents could not be producers. This became California law, but it did not apply to sport business. McCormack applied the MCA model of managing talent and then producing television shows and promoting events with our clients in them. Thus, the model of the full-service sport agency came to be.

McCormack soon showcased what this could look like when he added young phenom Jack Nicklaus and South African Gary Player to his roster. With these three imminently marketable golfers, McCormack coined "the Big Three," and created a made-for-TV series of matches by the same name featuring the trio. The synergy of television and sport was still emerging, and McCormack put IMG in a position to sell TV rights to the British Open and Wimbledon. That in turn led to the formation of IMG's television business, both production and distribution. McCormack hired one of MCA's producers, Jay Michaels (father of universally admired broadcaster Al Michaels), to head up IMG's media business.

360

OUTWORKING ADVERSITY

Gary Player

Gary Player, the international leg of IMG's made-for-TV "Big Three," fulfilled a promise and realized his dream through an indomitable work ethic—a critical attribute in any sport entrepreneur. Known as the "Black Knight," Player won nine major championships, plus six majors on the Champions Tour and three Senior British Open Championships during his career, and became the first non-American (and one of only five players ever) to win the career Grand Slam. The 1974 World Golf Hall of Fame inductee won more than 150 tournaments on six continents over six decades, along the way becoming a renowned golf course architect, authoring or coauthoring more than 30 golf books, and adding business interests that include licensing, events, publishing, wine, apparel, memorabilia, and Thoroughbred breeding. He operates The Player Foundation, which promotes underprivileged education around the world.

Overcoming adversity is essential in one's path to success. Whether in sport or business, at some point along the way, one will have to face adversity head-on. It comes in many shapes and forms. However, if you manage to handle its ugly face, it's a game changer.

When I was 8 years old, my mother was diagnosed with cancer. No doubt it is a traumatic experience for anyone to see his mother endure all the pain and suffering that comes with this terrible disease. But I believe how I responded to her passing put me on the path to success.

You see, I made a promise at her bedside. My promise was to work as hard as possible in whatever it was I chose to do. This ended up being golf. But at that point, I was still a young boy not knowing what the future would hold. One thing was certain—I wanted to become a professional athlete. And being small, I would have to outwork everybody to do so.

I was hit with adversity yet again, when a short time after my mother passed, my brother informed our family he was heading off to fight in World War II alongside the Americans and British. At the same time, my sister was attending boarding school and my father worked from sunup to sundown in the gold mines, thousands of feet underground, to support his children.

Many nights I sat alone in our house wishing I was dead. How was I going to make something of myself? What could I do to help my family at such a young age? I was lonely, sad, and disillusioned. But determined to honor my mother too.

By the time I reached my teenage years, I truly believed I was going to become a world champion because of my work ethic. At age 14, I took up the wonderful sport of golf. It was my father who first got me into the game. I was hooked immediately and quickly came to the realization I could play this sport for a long time. Practicing harder than my peers would surely lead to my success.

But that wasn't the end of adversity. During my career as a professional golfer, being from South Africa in the apartheid era, I faced scrutiny and criticism every step of the way. But I didn't let the naysayers stop me from my mission to become a world champion.

Now in my 80s, I can say with confidence that overcoming adversity was my game changer. Life is about how you react to it. Sometimes you face difficult decisions, and how you respond to those decisions can make or break your goals, your business, your family, or your life.

Because of the clients we represented in golf and later tennis, we kept seeing opportunities for promoting events and television properties. Often we couldn't sell our ideas to any promoters or any of the three networks, so we started creating events and TV shows ourselves. This was simply a way for us to fill the needs of our clients, but it resulted in massive growth for our business. The examples are endless, as filling needs in your sphere of influence can be when people are invested in finding them. Here are a few:

- One of the first events that IMG owned and operated was the World Match Play Championships. McCormack wanted to promote a World Match Play event. He believed in the format and thought it would showcase IMG clients. The problem was that there were none left in the world of golf. So IMG created the World Match Play Championships in London. It is still a big event on the European Tour.

- In 1983, in the lead-up to the upcoming Sarajevo Olympics, it was clear that figure skating would be the most popular sport. I was looking for a new challenge so I asked McCormack if we could jump into the skating business. At the 1984 Games, American Scott Hamilton won the gold medal, and East Germany's Katarina Witt beat out American Rosalynn Sumners for the gold. Figure skating was by far the highest-rated Olympic sport, but at that time the only career choice for an Olympic champion was Disney on Ice with Mickey Mouse or Ice Capades with the Smurfs. We set out to establish a wonderful professional sport for these great athletes. I signed Hamilton as our lead client. I remember pitching him that we would make him the Arnold Palmer of figure skating. Today I think he is (see the sidebar by Hamilton later in this chapter). By 1987, Hamilton and I created Stars on Ice, with IMG promoting the tour. Throughout the 1990s, it traveled to more than 70 North American cities. IMG also created skating television programming that ran every weekend in the winter to counter football and basketball. Stars on Ice is still playing in the United States, Canada, and Japan. This story has a very personal angle to it that I will share in the takeaway lessons near the end of the chapter.

- I went to Bradenton, Florida, in 1985 to sign the hottest tennis coach in the world, Nick Bollettieri. He went with another agency, but two years later he was unhappy and called me. I went back to see him; this time I had a much bigger arrow in my quiver. I said that IMG did not want to represent him; we wanted to buy the Nick Bollettieri Tennis Academy, all 27 acres, 50 tennis courts, and its dormitories. I thought it would be a nice extension to our tennis client and event expertise. Bollettieri was training a lot of great players, including Andre Agassi and Jim Courier. His academy also appealed to the serious juniors who sought college scholarships. Some 30 years later, Bollettieri is still coaching there; it is now a 300-plus-acre IMG Academy with well over 800 students living and training and going to school, for not just tennis, but for golf, soccer, baseball, football, lacrosse, and more. Another need filled.

- In 1987, Butch Buchholz was a former #1 American tennis player who had just finished his term as CEO of the ATP. He and I had a close friendship, and he asked me if we would be interested in helping him create a Players Championship for men and women in Miami, similar to the PGA Tour's Sawgrass event. He led the way, we helped, and some 15 years later IMG bought the event from Butch, where it became the #1 event asset in IMG's world. Another need filled.

- Since we were managing the best golfers and tennis players in the world, we had to become experts at endorsements and licensing (read more about licensing and sport in chapter 19). We felt we were the best at this, so why not start adding football, baseball, and basketball players to our client list? We decided we needed specialists in each sport to compete. By the 1990s, before consolidation really took hold in sport agency, we had the biggest team sport agency in the world. One of our early football clients was Archie Manning. He was still a client when his sons Peyton and Eli turned professional, and IMG signed them as well.

- Around that same time, IMG had a struggling small model agency. I asked McCormack if I could put a colleague of mine, Chuck Bennett, in charge and we would drive it. Within a decade, IMG Models had bought New York Fashion Week, created other Fashion Weeks around the world, and it was the #1 agency in the world. We applied what we had learned in sport to another business that was international and also wasn't restricted by language barriers.

That list should give you a good sense of how the simple but deceptively difficult act of finding niches to fill can lead to directions you never dreamed of. In the next sections, we will explore how to become better at finding those openings. I end this section with a quote by someone who was not a fan of my former boss, who died in 2003 and led to me becoming president and co-CEO of IMG Worldwide. Palmer's biographer, Tom Callahan, thought the agent expected too much in appearances and promotions from his clients, running them ragged in the process. But even the famed golf writer gave McCormack due for his vision.

"*Golf Digest* named McCormack the most powerful man in golf. *Tennis* magazine named him the most powerful man in tennis. *Sports Illustrated* named him the most powerful man in sport. His International Management Group stretched out into 80-some offices in 30-some countries, but Palmer stayed the primary client, even after Margaret Thatcher and Mikhail Gorbachev came aboard. In his middle-80s, without hitting a single golf shot that counted, Arnold was still earning $40 million a year under his perfect logo, an umbrella" (Callahan 2017, p. 103).

SEEK THE HORIZON, AND INVITE OTHERS TO JOIN YOU

Innovative thinking is required to anticipate the needs and desires of others. Innovation is really a progression, a series of consistently stepping outside of your comfort zone that allows you to glimpse the possibilities and decide which

GAME CHANGER

FINDING MY NEXT ACT AFTER OLYMPIC GOLD

Scott Hamilton

Scott Hamilton filled an industry need with Bob Kain by being professional and not letting someone else's preconceived notion of him dictate his path. The most recognized male figure skating star in the world, and figure skating's voice of authority in the United States, Hamilton captured the attention of the world with his Olympic gold medal performances in Sarajevo in 1984. Since then, he has shared his love and enthusiasm for the sport as an analyst, performer, producer, and bestselling author (*Landing It,* 1999; *The Great Eight,* 2009; *Finish First: Winning Changes Everything,* 2018). He further inspires others as a speaker, humanitarian, and a cancer and pituitary brain tumor survivor. Scott currently heads the Scott Hamilton CARES Foundation (Cancer Alliance for Research, Education and Survivorship) and the Scott Hamilton Skating Academy. In what

Courtesy of Scott Hamilton LLC. Photo credit: Michael Gomez, Gomez Photography.

little free time remains, Scott can be found on the golf course and enjoys spending time with his wife Tracie and four children at their home outside Nashville, Tennessee.

My success in professional skating happened in a way that many success stories in business happen. Out of devastating, horrible circumstances.

My first job as a professional skater came in a very traditional form. Right after I won my Olympic gold medal in 1984, a huge professional ice show that had been in business for almost 50 years gave me a two-year contract with a third-year option. I was the new "cog" in the giant machine.

The president of the company was hesitant in signing me because they had never had a male star. He even went as far as to tell me, "It's a great thing you won an Olympic gold medal, because you're too short to be in the chorus line." Another fact he shared with me was that he didn't like paying stars because they weren't reliable. They constantly missed shows and press obligations and made life difficult for management. When a star is "out," customers get upset and in some cases want their money back. He shared that with me not as a warning, but just because they were expecting me to be the same as those who had come before me.

(continued)

GAME CHANGER   *(continued)*

After two years of never missing a show, skating at a very high level, and never missing a press or media opportunity, I was dismissed. The reason given was that the ice show company was going through a sale and the new owner didn't want to present male stars. Only female.

To this day, I am grateful I had proven myself as a reliable professional, because another opportunity came to me in the form of a start-up. Would I be interested in starting a new touring ice show?

After checking my schedule and realizing that I had the rest of my life pretty wide open, I jumped in with all the ambition and intensity imaginable.

Stars on Ice was born!

I was able to skate in ways I had never thought to dream of. It was simply the greatest opportunity I could have been given and I wouldn't allow it to fail.

The first few years were spent proving the concept. And then something wonderful happened. Stars on Ice became the professional destination for practically every Olympic and world champion–level skater from then on.

I took the opportunity very seriously and spent 15 wonderful years skating in sold-out buildings from Seattle to New York, Los Angeles to Boston. I stayed for as long as I wanted and was able to retire on my own terms. It was time to move on to a normal life as a husband and a father.

The success that came from being "let go" was something I never could have anticipated.

To this day, I am grateful for the opportunity to build something new: An ice show tour that suited my abilities. It was all much more than I could have done had I been kept at that first opportunity.

Good things come when we least expect them!

---

ones to leap for. McCormack was able to do that, and just as importantly, to (1) hire people who were willing to do that, and (2) allow them to do that. If you want to prepare for what's on the horizon, you better be willing to hire those whom you want to look out into the distance with you.

I'm proud to say I was one of those hires. If I sound boastful, understand that I quickly realized I was surrounded by an organization and a mentor that believed in me, which only made me believe in myself all the more even when I made mistakes.

I joined IMG in 1976 as an agent, the company's third employee on the tennis side of the business. Already well known as a golf and television agency, IMG had fewer than 100 employees worldwide, in Cleveland, New York, London, and Tokyo. I remember doing projections for the tennis division early on when gross revenues were $600,000. Two decades later, my tennis division was doing more than $100 million in revenues. There's a lesson for you. It is better to be a competent executive in a booming business than a superstar in a flat or declining business. Find that next rocket ship and climb on board!

I went on to lead the creation and building of IMG's Academy business, model and fashion business, and figure skating business, and was chairman of our financial planning business. I became president of IMG North America and South America. I pretty much tried to lead IMG in all areas besides golf, and McCormack kept giving me those opportunities. In 2003, McCormack passed away and I became president and co-CEO. In 2006, when I retired from IMG, we had approximately 3,000 employees in 60 offices in 30 countries. We were managing more than 1,000 clients, were involved in more than 1,000 events, and were producing and distributing more than 10,000 hours of television programming, creating revenues just under $1 billion.

McCormack set the tone for that ambition with a skill set that made him a unique leader. He was an optimist who could fly at 30,000 feet trying to figure out new opportunities. But lots of visionaries do that. He combined the vision and smarts with an unbelievable ability to micromanage his own projects and clients. For example, he was lead executive for the British Open and Wimbledon until the day he died. He managed those clients so thoroughly and in such detail that I still am amazed by it. No matter how big IMG got and how much in demand he was, he never stopped handling his clients' details. What a great lesson that was for us younger executives in how to manage a client or project. It taught us we would never reach a level where we were just overhead; we would always be expected to manage specific projects or clients.

Still, McCormack never micromanaged his employees. He hired us to dream big, and time after time, McCormack let us follow our ambitious ideas.

THE GLOBAL MINDSET

When Palmer traveled to the British Open in 1960, it was a huge deal. Americans simply didn't go across the pond for that hallowed event back then. McCormack saw that, and I believe it helped frame his early thinking. He had always considered sport in general, and golf specifically, as a global business that didn't face as many language barriers as more traditional industries required to consummate. McCormack firmly "believed the popularity and marketability of athletes could transcend borders, cultures, language, even sport itself. McCormack-managed athletes were the first to endorse clothing, watches, and motor oil. They played exhibition matches around the world. They gave inspirational talks to business at a hefty price tag" (US Legal 2016).

To appreciate his vision, understand that 50 years ago sports were just a couple of pages in the daily newspaper and, on television, maybe 3 hours over a weekend on just three networks. Most countries had only a government-controlled network. The small number of sport agents usually worked only in the home country that was theirs and their athlete's. By the late 1960s, McCormack had spent considerable time in Europe, particularly the United Kingdom, and he signed his first institutional clients, the Royal & Ancient Golf Club, which hosted the British Open, and Wimbledon. IMG began selling their global television rights and their sponsorship rights. Surprising as it sounds today, these seminal events had never had real representation. When McCormack's first client, Palmer, died in 2016 at age 87, three of IMG's biggest clients remained Palmer, the British Open (now referred to as The Open Championship), and Wimbledon—all signed during an era when the globalization of sport was decades away from being a buzzword.

With IMG established in the United Kingdom, McCormack was able to sign Formula One World Champion Jackie Stewart and Jean-Claude Killy—who in 1968 became the only skier ever to win Olympic gold in the downhill, giant slalom, and slalom. The global agency had entered the motor racing and ski worlds as well, expanding the global reach of all these sports in the process.

By the mid-1960s, McCormack saw Japanese interest in golf and opened an office in Tokyo to sell and service endorsements and licensing deals for the Big Three. IMG started selling TV rights worldwide, and with an Asian base of operation we could staff it when tennis became a hot market there. I remember accompanying Bjorn Borg on his first trip to Japan. Everywhere we went the press and teenage girls seemed to follow, trying to get a glimpse of the Swedish great and his flowing blond locks.

> McCormack had a sensational long game. With amazing vision and foresight, he could see all the way to Australia and Japan. He pictured Arnold Palmer teashops on the Ginza, and made plans for the private airplane he knew was coming before Arnold did (the one with the initials AP on the fuselage), not to mention the streams of jets that followed. Then, with Palmer's permission, he brought Player and Nicklaus into the fold, if not technically creating "the Big Three" (and a TV show of the same name), then promoting them to a tee. (Callahan 2017, p. 102)

IT'S A DIFFERENT WORLD

Well into the 21st century, it is easy to say that global thinking is an obvious business imperative. Sure, McCormack found fertile fields abroad to grow his business when no one else was paying attention, but what can we learn from his approach today? The sport industry is wildly more mature and sophisticated around the world than when McCormack revolutionized the work of sport agents. I'll give you an example. My admiration for his business skills, work ethic, and vision is immense, and I loved spending my career with IMG. But I would be remiss if I failed to mention that he did not bat 1.000. How McCormack entered the tennis business shows you how different the agency business is today. After Rod Laver won his first Grand Slam in 1962, he wrote and asked McCormack if he would be interested in managing him. McCormack said no thanks. Tennis began the open era in 1968, and in 1969, Laver won his second Grand Slam, and the only men's Grand Slam in open tennis history, making him arguably the greatest tennis player of all time. Laver again wrote McCormack, and this time IMG's leader jumped at it. Tennis became a fledgling division. IMG could recover from that oversight then because the competition was not yet stabilized. Today, a company would not get a second chance to rectify that mistake. In today's busy, ambitious landscape, you must anticipate having many misses as well as hits.

Filling needs may seem perhaps not as easy to do now, but don't forget that the sport business is tens of thousands of times larger now. The world keeps changing and new opportunities are out there (for example, esports). You must be creative in finding them, which is no different than for McCormack in that Sporting Stone Age when he unleashed a whole new way of thinking about marketing, licensing, and agency. Consider what I said at the start of this chapter: To fill needs, you have to identify what people want before they do. And never forget that when you are looking for new areas to enter or new ideas to test out, don't look far. Look around you. The areas closest to you are the areas where you will see a need and be able to calculate the odds of success. You see that lesson many times in IMG's incremental growth in so many interrelated areas. Here are a few examples from IMG's illustrious history of signing clients that provide takeaway points you can use to promote innovative thinking.

LOSSES CAN BE WINS

My first recruiting effort in figure skating was to sign Rosalynn Sumners, 1983 World and U.S. Champion, and soon-to-be Olympic silver medalist. After what I thought was a great recruiting meeting at her home with her mom, we were sure Roz would be our first big skating client. Two weeks later, we got the call that she was signing with Peggy Fleming's agent. But this was another loss that turned into a big win. My second recruiting meeting was with Scott Hamilton and his lawyers. If I had signed Rosalynn, Scott would not have been interested in me. They were the two U.S. stars coming out of the 1984 Olympics, and Scott wanted his own manager. Hamilton was four-time U.S. and World Champion and had just won Olympic gold. It turned out his lawyer and I both belonged to Pine Valley Golf Club. On top of that, two of my clients, Borg and Evert, were two of Hamilton's heroes. I walked out of that meeting with a new client, and as mentioned earlier, we created Stars on Ice together, plus many network skating events. He became the biggest star in the sport, and an influential person in my life. He later made me hire Sumners when we started Stars on Ice, and eventually she became my wife as well! I was best man in Hamilton's wedding, took him to the Cleveland Clinic for his cancer and brain tumors, and helped him start his CARES Foundation.

I spent 18 months trying to sign young tennis superstar Tracy Austin. I visited Tracy's parents numerous times, always sitting in the same chair, always getting dog or cat hairs on my blue blazer! It was a crushing loss when I heard she was signing with our arch-rival. The good news is I signed Chris Evert and Martina Navratilova in the following year, and they dominated women's tennis for the next decade. Two of my biggest failures in recruiting led to some of my biggest recruiting wins!

RELATIONSHIP BUILDING IS CRUCIAL

And speaking of Chrissie Evert, when I first came to IMG I was given a tennis player to manage by the name of Kristen Kemmer. She was not a great pro, but a nice young player and a wonderful person. It just so happened her best friend on tour was Chris Evert. I worked hard for Kristen and she appreciated it. About two or three years later, when I was recruiting Chrissie, one of the biggest reasons she liked and trusted me was the recommendation of her buddy Kristen.

MAKE YOUR BREAKS

In 1978, we created one of the first major women's professional tennis events in Tokyo, the Grand Slam of women's tennis. It included just four players, and one of them was Martina Navratilova. I knew Navratilova was being managed at the time by a friend of hers, and I also knew that as she was becoming a global star she needed someone with more experience. She, however, wasn't too interested in meeting. At this event, we had tournament transportation to and from the hotel. Traffic was always horrible, so I figured if I could get in her transport car I would have her trapped for an hour. I sat around the transportation area for an hour waiting for Navratilova to show up and asked her if I could bum a ride. An hour later after nonstop selling by me, we arrived at our hotel and she had agreed for me to come see her back in the United States to further our conversation. Two months later, she became a client!

STAY OPEN AND RECEPTIVE TO NEW IDEAS

By 1987 we owned the Nick Bollettieri Tennis Academy, and young Agassi lived and trained there. I asked Nick if he could set up a meeting for me with Andre's dad. I flew to Las Vegas and met Mr. Agassi at his favorite Denny's. He was about to re-sign Andre with another management company, but he was upset that the company wanted to commission Andre's Nike deal even though Mr. Agassi had done it. He then pulled out this company's representation agreement with the clause in it. I crossed out that Nike clause. I also crossed out the name of the company and the agent's name and wrote in IMG and my name in their place. A week later I had a signed agreement with Andre, and after Mr. Agassi saw our expertise, he asked us to handle Andre's future Nike deals.

Lessons aren't always learned in the big negotiations. Sometimes, the wonderful people we surround ourselves with make us see things just a little bit differently. McCormack used to tell the story of having lunch with Jean-Claude Killy, when the great French skier ordered a glass of wine. The American agent commented on how he was surprised that Killy would order wine at lunchtime. Killy replied, "What, you rather I drink milk and ski like an American!" Killy was a wonderful person and client. He later hired IMG for marketing services when he was CEO of the 1992 Albertville Olympics that were held in his home country.

UNDERSTANDING THE POWER OF NUMBERS

Dan Towriss

Sometimes the need you strive to fulfill isn't about more profit, but rather relates to the need of a community. Dan Towriss has pushed for the latter through his years as chief executive officer of Group1001, a financial services group focused primarily in retirement and protection markets. An insurance industry veteran of 24 years, Towriss has been active in the acquisition and revitalization of insurance businesses, returning them to growth and profitability. Mr. Towriss helped to start and later led the insurance group at Guggenheim Partners and has held various executive positions with long-standing insurance enterprises such as Aegon, ING, and Lincoln National.

From locker rooms to boardrooms, small-town fields to franchise headquarters, sport has the power to unite and drive passionate individuals to achieve more. The athletes, the managers, the franchises, and the fans may be diverse, but they share the same spirit of competitiveness, loyalty, pride, passion, and commitment.

It's those traits, learned through participation in amateur sport, that have helped me to meaningfully shape my professional life and drive me to continuously look for new challenges. Character-building events experienced at a young age would form the foundation for future success, helping me bring people together to serve the collective whole in good times and bad.

As CEO of a leading insurance group, I have seen the potential of this collective spirit to deliver amazing results. Our group has been proud to harness the collective power in numbers to create life-changing opportunities through sport around the country. We will leave a lasting legacy in the areas we serve by encouraging sporting opportunities that inspire, connect, and shape communities. We will also continue to look for new ways to encourage young people, women, and athletes of all abilities to get in the game and pursue their goals.

Opportunities can arise when we least expect them. While attending an event in Oklahoma City we learned of communities battling in at-risk areas where gangs often start recruiting children at the sixth-grade level. We knew we wanted to do something to help give children a better option. Youth sport and education are among the few remaining ways to reach at-risk youth for positive social change. To this end, Group One Thousand One began to invest in and support Fields & Futures, a program on a mission to grow student participation in sport by rebuilding athletic fields and creating new opportunities for students to join a team and benefit from that experience.

We are not alone in our mission. At the intersection of business and sport, there are countless inspiring and yet untold stories that should be shared. To encourage more businesses and individuals to step up, it is essential we showcase these stories, displaying the power of our numbers to inspire positive change.

Business and sport are now symbiotically linked. We need to harness the power each can bring to create even more opportunities for change. The lessons learned through sport prepared me for life beyond the field and beyond the classroom, and I am committed to elevating opportunities so more communities can have that advantage as well.

BE KIND

McCormack had a wonderful story about how he learned from Palmer early on. The two were having a shower after a round of golf and there were no towels in the locker room. McCormack was screaming to the universe for towels, and then screaming directly at the locker attendant. When they left the locker room, Palmer told McCormack, "I don't treat people that way, and if you are going to represent me you can't either!" Mark never forgot that lesson.

START WITH SALES

When I spoke to students at the University of Massachusetts' Mark H. McCormack Department of Sport Management, where the Mark McCormack papers are located, they wanted to be in just about every job in sport . . . except sales. I made a big deal about sales being the most important thing they need to learn. You can't get a job if you can't sell yourself. You can't negotiate a good contract if you can't sell. You can't get a client if you can't sell. You can't consult effectively if you can't sell your ideas.

CHANGE IS THE CONSTANT

The example that opened this chapter shows visionary thinking. This can occur in any conceivable area when innovation and expanding boundaries are standard operating procedure. Whether demographic, global, or technological, there are tens of thousands of needs to be filled in sport. Don't believe me? Consider how much the Olympics have changed in the past 30 years, in terms of number and type of competitors, and the type of sport. Consider the advances in performance and viewing consumption thanks to advances in technology. Think of the rise of esport and Ultimate Fighting Championship. Who would have thought the sport apparel business needed a new player when Under Armour came along? Did your parents foresee the X Games way back in, say, the late 1980s? Maybe they didn't . . . but somebody sure did, because by 1995, the first X Games was held in Newport, Rhode Island. Unfortunately, IMG didn't fill *that* need.

Fortunately, there are enough needs to go around. McCormack was thinking global when that seemed completely unnecessary or impossible. Always think beyond what you can see at the moment. That is how you find the next rocket ship.

References

Callahan, T. 2017. *Arnie: The Life of Arnold Palmer.* New York: Harper.

US Legal. 2016. "Sports Agents: History and Law." https://sportslaw.uslegal.com/sports-agents-and-contracts/sports-agents-history-and-law.

CHAPTER 6

Building a Championship Brand

Tom Ricketts

Tom Ricketts is the executive chairman of the Chicago Cubs and a long-time fan of the team. In 2009, he led his family's acquisition of the team from the Tribune Company. When Tom and his family were introduced as the new owners of the Chicago Cubs, he outlined three goals for the organization: to win the World Series; to preserve and improve Wrigley Field for future generations; and to be good neighbors, giving back to the city and the team's North Side neighborhood. The Chicago Cubs won the 2016 World Series and were named by *Baseball America* as the 2016 Organization of the Year. Ricketts is on the executive council of Major League Baseball.

Ricketts is also the chairman of Incapital LLC, which he cofounded in 1999. Incapital is an investment bank with underwriting and distribution expertise in a wide range of securities. Incapital has underwritten more than $400 billion of securities including corporate bonds, U.S. agencies, preferred stock, certificates of deposit, mortgage-backed, structured notes, and market-linked investments. In 2010, Tom was named Ernst & Young's Midwest Finance Entrepreneur of the Year for his work with Incapital LLC and was on several occasions named by *Institutional Investor* magazine as one the 40 most influential leaders in electronic finance.

Ricketts is on the boards of Meijer Inc., NorthShore University Health-System, Choose Chicago, the Field Museum, the Executives' Club of Chicago, the Economic Club of Chicago, and the Wood Family Foundation. Prior to Incapital, he worked at ABN AMRO, The Chicago Corporation, and Mesirow Financial. He was a market maker on the Chicago Board Options Exchange from 1988 through 1994.

Ricketts has an AB in economics and MBA in finance from the University of Chicago, and he was named the Business School's Young Alumnus of the Year in 2005. Ricketts and his wife, Cecelia, have five children.

My sister Laura, my brothers Pete and Todd, and I are Cubs fans. We were bleacher bums when we were young. In fact, I met my wife in the center-field bleachers. I came to Chicago for college in time to enjoy the 1984 playoff run. We wanted a championship, we love Wrigley Field, and we love Chicago. We drew upon our life as fans as we took over the role as owners.

On the day we introduced ourselves to the Chicago media when we bought the club in October 2009, I said that the Ricketts family promised three things: (1) to win a World Series, (2) to preserve and enhance Wrigley Field, and (3) to be a good neighbor to Wrigleyville and the entire city of Chicago. My family and I declared an end to the era of the lovable loser and talk of curses.

On the drizzly morning of November 3, 2016, in Cleveland, the entire Cubs organization delivered on that promise of winning the World Series. It really was an incredible experience for our fans, ending a 108-year championship drought. To get there required clarity among everyone involved in our organization about how to build a winner and the image we expected to portray to the world.

That morning in Cleveland finally put an end to the notion of "lovable losers."

As someone who had a career in finance before we became baseball owners, I would never have thought I'd be writing a chapter in a book about brand management. But upon reflection, I've learned a few things as we've turned the Chicago Cubs from a team known as the lovable losers who played in the most beautiful ballpark in the world to a championship team with global reach.

Not everything we've tried has gone according to plan, but if there is one thing we've done right since we bought the Cubs, it's been to focus first on our fans. If the brand is a promise, then we've been very true to our brand. We're a team with intensely loyal fans, owned by loyal fans, all of whom were rewarded with a long-awaited championship.

TRANSPARENCY

For decades, our fans, instead of fraying at the seams from unmet expectations, bonded over losing teams. Since 1945, we had made the playoffs only seven times before 2015. Fans stayed with the club through thick and thin, and embraced it. For decades, instead of a championship tradition, Cubs fans bonded over day baseball at Wrigley Field and rosters of players who wanted to play in Chicago for the quality of life instead of the quality of wins.

But in the modern era, things began to change. The Cubs got close enough to the promised land—from the playoffs in 1984 to five outs away from a World Series berth in 2003—that fans got to be a raw nerve. The three times we made the playoffs in the 2000s left them frustrated because they were so close yet so far from a championship. So, Cubs nation bought into our three goals and wanted to know how to get there. They had finally gotten to the point where they were tired of having their hopes dashed.

After spending our first season as owners understanding how the Cubs came to embrace mediocrity on the field, we knew we had to rebuild the organization from the ground up. Our minor leagues were in sorry shape and we had no prospects on the horizon. Our spring training facility was basically an Arizona Park District field and our Dominican Republic Academy was the worst in baseball. To achieve our goal, major change was needed. We caught a break when we learned we were able to hire Theo Epstein, who had brought his hometown Boston Red Sox two world championships after their 86-year drought. Within 10 minutes of meeting, I knew Theo was the right person for the job. We signed him in the fall of 2011 and he brought in his team led by Jed Hoyer and Jason McCleod. We proposed something radical to Cubs fans. We're going to build a winner the right way. To achieve sustained success we would build the best minor league and international player development system and facilities and we'd forego short-term wins for long-term success by developing our own young talent.

Over the next three years, we traded away veteran players for young talent and lost 286 games. We were retooling for the long haul. As part of our brand, we were honest with fans, and they repaid us with support. While sportswriters derided this phase as "tanking," I spoke with fans every day as I walked around the upper deck and the bleachers of Wrigley Field. They knew we were executing our plan. I can't thank Cubs fans enough for their patience. We are in this together, Cubs fans seemed to say: We're a family and we've made it this far. We can make it a few more years until we get that title. They appreciated that for the first time in team history, ownership, baseball operations, and business operations were all aligned on a plan to build the best organization in baseball. I think this communication with fans was critical to building our brand and to keeping our fans engaged.

A SENSE OF PLACE

You can't talk about the Cubs without talking about Wrigley Field. Even when we were the doormat of the National League, Wrigley was one of the top tourist destinations in Illinois. The sunshine, the ivy-covered outfield walls, and the iconic old scoreboard were beloved. But Wrigley Field's infrastructure was crumbling beneath our feet. Fans in the 200 section had nets overhead protecting them from falling cement. Previous owners had allowed Wrigley to fall behind the times in player facilities, fan amenities, and revenue opportunities.

In fact, a once-quaint WGN-TV shot of fans on neighboring three-flats setting up lawn chairs on the roofs to peer over the outfield walls turned into major commerce. Rooftop businesses were created and those businesses sold ticket packages to our fans and lobbied city government to protect their views, inhibiting the ability to modernize. We took fans on this public process as well and directly shared with them how the time had come to reinvest in Wrigley Field. We asked them to appeal for city government to support us in our efforts to spend several hundred million reinvesting in and expanding Wrigley Field.

We have always told fans we considered ourselves stewards of Wrigley Field. When we introduced a 42-foot-high (12.8 m) video board at Wrigley Field in time for the 2015 season, we didn't try to make it the biggest, loudest, or

GAME CHANGER

ONE QUESTION PAVES THE WAY TO COMPELLING STORIES

Ross Greenburg

Ross Greenburg is one of the sport world's masterful storytellers, and he knows the key question to ask to successfully communicate your message. Greenburg worked at HBO Sports from 1978 through 2011, becoming president of HBO Sports from 2000 to 2011. During his tenure at HBO he created *Real Sports With Bryant Gumbel, Hard Knocks,* the *24/7* series, *Costas Now,* and *Inside the NFL* and produced Wimbledon for 21 years. He also created and produced more than 75 sport documentaries at HBO during that time. In 2011, he launched Ross Greenburg Productions and has supplied Showtime, NBC Sports Network, Golf Channel, CBS, NHL Network, Epix, and others with documentaries and sport reality series since the company's founding. Ross Greenburg also produced two heralded films, the award winning Billy Crystal collaboration *61*,* and one of the most acclaimed sport movies in history, *Miracle.* He has won 54 Sports Emmys and 8 Peabody Awards during his illustrious career.

Ask "Why?" The art of storytelling always begins with the question "Why?"

- Why was the 1980 "Miracle on Ice" United States Olympic hockey team's win over the Soviet Union such a big deal?

- Why did the 1999 United States Women's World Cup soccer team capture the attention of the world when no other women's team had done so before?

- Why did the rivalry and relationship between Larry Bird and Magic Johnson transcend the NBA and the sport world? Why did their relationship seem to change over the years?

It all starts with and comes back to that one word, that one question: Why?

When I first started my career, I worked long and hard to try and foster, develop, and create stories. In each story that I tried to create, I wanted a beginning, a middle, and an end, as you find in any good book. I wanted to take people on fun, special journeys through stories in the sport world, capturing the mind, heart, and emotions of my viewers. I knew that I wanted to do something other than simply throwing interviews against the wall with some highlights mixed in; I wanted to do something unique.

My breakthrough style developed in 1990 with the production of *When It Was a Game.* That story was meant to look back at the early years of Major League Baseball, so I chose to use only 8-mm and 16-mm film taken by players and fans from the 1930s through the 1950s. All through the creation of that film, and during the production of all my subsequent films, I was asking myself "Why?" Why was this story important? Why was I doing what I was doing, laying out and producing the story the way I was?

My primary goal has always been to simultaneously entertain and create change in the world. Sport is always a microcosm of what is happening in the country and the world. Because of that, I like to take sport seriously. Telling stories this way is unique because each one means something different to each person. One story might be more reflective and rekindle a certain feeling or emotion for a person who watched it unfold before her own eyes, while for a little kid who might not have even been alive at that time, that same story will mean something entirely different. Questioning why the story at hand is important not only allows me to dive into the narrative, but it lets me tell it in a way that will hopefully resonate with everyone who watches it.

Continually asking "Why?" is not always easy. You must work to build trust with your subjects, bringing viewers inside the locker room before and after games, helping them to understand the raw emotions of winning and losing in that moment. When Steve Sabol of NFL Films and I introduced *Hard Knocks*, the all-access show that has become a staple of NFL preseason programming, we understood that we were setting the tone for the future of TV. We were lessening the impact of language and emphasizing the authentic power of the visual. Viewers want to be taken where they haven't been before, and even then, well before virtual reality took hold, we were moving dramatically in that direction.

It all starts with and comes back to that one word, that one question: "Why?" Continue to ask it and maybe you can create something big, or fix something in society that needs fixing. One might even say that question is just as significant in determining your career and your decisions on the job as it is to storytelling.

Used with permission of Ross Greenburg.

---

busiest. We avoided Kiss Cams, Limbo Cams, and a team staffer chatting with fans for between-innings contests. We use our new left-field video board to honor the legacy of the Chicago Cubs, and of course we use it for instant replay—a must for fans of today's Major League Baseball, where manager challenges and second looks are very much a part of the game itself. We continue to use our historic, landmarked center-field scoreboard for runs, balls and strikes, other scores around the major leagues, and the old-style clock face crowning the top. The new video boards created a better fan experience and helped us catch up to the rest of the league in terms of revenue opportunities. Corporate partners are willing to pay a premium for the chance to reach fans in our iconic ballpark.

As fans, my siblings and I understand there is something special about Wrigley, so we put a premium on the fan experience and respect for tradition in everything we do. We balance this with each new amenity we add.

For a century-plus-old ballpark that didn't even have lights until the final months of Ronald Reagan's presidency, it goes without saying that Cubs fans embrace a more unplugged experience. A ballgame at Wrigley is a nod to tradition. Sure, fans want information about the game and our players, and we use

CUSTOMIZING A MESSAGE FOR FANS: THREE STORIES

Frank Luntz

Fans feel a sense of pride and place when you make them a priority, as Dr. Frank I. Luntz shares in these three anecdotes. Luntz has conducted surveys, focus groups, and in-depth language sessions for more than two dozen professional football, base-ball, basketball, and hockey teams over the past decade. He has worked with owners, team presidents, CFOs, general managers, coaches, and players to strengthen reputations and maximize fan engagement.

It's all about the fans.

You cannot create effective marketing or advertising without understanding the culture and character of a team's fans. Every community is different, even if the sport is the same. And every team is different, even when they share the same community. Team owners have learned the hard way that the stunning new arenas, the most engaging in-game entertainment, even the greatest players in the sport will fail to attract fans if you fail to give fans what *they* want and need. Just ask the ex-owner of the Florida Marlins, who built a beautiful, brand-spanking-new stadium for fans who couldn't care less—and proved it by staying away. What Marlin fans really wanted most was *love*—and that the former owner could not give.

I have polled or focus-grouped fans in just about every sport and every city—and no two places are alike—but there are three examples of fan culture that stand out.

1. In 2009, I attended a Monday Night Football game in Philadelphia at the invitation of Governor Ed Rendell. Earlier that day, I was a guest on Fox News, where I held up World Series tickets on air and boldly predicted that the Yankees would defeat the Phillies. That night, I was taking my seat at the football stadium when a woman—yes, a woman—stood up and started screaming at me: "Hey Luntz, you piece of sh*t. I saw you on Fox. Phillies rock. You suck. I'm going to kick your ass." I pointed to the governor and said, "Ma'am, perhaps you'd like to say that to the governor." Her response: "I'll kick his ass, too." The entire section cheered. Philly fans are the most passionate, unforgiving fans in America, and they expect that same unwavering commitment from every fan. No exceptions.

2. That winter, I was lucky enough to get tickets from boxing hall of fame sportscaster Jim Gray to the Olympic Gold Medal Game in Vancouver, where I learned the difference between the two nations. Americans love hockey. Canadians live and die for hockey. And unlike their American counterparts, there is a hospitality to Canadian fans that you won't see in most American cities. Our section had a fair number of Americans, and even though we were the focus of continuous jeering, it went something like this: "We're going to break you. We're going to crush you. We're going to make you cry. Can we buy you a beer? Who wants pizza?" There is a special camaraderie among

hockey fans that transcends cities and even countries, and the most effective hockey ads feature the fans celebrating a win together.

3. The single best sport ad I ever developed never made it to air. It was for the Los Angeles Dodgers and it featured a 10-year-old boy speaking straight to camera to his mom—knocking on the camera lens to get her attention:

> *"Mom. I know you get mad at me, and I know it's usually my fault. But Mom, the Dodgers are in town this weekend, and I really want to go. Please Mom. I promise I'll make my bed, and I won't tease my sister—at least for a few days. And Mom, if you take me, (slower) I promise to tell you and Dad 'I love you,' (pause) and we'll remember this day forever. Okay Mom?"*

No fan is more important than Mom, because she determines the sports her kids will watch, play, and attend. And nothing matters more to moms than making unforgettable memories that last a lifetime. If you win Mom, you win.

Note: The ad was never produced because the internal organization could not agree whether Moms or Latinos were a better ticket sales target. For the Dodgers, the correct answer is both.

---

technology to provide it. But if we weren't thoughtful about the relationship our fans have with our ballpark home, we could have gone with a more modern strategy, typical of the stadiums built in the past 25 years. We decided to focus on the game and give them replays, but we didn't want to overuse them and create a distraction to the game. Our goal was to be respectful about what fans appreciate about Wrigley Field while also enhancing their experience. I think it's been extremely well received. That's an area where we could have made a huge mistake if we had not been so careful about our video board programming.

CONNECTING WITH COMMUNITY

We made our quickest progress in our off-the-field efforts to be a good neighbor. Cubs Charities was a small but well-intentioned organization that, like everything about the Cubs when we took over, had lacked resources. We immediately jump-started our charitable efforts. My sister Laura leads our family's efforts. We now raise more than $10 million each year, give away millions, and help more than 135,000 Chicagoans by supporting organizations all across Chicagoland. We built the first new baseball field for Chicago Public Schools in more than 30 years with Kerry Wood Cubs Park at nearby Lane Tech High School. We've awarded more than $500,000 in college scholarships to area young people, and we help encourage playing baseball by building baseball fields and supporting baseball and softball teams for boys and girls.

John Spanos and A.G. Spanos

Like Tom Ricketts with the Cubs, John and A.G. Spanos of the Los Angeles Chargers see a responsibility to blend their franchise's history with a forward-looking ethos. John is president of football operations for the Chargers, and A.G. is president of business operations. John is in his 20th season with the team, having risen through the ranks and served in all areas of football operations. Key roles included pro and college scout, assistant director of college scouting, and director of college scouting before becoming executive vice president of football operations in 2013. He also serves on the board of directors for National Football Scouting. A.G. has been in the Chargers' front office for 18 seasons. He oversees the day-to-day business operations of the organization, including marketing, sales, public relations, digital media, and community relations. He has held these responsibilities since 2011 when he was named the executive vice president–chief executive officer. He served three years as executive vice president–executive officer (2008-2010) and five seasons as the team's director of marketing programs and business development (2003-2007).

Our grandfather, Alex Spanos, fulfilled a lifelong dream when he purchased the Chargers in 1984. Ten years later, he named our father, Dean Spanos, president of the Chargers and entrusted him with control of the organization's day-to-day operations. While currently our controlling owner and chairman of the board, in 2015, our father handed over the reins of day-to-day leadership to us. After our family's three-plus decades in the NFL, we are excited to lead the Chargers into a new era of NFL Football in Los Angeles, our original home, while continuing to build upon our grandfather's vision for the family business.

Chargers culture is based upon family values and service to the community, both of which have been passed down from generation to generation. Look no further than our grandfather, Alex Spanos, to see where it all began. His life is, quite literally, the epitome of the American dream. From humble beginnings, growing up with practically nothing, he built three successful businesses through hard work and sheer determination. First, he turned an $800 loan into a successful catering business in California's Central Valley. From there, he rolled up his sleeves once again and built one of the leading real estate and development companies in the industry, ultimately enabling him to purchase an NFL franchise. He is someone who, our entire lives, has preached to us the importance of family and the importance of hard work. Growing up with his example has played a defining role not only in our lives, but in the culture of the organization we are now entrusted to run.

While football rightfully dominates the day to day of our current roles with the team, we also particularly enjoy the opportunity to further our grandfather's extensive philanthropical legacy. This runs deep in our family and organizational DNA. We believe the Chargers' north star is twofold: (1) to bring the Lombardi Trophy home to Los Angeles, and (2) to make a positive impact in the community. If we can live up to those ideals, we know we will have built a championship organization.

As we usher in a new era of Chargers football, the pillar of our modern legacy is the franchise's new home—Los Angeles Stadium at Hollywood Park. Not only does the 70,000-seat, open-air facility slated to open in 2020 provide us much-needed direction as we approach the end of the decade, but once completed, it will be North America's, if not the world's, premier sport and entertainment venue. The multibillion-dollar stadium, already slated to play host to the Super Bowl, College Football Playoff, and 2028 Summer Olympics, will be the cornerstone of events that the entire world will be watching and push the Chargers brand forward, both at home in LA and abroad across the global market.

Between our iconic uniforms, rich tradition, Hall of Fame players, and founding principles that emphasize the pursuit of football immortality while making the community we live in a better place, we believe the Los Angeles Chargers are positioned for success today, tomorrow, and for years to come.

From John: The best career advice I can give is that if you remain focused on the task at hand, and are doing your current job to the best of your ability, you will get noticed. The people that I have seen rise through our organization the fastest are the ones who have done a very good job addressing their specific responsibilities—and doing so exceptionally well. If you start worrying about what the next step is and how to get there, that will be a distraction and can affect how you perform in your current role. If you focus, first and foremost, on doing the task at hand and doing your job to the best of your ability, I promise, you will get noticed.

From A.G.: I recommend talking to as many people in the industry as possible. Pick people's minds. Seek out opinions and advice. If you just called the main directory of a sport organization, you'd be surprised; it's crazy who you can sometimes get ahold of. It's a very welcoming culture. People will give you honest feedback, and it's a great way to learn more and make an educated choice about your career.

Used with permission of John and A.G. Spanos.

This culture of giving back is embraced by our manager and players. Joe Maddon is very generous in Chicago and in his hometown of Hazelton, Pennsylvania. Our players support the community. First baseman Anthony Rizzo and pitcher Jon Lester have raised millions of dollars to fight pediatric cancer, and outfielder Kyle Schwarber raises money for first responders. They lead a clubhouse of players who all get involved in the community. They are champions on and off the field. It's another touch point for us with our fans.

THE "C" ON THE CAPS

We started with a vision to become the best organization in baseball. We hired great people like Theo Epstein while investing in Crane Kenney's business operation to allow him to hire great business talent. Every day we were single-minded in our goal of delivering for our fans. We changed the lovable loser narrative in 2016 and had a deep playoff run in 2017. I feel as if we could be one of those teams that is consistently in the hunt for a title. When you look at the great sport organizations around the world, such as Real Madrid, Manchester United, or the All-Blacks, they are known for winning. We were known specifically, and fairly, for losing. If we can win consistently, if we are in a place to win championships on a regular basis, that "C" on our caps can stand for commitment to each other and to our fans. More than that, the Cubs could one day be known as one of the great global sports brands. We already have a large following around the world. But the only way to become a recognized top global sports brand is by winning. Good teams win the World Series. Great teams get there on a consistent basis. We have to prove we're one of those teams. If we do that, we have the chance to be one of the highest-profile sports teams on the planet.

CHAPTER 7

A Mindset of Authenticity: The First Step in a Successful Sport Business Venture

Jack Nicklaus

No name is more synonymous with greatness in golf than Jack Nicklaus, and no single person has changed the face of the sport more—as player, golf course designer, businessman, philanthropist, and goodwill ambassador. Named Golfer of the Century or Golfer of the Millennium by almost every major golf publication in the world, he was also named Individual Male Athlete of the Century by *Sports Illustrated,* and one of the 10 Greatest Athletes of the Century by ESPN. Known globally as the Golden Bear, Nicklaus is one of only 16 individuals over a 240-year history to have been awarded both the Congressional Gold Medal (2015) and the Presidential Medal of Freedom (2005)—the highest civilian awards in the United States. Nicklaus' competitive career spanned five decades, and his legend has been built with 120 professional tournament victories worldwide and a record 18 major championship titles (six Masters, five PGA Championships, four U.S. Opens, three British Opens). He is one of only five golfers who have won all of golf's modern majors—referred to as the career Grand Slam—and the only golfer to have done so on both the regular and senior tours.

His postplaying legacy equals his extraordinary accomplishments. Cochairman of the privately held Nicklaus Companies, Jack has designed more than 300 golf courses over a six-decade career, and he was voted 2017 Golf Course Designer of the Year by the World Golf Awards. His firm, Nicklaus Design, is considered the industry leader, with 415 courses in 45 countries. Jack is the architect of a global brand; the Jack Nicklaus– and Golden Bear–branded lifestyle collection of products include golf academies, ice cream, restaurants, beverages, wine, beverageware, home appliances, flooring, cabinets, apparel, footwear, and golf equipment.

Tireless philanthropists, he and wife Barbara are the guiding light for the Nicklaus Children's Health Care Foundation, which supports numerous pediatric health care services in South Florida and nationally. It has raised more than $85 million since its inception in 2004. In 2015, Jack and Barbara's efforts in pediatric health care reached a significant milestone when Miami Children's Health System renamed its flagship hospital Nicklaus Children's Hospital. In November 2017, Miami Children's Health System underwent a systemwide rebranding and became Nicklaus Children's Health System. In October 2010, Jack and Barbara were inducted into the International Pediatric Hall of Fame.

Focused on growing the game of golf, Jack has spoken before the U.S. Congress three times on the character-building aspects of the game. He is a trustee and national chair of The First Tee, and in 2017, Jack and the Nicklaus Companies became a trustee of the PGA of America, where Nicklaus is a spokesperson for PGA REACH—the charitable arm of the PGA of America, with a focus on youth, military, and diversity and inclusion. Residing in North Palm Beach, Florida, since 1965 and in the same home they have lived in since 1970, Jack and Barbara Nicklaus are parents to five children and grandparents to 22.

Over the course of my adult life, I have been fortunate enough to be a part of a variety of business ventures, and even more fortunate to say that many have been a success. As a result of this, I'm quite often asked about the launch of a business, growing one, and, what can sometimes be the greatest challenge, sustaining one.

I try to draw as many parallels as I can to my competitive golf career and what served me well on the golf course. But ironically, there is one critical element to success in business that might be considered the antithesis of what perhaps attracted me the most to the game of golf and eventually separated it from all the other sports I played and enjoyed in my youth.

What I loved about the game of golf was that to play or practice it, I didn't need someone to throw or catch a ball; I didn't need someone to defend me; I didn't need to stand on a dusty ballfield on a hot July afternoon in Ohio, waiting for a bunch of others to show up before we could play. In golf, it was me against the golf course and me against myself and my own limitations. My success was often determined by how much time and effort I put into my game.

But in business, at the end of the day, it comes down to people—at least in the most simplistic sense. After all, if you align and surround yourself with talented and dedicated individuals often enough, for long enough, their skill, intelligence, and commitment will eventually rub off on whatever it is you are working on. You also have to empower those people to make decisions—and sometimes mistakes—on their own, and allow them to grow and to feel a sense of ownership in whatever it is you are doing.

As they say, few great things in life are accomplished alone. Golf is perhaps an exception.

So, yes, I've been incredibly blessed over the years to be able to work with some unbelievably talented individuals, and I owe them much of the success I've enjoyed during that time. But it's unlikely you picked up this book willing to walk away feeling satisfied with advice that can be whittled down to one word—people.

Rather, there is a second thing that I frequently tell aspiring businesspeople when they ask about launching a product, or a business, or whatever venture they want to get off the ground. And interestingly enough, it goes back to something I learned long before I ever entered a PGA Tour event or my first boardroom.

I will tip you off now that the second thing will be the basis of the rest of this chapter. The discerning reader will likely already have picked that up.

REACHING FOR A-I-R

Whether it is my Midwestern upbringing or the influence of my parents, I am a firm believer that authenticity is the common thread linking all successful endeavors—business or otherwise. The reason for this is blindingly simple, but it permeates everything you will ever do as a business owner, executive, or decision maker. Let's call it A-I-R: Authenticity. Integrity. Resolve.

I have found that the vast majority of consumers are most attracted to people, places, things, and ideas that they perceive to be authentic. Ones they perceive to be *real*. No one wants to associate with someone or a brand that is trying to be something it is *not*.

This is a wonderful place to start and a key part of a foundation when you are getting a business off the ground. Too many times, people enter a business venture trying to figure out what the mass population wants. Nine times out of 10, at least in my opinion, ventures that start in this manner fail. The reason is obvious: It is impossible to feel an intimate connection to a business or a brand if it was born out of a desire to appeal to a mass audience—to be everything for everybody.

This is especially true in the business of sport. Everything in this industry is driven by grassroots passion and extreme fan support. If your idea is not authentic, sports fans will sniff you out and dispose of you rather quickly.

This is why authentic passion is so crucial when you are formulating your mindset. The business of sport is a tough one. Very tough. Regardless of what sector of the industry you want to work in, you will have to work on weekends. You will have to work unusual hours. You will have to be comfortable working in an industry that is ultra-competitive.

Once things get tough, and trust me, they will—no matter how much start-up capital you might have—you absolutely must have your own authenticity, values (integrity), and passion (resolve) to fall back on in the worst or best times. Plus, you have to be willing to push on for the sake of your unique idea, not the money that might or might not materialize.

FROM HUMBLE BEGINNINGS TO PGA CONCESSIONAIRE

David Lee Cook III

David Lee Cook exemplifies the power of perseverance. Cook, known as "Dave," owns one of the most distinctive catering, concession, and merchandising companies in the country, the Americana Group. Dave was born the second of eight kids in Charlotte, North Carolina. At just 10 years old, he started carrying two bags (a double) as a caddy, which is difficult even for adults. Cook, always dedicated to family, would walk to a local grocery store, ParknShop, to buy a chicken, a bag of potatoes, and a loaf of bread to feed his entire family. After high school, he joined the Marine Corps and became one of the youngest sergeants during the Vietnam era, making that rank in 17 months when it normally takes five years. His love for sport and entertainment law led him to a career in golf concession and merchandising that spans almost four decades.

Courtesy of David Cook. Photographer: Joy Cook.

When I started my company working in professional golf, I was one of the only people of color on the course. Any other African Americans were cleaning the restrooms, cutting the grass, and washing the dishes. As a young kid on the golf course, the caddy shack was the worst place for a young kid because of the gambling and cursing. My dad was a Baptist minister and it was off limits to us. But from humble beginnings came a fantastic future in the sport.

At the age of 8, I started sneaking onto the golf course with neighbors and made 50 cents a bag shagging balls. At 10, I started carrying bags, receiving a mere $2.30 per bag for 18 holes. The money I made was helping my family and me buy school clothes and give lunch money to my siblings. My dad looked the other way from what he saw as the dysfunctional nature of golf course culture at that time because he looked forward to my monetary contributions.

After high school, I went directly into the Marine Corps. I went on to college and then to law school. John Weistart, my sports and entertainment law professor at Duke University Law School, was so engaging I immediately was hooked on sport law. Through researching the field, I discovered that sport concession was a lucrative business with no African Americans in leadership roles. I was able to get contracts with the Atlantic Coast Conference (ACC) to provide merchandise and concession. From the ACC Tournament, I was able to get the concession contract with the Carolina Panthers.

I met Joe Polidora with Restaurant Associates (RA), and he hired me to handle professional tennis and golf in 1992. We formed the Americana Group then, and though RA is now under different ownership, to this day merchandise and concession at all PGA events are handled through that original partnership. I like to think that my company and I joined great players like Calvin Peete, Lee Elder, and Bill Spiller to give golf a presence for people of color before Tiger Woods ever swung a professional club.

My defining moment with the PGA was the 1999 Ryder Cup. Until that time we had only concession carts and beverage stations, but Polidora said he observed me and wanted me to operate one of the main food locations. We facilitated the first full-service concession stand for the PGA at the Ryder Cup in Brookline, Massachusetts, that year. Reluctantly, I took on the challenge and superseded my monetary goals by $70,000. Not only did I work the most famous Ryder Cup of all time, but from that day on if you wanted to find Dave Cook, you would just go to the biggest and busiest on-course concession stand and would find him there. Since 1992, the Americana Group has been the "go-to company" on the course for PGA of America and five Ryder Cups—and 18 PGA Championships later, we are still kicking.

Golf has been very, very good to me!

PASSION AND THE "INSIDE-OUT" APPROACH TO SPORT MARKETING

I have never stepped into a single business opportunity without asking myself if the venture involved was something I was truly *passionate* about. Or something I cared about on a deep level. Since the mid-1970s, one of my primary areas of focus in the business realm has been golf course design. I did not enter the business of designing golf courses because I thought I would make loads of money. And I did not do it out of a desire to attract the interest of a wide, massive audience.

I entered golf course design simply because I enjoyed the opportunity to express myself on a piece of ground and express my vision of how the game should be played. I love the game of golf beyond its being a vehicle for me to compete, and through course design, I could help introduce and grow the game around the world. And I could do so by creating quality golf experiences that people could enjoy while servicing the needs of a developer—be it a residential community, a resort, or a private club. This "inside-out" approach to appealing to the market is, in my view, what has allowed me to stay engaged in my work for more than 50 years.

As opposed to wondering what the market wanted and, in reaction, creating a product or business, I would rather see what kind of unique talent, experience, or perspective I can bring or my company can bring to the market, and then tailor a product or service around that. Next to having a mindset of authenticity, this could be the most important step in launching a business in sport, simply because it goes back to the *very nature* of sport business. People in this industry achieve success when they have brought something to the market that not only was desired by the market, but also was deeply rooted in the company's values and grassroots appeal. They *brought something unique and personal to the market,* and then tailored that idea to the market conditions surrounding them.

I remember that when we launched Jack Nicklaus Ice Cream in 2015, golf writer Jaime Diaz—a long-time friend who has written for *Sports Illustrated, Golf Digest,* and now Golf Channel—joked that this might be the most authentic product launch in sport. There is no doubt that I have always loved ice cream, and I am not sure I have ever been so hands-on (and spoons in) with product development as I was with our ice cream.

Now, let me be clear here: There is nothing wrong with trying to fill a gap in the market or appealing to the Average Joe or Josephine. Quite the contrary, I feel that connecting with the Average Joe is a key part of being a successful business owner. But you must, must add that first layer of authenticity, of unique perspective, and of personal passion before you connect it back to a wider audience.

Yes, I know this sounds inherently risky. But what has the theme been to this chapter to this point? *Nothing good in life ever came from surrendering to the whims of a mass audience.* And there is nothing "safer" than adhering to what a mass audience wants. "Safe" ideas go nowhere in this world. It is the risky ones, built on pride and personal commitment, that truly take off, and that is almost invariably because those ideas tend to be unique and authentic.

Become comfortable with that risk. Learn to make peace with that risk. That risk is what will give you a chance at finding real success.

PUTTING AUTHENTICITY INTO PRACTICE: THE ART OF ATTENTION TO DETAIL

I am often told that I have an obsession with small details. A lot of folks that I work with will tell you that it is a hallmark of my personality. And it's the truth: I have always been this way. Golf taught me to pay attention to the little things over the years. In the game of golf, the smallest adjustment to your swing can yield massive results and dividends on your scorecard.

I will never forget the 71st hole of the 1972 U.S. Open at Pebble Beach. I stood on the 17th at Pebble Beach, the famed par 3 that borders the Pacific and, particularly on this day, plays into the teeth of an angry wind. I had a three-shot lead with two holes to play, and with 219 yards to the pin, went with my trusty 1-iron. On my backswing, I actually felt myself closing the clubface and working too much inside my target line—all spelling a hook. My timing and tempo were so good that week that I was able to make a small adjustment and was able to correct my swing on the way down. The ball pierced the wind, and although I couldn't see the result, the crowd's roar told me all I needed to hear.

SUCCESS: THE INTERSECTION OF TALENT AND PASSION

Pat Williams

Courtesy of Orlando Magic.

Just as Jack Nicklaus identified personal passion as necessary for any venture he embarked on, so Pat Williams describes the importance of passion combined with talent. Williams is a basketball Hall of Famer, currently serving as cofounder and senior vice president of the NBA's Orlando Magic. One of America's top motivational, inspirational, and humorous speakers, Williams has addressed employees from many Fortune 500 companies and is author of many titles, most recently *Coach Wooden's Forgotten Teams*, which highlights the secrets to peak performance. Since 1968, Williams has been general manager with teams in Chicago, Atlanta, Philadelphia, and Orlando, including the 1983 World Champion 76ers. In 1996, he was named one of the 50 most influential people in NBA history, and in 2012, he received the John W. Bunn Lifetime Achievement Award from the Naismith Memorial Basketball Hall of Fame. He and his wife, Ruth, are the parents of 19 children, including 14 adopted from four nations. They have been featured in *Sports Illustrated*, *Reader's Digest*, *Good Housekeeping*, *Family Circle*, *USA Today*, and the *Wall Street Journal*. Williams was diagnosed in February of 2011 with multiple myeloma, an incurable form of cancer. However, after several rounds of chemo, his doctors told him that they were unable to detect any myeloma in his body and gave him a clean bill of health.

Some years ago, I was having dinner with legendary UCLA basketball coach John Wooden. During our conversation, I said, "Coach, if you could pinpoint just one secret of success in life, what would it be?"

He said, "The closest I can come to one secret of success is this: A lot of little things done well." That was a eureka moment for me. I later turned that seven-word phrase into a book called *Coach Wooden's Greatest Secret* (2014).

Soon after that book was published, I met with my editor, Andrea Doering, and she said, "Pat, you asked Coach John Wooden for his secret of success. Now, I'm going to ask you that same question: What is your secret of success?"

I didn't even have to think about it. I said, "When your greatest talent intersects with your strongest passion, you've discovered your sweet spot in life. That's how I define success."

(continued)

360 *(continued)*

Andrea said, "You need to write a book about that." So I did. Published in 2017, the book is called *The Success Intersection: What Happens When Your Talent Meets Your Passion.*

The book begins with the story of my career as a sport executive. I have always been a sports fanatic, and my first love as a sports fan was baseball. I played baseball at every opportunity, from age 7 all the way through Wake Forest University and on into the minor leagues in Miami, Florida.

During my two seasons of minor league ball, I discovered that while baseball was my greatest passion, it was not my strongest talent. It quickly became clear that my career as a professional baseball player had reached a dead end—but my career in pro sports was just beginning. I discovered that I had a talent for leadership, sales, and promotion. I had strong front office abilities to match my passion for sports.

For more than 50 years, I've had an exciting career in sport—not as a player but as a sport exec, first in minor league baseball and later in the National Basketball Association. I've helped build a championship team (the 1982-83 Philadelphia 76ers), and I cofounded an NBA expansion franchise (the Orlando Magic). My life has been an absolute thrill ride.

Over the years, I've met successful people in every walk of life, and I've recognized in all of them a quality I see in myself: These successful people have merged their greatest talent with their strongest passion. They're doing what they do best and love most—and that's why they're successful.

If your greatest passion and your strongest talent are focused on a single goal, you can't miss. That's my secret of success—the intersection of talent and passion.

The ball had taken a couple of hops, hit the flagstick, and stopped 6 inches from the hole. I birdied the hole en route to my third U.S. Open title.

As I've learned in the world of business, the tiny details can make an incredible difference on your bottom line.

I had known about the power of small details—in golf or business—long before that U.S. Open victory or my first major or first golf course design. As you look for more "practical advice" prior to launching your business, the small details are what I would encourage you to pay attention to the most.

Why, you might be asking, are small details so important? As the aforementioned story might help illustrate, we live in a very competitive world, and beyond the golf course, our world can be very homogenized or standardized. Think about all of the ideas that are floating out in the wild. The incredible competition that exists in the marketplace, combined with the utter "sameness" that is inherent to a consumer-driven economy, means that very small features can make a very large difference in terms of helping you stand out in the market. And as we discussed earlier, standing out and being unique are important attributes to possess in the world of sport business.

To illustrate, let's pretend you are a former PGA Tour pro looking to get into the world of golf course design. You probably have tons of ideas rolling through your head of ways you could make your first course design fun and unique. But here's the rub: Most of the larger-scale design features you come up with are likely to have been dreamed of or implemented by someone else, somewhere. You should always, always assume that no matter how distinctive your idea is, somebody somewhere has dreamed up something close to it.

So let's further assume that someone *has* dreamed up a golf course design that is highly similar to yours. And let's say that that competitor is going to build her course across the street from yours. How do you stand out? How do you deliver a unique experience in a competitive and homogenized world? You do it by letting the small details add up and differentiate you. Even though you and your competitor's course might have the same basic look or feel, you can separate yourself with sounder strategy, better shot values, and unique design features. Or perhaps it is making certain that the overall guest experience is better—be it exceptional service from arrival to departure, caddies and a staff that go that extra mile, or maybe just an unforgettable burger at the turn.

On their own, these details may not seem all that important, but when you compound them, they make a world of difference. And in the business world, *especially* the sport business world, this is the only way to truly get ahead. Everyone has the big ideas figured out. The big ideas are easy to come by. It is the blood, sweat, and tears that go into the small details that make the biggest impact at the end of the day, and it is here you can create real value for your customers and fans.

NEVER DEVIATE FROM WHO YOU ARE

There is a classic case study that gets passed around in business classes nowadays that some of you who are reading might be old enough to remember. This, of course, is the story of "New Coke."

I haven't had a soft drink for more than 25 or 30 years, but I know the story of "New Coke." For those who are unaware, "New Coke" was a reformulated version of Coca-Cola launched in the mid-1980s that ended up failing miserably, so much so that the Coca-Cola of nowadays is still referred to as "Coca-Cola Classic" on the can to differentiate it from the New Coke debacle. Or from Diet Coke or Coke Zero.

New Coke was launched as part of an attempt by Coca-Cola to compete with Pepsi, a company whose cola brand was rising in market share at the time and eating into Coca-Cola's profits. Despite still having a successful cola that was putting up massive numbers in the market, Coca-Cola decided to reformulate their age-old product to taste more like Pepsi, thinking it would lead to record profits.

As one can imagine, the absolute opposite happened. New Coke fizzled, it created a public outcry, and Coca-Cola was forced to bring back the old formula, all while enduring damage to their brand that took years to recover from.

If you've learned anything from this chapter, you should be able to see exactly *why* Coca-Cola's "New Coke" move represents the final lesson I have to offer you: Stay true to who you are!

This story is one that is so common it makes you wonder how and why businesses continue to make this mistake over and over again. But alas, every year, it happens.

In the business of sport, you have to understand that your brand, and more specifically, the *public perception* of your brand, trumps every other decision you make in your marketing mix. The New York Yankees, Dallas Cowboys, Augusta National, Pebble Beach, Nike, Under Armour . . . all of these brands are successful because of the way they are perceived. Fans of these brands have a strong, positive, grassroots-driven feeling for each, and if any of those six brands were to lose that grassroots passion, they would have nothing. There would be no fans in the stands, and there would be no kids walking around in $120 basketball shoes. Authentic brands do not deviate from what originally earned them success or notoriety. The brand *itself* is what makes these companies successful.

As the founder of a business, you are thus the source of this brand passion and of authenticity. It emanates out of the decisions you make, and this is why you must never make the New Coke mistake. Coke had a very well-developed brand with a well-developed personality that took *decades* to cultivate. Along with that personality came a rabid and loyal fan base, whose passion could match that of the fans of any professional sport franchise. And when those Coke fans got a taste of New Coke, they felt betrayed. They felt as though Coke was changing the very fabric of what made Coke.

Use this as a lesson as you work to launch your business and build that business or brand. At every step of the way as you grow your enterprise, you will be faced with decisions that test your ability to stay true to who you are. Perhaps you'll be offered money at some point to change a product logo in a way that doesn't fit your original brand conception. Perhaps you'll be told by an advisor to pursue a new audience that you don't identify with. If you've learned anything from this chapter, you already know the correct decision to make in both cases.

There are a variety of strategies that you can employ to ensure you never deviate from your inner values. In many ways, this can be accomplished by putting yourself in the shoes of the consumer you are targeting. Instead of targeting the Average Joe or Josephine, *imagine yourself as the Average Joe or Josephine you are targeting.* If you yourself wouldn't buy the product you are launching, that is not a product you should launch. If your product is poorly designed or poorly tested, would you still use it? Of course you wouldn't. Strive to create products and services that you yourself would be proud to use or consume.

This ends up extending out to every decision you make for the business. Those small details I talked about earlier become important, because those small details

GAME CHANGER

ONE GOOD DEED LEADS TO ANOTHER, AND ANOTHER, AND ANOTHER . . .

Cal Ripken Jr.

A life of integrity, one of Nicklaus' guiding principles, can last beyond a person's lifetime, as chronicled here by Cal Ripken Jr. about the influence of his dad in inspiring a game-changing family decision. Known as the "Iron Man," Cal Ripken Jr. is synonymous with longevity in baseball because of his streak of 2,632 consecutive games played. This was the crowning achievement of a career that created a new template for shortstops and included 19 All-Star Game appearances, two American League (AL) MVP Awards, and an AL Rookie of the Year Award. He was elected to the Hall of Fame in 2007 with the fourth-highest voting percentage (98.53%) of all time. Ripken is a bestselling author and the president and CEO of Ripken Baseball Inc., whose goal is to grow the love of baseball from a grassroots level. Since his retirement, he has purchased three minor league baseball teams. He has been active in charity work throughout his career and is still considered an ambassador of the game.

When we lost Dad to lung cancer in 1999, our family wanted to pay tribute to him and recognize what he loved to do most, teach the game of baseball. We had always had Dad, who we called "the encyclopedia of baseball," to teach us the game, but we knew that most kids didn't have such a great base of knowledge and support in front of them, every day, so in 2001, we established the Cal Ripken Sr. Foundation. Today the foundation is a national nonprofit that helps build character and teach critical life lessons to at-risk young people living in America's most distressed communities.

When we started the foundation, we would have been happy to impact a few hundred kids in our home state of Maryland and honor Dad that way. But the foundation really took off over the last decade, and it amazes all of us when we see the reach and impact that the foundation has had.

At the beginning it was all about programming and using the sport we knew and loved as a way to get in front of and engage with underserved kids who didn't have the advantages that, thanks to Mom and Dad, we had.

Our programs are still at the heart of the foundation's work, and the one that we are most proud of and that seems to have the greatest impact is called Badges for Baseball. It is a simple concept of pairing up law enforcement with kids in areas of need in an effort to repair strained relationships in the community, and it has really worked and continues to grow.

We like to say that we could do great work on our own but we can make a real difference when we partner with others, and we have done just that. With Badges for Baseball we have partnered with police departments across the country and Attorney General offices in many states to make the program effective. In addition, we partner with wonderful youth-serving organizations across the country, such as Boys & Girls Clubs, Police Athletic Leagues, and YMCAs. These fantastic

(continued)

organizations already have kids they are working with and they need additional programs and resources to help these kids in myriad ways, and that's where we come in.

As the programs were growing and we were traveling nationwide with the foundation we noticed that there was a dearth of parks, fields, and safe places to play for these kids, something we took for granted but saw as an area of great need, especially in our cities across the country. We decided to try and rectify this problem.

In 2010, we had a goal of building 50 of these parks across the country. These are multipurpose turf fields that cost, on average, $1 million each. We call them youth development parks because the foundation's work is never about creating ballplayers or athletes but about using the basic message of sport to help create better people, teach life lessons, and give young people the best chance at success.

I thought that this goal was way too lofty and, frankly, unreachable, but off we went. Well, it turns out others agreed that this was a need that had to be addressed, and I was so proud to cut the ribbon on our 70th youth development park in the fall of 2017, with many more in the making!

Looking back, I am sure Dad would be amazed and proud of the effect that the foundation bearing his name has had on more than a million kids across the nation. Actually, he would probably say we were "getting too big for our britches," but I know that our family is proud we could do something that helps so many and reflects so well on Pop and all that he stood for.

---

and fine personal touches become a reflection on you as a business owner. When you choose your business partners, choose only ones that you trust and that you feel hold the same values you do. Because guess what? If they break those values, it is a reflection on *you* and your *entire brand.*

You must remember that as a business owner, you are your brand, and your brand is you. If you betray the values that brand claims to hold, you are by extension violating your own values. And with consumers being smarter than ever, they will sniff out the inauthenticity and put you right out of business. Integrity wins in this industry, folks; never forget that.

PASSION + AUTHENTICITY = SUCCESS

The business of sport is difficult, just as sport is for professional athletes. It is taxing. It demands every inch of your capacity to focus, and it will test your character in ways you never thought imaginable. It is also one of the most rewarding businesses to operate in, because of the sheer passion and fun shared by the individuals who make the industry tick, as well as the fans that support the industry in full.

In order to operate effectively in this wild, competitive realm, you have to be authentic. There is simply no other way to do it. Sport is a field that thrives on passion, hard work, integrity, and unique ideas. If you truly love sport, and the business of sport (why else would you still be reading?), you have what it takes to make it in this industry. Passion is the first requirement. If you can take that passion and combine it with a unique, authentic idea that you are willing to commit your very identity to, you will find success.

I was never formally trained in business. But I managed to get by for more than 50 years by staying true to the traits I outlined above. No matter what any fancy business textbook tells you, mindset *counts,* and authenticity counts even more so. If you can learn that now, before you launch your empire, you will be that much better positioned to find success.

References

Williams, P. 2014. *Coach Wooden's Greatest Secret.* Ada, MI: Revell.

Williams, P. 2017. *The Success Intersection: What Happens When Your Talent Meets Your Passion.* Ada, MI: Revell.

Courtesy of NHL.

CHAPTER 8

Handling Crises Calmly and Capably

Gary Bettman

Gary Bettman is the longest-tenured commissioner in North American pro sport, having served the National Hockey League since February 1, 1993. He has been at the league's helm for more total regular-season and playoff games played than all his NHL predecessors combined and has guided the world's top professional hockey league through an era of unprecedented growth on and off the ice. Record revenues, record attendance, and numerous fan-friendly and community-minded initiatives are among the ways Commissioner Bettman has brought the NHL to a broader audience than at any time in league history.

Bettman has fostered unprecedented economic stability for the league's member clubs by negotiating a long-term collective bargaining agreement and long-term, multibillion-dollar national broadcast rights agreements in the United States (NBC Sports) and Canada (Rogers Communications) plus a landmark digital rights agreement with Major League Baseball Advanced Media. League revenues have increased more than 10-fold during Bettman's tenure and franchise values have increased exponentially.

Trademark competitive balance and innovative signature events—including iconic outdoor games—have helped drive fan engagement and sponsor participation to unprecedented levels during Bettman's tenure, positioning the NHL for sustained momentum in the future.

It has been my privilege to serve the National Hockey League as commissioner since 1993. The longer you do a job of this type, the better you understand the nature of what you're doing. Perhaps most significant, you understand what's important and what isn't, how to make the right decisions. The most important thing that I've found: *Do what you think is right.*

People will criticize. There is never any shortage of criticism; it comes with the territory. Some people will say you're great and some people will say that you're an idiot—and, by the way, they're all wrong. Which is why, if you want to sleep at night and you want to have success, you've got to be comfortable that you're doing what you believe is the right thing.

You can't worry about playing politics or doing what you think is popular because, with all due respect to the media, they'll present a suggestion one day as the greatest idea, and if you happen to follow it and it turns out not to be a good idea, they'll say, "That was ridiculous. You *never* should have done that."

It is virtually impossible to do a job of this type, particularly in a very public industry, if you have a thin skin. You have to decide that if you know the facts and the truth, and you're comfortable in your own skin, it doesn't matter what the media, or your adversaries, are going to say. While I focus on the fans and the game, I also report to the owners of our teams. The goal is to satisfy all the constituents at the same time.

Satisfying all constituents at the same time is no easy task. This was never more true than in the summer of 2004.

PRELUDE TO THE LOCKOUT SEASON, 2004 TO 2005

Walking into a news conference to announce the cancellation of an entire season certainly was not a highlight. However, we had no choice and I knew we were doing the right thing. I was firmly of the belief that the NHL could not continue on the path it was travelling. Our teams were not healthy. Our game was not competitive. There were lots and lots of "Skating on Thin Ice" headlines and commentary, probably because we had a number of teams losing millions and millions of dollars.

Still, the enormity of that moment was terrible—not only for our fans, but for the tens of thousands of people who make their livelihoods from working in our game and the people who work in the arenas, restaurants, bars, and parking lots that surround the arenas.

Putting aside that we had franchises that were in trouble, the game itself wasn't going to survive. The 2003 to 2004 NHL season was referred to in many quarters as the epitome of "the dead puck era"—and for good reason: the clutching, grabbing, hooking, and holding that were taking place on the ice. Our game was receiving a lot of criticism, justifiably.

There was a tremendous disparity in player payrolls—a range from $20 million to almost $90 million—and, as a result, there was a similar disparity in player talent. I asked the coach of one low-payroll team, "How are you competing?" He said, "Do you really think we're competing? To compete against a more skilled team, we clutch, we grab, we hook, we hold, we neutralize their skill for 50 minutes and then we try to steal the game."

Well, that doesn't make for a very competitive or, more importantly, entertaining game.

We kept telling the NHL Players' Association that the game was not healthy and there were teams in dire straits. Their response was somewhere between "We don't care" and "We don't believe you." The attitude was "It's *your* problem. Franchise goes out of business? *Your* problem. Franchise losing money? *Your* problem." Until . . . I'll never forget: I had to make a call to the union's executive director to say, "By the way: payroll next week for this club? They're not going to make it." And there was a long gasp on the other end of the phone, as well as lots of questions and expressions of concern. We made sure the players were paid, so ultimately it didn't change the dynamic or the mindset.

ACCURACY AND TRANSPARENCY

Against that backdrop, I reached out to Arthur Levitt, who from 1993 to 2001 had been chairman of the U.S. Securities and Exchange Commission. During his tenure, he was very well respected—particularly in the areas of accuracy and transparency in accounting. I asked him to go through all our financial books.

As he was considering whether to assume the project, Mr. Levitt said, "Who do I report to?" I said, "You report to the world—whatever you find."

He said, "You have to pay me up front, so there's no issue about you owing me money." I said, "Fine."

Then he said, "And what happens if I find out that the problem isn't as bad as you think it is?"

I said, "I certainly would like to know that!"

He took the retention. He brought in Lynn Turner, formerly the chief accountant of the SEC, and an accounting firm (Eisner LLP) that was unconflicted by any other professional hockey clients. In the 10-month period that began in April 2003 and concluded in February 2004, they went through all the clubs'—and the league's—finances. Mr. Levitt then held a news conference, at which he said that the NHL was losing tremendous sums of money and we were "on a treadmill to obscurity" because our economics were unsustainable.

He said some other things, both to our board of governors on February 7, 2005, and to the media at the news conference five days later: that our accounting practices were, in fact, sound; that our clubs had lost $273 million on revenues of $1,996 billion during the 2002 to 2003 season; that "businesses of this size cannot sustain losses of this magnitude and be viable"; and that player costs of 74 percent of revenues ($1,494 billion) were "inconsistent with reasonable and sound business practices."

Mr. Levitt concluded his news conference by saying. "I have to say I would neither underwrite as a banker any of these ventures nor would I invest a dollar of my own personal money in a business which, to me, appears to be heading south."

The union's reaction was "Who's Arthur Levitt? What does he know?" When Arthur offered to meet with them, the union refused.

Collective bargaining was not progressing. I suppose the union never believed that we would cancel a season. It had never been done before in major North

American pro sports, and it has never been done since. That it ultimately had to be done underscored the number of issues and the complexity of those issues, bringing me to the podium to make the announcement at the Westin New York at Times Square on February 16, 2005.

There was no playbook for what was about to happen, no "how-to" manual covering labor disruptions that cause an entire season to be lost. The words on these pages should not be construed as a "one-size-fits-all" strategic blueprint for a work stoppage in a sport business. This was a moment I had wished would never come, and my hope is it will never be repeated—in our industry or any other. While this was a difficult path, perhaps the most difficult, I knew we had no choice and I was doing the right thing. I also knew we were as prepared as possible to deal with what was about to unfold. The criticism would be relentless. The scrutiny would be constant. The challenges—the expected ones and the unexpected ones—would come from everywhere. However, the challenges were instructive.

CONFRONT ADVERSITY

When there's adversity, you deal with it and you move on. You don't ignore it, you don't gloss over it. You must confront it. *Adversity is not an excuse.* You can't be afraid of it. If anything, you have to learn from it.

The system was broken. The game was broken. And team economics were broken. We had to have a system in which all teams could afford to be competitive and we needed to achieve such a system in collective bargaining with the players. We needed a salary cap and revenue sharing as the major components of a completely overhauled economic system. We needed to fix our problems—not simply implement some stopgap measures that would buy us some time, only to have the same issues resurface in a few years. "Bandages" had been applied a few times in the past and none of them had worked; it was time to chart a new course.

COMMUNICATE

The person who said "Silence is golden" never faced a challenge of this magnitude. In a crisis, silence is one of your deadliest enemies.

Our business partners were hurting. In our case, business models were based on our league playing games. But when you have good partners who understand your business and understand that you're not running off and having work stoppages just because you think they're fun to have—that there's a real important purpose to having them—there is understanding. We communicated constantly, made sure all questions were answered.

Similarly, most of our fans understood what we were doing—no small accomplishment when you remember the time period involved. The opportunity to communicate directly with our fans was profoundly limited: Facebook had just reached the Internet; Twitter didn't arrive until 2006. The first iPhone didn't hit the stores until 2007. It was essential (and of course it still is) that we do every-

PREPARATION HAS ALWAYS BEEN A HALLMARK OF BAA

Tom Grilk

Tom Grilk dealt with a very different type of crisis than Gary Bettman, but similar principles, such as communication and preparing for the difficult decisions, apply just as well. Grilk is the chief executive officer of the Boston Athletic Association and Boston Marathon. He served as president of the Boston Athletic Association Board of Governors from 2003 until 2011. In addition to his duties as CEO, he served as the marathon's finish-line announcer from 1979 through 2013, and he is a former marathon competitor, with a personal best of 2:49 and a personal best at Boston of 2:54. He was for many years a corporate and business lawyer, both with the Boston law firm Hale and Dorr and serving as counsel and general counsel to Boston-area technology companies. He is a graduate of Cornell University and the University of Michigan Law School.

For all of the thrills and the joy that can come with what has become the business of sport, there will inevitably be trouble. Sometimes it will be small, sometimes large, and on rare tragic occasions it will be catastrophic. We saw the last of those at an English Football match in Hillsborough in 1989, at the Olympic Games in Munich in 1972, and at the marathon in Boston in 2013. Whether the issue is large or small, our response to it may become a far larger piece of our legacy than all of the good days put together, for it is in trouble that our commitment to those whom we serve is most tested.

When two bombs exploded in Boston in 2013, a great many people from Boston responded, and did so in a way that resonated and inspired people around the world. For some—spectators, runners, passersby on the sidewalk—it was visceral and immediate: They saw people in need and ran toward them, at the risk of their own safety and their own lives. That immediate resilience became the essence of what came to be known as "Boston Strong." That essential determination that people will live their lives as they choose, no matter what someone does to try to stop them, is innate and cannot be taught.

For everyone else—police, fire, EMS, ambulance services, nurses, doctors, hospital staffs, and the thousands of Boston Athletic Association (BAA) personnel and volunteers—there has to be a plan, together with an immense degree of collaboration in crafting all elements of it.

For us at the BAA, overall responsibility for the entire event rests with us. Among the most important elements of that responsibility is creating and fostering an environment in which the many people and agencies involved in the marathon are most effectively able to carry out the roles that they so enthusiastically embrace. In order to address that responsibility the BAA has in place written protocols for dealing with crisis, as well as for our approach to communications in crisis. They proceed from three principles: Focus on those to whom we have the greatest obligation, focus on the things we can control, and don't be distracted by the things we cannot.

(continued)

Those principles apply for us both at the time of a crisis and, no less importantly, in the planning process. The core concept that underlies it all for us is discipline; we learn about it from all the groups with whom we engage. The planning processes involve a series of exercises both driven internally and coordinated externally with many others, such as the Massachusetts Emergency Management Agency, which brings together state, local, and federal agencies in a wide array of collaboration exercises.

Perhaps the best known and most widely observed example of the benefits of that preparation and collaboration comes in the planning for medical services at the time of the marathon. The BAA is responsible for ensuring that the necessary facilities and equipment and, most importantly, people are in place on the day of the marathon. That means two medical tents with 200 and 80 cots, respectively, plus all of the equipment needed for whatever situation may arise, plus transport vehicles, plus careful coordination with Boston EMS and the hospitals to deal with emergency, plus the medical and other professionals in those tents.

Those facilities have been refined over the years to be ready for anything, and the people who staff them, led by our medical coordinator and our medical directors, have honed their training and techniques to that same end. The planning and rehearsal and experience of all of those people are the key elements in shaping the most essential component of our ability to respond: preparedness, a readiness for anything.

In Boston in 2013, a broad array of medical tent service assets set up principally to address runner problems—damaged joints, not enough water, too much heat, a cardiac irregularity—were instantly transformed into a major trauma center. Every person who went into that tent alive is still alive today, and each of them was in an ambulance or emergency vehicle and on the way to a hospital within 30 minutes. Three people whose lives were so tragically lost were deceased before they could be moved.

The ability to save so many lives was due entirely to a level of planning and preparedness, years in the making, that must lie at the heart of any system of planning for trouble and crisis at a sporting event. Our emphasis at the BAA is on a few simple principles, centered around focusing on those to whom we have the greatest responsibility and helping to enable the magnificent actions of many others, whether trained professionals or people simply infused with the best of the human spirit.

"Boston Strong" didn't emerge for the first time in 2013. It has been there since the days of the American Revolution, going back to 1775. The job of anyone engaged in organizing sporting events is to make certain that the planning has been done to ensure the highest degree of preparedness needed to address whatever sort of trouble may arise, and to do so in a way that engages all of the people whose resilience will be so essential to dealing with crisis. The time and effort involved in doing so is vast, but the results can be inspiring.

And it is in our response to crisis that many in the business of sport will be remembered. Few people will think of the organizers when an event goes well or their team wins the Super Bowl or the FA Cup. But they will remember when there is trouble, and they will remember whether the planning and disciplines that were needed were in place.

REBUILDING AFTER KATRINA

Doug Thornton

Doug Thornton didn't let adversity be an excuse when he spearheaded the Louisiana Superdome's central role in New Orleans' post-Katrina recovery. Thornton is executive vice president with SMG, one of the nation's largest private facility management firms. He oversees a portfolio that includes the operation of six NFL stadiums, two collegiate stadiums, 65 arenas, and multiple performing arts theaters. During his 21-year tenure with SMG, Thornton has helped attract, host, and produce numerous major special events while being involved in other key aspects of the sport and entertainment business including sports team negotiations and facility development. He originally joined SMG as general manager of the Superdome and New Orleans Arena in 1997, where he would later lead the unprecedented $225 million reconstruction and reopening of the Superdome in 2006 after it was destroyed by Hurricane Katrina—a project that was widely viewed as playing a substantial role in the city's recovery. Under Thornton's leadership the Superdome has benefited from multiple upgrades and remained one of the top venues in the country.

Courtesy of Doug Thornton.

As a long-time resident of New Orleans, I had been through many hurricanes before. But I knew this one was different when Mayor Ray Nagin and Governor Kathleen Blanco issued a mandatory evacuation of the entire City of New Orleans. At 6:30 a.m. on Monday, August 29, 2005, I watched as the Mercedes-Benz Superdome's 9.6-acre roof was ripped apart by Hurricane Katrina's unmerciful winds. Then, over the course of the next week, the world watched as more than 30,000 evacuees struggled to survive in the squalor and deplorable conditions as the Dome was pressed into service as a "refuge of last resort."

Within the blink of an eye, the Superdome, the stadium where so many great moments in sport history had taken place, was unexpectedly seen as the poster child for misery and suffering. It had now come to represent horror, devastation, and despair. How could this be? A facility that had meant so much to a community was now on life support—and its future was in serious doubt.

The story could have easily ended right there, but it didn't. What happened over the next several months was unprecedented. The Superdome would become the largest stadium reconstruction project in American sport history. A $225 million project of monumental scale that many thought was impossible would be completed

(continued)

in just one year, allowing the New Orleans Saints to return and inspire the recovery of one of America's great cities.

No doubt, the 12 months after Katrina turned out to be the most challenging period of my life—on both a personal and a professional level. My home had been flooded with nearly 7 feet (2.13 m) of water, the facility where I had spent so much of my career had been devastated, and there were doubts about our city's recovery—it was a difficult time.

But what I learned during that period are real life lessons that I still appreciate and practice today.

Sometimes, Out of Disaster Comes Opportunity

Just when you think the clouds can't get any darker, try to find a reason to be optimistic. There may be a silver lining if you look closely enough. In 2005, just prior to Katrina, we were struggling to decide whether to renovate the Superdome or build a new stadium. What we didn't realize until later is that Katrina actually forced us to deal with the stadium issue. It provided us with an opportunity not only to repair the damaged facility, but also to upgrade it to modern standards better than before.

I will always remember the inspiring words of NFL Commissioner Paul Tagliabue, who said to me during those early days of uncertainty, "[I]t can't be the same old Saints in the same old Dome. Now is your chance to do something different and make it a better place. This is your chance to erase all of those horrible images of Katrina." Boy, was he ever right about that. Our sports teams and all the major special events—the Super Bowl, NCAA Final Four, Sugar Bowl, and College Football Championship—have all come back, generating huge economic returns for the city. These events would have likely never occurred without the improvements we made to the facility after Katrina.

The Power of "Unity of Purpose"

What I saw in New Orleans in the months after Katrina was truly remarkable. The city had been completely devastated, yet the spirit of the people who returned to rebuild was unbroken. That same spirit and resolve is what enabled our project team to have the Superdome ready in just 12 months when others thought it would take at least two years. Despite the seemingly insurmountable odds, I watched the pace of the project actually accelerate once we were under way. At one point, there were 850 men and women working six or seven days a week, 10 hours a day, all with a purpose to achieve something very special—to play a football game on September 25, 2006. There was total "unity of purpose." Our project team was made up of mostly local firms from the New Orleans area, many of whom were dealing with their own personal rebuilding hardships at home. Some of these individuals had fathers who had worked to build the Dome back in 1975. This was no ordinary job for them; you could feel the strong sense of civic pride. Everyone was determined not to fail, because we all felt the city's future (and the next generation's future) hung in the balance. Never underestimate the power of the human spirit and what a deeply committed group of individuals can accomplish when there is unity of purpose.

Have the Courage to Accept Life's Challenges

You never know when life is going to present an unexpected challenge, whether it's a natural disaster or a personal tragedy. It could be anything that knocks you off balance and turns your world upside down. The real question is: How will you respond? Will you get back up?

Given all the hurdles, it would have been easy to quit, move to another city, or just let someone else do it. On September 25, 2006, New Orleans came home, and one the most meaningful football games in the Dome's colorful history was played that night. Yes, the Saints did their part by beating the Falcons 23-3. But for every New Orleanian, this special night was not just about football. It symbolized so much more. It was about recapturing something that had been lost. It was about planting a stake firmly in the ground and sending a message to the world: New Orleans is going to make it.

The men and women who were part of the Dome rebuilding effort had the courage to stare adversity in the eye and prevail. While the fate of a building, even one as special as the Superdome, cannot be equated with the fate of the many who lost so much during that storm, we locals understood the importance of persevering in our task. As challenging as it was to go through, I believe those of us who were part of the effort to rebuild the Superdome realized a sense of destiny and the consequences of failure. Even though it was incredibly difficult, I wouldn't trade the experience for anything in the world. It has made me a stronger and better person. I am sure the many men and women who shared the struggle with me would say the same thing.

---

thing possible to communicate directly with our fans and make sure there was maximum transparency on the issues as we saw them. Absent the social media outlets that are so pervasive today, we created our own information website, NHLCBANEWS.com, on which we posted frequent updates explaining our position and the status of negotiations and posted responses to some of the letters we received from our fans.

We held town hall meetings and fan forums in our franchise cities. We also did research and public opinion polls. This was a management lockout, and yet, overwhelmingly, the fans sided with us. The media didn't, but our fans did overwhelmingly, because we have the best-educated fans in all of sport, the most passionate fans in all of sport; they understood what our issues were and what we were doing to fix them. Being able to communicate effectively is essential when you are facing disruption.

CONSISTENCY IS KEY

There is an old saying: "The only way to be tough is to be tough. And, when you decide to embark on a course of action, you must make clear that you will stick to it." For example, at one time there was a perception in professional sport of the owners ultimately capitulating in collective bargaining. The union dynamic:

Wait until capitulation and you'll get what you want. When we cancelled the season, the union was stunned because no one had done it before. Now, no one should doubt our resolve as a league. In the course of a negotiation, you must preserve your credibility in what you say and what you do.

KNOW YOUR CONSTITUENCY

I always try to read the attitude of my board. Depending on a variety of things—philosophical bent, background, market size, you name it—you may get differing views. It is my job to lead and build consensus. It is imperative that the people who are doing the negotiation are leading and are empowered to negotiate and reach a deal.

Our owners care passionately about the game. Our owners believe in the game, are committed to the game. And so their concerns, and what they want for the fans, do not differ from what the fans want for themselves. Our owners are all sophisticated people with substantial investments who care about the game. They could take their money and invest it in a hundred other things and probably make more money. Do the big-revenue clubs love revenue sharing? No. They hate it. But they do it because they know it's good for the league. Achieving that understanding is all part of the consensus.

Did we like having a season-long work stoppage? Of course not. But we have the best competitive balance in all of sport—not only in the history of our game but in all of sport. In the 2016 to 2017 season, nearly half the teams in the playoffs (7 of 16) had missed the playoffs the season before. And of those seven teams who had missed the playoffs the prior season, four had been in the bottom five teams in the entire league. In 10 of the past 12 seasons, we have had a playoff turnover of at least five teams. Nearly 70 percent of our games in 2016 to 2017 were decided by two goals or fewer, and the Pittsburgh Penguins became our first repeat champions in nearly 20 years.

We have a regular season that is meaningful right from opening night, because teams are making the playoffs by a point or two, and a win on opening night can make the difference. We have a playoff season that is unbelievably competitive: Once again in 2017, we had a #8 seed, the Nashville Predators, reach the Stanley Cup Final. Our fans know that if their team can make the playoffs, they have a chance to win it all. And at the root of it all is the economic system that allows all the teams to be competitive—the one for which the players, the teams, the fans, and all constituent groups paid such a high price.

We had a vision as to what would make the game strong and healthy and enable us to grow. We had a vision for the right economic system, and the owners all embraced it. And there were owners who didn't need it; they could have lived under any system, but they understood that they would be in a six- or seven- or eight-team league. In the North American pro sport landscape, you can't be competitive in eight markets. You have to have a North American footprint if you're going to compete for media attention and if you're going to compete for sponsor attention and activation and licensing and everything that constitutes a sport league these days.

My job is to understand every team's position, every team's issues, and then try to address them. Ultimately, after the work stoppage, we made the deal that we were always prepared to make. Hopefully, the players understood that if we worked together this would be good for everybody. If we had gone through the ordeal of losing a season and then had failed to come back with a system that truly fixed the problems the business faced, people probably wouldn't have forgiven us.

In fact, we returned to record revenues and record attendance. And while missing a season was the last thing any of us wanted, the positives remain: We celebrated our year-long centennial—100 years of NHL hockey—by welcoming our 31st franchise, in Las Vegas. The average player salary, which was $300,000 in 2004, is approximately $3 million. We have long-term national broadcast agreements with NBC Sports in the United States and Rogers Sportsnet in Canada. We negotiated a groundbreaking digital rights agreement with MLBAM (MLB Advanced Media).

Our players are more skilled than ever. Our game is faster than ever. The NHL is more appealing than ever to sports fans, team owners, and business partners. Our games are available to a greater global audience, through more media options, than ever. By every metric, we are skating toward an extraordinary future as we launch the second century of our history.

Too many times to count, I've been asked if that year-long work stoppage was worth it. The simple answer: We had no choice.

CONTINUE TO EVOLVE

I'll tell you a story:

All three of my children, and one of their spouses, went to the Cornell School of Industrial Labor Relations, as I did.

During the work stoppage, my youngest daughter was accepted "early decision." The time frame for early decision is November through December.

A friend of my daughter's got into Cornell in April, and the friend said, "I'm driving up with my parents to see the campus. Do you want to take a ride?" My daughter said, "Sure."

So she went up and they go on the campus tour. The campus tour leaders are generally students, who can be very irreverent and sarcastic, and this particular tour leader had no idea who my daughter was—which was just fine. I'll also throw in that, at the time, I was chairing the school's advisory committee to the dean.

They get to the School of Industrial Labor Relations building, Ives Hall, and the tour leader says, "This is Ives Hall, home of the School of Industrial Labor Relations. Among its notable graduates is Commissioner Bettman, Commissioner of the NHL, who obviously didn't learn anything while he was here. . . ."

The ILR education includes a focus on industrial labor relations, as the name would have you think, but it really is a very, very intense social science

PROACTIVE SAFETY MEASURES ESSENTIAL TO YOUTH SPORT

Jon Butler

Jon Butler and the organization he leads know very well their constituents' needs. Butler has served as the executive director of Pop Warner Little Scholars for 27 years. He introduced coaches' education programs for volunteers on sporting behavior, coaching techniques, and respect for youth. Seeing the need for athletes with special needs, he launched the Challenger Division flag football and cheerleading program to provide the Pop Warner experience to those athletes. In 2014, he was elected president of the National Sports Concussion Coalition. Butler serves as vice president of the National Council of Youth Sports, is on the advisory committee to Heads Up Football, and is on the board of SAFE (the nonprofit arm of the Sports Turf Managers Association).

In youth sport, the first priority must be safety. It's incumbent upon all youth sport organizations to maintain their program with the safety of their young participants as the number one concern. As an administrator, you're taking someone's most precious child for a significant amount of time, so you owe a duty of protection. Multiply that child by 350,000, and that's our programmatic challenge—keeping them safe!

Pop Warner was founded in 1929 and has long made safety a top priority. In the 1950s, it adopted an age–weight schematic for safety reasons. All players are matched by both age and weight to ensure no great size disparities on the field.

Fast-forwarding to more current times, Pop Warner was the second national youth sport organization to mandate background checks for all volunteers—coaches and administrators—beginning in 2003. Those checks must be performed annually.

When Washington State enacted the Zackery Lystedt Law in 2009, it was the first state law addressing concussion management. Pop Warner then established a medical advisory committee in early 2010 and became the first national youth sport organization to enact its own concussion rule in 2010. That rule requires any participant with a head injury to be removed from participation, and that player cannot return to participation until signed off on in writing by a medical professional trained in concussion recognition and treatment.

In 2012, Pop Warner became the first football organization at any level to reduce the amount and type of contact allowed at practice. No more than one-third of practice time could involve full-speed contact drills or scrimmaging; in 2016, we reduced that further to one-fourth of practice time (overall practice time is limited to a maximum of 2 hours a day). A second rule prohibited full-speed, head-on drills in which the players start more than 3 yards (2.7 m) apart. And in 2014, Pop Warner mandated that all football coaches take and pass the Heads Up Football training course.

The Datalys Center for Sports Injury Research and Prevention in Indianapolis published a peer-reviewed research study (Kerr et al. 2015) showing that Pop Warner teams, when compared with non-Pop Warner teams that don't teach the Heads Up Football program, have 87 percent fewer overall injuries in practice and 76 percent fewer concussions in practice. Even compared to non-Pop Warner teams that use Heads Up Football, Pop Warner teams had over 20 percent fewer overall injuries and concussions in practice.

Through risk management, background checks, coaching certification, and first aid and CPR training, Pop Warner takes safety of its participants as seriously as ever. Like many youth sport organizations, Pop Warner is volunteer driven, and therefore meaningful changes take some time. Despite the challenges, I knew that we were positioned to be a leader in rules and policies to safeguard our young athletes. We've made the commitment to be on the leading edge of the safety movement, and now, for the first time, we have evidence-driven data that confirm the efficacy of the changes we've made. Be assured that we'll continue to change as new research indicates the need.

curriculum. It's basically an education that teaches you how to figure anything out, how to deal with complex situations. I learned every day at Cornell, and I've learned continually during the 25 years I've had the honor of holding this position. There are challenges, every day, and among your legacies will be the consistency with which you approach them, and the clarity on which your decisions are based, in the best interests of the owners who trust you, the fans who support you, and the sport it is your honor to serve.

References

Kerr, Z.Y., et al. 2015. "Comprehensive Coach Education and Practice Contact Restriction Guidelines Result in Lower Injury Rates in Youth American Football." *Orthopaedic Journal of Sports Medicine* 3(7): 1-8. https://doi.org/10.1177/2325967115594578.

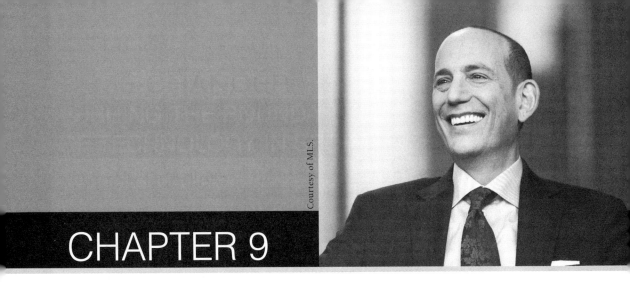

CHAPTER 9

Building a Brand That Reflects Your Core Values

Don Garber

Don Garber was named commissioner of Major League Soccer, the premier professional soccer league in the United States and Canada, in 1999. During his tenure, MLS has expanded from 10 to 25 clubs, added 23 new owners, and secured long-term broadcast agreements with ESPN, FOX, and Univision and major broadcasters in Europe, Asia, and South America. Garber has also led efforts to develop 20 soccer stadiums in the United States and Canada, and three more soccer venues will open in the next few years.

Early in his tenure, he created MLS WORKS, a league-wide community outreach initiative dedicated to addressing important philanthropic and social issues.

In 2002, Garber created Soccer United Marketing (SUM), an affiliate of MLS and one of the world's leading commercial and media soccer companies. SUM represents a wide variety of soccer properties, including the United States Soccer Federation and the Mexican Soccer Federation.

Prior to joining MLS, Garber spent 16 years in a variety of sales, marketing, programming, and event management positions at the National Football League. In 1996, he launched NFL International, a division he managed that was responsible for all aspects of the NFL's business outside the United States.

Garber serves on a variety of professional and philanthropic boards, including the board of directors for the United States Soccer Federation and Hope and Heroes, an organization raising funds and creating programs for pediatric cancer patients at New York Presbyterian Hospital.

There is a singular goal that drives us every day at Major League Soccer, and that is to be one of the top soccer leagues in the world.

We will not be satisfied until we join the ranks of England's Premier League, Germany's Bundesliga, and Spain's La Liga as one of the elite properties in the world's most popular sport. There are three things we believe will get us to our goal: (1) the highest-quality product on the field, (2) the most engaging fan experience anywhere in state-of-the-art, soccer-specific stadiums, and (3) cutting-edge, compelling content via our domestic and international media partners and social media channels. Whether an individual works for the MLS League Office or for one of our clubs, this is the shared mission among us. It is a vision shared by our owners and demanded by our fans.

For a professional sport league in just its third decade of existence, the progress on and off the field has truly been staggering. MLS was founded in 1996 with just 10 teams. Today we have 24 teams and will be at 28 in the coming years. The original business plan called for our clubs to be tenants in large NFL and college football stadiums. By 2019, 20 of our clubs will play in soccer stadiums that are appropriately sized and strategically located to be accessible to our young and increasingly urban fan base. We have more than 2,000 employees and more than 600 players; and we are particularly proud of the fact that now every MLS team has youth development academies and facilities that rival those of many of the top clubs from around the world. And almost 15 years ago—when we saw a rapidly growing interest within the business community in the sport here in North America—we created Soccer United Marketing, a comprehensive commercial soccer company that represents a wide variety of soccer properties in sponsorship, marketing, media, and game promotion.

It is particularly striking that this growth has taken place in the most competitive sport market in the world, with the added pressure from international soccer leagues and properties as well as countless entertainment options available to fans.

At the league office in New York City, we have hundreds of committed executives in many different business units that come to work every day knowing that they are delivering on the hopes and dreams of millions of soccer fans while working in an industry that provides great opportunities for personal and career growth. We recognize the unique and special relationship our employees have with the league and the sport of soccer. And we regularly empower them to take ownership of our vision and have responsibility for helping us achieve our goals.

WHERE WE WANT TO BE: OUR VISION

Like all forward-thinking companies, MLS established a vision to guide and focus our growth and serve as a "North Star" on that path.

We created our current vision almost 10 years ago when we were working with the United States Soccer Federation to bring the World Cup to our country in 2022. As part of that process, we wanted to establish a "future state" for the league should we win the bid.

GAME CHANGER

WHY NOT?

Donna Orender

Whether as an athlete, a sport executive, or a nonprofit leader, Donna Orender has always given shape to visions she seeks by asking a single question; whereas Ross Greenburg in chapter 6 exhorted you to ask "Why?", Orender asks "Why not?" Orender is founder and chief executive officer of Generation W, a nonprofit whose mission is to provide a platform for women and girls to be educated, inspired, and connected; learn how to effect change for themselves, their communities, and the world; and inspire women's leadership. She is creator of *WOWsdom! The Girl's Guide to the Positive and the Possible.* Previously, she was president of the WNBA and senior vice president of the PGA, as well a three-time All-Star and one of only 20 women to play all three seasons of the Women's Pro Basketball League.

When I got a phone call from Adam Silver, then NBA Deputy Commissioner, in 2004, asking if I would be interested in being president of the WNBA, I was quite intrigued but still filled with mixed emotions. Basketball was a forever passion of mine. I had competed at the highest levels, having played in the first women's professional league and being part of history as a starting guard in the first women's game ever played in Madison Square Garden. Ah, but life had moved on, and now I had a successful career at the PGA Tour. I had earned a spot as one of our top executives in the office of the commissioner, successfully leading media negotiations, providing strategic and creative direction, and launching new business initiatives. My family was nearby, and the tour was at long last on the cusp of exponential growth. So why would I leave? There were lots of whys to consider. The whys made me tentative, but I finally changed the question to one that has worked for me my whole life, "Why not?"

Why not return to where I learned how to be strong and courageous, and proudly and determinedly compete head-to-head? It was time to utilize all the lessons and business relationships developed over 17 years at the tour and three years in sport television to make a difference in sports in which the athletes were as talented and determined but just happened to be women. My peers looked at me as if I was crazy. Tiger was new on the scene; how could I leave now? And all I could think of was *why not* leave now? At my going-away lunch when I tried to answer why I was doing this, I pointed to my male colleagues who had daughters and said I was doing it for them. I also reminded them that I was doing it for my two sons as well. Women basketball players, with their grace and grit, are not just role models for young girls.

It was not the transition I anticipated. The sport work was to be expected, but it was the pushback on issues of gender and race and sexuality that was troubling. I experienced a lot of humanity at its best as well as at its worst while at the WNBA. I did not anticipate the harsh judgments and the stiff resistance that came from places that did not seem rational. I felt like a social anthropologist on the front lines of commerce and culture. I learned how men felt about women, politically, economically,

(continued)

GAME CHANGER *(continued)*

and socially. I saw how women felt about women, and I learned more about how I felt about myself, my doubts and dreams forged through a career of pioneering.

I look back at my life in sport and the business of sport, and the patterns emerge. As a tennis player I became the first girl to earn a spot on a boys' varsity team in the state of New York—that was when the first and defining *why not* was uttered. Why not play on the boys' tennis team? Thank goodness for an open-minded coach who gave me the chance to earn my way, to try out and prove I belonged. It is such an important lesson, being open to what is possible and supporting others' opportunities even when you can't clearly see the opportunities yourself.

With the benefit of hindsight, I can see now that all of this was a prelude to my work as founder of Generation W, which champions opportunities and amplifies the voices of women and teen girls. Generation W, Generation WOW, our teen girl mentoring program, and now *WOWsdom!*—a unique, engaging book that unites the Wow of girls with the Wisdom of women—are all about creating and respecting the unique human condition that is all of us. I suppose at its essence that is what sport is all about. It is a place where personal growth is forged, which hopefully translates into professional growth and creating better and stronger communities.

I am a work in progress, and so are all the organizations I have been part of. If you believe in people and in yourself, then do you want to be a game-changer?

I can answer that for you: Why not?

Used with permission of Donna Orender.

The vision we created was very simple: *to be one of the top soccer leagues in the world.*

While we were not successful in winning the bid to host the World Cup, the vision proved to be relevant and enduring—even while we have shown flexibility on the path to achieve it. The ever-increasing rate of change in our world demands strategies that recognize demographic shifts and marketplace and technological changes. Companies need to be flexible, responsive, and nimble. We believe that has been a critical component of our success.

HOW WE GET THERE: OUR MISSION

Even as our plans may need to be modified, the goal is always aligning all areas of the company to ensure that we are moving closer to achieving our long-term vision. And while a vision is what a company wants to be in the future, a mission is what a company needs to do now. In the case of MLS, we have established a mission—essentially a blueprint—that guides all our business plans, decision making, and activities.

Our mission is action-oriented and direct: to make MLS the league of choice for fans, players, and the business community here in North America.

Soccer is the world's most popular sport, and North America is the most valuable sport market. But while the opportunity to create a valuable and impactful business is massive, the task is complex and challenging. There are almost 80 million soccer fans in the United States alone, yet many of them are not engaged with our players and clubs. And while corporate sponsors and media outlets are involved in the sport at the same levels as they are with the other major professional sport leagues, there is still tremendous opportunity for growth. If we can convert this huge "soccer market" into committed and valuable MLS fans and commercial partners, we are convinced that would position Major League Soccer as one of the top leagues in the world.

THE WAY WE ACT: OUR CORE VALUES

Almost 10 years ago, we met as an organization to establish a set of core values for the MLS League Office. Core values are the fundamental beliefs of a person or organization. Essentially, these values help establish an organizational culture that guides behavior and can help companies determine if they are on the right path by creating an unwavering guide.

Our core values are prominently displayed on the walls at our office so every single employee knows what we stand for.

Our core values include these: *Diversity, Innovation, Passion, Teamwork, Brand. And Results*

One of Major League Soccer's key positioning statements is that we represent "A league for a New America"—a country that is diverse, global, and driven by empowered and engaged young people who have grown up with the sport of soccer. We believe it is critically important to have the *diversity* of our country reflected in our players and staff. Today, we have players from nearly 75 different countries and staff that are racially and ethnically diverse and increasingly bilingual and bicultural. We believe that a diverse organization drives success at all levels, including at the bottom line.

We strive to create an environment with leadership that drives and embraces *innovation*. We want to instill a culture that is vibrant and invigorating with our entire organization, looking not at what has happened, but at what needs to happen. And we want to challenge the status quo by encouraging creativity and critical thinking.

For many of us at Major League Soccer, working at the league and its clubs is a life mission, a *passion*. If you are going to succeed in MLS, you must be passionate about the sport, believe in our vision and mission, and be ready to celebrate our successes but also have the strength and conviction to work through our challenges.

One of my favorite quotes is from John Lennon: "A dream we dream alone is just a dream. But a dream we dream together is a reality." *Teamwork* is not a

RECTIFY MISTAKES QUICKLY: THE HOUSTON DYNAMO CASE STUDY

Oliver Luck

Oliver Luck had a rude awakening with one of the first decisions he made in MLS, but he acted quickly to understand the values and passion of his fan base and the league and correct his mistake. Luck was the NCAA's first executive vice president for regulatory affairs and oversaw all NCAA regulatory functions—enforcement, academic and membership affairs, and the eligibility center. He was also involved with the NCAA's strategic partnerships. A former NFL quarterback for five years, Luck graduated Phi Beta Kappa from West Virginia University in 1982 and earned a law degree from the University of Texas at Austin, graduating cum laude in 1987. He became CEO and commissioner of Vince McMahon's new XFL in 2018. Luck previously worked with the NFL, including the start of the World League of American Football as Frankfurt's general manager in 1991 and as president of NFL Europe.

Courtesy of NCAA.

Mistakes don't have to kill your career. Which is good, because you are bound to make some. I learned this as a college football player and in a long career in the competitive and chaotic world of amateur and professional sport. I also experienced my biggest and most public mistake rather late in my career. I made a doozy at the start of a new job that threatened to derail our whole organization.

What is critical for you to remember is to acknowledge the mistakes you inevitably will make and correct them as soon as possible. In my situation, my boss, one of the nation's wealthiest and most successful businessmen, helped me quickly rectify it.

Late in 2005, the Anschutz Entertainment Group (AEG), owner and operator of the San Jose Earthquakes, announced it was relocating the franchise to Houston. This decision was not taken lightly. San Jose was one of the founding members of MLS and had a passionate fan base. But given the challenging politics in California around taxpayer subsidies for sport and entertainment venues, the ownership group was not able to solve the existential stadium problem that confounded every MLS team—how to get a stadium built with significant public money.

Houston, of course, was a very attractive location. It was the country's fourth-largest city and the biggest metropolitan marketplace without a MLS franchise. It boasted a diverse demography that was ideal for soccer coupled with a booming economy, particularly in the health care and petroleum sectors. At the time, I was the president of the Harris County-Houston Sports Authority, the governmental entity charged with financing and building the sport venues in Houston's Minute Maid

Park, NRG Stadium, and Toyota Center. AEG asked me if I would be interested in running the new soccer franchise, and I agreed, knowing full well that launching the team was going to be a massive task given the incredibly short timelines. My first day on the job was January 1, 2006. Our opening day was April 2. Needless to say, every minute counted.

As the president and general manager of the new team, I faced numerous challenges—hiring a staff, finding office space, negotiating a stadium lease, identifying a practice facility, relocating players and coaches, securing sponsorships, selling season tickets, and perhaps most importantly, building political and civic support in the community for the team and for a new stadium.

The most pressing issue was giving the team an identity, a name. After conducting a handful of harried and cursory meetings with local soccer officials and league personnel, we decided, in a clear nod to the European tradition of naming soccer clubs after the year in which they were founded (think Hannover 96 or Schalke 04), to christen the team Houston 1836, the year in which the city was founded. Of course, there were examples of the "number name" in U.S. sport as well, the most notable being the San Francisco 49ers and the Philadelphia 76ers. And if you looked into minor league U.S. sport you would quickly find teams like the Oklahoma City 89ers and the Phillips 66ers.

But Houston 1836 did not go over well. Almost immediately after making the announcement, our young staff was faced with negative feedback bordering on contempt and outrage. What should have been a joyous celebration and a shot in the arm for the brand-new franchise almost instantly became an albatross. "Insensitive," "boorish," and "stupid" were just some of the adjectives hurled our way. The name was a slap in the face to many of the very people we wanted to attract to our matches.

To put it bluntly, we screwed up. Although 1836 was unquestionably the year of Houston's founding, it was also an "annus horribilis" in the eyes of a sizable portion of the Houston community, namely those Houstonians of Mexican descent. In 1836, Texas was a province of Mexico. Three events in that eventful year changed Texas (and arguably American) history forever, namely, the Battles of the Alamo, Goliad, and San Jacinto. And in that last battle, contested in a rain-soaked field just outside of today's Houston city boundaries, General Sam Houston defeated the Mexican forces under the leadership of General Santa Anna, and Mexico lost its province of Texas.

It didn't take long to realize that our fledgling franchise, by not properly vetting the new name, had just insulted a demographic that was hugely important to our success. Sure, those of us who were working frenzied 16-hour days preparing for opening day knew we had done this unintentionally. We knew it was just a result of this incredibly truncated "launch" process, which did not allow enough time to consider all the unintended consequences of our rapid-fire decision making. We knew we didn't mean to insult anybody, we just tried to honor the city—and all of its residents—with the new name. But that didn't matter. As William Faulkner once said, "The past isn't dead, it is not even past."

Over the next week, despite our outreach efforts to leaders within the Hispanic community, the criticism grew louder. The word "boycott" was tossed around. Things were getting worse. As I was questioning my own leadership in terms of how we could solve this imbroglio, my cell phone rang.

It was my boss, Phil Anschutz, founder and owner of AEG, and one of America's most renowned businessmen. Mr. Anschutz, whom I had not yet met, was also a

(continued)

360 *(continued)*

man of few words. He made Josie Wales look chatty. Obviously, he wanted to know my assessment of the situation. I told him I thought it was serious. "Houston," I said, "is one of those places where people of all races and ethnicities take pride in getting along. It's a so-called majority–minority city and the new name is hurting us."

Mr. Anschutz pushed back, telling me that his executives in Los Angeles, all smart and accomplished individuals, believed that the controversy would blow over and that the franchise could ride it out. "No," I responded, "This is like a burr under the saddle and the longer we ride the worse it will get. It is not going away. Mr. Anschutz, I have been on your payroll all of three weeks. You hardly know me. But I feel very strongly about this."

The line went quiet for a few seconds, and then Mr. Anschutz said matter-of-factly, "Well, change the name." So my boss, a man I had not yet met, trusted my judgment on this incredibly important issue. His decisiveness—in real time, mind you—allowed us to cut our losses, rectify our error, and return to promoting our team and its inaugural season.

And what a season it was! After a stunning 5-1 opening game victory over the Colorado Rapids before a crowd of more than 25,000 fans, the Houston Dynamo went on to win the MLS Championship. And six short years later the Houston Dynamo opened its 2012 season in a brand-new stadium, BBVA Compass Stadium, jointly financed by the Dynamo ownership group and the Houston community.

Moral of this story? Don't be stubborn, keep an open mind, and never be afraid to admit to making a mistake. And learn from leaders like Phil Anschutz.

Based in part on material first published in *20 Secrets to Success for NCAA Student-Athletes Who Won't Go Pro*, by Rick Burton, Jake Hirshman, Norm O'Reilly, Andy Dolich, and Heather Lawrence. © 2018 by Ohio University Press.

new or particularly flashy idea, but it's absolutely true that the most successful companies have employees who share the organizational vision and not only respect each other, but also take pride in supporting their coworkers' success and failures. I'm proud of the "all for one and one for all" mentality within the league office, but also in our interactions with the thousands of people who work in a variety of roles at our clubs. Our organizational strength lies in collaboration and effective communication among all our league-wide employees.

We also have created a department to specifically foster collaboration among our clubs—the Club Services department. This group facilitates workshops for the teams on ticketing, sales retention, marketing, digital and social media, communications, and fan engagement. Our clubs share best practices with each other on everything from managing the ever-evolving "supporter culture" to creating the game-day atmosphere in sport.

A great example of this in action was when David Beckham and the rest of the ownership group for our new team in Miami wanted to learn more about how existing MLS clubs became successful; Sporting Kansas City opened its doors to share best practices of every aspect of its organization.

As we grow and expand, we always need to keep the Major League Soccer *brand* front and center. Who are we? What do we want to represent to our fans, our communities, and the influencers who can help us achieve our goal? We believe that MLS is perfectly positioned for a new generation of sports fans: a sport that is diverse, global, and digitally native. These are not just buzzwords; they are at the very core of our decision making and ultimately, our forward-facing positioning and brand. As we venture into new initiatives, experiment, and push ourselves to the limits, this focus on staying true to our brand will never change.

Finally, sports are about measuring wins and losses. They are about *results*. We're not in this to be second best. We're in this to win. There are hundreds of soccer leagues. Our vision is not to be one of the good leagues; it's to be among the best leagues. Key Performance Indicators (KPIs) really matter, which is why we take great pride in the enormous rise in our club valuations by Forbes; in the high rankings we receive in sponsor loyalty surveys; in the development of world-class soccer stadiums, training facilities, and academies; and in the continued increase in attendance, viewership, and fan engagement.

I am proud that we have built a strong culture and a value system that is steeped in integrity, respect, collaboration, and results. It is fundamental to our success that we maintain these values and that they provide the foundation for everything we do.

BRINGING IT HOME: OUR PARTNERS, OUR FANS, AND OUR COMMUNITIES

Corporate partners are among the economic drivers of success for any sport league or team. We believe in them because they believe in us. I currently drive an Audi because it's a great driving experience, but it's also because Audi is a corporate partner of our league. We have a symbiotic relationship with our partners, who share our culture and values and represent some of the most innovative brands in the world.

One such partner is Southern New Hampshire University (SNHU). Our research showed us that many of our players were leaving school early to pursue their dream of playing professional soccer, yet many of them wanted to complete their college degree. Our unique partnership with SNHU helps players earn their degrees while continuing to play. Since the partnership began in 2015, more than 180 MLS players, retired players, and staff have enrolled in degree programs with SNHU. Tesho Akindele, a forward with FC Dallas and member of the Canadian National Team, was the first player to graduate from SNHU and, I'm proud to share, is now working toward his master's degree.

The same goes for our current broadcast partners—in North America alone, they are ESPN, FOX Sports, and Univision in the United States and TSN and TVA Sports in Canada. MLS matches are also televised in more than 170 countries throughout the world on some of the most prominent networks such as SKY Sports, Eurosport, and Fox Sports Africa. Our broadcast partners, including the

PITCHER-AGENT HAS ONCE-IN-A-LIFETIME ENCOUNTER DURING COMEBACK

Steve Trout

Steve Trout had to reflect on his core values as he toed the rubber against his client. Trout, son of star pitcher Dizzy Trout, followed in his father's footsteps (and wrote about it in the 2002 book *Home Plate: The Journey of the Most Flamboyant Father and Son Pitching Combination in Major League History*) by pitching in the major leagues for 11 seasons, mostly in Chicago with the Cubs and White Sox. He has been a coach for professional teams and conducted baseball academies and youth clinics since his attempted comeback described here was over.

Here I am, a sport agent, standing on the mound wearing a Pittsburgh Pirates jersey, about to turn 40. I'm facing a batter who happens to be my client, which makes for a rather awkward encounter. If I weren't so competitive, and if agents were as morally bankrupt as we are often depicted, I might groove one for him. Instead, I bear down to do battle. All my life, long before I was a rookie for the Chicago White Sox in 1976, competition was what I enjoyed. I decide to be true to myself and make him earn his way on base. Julio Vinas, a catcher on the White Sox 40-man roster, flies out to shallow center field. We laugh about it over dinner later that day, knowing this had never happened in baseball before.

This comeback for me came in 1996, after eight years away from the game. I worked at obtaining baseball players to represent during my time away. Becoming an agent was a way for me to do life differently. I saw things differently. I wanted to erase the chalkboard and rewrite my love of my profession. Age can make a big difference in how you go about doing something. How I would go about this comeback would be different from how I prepared when my journey started at age 20.

There is lots to prove in a comeback, showing everyone it is not a joke; it is not a gift from the Pirates. I want to make a difference and help them win games. I want to compete at the highest level again, which can happen only for a major league player.

Baseball is my life. The son of pitcher Dizzy Trout, it is my upbringing and it is my identity. We all share that. What we do is how we are remembered. I know in order to prove that I'm serious about this comeback I must work harder, follow the rules, and be a leader. Some of those things I was not so good at when I was 20.

To respect, appreciate, and enjoy the ride I must cherish every moment. I have learned that the days are not guaranteed and at age 40 I have learned not to hurry up time, not to force things; and I have also learned that once it's gone it might not come back. Treat every day, every pitch, as if it will be your last one.

innovative alliances formed with new social media platforms, are engaged collaborators in the promotion of MLS, and many of their employees live and breathe our sport. We are a fan-first league because we understand that the growth of our sport is fueled by our passionate supporters. Our fans are younger, more diverse, and more active on digital platforms than any other fans in any other professional sport. As these young fans grow older, become more empowered, and make more decisions, they will prove to be the engine of growth for the next phase of the league's evolution.

And while our fans are the youngest in professional sport, they represent a wide swath of demographic, ethnic, and regional subgroups, and each segment has its own needs. It is important that we understand what motivates each group and deliver the experience that will not only engage them today, but also provide the motivation for them to continue to support the league for years to come.

In 2006, we conducted extensive consumer research to get a better understanding of what our current fans thought about the league and what things would they want to see to become more engaged. The most telling result of the research was that our fans told us they wanted to see more world-class stars competing for MLS clubs. Based on that research, our owners created the Designated Player Rule allowing clubs to sign a player outside of the normal salary budget. The first player signed under the new rule was David Beckham, one of the most iconic athletes in the world. World-class players like France's Thierry Henry, Spain's David Villa, Italy's Sebastian Giovinco, Mexico's Carlos Vela, and United States stars Michael Bradley and Jozy Altidore (among many others) signed with the league in the following years.

Since then, we've instituted other initiatives to sign more elite players who have elevated the quality of play during a period of expansion in which the number of clubs doubled in size. Whenever I'm asked what makes me proudest about my job, the answer is not what most people expect. It's not just the expansion of the league across the United States or Canada. And it's not the opening of so many world-class soccer stadiums or the increased respect for the quality of the play on the field. What fills me most with pride is the impact the league and our clubs have made in the *community* through our league-wide philanthropic effort, MLS WORKS.

I believe that professional sport organizations, along with our players and coaches, have an unprecedented ability to positively influence the lives of those in need and to improve the communities where we live and play our games.

Even during our earliest days, when MLS was challenged to find the resources to run our basic business, our league, our clubs, and our players have donated countless hours to community service in a wide variety of areas, from promoting diversity and inclusion, to supporting local volunteerism, to helping promote healthy lifestyles and programs that support the environment.

As we begin preparations to celebrate our 25th season in 2019, we have proven that we are not only a league on the rise, but a league that is delivering on and off the field. We have earned the respect of the sport industry here and abroad and continue to provide countless opportunities for fans, players, and executives to be part of building a true soccer nation in America.

Part III

Mastering Modern Media and Technology

The world of sport has benefitted greatly from technology and the power of modern media applications. This part of the book will help you grasp how our rapidly changing innovations need not be something for you to be afraid of. Instead, a willingness to embrace new products and platforms rather than fear them will give you the opportunity to guide your organization toward its goals. NBC Sports' Mark Lazarus opens by sharing, through the high-profile example of the Olympics, how his organization has embarked on harnessing modern media for immediate needs as well as long-range strategy. The father–son tandem of Ted and Zach Leonsis provide an intergenerational example of how embracing changing technologies is essential to respond to changing consumption patterns in our society. Analytics has been a buzzword for some time now, so much so that it is no longer a buzzword as much as an essential part of sport business strategy. Shawn Spieth and Kyle Nelson, cofounders of MVP Index, explain how using analytics and social media effectively can offer profound insights for your organization to leverage. Peter Moore understood the possibilities for translating technology into new markets in both North America and Europe even before our 21st-century tech explosion. His chapter closes out this part of the book with ideas for how this understanding can benefit you even if you aren't tasked with running a global enterprise.

CHAPTER 10

Harnessing Modern Media Strategies

Mark Lazarus

Mark Lazarus is chairman of NBC Broadcasting and Sports. He oversees the NBC Sports Group, which consists of NBC Sports, NBC Olympics, NBCSN, Golf Channel, NBC Sports Regional Networks, NBC Sports Radio, NBC Sports Digital, and two transactional sport businesses, GolfNow and SportsEngine. Lazarus also oversees NBC Broadcasting, which includes the NBCUniversal-owned television stations, affiliate relations, and affiliate marketing, as well as network operations and broadcast standards.

Lazarus was appointed chairman of NBC Sports Group in 2011. During his tenure, NBC Sports Group has secured and renewed numerous media rights, including the Olympics, NFL, NASCAR, Premier League, and the Indy 500, and has delivered the most-watched shows and events in TV history, including the 2012 Olympic Games, Super Bowls XLVI and XLIX, and the only prime-time show to rank first for seven consecutive years (*Sunday Night Football*).

Previously, Lazarus served as president of media and marketing for CSE, and served in a variety of leadership roles at Turner Broadcasting, including president of Turner Entertainment Group, where he oversaw all aspects of Turner Entertainment Group (2003-2008), and president of Turner Sports (1999-2003).

A graduate of Vanderbilt University, Lazarus is on the board of governors of the Boys & Girls Clubs of America and serves on the board of directors for the East Lake Foundation.

As the world congregated in Pyeongchang, South Korea, in February 2018, politics, global issues, and International Olympic Committee (IOC) controversy dominated the dialogue leading up to the Winter Olympics. What else is new?

North Korea was feared at first, then made peace, and sent a team of athletes, diplomats, and cheerleaders to participate in the Winter Games. Overwhelming talk about U.S. and North Korean relations was prevalent in every Olympic discussion. The IOC banned Russia from the Games for the systemic doping scandal during the 2014 Sochi Games, though Russian athletes could compete under the Olympic flag and the name "Olympic Athlete from Russia."

But when the athletes took the field, all of that went away and the world celebrated incredible stories and athletic accomplishments.

The Korean organizing committee (POCOG) delivered a great Olympics that was well run and held at terrific venues by a warm and welcoming people eager to display their country.

As for NBC, our audiences once again showed up in big numbers across every platform. The Games were the number one rated prime-time show, with record audiences when broadcast, cable, and digital viewing were added together. Our Total Audience Delivery (TAD) metric is now a baseline for measuring major event coverage.

I could provide similar context for most Olympics. The 2016 Summer Games began and ended amid a cloud of controversy—would Rio de Janeiro, Brazil, be ready? What about security? Was the water safe? Would Zika or crime co-opt the sports? Much of this angst was not realized, though the Games did close with an embarrassing web of false accusations by American swimmers who tried to divert attention from their robbery and vandalism, which resulted in news coverage that took away time from memorable achievements on the courts and fields. In between, tremendous athletes accomplished remarkable performances, and massive global audiences across every type of media platform were able to witness them.

At Rio 2016, NBC produced, marketed, and sold more than 6,800 hours of content over a 17-day period. As a reference point, the 1996 Atlanta Olympic Games consisted of 171.5 hours of coverage. That's quite a change in just 20 years.

NBC has broadcast the Olympics on and off since 1964—that's a lot of Olympiads in a time period that takes us to the early days of the Cold War and when Roger Bannister became the first human to run a 4-minute mile. We are the home for the Olympics through 2032, meaning that we are putting together strategies and doing our best to predict what audiences will want every two years as well as more than a decade down the line. Not every reader of this book is going to come and work for NBC, or even for a major network. I could share with you the deep belief that I and my team have that no single event brings the world's best athletes together in unity to compete and respect one another better than the Olympics. I could assure you that we try to capture that spirit through media for audiences of all nations who live in the United States. That is our intention in the thousands of hours of planning we do for each Olympic cycle. But what I wish to do here, for an audience of sport business professionals and students, is use our experience in Olympic coverage to help you understand where modern media is headed, and how you can use that knowledge to benefit your own career goals as well as your organizational goals.

The media landscape and consumer behavior are always changing. The world is becoming more enamored with technology and what it has to offer. That is no different than it ever has been, though the changes are more rapid. With the Rio and Pyeongchang Olympics in our rear-view mirror, let's look ahead. Here are three takeaways that will help you grasp how modern media executives think, not just from a production perspective, but also in working with sponsors and partners to make production possible.

BE AWARE OF TOTAL AUDIENCE, NOT JUST THE MAIN PLATFORM

Once upon a time, we had three networks and three channels. Everyone watched TV. Today we have hundreds of networks. To master modern media, you have to understand the various platforms and the rate of change that is happening every day. Everyone wants personalized content. Everyone wants to stream or download or binge. This is reality. This has obviously been building for some time, but Rio in 2016 became a Games for change—a true sea change for how we count audiences going forward.

If you take nothing else from this chapter, make sure to take this: When negotiating, whether as media provider or as a sponsor, be aware of total audience, not just the main platform.

The press loves to focus on prime-time ratings, and as you can see in figure 10.1, which shows our prime-time audience across all platforms, we found

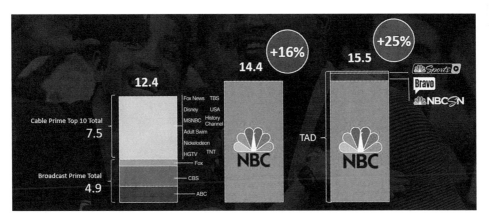

Figure 10.1 Top 10 cable networks: Fox News, Disney, HGTV, TBS, History Channel, USA, Adult Swim, Nickelodeon, MSNBC, TNT.

M-Th 10a-5p/Sa2 10a-6:15p/su2 8a-6p) versus prime time (aggregate across NBC, NBCSN, USA, MSNBC, CNBC, Bravo, and Golf). Total Audience Delivery measures broader Rio Olympics consumption by calculating average minute viewing across broadcast, cable, and digital.

TAD viewers / reach

Events on cable: team sports, non-USA

Events on Bravo: tennis

THE VALUE IN THE VALUES OF THE GAMES

David Baker

David Baker recognizes that sport has always appealed to something deep within us. When the media provide access to these stories, we will continue to watch. Baker's leadership has transformed the Pro Football Hall of Fame in Canton, Ohio, and dramatically expanded its brand by focusing on the mission to "Honor the Heroes of the Game, Preserve Its History, Promote Its Values, Celebrate Excellence Everywhere." Baker is also

Courtesy of Pro Football Hall of Fame.

David Baker (left) leads a discussion in Canton, Ohio.

leading Johnson Controls Hall of Fame Village, an $800 million mixed-use development project under way in Canton. Baker played professional basketball in Europe. An attorney by trade, he was elected mayor and councilman of Irvine, California; served as the Arena Football League Commissioner; and was the managing partner for Union Village, the first integrated health village, located in Henderson, Nevada.

"Spanning the globe to bring you the constant variety of sport . . . the thrill of victory . . . and the agony of defeat . . . the human drama of athletic competition. . . . This is ABC's Wide World of Sports!"

As a young boy, I was brought up on those words of Jim McKay as I devotedly tuned in every week to watch everything from ski jumping, track and field, bobsled racing, car racing, and billiards to team sports. Anything that had winners and losers. But more importantly, anything that involved competitors.

As a father, I found out that the values learned in competition far exceed what happens on the field. It is a laboratory for character development that helped my boys become better husbands, fathers, and citizens.

As a commissioner of the Arena Football League, I learned that the game is more than entertainment. Sport is a church where surrendering yourself personally to a team makes you more relevant and not less. And the "human drama of athletic competition"? It is full of invaluable lessons on perseverance, discipline, commitment, dedication, diligence, passion, courage, respect, nobility, honor, grace, and even compassion and love.

As president of the Pro Football Hall of Fame, I observed that true excellence is not pristine or perfect. Excellence is a fight. It is snot coming from your nose and blood dripping from getting smashed in the mouth. It requires constant and sustained courage and a lifetime of character.

Focusing on the values in the game actually makes the game *more* valuable! Every great empire was built on the values of competition. The Greeks had the Olympics, the Persians their equestrian events, and the Romans their gladiators. But when those events began to appeal merely to the prurient interests of entertainment, the thumbs-up or thumbs-down in the Colosseum, that's when the empire began to crumble.

Today, I have maybe 1,500 television channels at home and countless more platforms competing for my time and treasure on the Internet. Still, it seems as if there is nothing of true *value* worth watching. I'm not at all sure why I should be *Keeping Up with the Kardashians* or at all interested in the *Housewives of Orange County* . . . *Atlanta* . . . *New Jersey* or anywhere else.

But in every competition, hidden just behind the entertainment, there are life lessons, virtues, and values; there are heroes and villains, winners and losers, hope and despair, trust and love.

Show them the values and they shall show you how very much they *value* them.

tremendous success with our Rio ratings. But what they leave out is the total consumption across all dayparts, platforms, and forms of media.

Those best suited to judge the scale of the audience are the marketer or advertiser. It is with this group that we made a deal or promise to. They committed tens of millions of dollars to reaching our audience. The only way we maintain our strong partnerships is to deliver what we promised and pay off the trust they showed in NBCUniversal and the Olympics. Marketers care about the bottom line, and we delivered the audience we promised. We, the media, and the marketing community are changing as we speak. Our currency is shifting in response to consumer behavior change and technology advancements. The industry must shift to count for total audiences that consume content, whether it is linear, digital, broadcast, cable, social, or something we have yet to experience. Today we have to achieve this in a manual way by utilizing the syndicated research available from various ratings compilers. As an industry we expect to be able to count the audience. In fact, if we can't, our models for content and marketers will not survive.

What we proved with the 2016 Rio Olympics is that massive consumption and dominance in the media landscape pushed us and the industry closer to a currency and complete audience tabulation solution.

BE CREATIVE IN MAXIMIZING YOUR PROPERTY

Keep reading about what big media players are doing. NBC is not the only company that is innovating, but our Olympics illustration provides excellent examples to draw from in assessing how media is changing. We went into the Games with record advertising sales for both linear television and broadcast and cable, on digital and social media platforms. Each has its own reporting metrics

GAME CHANGER

GOING THE EXTRA MILES CAN PUT YOU ON THE MAP

Ken Solomon

Ken Solomon explains how with creativity and commitment, a property holder and media outlet can partner to create impressive results. Solomon is president of Tennis Channel (which comprises the cable channel, Tennis Channel Plus streaming service, and TennisChannel.com) and led the acquisition and integration of media siblings *Tennis* magazine and Tennis.com. Under his watch the channel grew from less than 4 million households into one of television's most successful, fully distributed independent networks, leading to its 2016 purchase by Sinclair Broadcast Group. Solomon has four decades of entertainment industry experience, with top posts at Walt Disney Company, Universal Television, and News Corporation. He is on the board of the International Tennis Hall of Fame and the advisory boards of the USTA Foundation.

Ken Solomon (right) has a laugh with Hall of Famer Martina Navratilova and all-time French Open champion Rafael Nadal.

Fred Mullane/camerawork, usa

In 2006, Tennis Channel had the chance to bid for media rights to the French Open (Roland-Garros), one of the world's top cultural and sporting events. The tournament had been negotiating an extension with its cable rights holder for months but hadn't reached an agreement.

To say this was an unheard-of opportunity for our three-year-old channel would be an enormous understatement. Single-sport networks are not known for coverage at their most important championship events. Tennis Channel was an even less likely candidate given our small reach at the time, just 10 million homes, versus the 90+-million-home incumbent.

But we had introduced ourselves to the French Tennis Federation (FFT) a year before and let them know of our plans for growing the sport on TV. So, when this door opened I immediately hopped on a plane and flew overnight to Lake Geneva, Switzerland, to meet with their media director.

The trip was a 36-hour whirlwind. We had just one day to work something out. Starting at lunch and wrapping up an hour or two after dinner, we crafted and signed an agreement, in what we later called our own Geneva Convention. I was stunned: We had actually closed a long-term deal to be the U.S. home of the French Open. As the ramifications hit me I spent the entire night walking the streets of Geneva.

The arrangement not only put Tennis Channel on the map; it fundamentally changed the trajectory of our network, the shape of tennis on TV, and, some might say, the sport itself. Our mission was to build a dedicated media destination that captured all the excitement of the sport's 24/7/365 schedule in order to grow the game. We never imagined we'd be able to use Roland-Garros as the catalyst for this, but that's exactly what happened. Then, we partnered with the event's former broadcaster to build a better model with more coverage than ever, which now includes all four of the majors and other top events. Within 36 months we had created immense short-term asset value for all of our stakeholders.

But most importantly, tennis fans went from seeing only 5 percent of pro tennis to enjoying almost the entire sport. The impact is clear: In the past five years tennis interest has grown 50 percent, according to the 2016 Nielsen Sports SDNA. And all of this precipitated Tennis Channel's evolution to a point where Sinclair Broadcast Group decided to purchase the network outright in 2016, expanding the channel from 35 million homes to 60+ million today. We've also added *Tennis* magazine and Tennis.com, and launched our Tennis Channel Everywhere app and a stand-alone digital subscription service, Tennis Channel Plus.

Looking back at that exciting, unpredictable moment, I see universal life lessons. First, never limit yourself. We believed in what Tennis Channel could be, even getting the rights to cover the majors. People say it all the time because it's excellent advice: Dream big. We visualized the ideal, rather than just a next step, and then engineered how to get there.

Second, just show up. You can't overstate the power of being there in the flesh. Don't assume. Don't send an email or leave a voice message. Just go. It's actually a very hopeful thought to me, that telephones, email, and social media will never usurp the power of personal trust and looking someone in the eye. Technology is a tool, but partnerships come down to belief in each other.

These ideas let our potential partners know we meant business. When we learned that year-round renewal negotiations left the FFT open to the idea of a different partner, we were prepared to move and were on a plane the next day. Sometimes you need to go the extra mile.

Or in this case, the extra 5,896 miles.

for our very long list of prominent advertiser partners—household names like Proctor & Gamble, Toyota, General Motors, Visa, McDonald's, Comcast, just to name a few.

We had high expectations for Rio 2016 audience levels and promised as much to our advertisers. We expected large television audiences (broadcast and cable), strong digital consumption, and a growing social media following, and we got that. What we missed was the balance or makeup of each of those media platforms and their audiences as parts of the total consumption. As you saw in figure 10.1, we averaged a 14.4 rating, making it the number one show for all of 2016. We provided more than 50 hours at this rating, the equivalent of an entire second NFL prime-time season.

For the first time, we leveraged this interest and produced cable prime-time live content. Both NBCSN and Bravo had live events in prime time, therefore splitting up—or better said, adding to—the prime audiences. The Rio time zone allowed for so much content to be live in prime time that we chose to use multiple networks.

In addition to the broadcast and cable coverage, we also streamed every event live on NBCOLYMPICS.com and on our NBC Olympics apps. This led to huge digital growth and notably the rise of connected TV devices such as Apple TV, Roku, and Amazon Fire, and the connected TVs made by set manufacturers had a lot of viewership.

This new technology brought people back to good old-fashioned large-screen TV viewing in a communal, multigenerational environment. They streamed through our app, but to the big screen in their living room, and watched in accordance with the family coviewing habit. Even in today's rapid-fire digital age, a "back to the future" approach can be successful when you stay aware of what your audience wants to see and where they want to see it.

DO YOU BELIEVE? . . . YES!

It's not exactly believing in miracles to think the Olympics can be a broadcast success, but as with anybody in sport business and the media industry, if we don't stay aware of the landscape and our product, we will struggle. There were plenty of reasons to be concerned about the news narrative prior to Rio and Pyeongchang, but we were confident in our approach and we continue to believe strongly in the Olympics.

The media world is hard. It changes every day, which is probably something you also experience, whether or not you are in media. Your job and expectations and skill sets are changing every day. You may see how things are changing from 30,000 feet in the air, and it may be difficult to keep up. But you have no choice. We have the Olympic broadcast rights through 2032. So many of the upcoming Olympics require vertical integration across time zones. This is a strategic issue to contend with, and we must be able to be proactive in both the short and long term. We try to be knowledgeable about how people will consume content in the near future, but what about a decade down the line? Maybe nobody will

360

SPORTS REQUIRE QUICK THINKING FOR SOLUTIONS

Jim Ganley

Sport production has evolved dramatically over the past half century. Here, Jim Ganley tells a humorous story to remind us of the value (and perils) of live television that makes sport a perpetual favorite, whether old-school plugged-in viewing or streaming from your smartphone.

The sport business is for innovative people who like to do the impossible. Innovation in the broadcast industry has changed how fans view sport, and how new technologies create new businesses. Who would have thought 50 years ago that sport would have changed as dramatically as it has?

The real-time aspect of sport has always been attractive to advertisers, even more so when video recording became popular, as people didn't want to just tape the games and watch them later, which would have meant fast-forwarding through the ads. They wanted to experience it as it happened, and not have the result accidentally spilled to them before they got to watch it. To accomplish a sport production, many changes have taken place in the games themselves.

Television has had a major impact on how and when the game is played. Start times and attempts to control the length of games are examples of broadcasters wanting to maximize advertising revenue.

A wrestling match in the mid-1980s during my time at Request TV (iN DEMAND TV) showed me how technology can directly affect a sporting event.

At the start of the pay-per-view business, the technology that cable operators used was (one-way) addressable cable set-top boxes located at the cable (subscriber's home). The technology Request used was scrambled satellite signal—the first scrambled satellite signals used in commercial TV to deliver to cable systems. We first authorized the cable operator's downlink and a decoder. That gave the cable operator the feed. Then the operator used a personal computer Request prepared for him in order to control his feed and timer from the cable headed to the subscriber's home cable box. Everything was set to cut off at exactly the top of the hour . . . everything except the wrestlers!

As usual for a live event, we had our broadcasting operations manager on the phone with the production team located at the arena where the event took place to make sure everything was going according to schedule.

The wrestling group had never put on a show with time restraints. During the final wrestling match—a battle royale with about 10 wrestlers competing—there were still at least 7 wrestlers in the ring and only 5 minutes left in the allotted time frame! Our operations manager alerted the production team. All of a sudden, wrestlers were flying out of the ring, and a winner was declared with only seconds to spare before the signal was cut off.

even be reading this book—or any other book—by then! Whatever I write may be dangerously close to being obsolete by the time this book comes out. I can only give you the flavor of our experience and our move to an expanded NBC platform, plus what we want to achieve in the years ahead. You have to carve out your approach based on your organizational goals.

LOOKING AHEAD

At NBC, we must incorporate the lessons from South Korea and Brazil to ensure our advertisers and viewers stay with us. We already can't wait for Tokyo 2020. I am proud of what we do each Olympic cycle, but I am also humbled by the Olympic spirit. The Olympics is the last great multisport, multiday, multicountry, uber-patriotic event in the world, challenged only by the FIFA World Cup. Regardless of how media platforms and viewing habits change, the Olympics will prevail . . . and matter. I believe that. The question for you to consider is whether your organization and your cause will stay relevant. What can you do to ensure it does so?

Courtesy of Monumental Sports & Entertainment. Photographer: Ralph Alswang.

CHAPTER 11

Changing Technologies, Changing Consumption

Ted Leonsis and Zach Leonsis

Ted Leonsis is founder, chairman, majority owner, and CEO of Monumental Sports & Entertainment, which owns the NHL's Washington Capitals, NBA's Washington Wizards, WNBA's Washington Mystics, AFL's Washington Valor and Baltimore Brigade, NBA G League's Capital City Go-Go, and the 20,000-seat Capital One Arena. The partnership launched Monumental Sports Network, a first-of-its-kind regional sports network for digital, mobile, and over-the-top platforms. It also operates Kettler Capitals Iceplex, the Capitals' training facility, and George Mason University's EagleBank Arena. Monumental also is co-owner of aXiomatic, which has controlling interest in global esport franchise Team Liquid; Ted is co-executive chairman of aXiomatic.

As cofounder and partner at Revolution Growth, Ted and his partners make a select group of speed-up capital investments in businesses each year, typically investing $25 to $50 million per deal.

Ted is the founder and chairman of ViewLift, a full-service content distribution platform for the web, over-the-top (OTT), and mobile, and SnagFilms, which has more than 5,000 movies and TV shows in its free online library. As a filmmaker, Ted has produced five documentaries, including *Nanking,* which won Peabody and Emmy Awards.

Numerous charities are served through his philanthropic efforts, and he is chairman of the board of DC-CAP, which is dedicated to encouraging and enabling D.C. public high school students to enroll in and graduate from college.

The chapter opener photo shows Ted (far right) and Zach Leonsis (second from left) with Zach's wife Melissa (far left), Ted's wife Lynn (third from left), and Ted and Lynn's daughter Elle.

Zach Leonsis is senior vice president of strategic initiatives for Monumental Sports & Entertainment and general manager of Monumental Sports Network, a first-of-its-kind regional sports network for digital, mobile, and OTT platforms. Zach led the transformation of Monumental Sports Network—co-owned by Monumental Sports & Entertainment and NBC Sports Group—from an ad-based blogging platform to a direct-to-fan service content provider.

Zach joined Monumental in 2011 and spearheaded the Monumental Sports Network, a premiere digital (web, OTT, and mobile) service that is a rapidly growing multisport media powerhouse. Under Zach's leadership, the network is an OTT pioneer and an Emmy Award–winning original content producer attracting attention for innovative programming, broad sport rights, extensive distribution footprint, and powerful packaging of content, ecommerce, and experiences. In 2017, *Sports Business Journal* recognized Zach as an RSN Power Player, citing his work with both Monumental Sports Network and NBC Sports Washington.

Zach's media expertise includes playing a key role in establishing a multibillion-dollar partnership with NBC Sports Group to guiding both strategy and operations that is elevating Monumental Sports & Entertainment's reach to among the strongest in U.S. sport.

In addition to overseeing Monumental Sports & Entertainment's media operations, Zach also oversees Monumental's growing esport division, sitting on the board of directors of Team Liquid, as well as overseeing Monumental's new NBA 2K League team, Wizards District Gaming.

Sports teams and talented male and female athletes deliver lifelong memories, and if we are lucky, the fond memories far outweigh the painful ones. Sport unifies us—families, friends, communities, and cities. It brings our nation together as we watch the Olympics and U.S. athletes competing at the highest level. Sport creates moments that bind us as one; it is the great convener.

I'm an only child. My father was a first-generation immigrant from Greece and a career waiter, my mother a secretary. I was a latchkey kid, heading to the basketball court every day on my way home from school—hoops before homework. We were a modest family, probably lower-middle class, though I didn't realize that at the time. Our luxury? My dad would save his tips and buy me New York Jets season tickets for my birthday. While my dad could barely afford it (it probably cost him $100 per season), it was an opportunity for him to spend quality time with me.

I felt extremely fortunate and never expected the heavy-underdog Jets, behind brash-talking quarterback Joe Namath, to win Super Bowl III way back in 1969. But they did. And days later I skipped school and was atop my dad's shoulders during the parade. That memory would bring tears to my eyes years later.

Sports are powerful. They are galvanizing. They impact the psyche of a city. They create everlasting memories. They make grown men cry. I feel blessed to be in the business of helping to create those incredible memories, memories that will last a lifetime and be shared by family and friends.

Sports—professional, collegiate, and even high school—hold a remarkable place in our local communities. They help define major cities as well as small rural towns. Often the morale of the community is in the hands of those teams. Win, and your next morning is a little brighter. Lose, well, your next morning mood might be somber.

Even though it wasn't easy, those Jets tickets were accessible to my dad, and I will never forget the memories that came with them. Yes, times and finances have changed, but our goal remains to make sport accessible to today's younger fan, though we have to do so in new and innovative ways.—*Ted Leonsis*

Today's sports are a much bigger business than during the Jets' Super Bowl–winning season. Tickets are expensive. The best games are sold out. Teams play seasons and games that are too long for many people, especially our younger generations. Roughly a third of Washington, D.C.'s purchasing population is composed of Millennial and Gen Z consumers. I predict our region will double in size within the next 15 years. High-speed Internet penetration is growing quickly to more than 90 percent in our region, and traditional TV viewing habits are on the decline around the country. Our younger consumers are cord shavers, cord cutters, and cord nevers. If our games are sold out and our younger fans aren't signing up for traditional cable TV subscriptions, how can we establish a touchpoint between them and our teams? How do we avoid losing a generation—or more—of fans? That is a challenge that confronts many of us in professional sport—meeting the changing interests and demands of our younger audience and fan base.

As the founder of Monumental Sports & Entertainment, which includes the NBA's Wizards, NHL's Capitals, WNBA's Mystics, AFL's Brigade and Valor, esport Team Liquid, the Capital City Go-Go of the NBA G League, and an equity interest in NBC Sports Washington, our goal is to make sport accessible to everyone.

One way is our Monumental Sports Network, an OTT, direct-to-consumer digital network. My son, Zach, is part of our executive leadership team and has day-to-day responsibility for our network as well as managing our relationship with NBC Sports Washington, our local cable TV rights holder. Collectively we are creating content and opportunities for younger fans to connect and engage with our teams.—*Ted Leonsis*

WHY IS MASTERING TODAY'S MEDIA IMPORTANT?

For the most part, today's viewing habits are not by appointment, as we set aside time on our own schedule to binge watch our favorite shows. Previously we had saved them to our DVR, but now we are more likely to use a streaming service and be perfectly content to watch using a laptop, tablet, or phone in place of a TV.

The major professional sport leagues along with the NCAA (primarily Division I football and men's basketball) find themselves at a unique intersection between traditional media rights and digital trends.

While time-shifted viewing becomes increasingly popular, live sport remains the final frontier of true appointment viewing. Fans have to go to great lengths

MEDIA, ATHLETES BOTH NAVIGATING INCREASED EXPOSURE

Harvey Greene

Harvey Greene agrees with Ted and Zach Leonsis that organizations with the ability to adapt to a changing marketplace will come out on top in sport business. Greene has served as a media relations executive at the major league level for more than 40 years. Most recently, he spent 25 seasons heading the Miami Dolphins' media relations department, including 12 years as the club's senior vice president of media relations. Before joining the Dolphins, Greene spent almost four seasons as director of media relations for the New York Yankees, where he was the main spokesperson for principal owner George Steinbrenner. He also was the director of public relations for the Cleveland Cavaliers and before that served in the same capacity for the Madison Square Garden Television Network. Internationally, Greene was an assistant venue press chief at three Olympic Games, two World Baseball Classics, and the 1994 Soccer World Cup.

In my 40 years in sport media relations, my bosses have included such legends as George Steinbrenner, Billy Martin, Lou Piniella, Don Shula, Jimmy Johnson, Nick Saban, and Bill Parcells, champions all. And I've been lucky enough to work with first-ballot Hall of Famers like Dave Winfield, Rickey Henderson, Dan Marino, and Jason Taylor.

So, to paraphrase a popular commercial, I've seen a thing or two. And one thing I've learned is that there is a consistency across the board that all winners have—a dedication above everything else to be the very best in their field. That hasn't changed over time.

But one thing has—the relationship between the players and the press.

Back in the "Dark Ages" of the late 20th century (and for 100 years before that), the media—newspapers, radio, and television—was the only way for the players to consistently interact with their fans. The athletes (and their teams) needed the media to get their message across to their followers, and the press needed the access to the players to get content for their various outlets. While there were hiccups along the way (I've had to referee some pretty heated disputes between players and the media), both sides benefited from that arrangement.

But with the dawn of the 21st century, that all began to change. With the advent of the web and the introduction of social media, players and their teams found another, more personal way to reach their audience. Using tools like blogs, Facebook, Twitter, and other similar platforms, they discovered that they could talk directly to their fans without the filter of the media.

For the first time, athletes could let their followers know exactly what they wanted to say without anyone or anything getting in the way. Similarly, teams discovered the economic benefits of using websites and social media outlets to generate revenue by bypassing the press to deliver exclusive content (including breaking news) to their fans.

Players and teams always had the content—now they're beginning to develop the distribution as well. So it's no surprise they're starting to ask, "Who needs the media, anyway?"

The fallout from that has been immediate, dramatically changing the interaction between players and their followers. For better or worse, fans have a much more intimate look at their idols, developing more personal relationships with them but getting increasingly exposed to the dark side of their personalities as well. And the mainstream media are starting to have a diminished role in that conversation.

Both sides have to learn how to deal with those changes, or the consequences can be harsh. Players are finding out that an inappropriate post or tweet can instantaneously destroy their reputation. Similarly, now that athletes have co-opted the media's unique ability to reach a mass audience, journalists need to find a way to deliver increasingly creative content if they intend to stay relevant.

So it's a Wild, Wild West out there, as players and teams figure out how to deal with this unrelenting and more open exposure, and media outlets either learn to change with the times or fold. But just as the champions and Hall of Famers I've worked with understood, one thing will always be constant—those entities that adapt best will be the winners in this new media world.

and disconnect from family, friends, and mobile devices to avoid learning the score of their favorite team. Plus, watching a game whose outcome already has been determined isn't the same as consuming it in real time, sharing the communal experience and engaging with second-screen content. Whose passion is the same when watching a game on demand compared with when it is actually live? Additionally, live sports content is the last bastion of programming for which consumers must subscribe to cable or satellite services to enjoy. If you're a Washington Capitals or Wizards fan, you must have a cable or satellite subscription in the Washington, D.C., area to watch games on NBC Sports Washington. In stark contrast, however, if you're a fan of a particular TV show, you can likely watch that show via a variety of different platforms or services including Apple TV, Netflix, Hulu, Amazon Video, HBO Now, and more.

For those reasons, sport is cable's and satellite's most valuable programming. Sports fans are inelastic. They will do anything to watch their favorite team play—either in person, on cable, or online. Sports are must-watch viewing in real time. The overwhelming majority of the viewership takes place in a live setting, not a time-delayed, on-demand environment. That's the polar opposite of most other video content that is consumed today.

Sports drive viewers to the traditional television networks and provide high-end value for cable operators as they furnish programming for linear and digital customers. Sport continues to play an incredible role in maintaining the cable bundle. It is fueled by passion—love and hate—a passion for a particular sport, team, or player. Many fans engage in fantasy sport leagues, or even gambling, which drives even further engagement with games that might not otherwise be deemed important to fan interest.

Contrast sport viewing with popular viewing habits. Many people set their DVR or connect to a streaming service and binge watch several episodes at a time. They watch at their leisure, on their time and when their life permits, avoiding commercials or fast-forwarding through them.

Not true with sport. Fans schedule life around sport viewing. They have to watch a game live. There is an anticipation, a buildup and a sense that you could see something you may never have seen before—or ever will again. (I don't envision anyone recreating "The Goal" Alex Ovechkin scored January 16, 2006, in Phoenix.) You also want to share that experience with others, in person and through your social channels. You can't adequately time shift that experience.

Live sport programming is mostly exclusive to cable through leaguewide national television deals or team distribution agreements with local cable regional sports networks. Live games are the staple for keeping the cable bundle together. Without live sports content, the value of a cable bundle plummets, and people could rely on programming from other platforms like Netflix, Amazon, Twitter, Facebook, Hulu, HBO Now, YouTube, and other digital-only sites.

As a result, the value of sport programming continues to rise. It's somewhat avoided what has troubled other TV programming. In 2016, my father was part of the NBA Media Rights Committee that negotiated a reported $24 billion TV contract. Our teams, the Wizards and Capitals, negotiated new local RSN deals in 2016, both of which increased significantly from the prior agreement.

The media rights bubble has long been rumored to be on the verge of popping, but we haven't witnessed it yet. What will be the tipping point? Will cable subscriptions erode and OTT platforms become more relevant? We have witnessed the mighty ESPN lose a substantial number of subscribers, which was followed by hundreds of layoffs, including well-known on-air personalities. Will that soon impact leagues, teams, and players who share in revenue? Will it impact the local cable distributer? How do Facebook, Amazon, Twitter, YouTube, Instagram, Snapchat, and emerging platforms factor into the equation? How will it impact the fan? Will there be accessibility issues? We believe in a future where linear cable networks can live symbiotically with new, emerging OTT digital networks, which is exactly what we have tried to craft here in the mid-Atlantic between NBC Sports Washington and Monumental Sports Network.—*Zach Leonsis*

ISSUES AND CHALLENGES: "I WILL NEVER USE TV"

Millennials, Generation Z, and the generations to come don't and won't have the muscle memory to sign up for cable the way my parents did. For example, when I went to college in 2007, my parents bought me a nice big TV (thanks, Mom and Dad!). I connected my shiny new TV to my in-room co-ax cable outlet as well as to my PlayStation. I was set. I had gaming and the ability to watch Washington Capitals and Wizards games. Life was good!

When my sister, Elle, went to college three years later, my parents felt she wanted and needed her own television as well (naturally, they had to treat their two children equally!). However, she scoffed at this idea. She said, "But Mom and Dad, I'll never use a TV, so please don't buy that for me. It would just be a waste of money. Could you buy me an iPad instead?" Demonstrating the changing times, Elle was moving into a new dormitory, which was built without co-ax cable outlets and instead was equipped only with high-speed wireless connectivity. Subscribing to cable wouldn't even have been an option for her. Frankly, it will never even enter her vocabulary.

This transition has come faster than any of us had predicted it would. So how do we reach customers like Elle and her friends? Well, they may not pay for cable, but they actually aren't averse to the subscription model. Take services like Spotify, Netflix, Birchbox, Jukely, or ClassPass, for example. Those businesses seem to be doing all right with younger customers. All feature recurring revenue models that are direct to consumer and available through a variety of applications where younger generations actually spend their time. And because these businesses are direct to consumer, this allows them to retarget individual customers who might churn out in the future. Cable networks sadly don't have this luxury because of disintermediation by multisystem operators like Comcast Xfinity, DirecTV, Dish Network, Verizon Fios, or Time Warner Cable, among dozens of other major providers.

If you aren't building your websites to be mobile and social first, you're missing a huge opportunity!—*Zach Leonsis*

THE POWER OF GOING DIRECT TO CONSUMER

For too long companies have had to forge through go-betweens to distribute their products. Think about a cable company providing you a bundle of channels, or a convenience store selling you a package of various products. All of those data are collected by the seller and not the producer. As a result, sellers have acquired more valuable data on consumers than producers have.

One great example of this is the movie business—when Episode XII of the *Star Wars* saga was released, Disney CEO Bob Iger enjoyed a hugely successful quarter. On the earnings call, everyone was thrilled at how much success Disney was enjoying. But Iger pointed to one key observation: While he knew that literally hundreds of millions (if not billions) of people had seen the new movie, he couldn't tell you who a single one of those people was. Movie theaters were the go-betweens in this value chain, and they never shared any of the data with producers.

This is a huge issue for businesses, but the ability to go direct to consumer is now growing, thanks to digital platforms and new consumer preferences. Custom Ink is a great example of a direct-to-consumer company, creating custom T-shirts and other apparel for audiences. I'm on the board of directors at Custom Ink, and every order is a one-of-a-kind opportunity for us. We have an online design

FILLING THE GAPS BETWEEN PLAYS

Jim Lawson

Recognizing the challenges of changing demographics as the Leonsis father–son duo does, Jim Lawson encourages young, ambitious sport professionals to use their contemporary views and interests to shape sport for the better. Lawson is both the CEO of Woodbine Entertainment Group and the chairman of the Canadian Football League.

As a professional athlete whose career was cut short by injury, I had the daunting task in the early 1980s of choosing that next career path. Transitioning out of sport is extremely difficult, especially moving away from the camaraderie I enjoyed my entire life and of course the love and routine of training, sport, and competition itself. Like so many, I was not prepared to make that leap, so with the further daunting prospect of attending law school, I thought that next step of attending graduate school might delay that transition; and on the upside, I could always practice sport law or pursue sport agency.

It has been many years, actually more measurable in decades, since I embarked on that transition. Along the way, I have learned much that has gotten me to the point where I am today, which is a life totally immersed in the sport world again.

Sport is fun, entertaining, and for so many in society, a welcome relief from the day-to-day challenges we all face in our lives. Yet make no mistake—it is a business and not unlike other businesses.

That truth is a difficult one to accept for many young people who opt to make their career inside it. The business of sport is not just the fun environment that we have come to understand as fans and as participants. As a young person hoping to use my education to jump back into the sport world, I thought it would be easy, exciting, and all about entertainment . . . spending time with the players and enjoying that "game-day experience" regularly. The good news is that is partly true; the bad news is that it mostly is not. Life in the business of sport does not include hanging out with the athletes or being in the dressing room.

Business, whether in or out of sport, requires you to bring developed skills and contribute to the success of the business. It feels as though I am stating the obvious, yet I am not. Many people flock to positions in sport, accepting internships or other roles demanding skills that one might not otherwise accept. The sport business should not be viewed through a different lens. Keep your eye on what you want your career path to be. You would not accept a position in a business that does not allow you to pursue your highest potential, career path, and self-fulfillment, and sport should be no exception. You can get too comfortable in the sport environment and get 10 years down the road and realize you have not challenged yourself. In the business of sport, people sometimes forget to look forward—complacency cannot be your friend.

Historically, sport organizations have been more static than those of other industries. The good news, for the industry as well as you, is that this is no longer the case. Sport business is increasingly complex, from food and beverage to information technology, digital applications, the distribution of content, and the development of contracts. We are constantly looking for ways to increase revenues and analyze consumer trends. There are many paths you can take to increase your knowledge base, challenge yourself, and make a difference in the industry.

Look no further than my home. I've spent a good portion of my professional career with Woodbine Racetrack and the Canadian Football League (CFL). Toronto is one of the world's most vibrant and diverse cities, with a crowded sport market. People have countless options on how to spend their leisure time. Woodbine and the CFL are more similar than you might think. They are both "bums in seats" businesses, meaning if we don't get people to show up, we don't exist. Our demographic is aging. This means we have to be strategic in generating exposure for these two enterprises. We have to analyze how a young generation consumes sport, and meet a demand for a reality TV mindset of highlights and shorter attention spans. We have to find meaningful ways to fill the gaps between plays or races. This is challenging, but it is also thought-provoking.

My question to you is, How do you fill the gaps between *your* plays? Are you putting in your time at your job, enjoying a few moments but dragging through most days? My suggestion is to use your time to get outside your comfort zone and be flexible in order to learn all you can about the emerging and varied aspects of the sport business. In a shifting sport business landscape, we need imagination and ideas to be filtered through a younger lens and for you to share those ideas if we are to attract and retain new customers. If you do reach out beyond your comfort zone and explore opportunities, then your career path will become evident and meaningful and you will be simultaneously making an impact on the sport industry.

Business, sport, and life are all about the people. There is no greater understanding of teamwork and working together to achieve goals than in sport. It is eminently true that world-class sport organizations are built on leadership and a proud culture of excellence that attracts top people. This means communicating, working together, and understanding that it takes a vast array of skills and people to come together in order to achieve success, including winning on the playing field. Embrace these values. The arena of sport businesses makes for a fulfilling career, and sure, you get to watch some sports along the way!

---

lab where customers have access to a huge library of fonts and art. Users upload their designs and our experts review them before going to print—100 percent satisfaction guaranteed and the elimination of a go-between.

All OTT networks, like Netflix, are direct-to-consumer businesses. These businesses are able to better gauge what's working and what's not and are more nimble when reacting to customer needs, which ultimately allows companies to create better and more valuable products for customers! Truly, a win-win.

Owning a portion of our local cable network, NBC Sports Washington, we worry about not being able to reach noncable subscribers. While other teams have equity stakes in their local RSN, ours is different in that NBC Sports also

GAME CHANGER
ATTENTION TO DETAIL, TOP TO BOTTOM

Mark Williams

Whether knowing your audience as a media executive or using technology to give your client a personalized pitch as an architect, as Mark Williams describes, attention to detail leads to results. Williams is a principal at HKS, Inc., serving as director of sports and entertainment business development. In 25-plus years as an architect, Williams says that his role with clients is to be "like the utility infielder. Clients can depend on me to show up and do what needs to be done for the project that day."

As a firm, we believe in doing the right thing. If you're going to spend millions or billions of dollars, we think that performing a broad and deep analysis of every single aspect of the building is the correct approach. This can involve things as simple as working with the food service operators to understand what they want to do and how to meet their goals. Any time we can plug ourselves in to similar entities, we can elevate the design. What this means to the client is having a broad understanding of the choices that can be made to improve the project, taking into account the implications from the schedule, budget. and experience standpoint.

Our job is to share with our clients all of the variables and advise them based on our experience so they can make informed decisions. To that point, we use 3D imaging and parametric modeling to help our clients visualize the design and explore options.

We used this technology to great effect in winning the design assignment for the new Rams stadium in Los Angeles. We presented our design concept to more than 30 competing team owners using our advanced visualization technique. By the end of that meeting, everyone had a pretty good idea of what we were proposing, and the level of engagement and excitement was high. Our plan was approved months later because we demonstrated that we understood the venue and had a holistic design that would activate the surrounding area, maximize revenue potential, and deliver a state-of-the-art entertainment experience.

Used with permission of Mark Williams.

has invested in our OTT network, Monumental Sports Network. Our live game programming—the Capitals' and Wizards' regular-season games, plus the first round of the playoffs—is by far the most valued on NBC Sports Washington. Where does an RSN go if the "S" is gone? So we want to play a role in the network's success as they take our product into millions and millions of homes. Monumental Sports Network complements NBC Sports Washington, providing subscription programming that includes live game coverage of the WNBA, AFL, AHL, G League, local high school sports, and a dozen other categories. This programming is not in competition with NBC Sports Washington; instead it provides content that otherwise would not be accessible to fans. We each have reciprocal board of director seats and our content strategy is a joint effort. And without a direct-to-consumer approach, we wouldn't even know who these people are!—*Ted Leonsis*

VIEWING ISN'T PASSIVE—IT NEEDS TO BE ENGAGING

Sitting back and watching a game—in an arena or from a couch in the living room—isn't good enough anymore. For years teams have aggressively increased their focus on in-game entertainment to keep fans interested between halves, periods, quarters, and innings. But that engagement now extends to the viewer at home.

The use of a mobile device, phone or tablet, when watching TV continues to quickly rise. According to Statista, in March 2017, 81 percent of Internet users in the United States were using another device while viewing TV. And I'm confident that percentage is even higher for those watching sporting events, especially among Millennials. Sharing content on social channels makes viewing sport more enjoyable for many fans.

Team-related apps, for instance, should support the live action, not distract from it. Content should be unique, add value, and be exclusive. These apps need to provide high-value content that also is easy to use and navigate. Fans are engaging with franchises during the game, and teams need to be a participant in that conversation.

A great example of this is our partnership with Kiswe Mobile, which was cofounded by Jeong Kim, a member of the Monumental Sports & Entertainment ownership group. Kiswe is focused on changing the game of live media for the next generation of sport and entertainment fans. Among other things, Kiswe transforms live digital video to make it interactive, personalized, and social, which is key to increasing fan engagement and loyalty. For example, Kiswe's multicamera technology SDK is integrated into Monumental Sports Network's video player developed by ViewLift to allow users to access the various game cameras that cover an event. Users have access to all video feeds and can select the view that is most appealing them; they become their own virtual producer. The user can clip video and share it on social platforms, increasing engagement with the live event as well as personalizing and distributing content.

Today's fans are a mobile-first audience, and short-form content that has built-in social sharing creates a personal, interactive, and transformative fan experience. It takes passive linear video and creates an engaging environment.—*Ted Leonsis*

EXPERIENCES MATTER

Nearly every study out there these days points to the same conclusion: Millennials and Generation Z consumers have a strong affinity toward experiences. We

Courtesy of Monumental Sports & Entertainment. Photographer: Ralph Alswang.

Washington Capitals owner Ted Leonsis hoists the Stanley Cup after his team's 2018 championship.

need to explore what we call "Millennial-sensitive programming"—experiences that are unique, are engaging, and connect our brand to our fans and potential fans. How do we effectively introduce virtual reality, artificial intelligence, more real-time data sharing, new camera angles, and increased engagement through the second screen? These experiences need to be digital, social, and personal. Today, the game and connection to teams and players demand an immersive experience, because for many, the game simply isn't enough anymore.

The intersection of sport and fan engagement is where modern media plays a critical role. One of our initial steps was to create a direct-to-consumer, OTT platform that addresses some of these challenges. We launched Monumental Sports Network, the first sport OTT platform, to take a regionalized approach, bundling hundreds of live games, hundreds of hours of original programming, and in-real-life events and experiences with Monumental's professional athletes and venues.

When we completed our long-term media partnership with NBC Sports and NBC Sports Washington, we realized that the largest audience still existed on cable, but we also knew the D.C. region had a particularly strong OTT presence. In fact, Nielsen named Washington, D.C., the #1 penetrated market in the United States for SVOD (subscription video on demand) services. SVOD services enjoy 61 percent penetration in our region compared with the national average of 53 percent. We partnered with NBC Sports to further develop Monumental Sports

Network as a sister network that would live solely on OTT platforms and work to develop and refine what a Millennial sports bundle could look like.

We package live games from the Washington Mystics, Washington Valor, Baltimore Brigade, Hershey Bears, esports, and hundreds of high school basketball, football, hockey, and lacrosse games with other original programming that is built either for social distribution or for longer, more in-depth viewing.

But our $9.99 per month VIP Membership also includes experiences. We create monthly experiential events that include access to our players, teams, and venues. For example, we held a December subscriber-exclusive open-bar mixology class with Wizards player Otto Porter. It made for some great new holiday cards for many of our subscribers.

Monumental Sports Network is direct to consumer, so we know what is working and what needs improvement. We work daily to make the network more relevant and valuable for Millennial sports fans and for generations that will come after them.

Monumental Sports Network is completely OTT with an AVOD (advertising video on demand) layer on top of an SVOD bundle. Everyone can enjoy some free content, and subscribers enjoy premium content with their paid subscription. We also need to be where our fans are, so the network is available via the web, iOS, Android, Windows 10 devices, Roku, Amazon Fire TV, Chromecast, Apple TV, and Xbox.

It's all about increasing accessibility to our teams and creating experiences for our fans. We believe in the need to adapt our profile to match that of our customers.—*Zach Leonsis*

MODERN MEDIA IS (STILL) PERSONAL

We have seen tremendous changes in the media landscape, and it will continue to evolve. One such shift is toward the niche bundles that allow for more personalization of content—no more paying for countless cable channels that have no meaning for a subscriber. And that is a sweet spot for sport broadcasting and the rise of hyperlocal coverage.

Cut out the go-between and deliver content direct to the consumer, and that's best accomplished with an OTT platform that focuses on content related to local sports. It also can provide a fully integrated viewing experience that includes on-demand shoulder programming, interactive in-game elements, and regular experiences that connect the subscriber to the team.

A granular approach to local sport broadcasting captures that excitement and sense of community by offering in-depth coverage of sports in the region, such as high school hockey, football, lacrosse, volleyball, and cheerleading.

As we have said, sport is the great convener. Outcomes impact our community. There are lifelong memories to capture, whether the 1968 Jets football season and subsequent Super Bowl celebration or the 2020 high school volleyball senior night match. I coveted that '68 experience with my father—eight games at Shea Stadium, seven of them victories. I felt an incredible sense of community pride after the Jets shocked Baltimore at the Orange Bowl. Unlike what was going on in the 1960s and '70s, however, today's media allows us to capture, share, and preserve these memories in countless ways. The memories of that high school hockey game, cheerleading competition, or lacrosse game can be shared instantaneously. These experiences were instrumental in forming the basis for my most recent book, *The Business of Happiness*. The joy of sport is critical for the consumer, but also important for sport media and sport business executives to be aware of if they are to make good business decisions.

We want those memories to be easily accessible, engaging, and delivered where and how a consumer wants to receive them. The future of sport broadcasting is hyperlocal. It's social. It's mobile.—*Ted and Zach Leonsis*

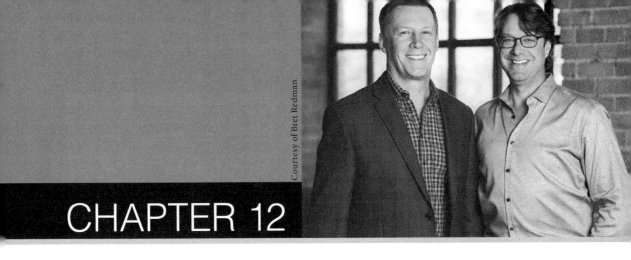

Courtesy of Bret Redman.

CHAPTER 12

Using Analytics and Social Media Effectively

Shawn Spieth and Kyle Nelson

Shawn Spieth and Kyle Nelson are cofounders of MVPindex. Spieth is president and has more than 30 years of experience delivering results for Fortune 500 and start-up organizations, serving in strategic sales and management roles at Anixter International, Williams Communications, Network ICE, Internet Security Systems (ISS), and MacroSolve. He delivered top sales, growth, and profitability performance for each of these market leaders. Shawn is the proud husband of Chris Spieth and a father to sons Jordan and Steven and daughter Ellen.

Nelson is chief marketing officer with more than 25 years' experience in technology sales and marketing. Kyle most recently exited LaunchFish, a social media marketing and outsourcing agency he founded in 2009, servicing public companies, media entities, and large small-to-medium-sized businesses (SMBs) and small-to-medium-sized enterprises (SMEs). Kyle is known as a social media thought leader and software entrepreneur, founder of OpenACircle, public-choice winner of DEMO 2008, founding member of Jobs.com, and founder of several marketing consulting service companies in his career in the software industry. Kyle is the proud husband of Beverly Nelson and father of three sons, Conner, Cameron, and Christian, and three step-children, Nico, Chloe, and Ainsley.

Imagine walking into the richest oil field in the world, only to discover nobody has ever drilled there before. The opportunity to bring the richness in that earth out belongs to you and you alone.

That's what we observed in social media in 2012, and that's when we decided to create the first real-time social media index for the sport and entertainment industries. In our case, rather than oil, we struck gold tracking the world of sport

Shawn Spieth (left) and Kyle Nelson, cofouners of MVP Index.

across social media—every team and athlete in more than 80 sports and more than 200 entertainment categories globally. What we discovered in tracking the engagement by fans is that the social media influencers in sport and entertainment have better-performing content related to their brand sponsors than the actual brands do across the same social media channels.

Until recently, social media had been a "throw-in" for most athlete endorsement contracts—a nice value-add for the brand, but with no actual value attached to it. Agents, not knowing what a client's social media real estate was truly worth, would dangle follower counts in front of brands as an additional incentive for an endorsement, but had no baseline measurement for social media exclusively for athletes and influencers.

In 2012, Shawn Spieth's son, Jordan, was gearing up for his pro golf career. When Shawn spoke to potential partners, he would ask about how athletes leveraged their social media presence with brands. Nobody could give him a good answer as to how the industry was valuing social media other than audience size. Even then, there was no clear index to determine which athletes were best at engaging their audience on social media. On the other side of the coin, athletes need to maximize their brand value while they can.

It's not often that you're presented with an opportunity to change the way an entire industry looks at sponsorship opportunities. At MVPindex, our initial focus was to index athletes to assist brands in ambassador selection and campaign alignment.

Everyone believed that the best athletes or teams on social media were the ones with the most followers. However, in many cases, those athletes were actually the ones scared to post as aggressively as those with perhaps fewer fans, but far more "personality"—or, at least, more personality than they were willing to share socially with their fans.

So, in order to showcase who was really engaging fans, we developed an algorithm that scores athletes on three distinct components: Reach, Engagement, and Conversation. An athlete's Reach is determined by his total audience (fans, followers, subscribers) on each social media platform, with more weight given to platforms where fans of the particular sport engage with athlete content. This means that if an athlete has 1 million fans on Twitter and only 100,000 on Instagram but fans of that sport engage more on Instagram, those 100,000 Instagram fans are considered more valuable than the larger Twitter audience.

Engagement measures the rate at which fans engage with an athlete's social content, including likes, comments, shares, retweets, and mentions. As with the Reach score, more weight is given to Engagement on platforms where the fans in that sport are most likely to engage.

The real "leveler" in value is something called Conversation. The Conversation score measures the number of mentions of an athlete across social media. Our team also monitors negative events in an athlete's life, both on and off the field, and adjusts the Conversation score based on the severity of the event. For example, an athlete might have huge Reach and Engagement scores, but if that athlete slips up and gets a DWI, gets caught doing performance-enhancement drugs, or commits any other indiscretions, our Conversation solution catches it and reflects the athlete's social "sponsorability" plummeting.

THE INDEX TAKES SHAPE

Modern analytics as we now understand the term—the analysis of business data, whether yours or your competitors', to drive forward the customer experience—is still in its infancy. Whether you're using analytics in social media or to solve other business problems, you must be flexible and inquisitive in effectively using information. An explosion of data is now available to even the smallest sport organizations.

Yet, even when you see a problem and create a solution, as we thought we did, you may find that the value you created is better served by addressing another problem or speaking to another audience.

We presented the index to agencies, teams, and brands for feedback and insights. At first, it was primarily a brand ambassador selection tool, helping identify which athletes rank highest with fans in the targeted sport and where the content engaged the broader sport audience on social media. We quickly realized that brands were our target market (because they write the checks).

Brands already using the services of athlete brand ambassadors could harness the power of our platform to discover everything about their market pertaining to the professional athlete, team, and league social media ecosystem. We had underestimated the value of our platform and thought it would be valuable for a wider spectrum of users than it was. We learned to target our primary audience more directly, but we could find that out only by going to market with the best product we could imagine at the time.

Before MVPindex, brands looking for information regarding the engagement of their ambassadors versus that of the competition were limited to social listening tools. Listening tools can track shares, likes, mentions, and so on, but don't differentiate between imposture handles and really don't index between competitors or performance for partners. The data can be overwhelming and cluttered without being pulled into buckets segregated by brand category, sport category, and so on. Essentially, it's just noise.

The distinct advantage of MVPindex is its wealth of past social media engagement data for all athletes, teams, brand ambassadors, influencers, and brands tracked in the system, along with a real-time view of the sport and entertainment ecosystem around our clients' marketing investments. By establishing key brand categories, as well as roles of the brand ambassador (e.g., PGA Tour player, actor, chef), brands are able to benchmark their campaign activations in real time to discover baseline expectations of each activation, uncover best practices across all athletes and brand categories, and measure the overall share of voice owned by that brand and its competition.

This ability becomes increasingly valuable as the media landscape shifts from a passive to a wholly participatory model. In the past, fans were able to consume sports content only at game time (either attending the game in person or watching on television or listening on the radio). Fans now spend more time engaging with athletes and teams across social media 24/7 than watching a specific event (game, concert, and so on).

In this current model, there are millions of content creators, so athletes have essentially become their own network, producing their own content and engaging millions of fans every day. High-profile athlete brand ambassadors like LeBron James and J.J. Watt (see figure 12.1) have audiences on social media that exceed those of the broadcast networks that host game coverage. Intelligent brands desire every ounce of data they can get their hands on regarding that valuable real estate.

The fact that social media is an always-on means of communication and content dissemination does not mean it's exclusively an ad platform. If accounts constantly posted content at their fans and followers using a standard ad model, the audience would quickly find more enjoyable entertainment. Brands and ambassadors that try to make social media an interstitial medium are at risk. Social media is never interstitial; in fact, it has become endemic to the sport world, a way for fans and athletes alike to participate in the greater conversation.

Social media is not an ad medium—it's a relationship medium. Brands that win on social media are the ones who find ambassadors with engaged audiences who live the brand. When this happens, everyone wins simultaneously: Brands get real exposure and engagement; athletes share the message of a product they love; and fans are entertained, informed, and motivated to take action.

Audiences are aware of this delicate balance. They know that for their favorite sports to exist, sponsorship is a necessary factor.

Athletes can use social media to market themselves to brands and to get additional benefits from sponsorship relationships. Some athletes have many sponsorship demands. One common requirement is that of "service days," with an athlete representing a brand at functions, charity golf tournaments, and executive retreats. These activities, while valuable, may not most effectively harness the influence of the brand ambassador.

Armed with these data, an agent representing an athlete can approach a brand and show the ultimate marketing value of that athlete's social media channels. This not only will earn that brand a better return on engagement but will provide the athlete with more time to focus on skills and upcoming competitions. Social hours in trade for service hours means reaching a broader audience with proven value, as opposed to limited face time with a select few customers. This approach creates a win-win for the athletes and their sponsors.

ANALYTICS IN PRACTICE

The following two case studies show social media analytics in practice—how one motorsport team used analytics to deal with a marketing challenge in its industry, and how one well-known sponsor gained deeper knowledge about its partnership with the NFL.

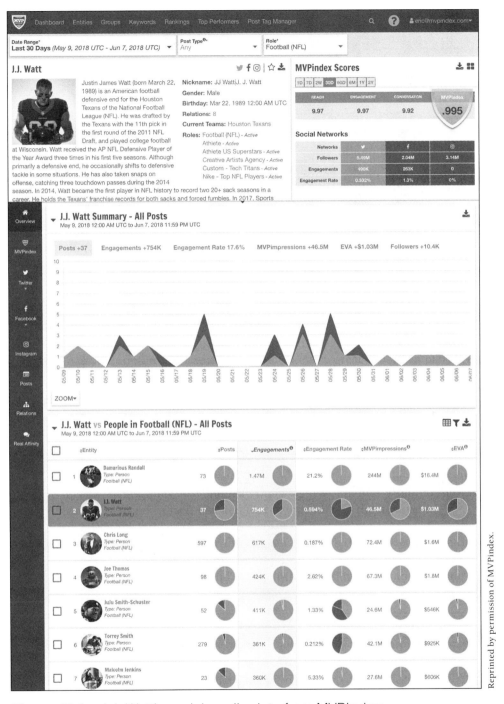

Figure 12.1   J.J. Watt's social media data from MVPIndex.

GROWTH OF ANALYTICS LEADS TO INDUSTRY EVOLUTION

Jessica Gelman

Jessica Gelman (right) with Daryl Morey and Billy Beane.

Like the chapter authors, Jessica Gelman has been at the helm of a company that has transformed sport at many levels through improved analytics. Gelman is CEO of Kraft Analytics Group (KAGR), a technology and services company focused on analytics, data management, and consulting that spun off from Kraft Sports & Entertainment (including the New England Patriots). Gelman is a *Sports Business Journal* Forty Under 40 and Game Changer honoree. A Harvard and Harvard Business School graduate, she cofounded and continues to chair the MIT Sloan Sports Analytics Conference.

Over the past decade, the sophistication of the sport industry has dramatically evolved as the money associated with the business has been accelerating. From player contracts to media rights to licensing to ticket prices, the cost of attending events and watching or supporting our favorite teams has increased. In parallel, fan expectations have grown.

In the early 2000s, I was fortunate to join the Kraft Group as the inflection of sport and analytics was about to take root. Under the guidance and direction of Robert and Jonathan Kraft, two of the leading entrepreneurs and innovators in sport, they empowered me to use analytics to imagine the business differently. This began a journey that transformed how we approached our business.

Our focus was on the customer to start. We began with fan surveys. Then, over time, it was possible to track behaviors at a customer-specific level. We were able to track ticket scans, email opens, customer service calls, in-venue purchases, and web visits, to name a few, which gave us an opportunity to customize our communications and influence fan behaviors. Cross-selling, upselling, and educating fans about various engagements they could have with the New England Patriots or New England Revolution became part of our fabric. Having a single view of our customers across all the myriad touchpoints and systems whereby they engaged with us was critical to prioritizing strategies, stadium investments, or new business creation. Analytics and customer knowledge drove our operations, too. We created new loyalty programs like Patriots365 and new stadium amenities like the Optum Field Lounge. We built forecasting and retention models to understand customer demand and then improve our supply of jerseys or amenities. Our business grew tremendously as our customer satisfaction ratings doubled. Fans engaged with us across multiple business areas, and our profits grew, too.

In short order, we outgrew the technologies and vendors we needed to support our efforts. To meet our needs, we invested in and built our own proprietary data management and analytics technology platform to better engage customers and understand our operations. Recognizing a gap in the market, in 2016, we spun off Kraft Analytics Group and now are working with teams in the NBA, NHL, and colleges and the broader industry.

Along the way, I cofounded the MIT Sloan Sports Analytics Conference to help accelerate the conversation around analytics and its applications. With attendees venturing to Boston each winter, what has become affectionately known as "Dorkapalooza" has grown from 150 people in 2007 to a two-day extravaganza with more than 3,500 attendees where analytics, innovation, and technology intersect.

From player evaluations, draft strategies, stadium improvements, and fan identification, analytics has become a critical tool for prioritizing strategy and decisions on the field. Today, the investments in and around sport are big, and the wrong decisions are costly. Analytics helps make sense of the data and the opportunities off the field. We are just beginning to scratch the surface of how analytics will continue to transform the industry.

Used with permission of Jessica Gelman.

HENDRICK MOTORSPORTS—UNVEILING THE SOCIAL COMPETITIVE LANDSCAPE

The pulse of sport relies on sponsorships, and no league realizes this more than NASCAR. With declining viewership numbers both in-venue and on TV, NASCAR realized that social media was the best way to keep fans of their teams involved and to grow their audience. In turn, they targeted motorsport teams to help them gain a better understanding of how their social real estate could be best used as a marketing asset to strategically drive more value for sponsors and increase fan engagement with sponsored posts.

The NASCAR audience understands the value sponsors bring to the sport more than the casual sports fan; they expect to see their favorite drivers endorsing products and services because that's what keeps their teams running each week. Before MVPindex, drivers and teams knew they had a significant impact for brand sponsors on social media, but there was no real way to measure the true competitive landscape for brands across sports and social platforms. Hendrick Motorsports approached MVPindex to do just that: demonstrate the advantages Hendrick Motorsports teams and drivers have on their social platforms over other comparable teams and athletes in all sports.

Now, imagine you're Hendrick, and up to this point, you'd never seen comprehensive, cross-sport social media intelligence. The only numbers you absolutely knew were the followings of your team and a general comparison across NASCAR teams.

With the MVPindex platform, you now know that not only are you definitively the most-followed NASCAR team on social media, but that all of your drivers are ranked in the top 20 in Reach, Engagement, and Conversation. Imagine going from knowing that your posts about Lowe's get a lot of Engagement to being able to *prove* that these are the most engaged posts about an insurance company across sports—and knowing the monetary value of those posts.

In the past, athletes and teams were ranked only by follower count compared to other, same-sport teams. With this new source of data, Hendrick Motorsports can clearly illustrate their strengths and show share of engagement against all of NASCAR, against teams and athletes from motorsport venues where events are held, or against the entire digital sport landscape as a whole. Hendrick can now see when fans are more likely to engage with content across different platforms, allowing them to better schedule their posts for maximum impressions and engagement with fans. Sponsors now have the much-needed assurance that their marketing dollars are going to get a great return on investment (ROI) beyond the sponsorship of the car on the track.

BUD LIGHT CAMPAIGN PUTS NFL LOGOS ON CAN, MVPINDEX PUTS VALUE ON SOCIAL MEDIA

Even for companies with experienced marketing departments, social media can present some unique hurdles that can make it difficult to get a complete view of campaign performance and ROI.

Anheuser-Busch InBev (AB), for example, is the official beer sponsor of the NFL and the majority of its teams. From Spuds MacKenzie to the Budweiser Frogs to the "Whassup?" guys, Anheuser-Busch has launched some of the most memorable ad campaigns in its history around the NFL. So, it was natural for AB to connect the brands directly to their products. In 2016, AB began putting NFL team logos directly onto cans of Bud Light and launched the #MyTeamCan campaign on social media.

The campaign was a great fit for social media across the league. The hashtag was useful in presenting stats from teams each week, but the imagery of the

Bud Light cans sporting NFL team logos also made for some unique creative opportunities. One of the top posts from the Indianapolis Colts was a photo of a Denver Broncos Bud Light can sitting crushed on the turf at Mile High while a Colts-branded can "stood" above it, unblemished.

However, with 28 NFL-related entities to track across multiple social media platforms, AB had found in the past that it could be cumbersome to manage and assess a campaign like #MyTeamCan. In past seasons, AB Experiential Marketing would manually track all social media posts and engagement for Bud Light natively on each network by monitoring the NFL's social media accounts along with the social media accounts of the 27 teams they manage.

By pulling together all of the social media data in-house, AB was able to see the Bud Light posts their team partners published, but they lacked context. They had no competitive insight on share of voice to tell them which teams and social accounts were generating the biggest impact. They couldn't see how that compared to campaigns run by competitors in the alcohol category or even to the typical post from the NFL or team accounts. Perhaps most importantly, they did not have the ability to put a dollar-figure valuation on social media achievements.

AB turned to MVPindex to find solutions to those problems and track the #MyTeamCan social media campaign. We delivered analytics around mentions, engagement, impressions, and valuation, and identified sponsorship social media results to AB's senior leadership.

During the 2016 NFL season, we produced comprehensive weekly reports showing social media performance and data of all of the Bud Light–sponsored teams and the league itself (see figure 12.2). AB could see each week how their social sponsorship compared to other brands activating with the league.

Using our platform's dashboards, the AB Experiential Marketing team could see how often each team posts included mentions of the #MyTeamCan campaign or included Bud Light branding, the engagement and impressions those posts generated, the top posts of the week, and the dollar value generated by the posts.

As the season progressed, we provided AB and their partners with a custom report for the first third of the season showing team performance competitive data. This report not only highlighted the top-performing teams in the campaign, but also provided best practices to increase engagement and reach for the remainder of the season.

The #MyTeamCan campaign proved to be a sweeping success for AB. Bud Light was mentioned in 543 posts during the season across all NFL accounts, representing 2.3 percent of all branded social media posts by the league and team accounts during that time.

With the help of these insights, the AB Experiential Marketing team was able to value the content in the campaign in a way they had never been able to before, allowing them to prove ROI on social media and attach a true dollar value to the content the league and its teams generated throughout the season.

That freed up AB's marketing team to focus their efforts on looking forward to their next big campaign instead of recapping the last one. They moved on to working on things like the medieval-themed campaign that included the

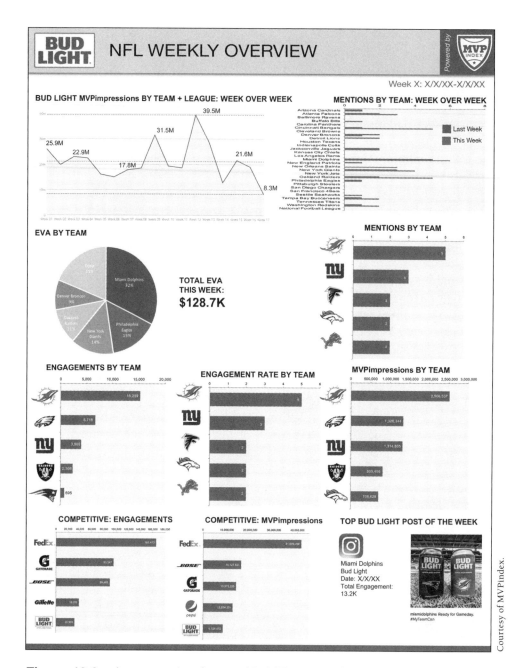

Figure 12.2 An example of a weekly NFL report for a brand such as Bud Light.

GAME CHANGER

PUSHING THE BOUNDARIES OF TECHNOLOGY IN SPORT

Angela Ruggiero

Angela Ruggiero challenges sport leaders not to lose the human essence of the sporting experience as technology continues to profoundly influence the industry. Ruggiero is a leading figure in global sport, having served as an elite athlete, educator, administrator, innovator, advisor, board member, and investor. She is cofounder and CEO of Sports Innovation Lab, the global leader in sport innovation intelligence, helping clients make sense of a complicated sports–tech market. Ruggiero is a member of the 2015 Hockey Hall of Fame and a four-time Olympian in ice hockey, winning a gold medal

Courtesy of Angela Ruggiero.

in 1998, silver medals in 2002 and 2010, and a bronze in 2006. She was a member of the International Olympic Committee and chair of the IOC Athletes' Commission. She currently serves on the IOC's Digital and Technology Commission and the Ethics Commission. Ruggiero is a graduate of the Harvard Business School (MBA), Harvard College (BA), and the University of Minnesota (MEd).

Sport technology is not new. People who suggest otherwise are recklessly narrowing their definition of "technology." People often conflate the concept of technology with the digital age—innovations since the development of the microprocessor—but the reality of the relationship between sport and technology is much older when you take a closer look.

For as long as we've played sports, we've looked to technology to influence how we play and how we watch. Some technologies have been adopted quickly, while others have faced negative pressure. Radio and TV broadcasts were initially seen as threats to ticket gate revenue, and coaches feared that helmets in American football would make the players soft (they didn't). Skates, bicycle derailleurs, jumbotrons, scoreboards, stopwatches, tickets, and the mobile phone: The list goes on, and it would be impossible to measure the impact of all technology on sport. The point is that sport and technology are inextricably intertwined, and always have been. In many cases, sport has served as the perfect breeding ground to test out new innovations.

Throughout this long and interconnected history, technology has been predominantly used to improve the fan experience, while the on-the-field competition remained the same. Sport was always seen as a competition among people, in-person, regardless of the degree of physicality, including hockey and chess and everything in between. Now, new technologies are giving athletes a sought-after

(continued)

GAME CHANGER *(continued)*

edge, providing a new platform for the fan to watch, and affecting the competition, even in the field of play.

Additionally, over the past decade, technology is forcing a dramatic reimagining of what sport even means. Innovations like virtual and augmented reality, advancements in robotics and body modification, and rapid global interconnectivity may change the very concept of human sport. Esports is, in many ways, already bearing this out, as video game players compete with digital athletes on screen, often across continents. It is an amazing meld of human and computer sport. Martial artists and boxers are exploring how the mixed realities could eliminate the physical danger of fighting in relation to sport. New leagues are experimenting with crowd-sourced coaching, as fans are encouraged to vote in real time on a team's play-calling.

As an Olympian, IOC member, and chief strategy officer for the Los Angeles Olympic bid that involved creating the "most innovative Olympics ever," I've spent a lot of time thinking about the relationship between sport and technology. Technology will allow the industry to connect to more fans, help more athletes reach their peak performance, and inspire the next generation of young people. That is the power of tech: a means to a greater end, a way to keep sport relevant at a point in time when other entertainment options are demanding more time and mind share. Technology may be the solution to keep sport relevant when Netflix and other forms of entertainment are grabbing the attention of the next generation.

With all of this innovation, we may look back on this book in 20 years and not recognize the sports being discussed. The marriage of sport and technology is not new, but the rate of change and the pace of technological development are accelerating. It is my great hope that even as we experiment with the role humans have in and the extent to which they are involved in sport, we never abandon the essential humanity that has driven sport throughout history. Technology may subvert and change our role as agents in the world of sport, but we must remember to embrace and hold fast to the spirit of competition, sorority, fraternity, and unity that has always made sport one of the most powerful cultural phenomena in the world.

introduction of the Bud Knight in the Super Bowl following the next NFL season. Dilly, indeed.

SOCIAL MEDIA VALUE—
THE FINAL PIECE OF THE PUZZLE

Your activation went off without a hitch. All of your ambassadors engaged authentically, and your campaign racked up Engagement the likes of which you'd never seen. Congratulations! Now, what's it all worth? How, at the end of the day, do you calculate the digital marketing value of a social media campaign?

Sure, you can estimate impressions per tweet and do some guesswork, but that's not going to convince anyone—especially a seasoned marketing executive—of the activation's inherent value in a campaign. For years, the market has clamored for a standard valuation, accepted as the digital marketing currency for social media from which an ROI or return on equity (ROE) could be accurately calculated.

With our access to the top five social media networking platforms, MVPindex was in position to develop that standard. That is how we developed the Engagement Value Assessment (EVA).

The true value of social media is that it allows fans to develop a relationship with brand ambassadors as never before. In the past, the only interaction between fans and athletes occurred when the fans watched games, read articles, and caught a glimpse of their favorite athletes in a commercial. Celebrity endorsements are great, but unlike the continuous stream of social media, these endorsements don't give fans the ability to know the athletes' true personalities and the passion they feel for their sport. That's why the first step in developing EVA was the decision to value the entire conversation, and not just each singular post.

EVA is now the emerging standard and the currency for estimating the marketing value of social media posts endorsing or promoting a brand. As shown in figure 12.3, it combines these elements:

- Published and proprietary statistical estimates of social media reach
- Engagement and sampled social and digital marketing cost-per-thousand impressions and cost-per-click estimates
- Proprietary social amplification factors to arrive at an estimated media spend equivalency for social posts endorsing or promoting a brand

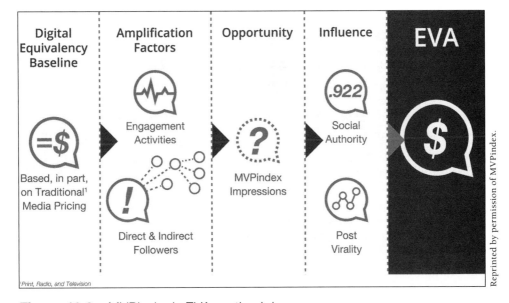

Figure 12.3   MVPindex's EVA methodology.

EVA IN PRACTICE

Two case studies show how EVA gets used—an NHL team that wanted to communicate its social media knowledge with sponsors and potential sponsors, and a shoe brand finding results in the emerging collegiate sport space.

CHICAGO BLACKHAWKS LEAD THE CHARGE IN USING SOCIAL MEDIA FOR SPONSORSHIPS

The Chicago Blackhawks, looking to monetize more than dasher boards and on-air advertisements, were early adopters with regard to using MVPindex to value their social media and showcase their social prowess to brand sponsors. Using EVA analytics, we were able to value the entirety of the Chicago Blackhawks' social media real estate across Facebook, Instagram, and Twitter during the 2014 to 2015 season, illustrating that the team earned more than 40 million total Engagements with their content and delivered an EVA of $5.7 million for the season.

ABI's Bud Light launched the #UpForWhatever campaign across sports that season. MVPindex data showed that the Chicago Blackhawks had the most engaging activation around that hashtag across all sports, netting the brand 285K likes, shares, and comments, along with more than 3.8 million total impressions. Using these insights, the Blackhawks were able to educate their partners on the actual value of their social media campaigns, as well as generate incremental sponsorship revenue.

When teams like the Blackhawks and partnering brands like ABI are able to value social from a single source of truth, they can constantly improve engagement and the value derived from it by listening to the data, and taking those best practices to other owned properties and their other partners—or even to entice new partners.

ADIDAS EXPLORES UNTAPPED POTENTIAL IN COLLEGIATE ATHLETICS

The increase in digital sports content consumption among sports fans, particularly Millennials and Generation Z, has driven collegiate athletic departments to incorporate digital assets as part of their overall media and sponsorship strategies, ultimately leading to additional revenue streams outside of traditional TV rights. This transition is forcing athletic programs to assess the value of their social media footprint and the opportunity it creates for their brand partners to best reach their target fans.

While there are a few pioneers in the space, universities are significantly behind professional sport when it comes to brand activations on social media. For example, in 2017, less than 1 percent of posts by athletic departments (where the majority of collegiate-branded content is posted) included a brand, while the

TOWARD A BETTER UNDERSTANDING OF SPORT MARKET ANALYTICS

Richard Lipsey

Richard Lipsey suggests what the future might look like for sport market analytics. Lipsey is founder, president, and CEO of Sports Market Analytics, a leading provider of sport marketing research that draws upon syndicated and proprietary market data, plus industry reports and licensed industry articles. Lipsey founded Sports Market Place in 1980, which became the standard for sport industry directory publishing, serving all segments of the sporting goods and sport marketing industries. While director of Leisure Time Research Division of Audits & Surveys Inc., a leading market research firm, he introduced the concept of syndication to the sport industry for consumer studies, and retail auditing programs for golf and team sport equipment. While at The NPD Group, he introduced a study of sport participation to the National Sporting Goods Association that is still the industry's leading continuing study on that topic. He has an MS from the Wharton School at University of Pennsylvania and an MBA from the University of Chicago School of Business, and he is author of *The Sporting Goods Industry*.

When reference is made to sport analytics, what do we really mean? To my way of thinking, sport analytics really has two components:

1. Sport performance analytics
2. Sport market analytics

Sport performance analytics is what captured our attention 20 years ago (with *Moneyball*) or even farther back (with Bill James' *Historical Baseball Abstract*). But that is changing. Performance analytics will continue to grow, and there's lots of data there for talent scouts as well as fans. But I believe that sport market analytics will rise to equal if not exceed the value of performance analytics' importance in the years to come, particularly among sponsors, agencies, and team marketing directors, because marketing analytics is what drive business decisions that lead to big media deals and better customer engagement in a viciously competitive marketplace.

Sports Market Analytics supports marketers to maximize the effectiveness of all facets of the marketing process. Sports Market Analytics enables sport rights holders, sponsors, and governing bodies to capitalize on the multidimensional media landscape that is revitalizing, if not totally changing, how sport organizations communicate with their fans.

Rarely have historic media strategies been an endangered species, but they are now, and sport market analytics needs to keep pace by analyzing the complex blend of broadcast media, social media, sponsor brand characteristics, and online and in-stadium technology that characterize today's sport media environment.

While big data technology facilitates dealing with massive amounts of data, the technology is of limited value in sport marketing because most fan surveys deal with only one aspect of marketing, making it necessary to combine data that come

(continued)

TOWARD A BETTER UNDERSTANDING OF SPORT MARKET ANALYTICS   *(continued)*

from a variety of sources; most all of these use different methodologies and sampling devices. This severely limits, if not entirely excludes, the value of an overall analytical approach.

The future of sport market analytics involves examining results of a single-survey approach that measures all sports fans' behavior across their sport-related behavior over a given period of time. Sophisticated analytical technologies can then be applied that will allow sport market practitioners to organize and examine this information for specific purposes, without having to worry about an "apples and oranges" approach using data from many different surveys with differing methodologies.

Teams can use the information to promote ticket sales by profiling their prospects. They can target logo apparel marketing to most likely prospects, and they can attract more viewers by targeting their streaming and social media broadcasts. Sponsors can use the information to match their brand with the sport or sports that best serve their ability to meet specific sales or awareness targets and to track how their competitors are performing in the sport marketplace. Marketing agencies can use the information to best help their clients achieve their specific marketing objectives.

Single-survey applications not only greatly enhance the value of the information but also greatly reduce the cost, while speeding up access to relevant information needed in today's superfast-paced sport marketing environment.

Our company, Sports Market Analytics, is devoted to providing single-survey applications for sport marketing. Our technology is based on a wealth of experience in the private sector over many years, spanning the spectrum of sport marketing from the 1970s to our current modern-day environment.

Used with permission of Richard Lipsey.

teams from the top five major leagues in the United States (NHL, NFL, NBA, MLS, MLB) averaged more than 5 percent.

Savvy brands activating in the collegiate market are starting to expect more out of their collegiate partnerships, including frequent and engaging social media activations to best connect with their target.

During the 2017 NCAA Men's and Women's Basketball Tournaments, Adidas ran a #CreateYours campaign with their respective teams, including the Kansas Jayhawks and Miami Hurricanes. According to MVPindex's EVA methodology, these social media campaigns drove more than $26,000 in value for Adidas. The Miami Hurricanes accounted for 30 percent of the value generated with a 16 percent amount of mentions. While Adidas' premier programs (Kansas, Indiana, and Louisville) mentioned #CreateYours only twice on their social media channels, to the surprise of Adidas, Utah Valley was the #1 school mentioning #CreateYours with 68 mentions, driving the fourth-highest amount of value for the brand. Their impressive ranking compared to larger programs was due to continuing the activation past the uniform reveal and using the #CreateYours hashtag when posting during their games.

The lack of activity by Adidas' premier programs led to a reevaluation of their future collegiate campaigns and the role of social media in them. One change Adidas made was having their teams use the respective campaign hashtag throughout the tournament, rather than only when the uniform was unveiled.

CONTINUOUSLY DIGGING FOR OIL

So just how deep does the oil well go? For those willing to dig, the opportunity never stops for teams, players, and brand sponsors. At MVPindex, we're adding new influencers every day: more than 85,000 at the time of writing this chapter. From draftees starting to make waves on the field and on social media, to esport influencers reaching niche audiences, not only do the players change every day—the game changes, too.

And, with a merger with Umbel (now known as MVPaudience) in 2018, MVPindex can not only rank, measure, and value the brand activation with influencers, we can dive in to understand who the audience is that is engaging with brand ambassadors throughout sport and entertainment. Understanding which brand ambassador is hitting a brand's target audience is key to realizing a higher ROI across these activations.

Social media platforms wax and wane, algorithms shift, formats like GIFs and video go in and out of vogue, but one constant remains: Social media presents unprecedented opportunity and value to those willing to measure and adapt their presence in this new real-time era of fan engagement.

CHAPTER 13

Translating Technology Into New Markets

Peter Moore

Peter Moore joined Liverpool FC as chief executive officer in June 2017, a role that brought the lifetime LFC supporter back to his hometown of Liverpool. Bringing his tremendous personal passion for sport, competition, games, and the Reds to the role, Moore is responsible for all business, commercial, and operational areas of the club—reporting directly to the club's ownership, Fenway Sports Group. Moore previously led EA's Competitive Gaming Division, where he brought to life new global competitions for EA franchises, including FIFA, Madden NFL, and Battlefield. Prior to that he served as chief operating officer of EA, providing strategic leadership for all global operations that enabled EA to bring products to market via retail and digital direct-to-consumer channels. He also previously held the position of president of EA SPORTS, overseeing the delivery of some of the top-selling sport video games from franchises including FIFA, Madden NFL, NCAA Football, and NHL. Moore also oversaw the growth of the FIFA Interactive World Cup, growing it into one of the world's largest gaming tournaments.

Moore has more than 30 years of experience in gaming, entertainment, and consumer products and has held leadership positions as the corporate vice president of the Interactive Entertainment Business of Microsoft Corporation, as president and COO of SEGA of America, and senior vice president of marketing at Reebok International Ltd. Moore holds a bachelor's degree from Keele University, United Kingdom, and a master's from California State University at Long Beach. He also currently serves as a VP of SpecialEffect, a nonprofit that uses technology to enhance the quality of life of people with physical disabilities.

When I look back on my upbringing and the journey I've been on as a business professional (Reebok, EA Microsoft, Liverpool FC), it's easy for me to see how important technology has been. It has been all around me in the products I've helped to market and sell, but I often wonder how I came to understand that technology provided the ongoing capacity to create market and career leadership.

A long time ago, in a small town outside of Boston, Massachusetts, at Reebok, we were trying things like "The Pump," whereby users would physically inflate the fit of their basketball shoe. The idea was ahead of its time and ultimately overpowered by the success of Nike's visible air concept, but I remember how hard we worked at making a commitment to dramatically change the basic foundation of shoe design. It made a great impact on my thinking and showed me that technology, done right, took brands to new customers and new markets.

Later, at Microsoft in Seattle and EA in San Francisco, technology was embedded in everything those companies did. In particular, the massive developments EA made in video game franchises like Madden and FIFA helped shape an entire industry.

Not surprisingly, per my most recent posting as CEO of Liverpool FC ("You'll Never Walk Alone"), technology touches everything we do, from player scouting to analyzing our game play, from all broadcasts to our marketing and sponsorships and more fully facilitating the fan experience of our global supporter base. In short, Liverpool FC can no longer exist without a commitment to immediate worldwide access.

Writing a chapter for this book about the translation of technology is interesting for me. Technology for the sake of using phrases like "We're leveraging technology to improve our product" misses the point. In today's fast-paced business world, technology, in all its many forms, must be a part of a brand's DNA. It must be in every discussion, in every meeting. Firstly, though, it must be understood, and that is dangerously difficult in an age when the rapidity of change is so dramatic.

But for this chapter, let me come at the topic like this: We live and operate in a global and digital economy. To not discuss technology is to simply ignore the realities of how every business must operate. Technology these days is a bit like oxygen. You can't survive without it. Even more importantly, and to give credit to Thomas Friedman and his late-2016 book *Thank You for Being Late,* the rate of change in technology is now so phenomenally fast that all CEOs, COOs, CFOs, and CMOs must stay intimately connected to their CTO.

HARNESSING PASSION THROUGH TECHNOLOGY

It wasn't always that way. When I started my professional business career in Southern California (as a commission-only sales rep for Patrick), I was selling shoes out of my beloved Toyota Camry: Patrick Keegan Golds, Michel Platini Super Golds, and John Doyle's. They were all magnificent boots, and I learned so much about selling. But I was doing it person to person with no scale. No appreciation for how big the stakes were (when parent company Patrick was compared to Adidas or the starting-to-boom Nike).

Looking back, that was probably the point in my life when I realized that while I loved football (I quickly learned to call it soccer), I also knew I didn't want to be the Brit standing in some pub whining about Yank beer. Still, Los Angeles in the early 1980s was amazing. It was a time of the Dodgers, Rams, Angels, the 1984 Summer Olympics, Disney, Hollywood, and amazing beaches. The electricity was always on, and business in every form leaped forward with TV advertisements, sponsorship deals, sold-out stadiums, and big broadcasts from the major networks and even the start of a technology breakthrough in cable television with ESPN.

Sports were very much a part of the American DNA, and I'd like to think the originators and visionaries at ESPN knew that. They grasped that a TV channel that offered sport 24 hours a day, every day of the year, was feasible. Of course, at the time, Americans and Europeans were gobsmacked by the idea. It broke the rules of how sport or a TV network should operate.

But that was exactly the point. The technology of cable television ultimately meant you could add a second revenue stream. You could sell ads. That was traditional. But you could also sell the subscription portion. If you put the right content on, people would pay to get that special "sports-only" channel.

Not immediately but eventually, cable changed everything. We didn't have just a sports channel, we had 500 channels, and the eclectic nature of content, as was also seen with the Internet, exploded.

When I arrived at EA in August 2007, coming down the West Coast from Microsoft and Xbox in Seattle, I realized where the technology spaceship was going. You wouldn't know this, but I had started out, way underage, on the beer-stained floorboards of my dad's pub in North Wales, the Red Lion, when I was only 11. Now, I was at Microsoft, and Bill Gates or Steve Ballmer would come pounding down the halls demanding that people expand their thinking and bring products to life faster.

Of course, everything had to work, but the point of that lifestyle was the very possibility of where ideation, inventions, innovation, and enigmas were going to take us.

So now I was at EA, as president of EA SPORTS, and we were going neck and neck with other video game manufacturers on designing the optimal soccer game. Andrew Wilson (now the CEO of EA) was part of my team and bravely declared, "We are going to stop and redo our game engine." For any organization, that kind of proclamation is a very dangerous thing. When you say, "We're going to hit Control-Alt-Delete," you are truly rolling the dice.

But Andrew and I knew that global football was growing and knew EA could be at the epicenter of that sporting revolution. We also knew that the video game, more so than Madden, could become much more than a successful video gaming title but rather could be a cross-cultural fully global, live, interactive service.

Translating technology into new markets: That was the moment we grasped that there were fans who would play our video game and always choose to control the joystick as Manchester United. But the transformational idea was saying, "Wouldn't it be cool if you got this player here and put that player there and instead of Everton it's Peter Moore United." Gamers could create their own kit

GAME CHANGER

HOW "MOONSHOT" TECHNOLOGY IN REGENERATIVE MEDICINE INFLUENCES THE BUSINESS OF SPORT

Jeff Conroy

The sport industry blends performance and business in many different ways. In this example, Jeff Conroy shows how Peter Moore's discussion of translating technology into new markets extends to sports medicine. Conroy is a life science entrepreneur and the chairman and CEO of Embody, a Norfolk, Virginia, medical device company reinventing the treatment of serious tendon and ligament injuries.

The worlds of elite war fighters and high-performance athletes are of course very different in that the one involves life-and-death stakes every day and the other is entertainment. But when it comes to injuries, and the incentive to help individuals recover quickly, safely, and with as close to full functionality as possible, similar business issues come into play. An emerging trend is the intersection of these two sectors in which regenerative medicine achieves advances in player health and recovery from serious injury. Increasingly, we are seeing Achilles and ACL injuries with the potential to end NFL and NBA careers. In fact, we now have a stream of potential career-ending injuries across sport happening in real time.

Elite war fighters such as U.S. Navy SEALs are multimillion-dollar assets based on years of training and specialization. Tendon and ligament injuries such as Achilles, ACL, and rotator cuff tears are some of the most frequent injuries affecting them. Existing surgical approaches often fail to fully restore preinjury performance. Consequently, the Department of Defense is highly motivated to develop innovative solutions to restore elite war fighters to preinjury performance levels.

In technology parlance, a "moonshot" is an attempt to develop groundbreaking, high-impact, high-risk solutions with the potential to achieve a 10 times improvement in outcomes. The Department of Defense has a moonshot factory called the Defense Advanced Research Projects Agency (DARPA) to develop ambitious, groundbreaking improvements across science and technology. DARPA has been at the forefront of funding and advancing regenerative medicine solutions to restore preinjury performance for American elite war fighters. Under DARPA's Atoms to Products program, Embody has been funded to develop our moonshot tendon and ligament technologies.

Embody is a great example of how modern technology has applications across multiple domains. For a sport business professional or entrepreneur, it is also a case study in how sport business is not just limited to a front office. We are a medical device company developing regenerative scaffolds for the repair of Achilles and rotator cuff tears. Longer term, Embody is developing an engineered collagen-based replacement ligament for the treatment of ACL injuries. Embody's approach is to deliver a collagen-based scaffold to be wrapped around the surgical repair of a tendon injury. Collagen is the major protein composing connective tissue in the body. Embody harnesses the power of collagen to create a prohealing environment enabling a patient's native cells to restore new tendon-like tissue over a surgical repair. The stimulation of new tendon-like tissue can minimize scarring and increase the patient's rehabilitation options. These advances will ultimately benefit elite war fighters, high-performance athletes, and sports medicine patients.

It is clear how technology developed for the best performers in a given profession, whether soldiers or athletes, can soon be used for the benefit of many more. The Department of Defense and DARPA, with the goal of driving innovation in medical care of serious tendon and ligament injuries for elite war fighters, has created high-value enabling technology for the benefit of high-performance athletes, player health, and rehabilitation across professional sport. In fact, these Navy SEAL–driven advances will immediately be available for all sports medicine patients, delivering innovation and advancement in rehabilitation options for sports medicine patients everywhere.

(uniform design), bring their own players in, start trading players, and engage similarly minded fans all over the world. And not just during the traditional EPL, La Liga, or Bundesliga season. All year long.

I guess it's safe to write that with that iteration of EA's FIFA, the concept of an ultimate team was born. That engagement platform made sense to millions of fans who started, collectively, spending billions of gaming hours.

Building your own team meant you had to understand who this guy is that plays left fullback for Real Madrid or center midfielder for AC Milan. I think this was quite like the scenario in Michael Lewis' book *Moneyball* (about Billy Beane and the Oakland A's) because now video gamers were thinking about how to get a "gold player" and then "sell" him in the marketplace.

What we were doing was not only imbuing a sense of love and passion for the game, but understanding what players were, who they'd been, who the legends were—because we all have our icon players—and then understanding the perspective of taking them very seriously while covering the world with this concept of the beautiful game . . . a game that you can play all day.

What we did was make EA's FIFA a living, breathing organism. It wasn't just something such that you put the disc in and you played the game only to forget about that specific game (when you won or lost). No, this was different. You were invested. You were on the phone, looking at players in the marketplace, auctioning players. Lots of hours. All in.

To my way of thinking, we had used technology to drive our product but we were teaching young people marketplace arbitrage. To some, that would be a gross exaggeration, but I've met so many young people over the years who told me that EA SPORTS and FIFA helped explain the business of professional football and inspired them in their studies at school.

So I'm all right with how we used technology. I lived through that period at EA when we were experiencing massive growth. All of a sudden, I'm looking at a gaming economy that is bigger than the GDP of a small African nation, all because we had built this incredibly sticky, innovative thing that was more than just playing a video game.

TRANSFERRING TECHNOLOGY LESSONS TO THE REAL WORLD

Coming to Liverpool as the CEO, I wanted to make sure that I didn't think of the team as just a Premier League side. Firstly, I wanted the chance to give back to this wondrous organization because of all it had given to me as a poor kid growing up. Not in a dollars-and-cents way but in the optimism and aspirational way that pro sport causes young people to dream. If I had a kick about in the street or on a formal pitch with my mates, I was inspired by what was possible for those who had reached the heights of playing at Anfield.

But secondly, and maybe more importantly, I wanted to use the technology lessons from Reebok, Microsoft, and EA to help shape Liverpool for the future. I don't doubt my ability to morph from one type of business situation to another because that's business. This particular business is based on success on the field. Our business at EA was based on the success of a particular game at a particular time. Our success at Reebok was based on how many units of shoes we sold and how we built our brand. The core elements are all very similar.

My predecessors at Liverpool brought us to 2017, and my hope is to build on their foundation. Of course, I'm going to do things differently. And I'm going to do things my way. I certainly hope I'm going to be more technologically energizing because I know where I've been. That being said, I hope I'm still going to have a beer or wine on a Saturday night after a match or find a pub where I can watch the game when I don't travel with the team.

At the end of the day, my job is to support our manager, his coaching staff, and the team director and to give them everything they need to be successful on the hallowed turf that is our field. That includes these elements:

- Stadium operations
- Commercial activity
- Game-day operations (we have 2,000 people who work for Liverpool in or around our stadium on game day)
- Expanding our retail sales and commercial licensing
- Influencing our role in the community and our charitable efforts
- Involving our team in community with kids, particularly in the Anfield area
- Trying to make those kids' lives better through Liverpool Football Club
- Growing our TV and social media activities and understanding that augmented reality and virtual reality will open new doors for Liverpool's worldwide fan base

RETAIL ANALYTICS OF THE FUTURE BENEFITS CONSUMER, COMPANY

Matt O'Toole

Matt O'Toole explains how lessons in technological innovation cut across many sectors, including retail, in this example from Peter Moore's former employer. A 25-year veteran of the sport apparel and equipment industry, O'Toole is the global head of the Reebok brand and has pioneered the company's return to its fitness roots. In 2017, O'Toole oversaw Reebok's move of its headquarters from Canton, Massachusetts, to the Innovation and Design Building in Boston to help drive innovation, collaboration, and creativity. He serves on the Adidas Core Leadership Group, supporting the Adidas Executive Board to accelerate strategic projects across both Adidas and Reebok brands. During his tenure at Reebok, Matt has forged unconventional alliances with organizations such as CrossFit, the world's fastest-growing fitness movement; Les Mills, the largest provider of group fitness classes and programming; UFC, the world's leading mixed martial arts organization; and Ragnar Relay, the largest overnight running relay series in the United States. O'Toole holds an MBA from the Kellogg School of Management at Northwestern University. In 2012, he summited Mount Kilimanjaro in Tanzania to raise money and awareness for Reebok's social purpose program, BOKS.

When people debate the balance between brick and mortar versus eRetail, they often forget a third alternative—a hybrid in which the physical retail trip is complemented by a brand's technology to create a better overall consumer experience.

Without question, the way consumers purchase products from athletic brands has evolved considerably over the last 50 years. Historically, Reebok's business has relied heavily on the wholesale channel, which will continue to be important. As we look at future purchasing behavior, however, consumers will expect to interact with our brand through a more accessible and dynamic multichannel experience. This future marketplace requires Reebok to engage consumers through and with more "direct-to-consumer" tools and touchpoints, which will complement our wholesale distribution and make our products and experiences more easily accessible. For Reebok and the rest of the industry, this a critical strategic shift, but one dictated by our consumer.

Our approach to the physical retail store will evolve to an environment where consumers can expect us to have a robust mobile experience through which they can learn more about our products, compare prices, order online, and check out without waiting in line at a register. In order to meet these new customer expectations, Reebok must embrace technology as part of our in-store offering. We have begun the implementation of Store Associate Mobile (SAM) devices in all stores to assist staff in giving our consumers a complete brand experience. This tool helps provide details on our brand ambition, product technology and inspiration, consumer reviews, and recommendations on which products meet an individual's fitness and lifestyle needs. These SAM devices will also facilitate inventory lookup in other

(continued)

360 *(continued)*

Reebok stores and at our wholesale partners' locations. They also enable our associates to process an online order, or to have product shipped to a customer's home from the closest and quickest location available. The possibilities are endless, and we aim to make our brand and products accessible to consumers where they live, play, and shop. SAM benefits the company and the consumer.

These technology tools also provide benefits for Reebok by giving us greater insight into our consumers through analytics. We "swim" in data today, but with the right lens, we can translate those data into actionable decisions in consumer targeting, product development, assortment management, marketing communication, pricing, and so on. This is the new way to "listen" to our consumer base and ensure that we are bringing products to market that people desire and are willing to buy. For example, knowing a consumer has interest in our running products based upon past purchasing or browsing behavior allows us to customize our future interaction to let that customer know when new offerings or experiences are available. Having a more personalized approach translates into a better relationship with our consumer and increases loyalty. We can capitalize on this trove of data by increasing our speed to market and get goods to physical shelves and virtual "shelves" in time to take advantage of trends and market dynamics.

While this new environment will likely pose challenges, we also expect it to offer great opportunity for Reebok to connect directly with our consumers, and evolve our offerings to not only keep up with competitors but also surpass our consumers' expectations. The brands that do this well will win, and we expect to be one of those great brands of the future.

On the latter point, many of the biggest sport leagues in the United States are trying to open new doors for their teams in countries like China and India and hoping that technology will be the vehicle that makes fan engagement affordable. In Europe, though, the biggest teams, the so-called megaclubs, are already doing that. Manchester United, Manchester City, Arsenal, Real Madrid, Bayern Munich, FC Barcelona, Paris Saint-Germain . . . these teams are worldwide brands and no strangers to leveraging social media or digital retailing.

All of this is good and the TV money for the broadcast rights is monstrous, but the danger we have as football clubs, all of us, is the potential of drifting away from the people who made us what we are and what we still should be. We must not lose connection with our fans, and technology must help us translate the transition from a team in a league in a single country (before the days of UEFA and friendlies in Singapore, Sydney, or San Diego) to a global team generating news content and events on a daily basis all over the world.

In the end, fan engagement means being able to walk down Dale Street or Old Hall, Castle, or Water Street in Liverpool and have a chat with a guy in a pub. I do that now but I can do that only so many times. But technology lets me engage millions, if not tens of millions, of our fans via social media.

FUTURE OF SPORT MEDIA IS ADDRESSING FANS WHO LEAN FORWARD

Chris Wagner

Chris Wagner has seen up close the change in fans' media behavior and, like Peter Moore, sees a future in which sports fans will expect more intimate experiences. Wagner is a technology expert who partners with investors, executives, and entrepreneurs to grow their professional brands, revenues, and customers. After spending more than a decade in the video Internet streaming industry, Wagner has developed an uncanny ability to start up new technology businesses and enhance existing enterprises through digitally enabled services. He cofounded Internet start-up NeuLion and helped grow the business to $100 million, which sold to Endeavor for $250 million in cash. His passion for technology and how to apply it to enable business success has created a network of followers interested in his views and how he might add value to their teams.

Courtesy of Chris Wagner, NeuLion.

When we started NeuLion in 2004, the idea that fans would watch live sports on anything but their television set was generally not an accepted idea—not with fans, sports networks, or cable companies. But three major developments have forever altered the business of distributing sports content: the rise of the connected fan, the resulting breakdown of traditional TV business models, and the development of sophisticated video technology that has made it ever more economically feasible to deliver a superior viewing experience over the Internet.

Consider first the sports fan. As technologists and entrepreneurs, we recognized in the very early days of NeuLion, even before we pivoted the company to focus on sport, that the distribution of entertainment content over the Internet would be far superior to cable and satellite. After acquiring video compression technology in 2005, we launched two Internet TV networks that couldn't have been more different: one focusing on Chinese TV and the other streaming New York Islanders NHL pre- and postgame hockey content. The opportunity in sport was quickly apparent. Unlike most other forms of entertainment, sports content is perishable and drives an intense desire to interact. This is the central insight upon which we built our business—and one that would transform sport viewership from a passive, "lean-back" experience to an immersive, "lean-forward" proposition in which fans would actively engage with sport programming. It's an evolution that will only intensify in

(continued)

the coming years. Today, the average American has 4.3 connected devices. By 2020, there will be more mobile handsets than people with electricity. What was once a broadcast business is now a live and on-demand, one-to-one conversation with fans.

Given the entrenched business models in those early days, it's amazing how far we've come. The primary constraints on Internet distribution weren't just the technology. Existing television advertising, cable affiliate, and retransmission fees defined the TV industry for generations and slowed its evolution. But the consumer's rejection of prevailing models has been swift and unrelenting, giving rise to an entirely new vocabulary—terms like "cable cutters," "cable nevers," and "cord shaving," which reflect consumers' ever-growing aversion to paying for anything other than exactly what they want, when they want it. Sport rights fees have only accelerated in response to changing preferences. In 2016, for example, Twitter bought the rights to 10 Thursday night NFL games for $5 million. One year later, the fee for the same 10 games was $50 million.

The key to this transformation, and the reason for NeuLion's growth trajectory, is the rapidly evolving technology that enables sports content to be distributed over the Internet faster, at a lower cost, and with a better fan experience in comparison to cable and satellite. As one example, when NeuLion made the jump from HD to 4K, our customers realized a four times improvement in picture quality at 30 percent less cost, thanks to advancements in our compression technology. Today our customers include the NFL, NBA, World Surf League, and Euroleague Basketball, to name just a few. As content owners, they are discovering that fans who are connected all the time tend to engage more, creating new opportunities to growth revenue.

I see a future where technology will generate more personalized experiences for consumers and businesses—and content producers, advertisers, and sport organizations alike will benefit from the unprecedented amount of data that is being generated, enabling them to design programming and experiences to a specific audience's taste. In this dynamic digital environment, sport business professionals must embrace a far broader view of what a successful career path can entail. Already, the business of sport rights and distribution is bigger than ticket sales, sponsorships, and merchandise sales combined. What happens outside sport venues is more lucrative than the business conducted inside. That's a major shift. Creative sport business professionals will ride this trend, creating new experiences for fans beyond the stadiums and arenas that have yet to be invented, helping new generations of consumers get closer and deeper into their favorite teams and games in ways we cannot yet foresee.

Yes, without question, I have to be careful. I have to be measured in what I say because the technology allows me freedom. And I love the discourse. The interaction. I love the jousting. I love the opinions. All who have a keyboard can tell me what they think now. And I'll go talk to them. That's the power of football. It's what draws us to the game. The indescribable connection that becomes all the more powerful because it's not said with an eye to rational, cold strategy. It's said from the heart . . . that place where most people are very real.

PERPETUAL, GLOBAL, INTIMATE CONNECTION

What does the future hold? It's almost impossible to suggest. But it is logical, given all of our supporter clubs in bars and pubs around the world, to imagine the growth of the aforementioned augmented or virtual reality allowing an executive such as myself or our coach or a player to appear in a setting via holograms or for the fans to sit in on meetings with us.

I think the fans want more interaction and more ability to join us behind the scenes. They want to know their team even better than they did 10 minutes ago. Therein lies technology's great ambition. Fifty years ago as a lad in North Wales, my ability to follow a side was limited to a bit of radio or the rare game on the TV, and newspapers limited the space they could dedicate to a fan's favorite team.

Today, technology makes access instant, and the limitations of space are hardly ever discussed. Going forward, we'll be able to better train our players, better explain outcomes to our supporters, and better present our most spectacular achievements; and we'll do it in real time and, most logically, with platforms that don't yet exist.

Sport is flawed at times, like the humans who play our favorite games, but there is nothing like it for unifying us. My sense is that technology will only bring us closer but it will create more engagement for our fans. One of my biggest fears is that I won't help bring fans back to the club as before. If we don't engage them in the way they want to be engaged, we'll lose them.

So our research must show how they want to connect with us. Phone, laptop, TV, Instagram, Twitter, Snapchat, Facebook, movie theaters, pubs, classrooms, homes, trains, planes, trams, ferries, cars, mountaintops.

If I do my job, we'll translate our digital data, our 1s and 0s, so that all fans stay connected, whether they are at the stadium seeing us live or whether they are on the other side of the globe in the middle of the night. It's a great challenge, but I know deep down that Liverpool FC is up to that challenge.

YNWA!

Part IV

Making Successful Deals

Deal making is an essential component of many aspects of sport business, as reflected in the eight chapters that make up this part. You will see concepts from parts I through III applied to the often complex and invigorating high-stakes world of negotiating, from ethics and relationship building, to effectively communicating, to knowing your brand goals and successfully selling your image, product, or idea.

Ivy League Executive Director Robin Harris' opening chapter is essential reading on how to develop business deals with your core values in mind. Donald Dell, ProServ founder and agent for many of the biggest names across a wide range of sports, offers key takeaways you can leverage when you understand how the arc of a deal transpires. Long-time multisport executive Jerry Colangelo shares tips on how to generate consensus when you are engaging a partner in a transaction. Contributing editor Rick Burton is the David B. Falk Endowed Professor of Sport Management in the David B. Falk College of Sport and Human Dynamics at Syracuse University. He presents the Falk–Michael Jordan–Nike nexus as a case study in how marketing properly understood and with the right partners can make a deal far greater than the sum of its parts. Ronald Norick, former mayor of Oklahoma City, uses the groundbreaking MAPS initiative there as a case in operating successfully across public and private domains to greatly enhance his community.

Joseph R. Castiglione Sr., athletics director at University of Oklahoma, hones in on deal making in the realm of licensing to ensure that both the property holder and the licensee work toward a win–win relationship. To close out part IV, veteran ad executive Tony Ponturo and Dallas Cowboys Chief Operating Officer Stephen Jones present two sides of the same sponsorships coin. Ponturo takes the sponsor's point of view and Jones takes the rights holder's point of view to help readers see the value in understanding the needs of both sides when securing strategic sponsorships.

CHAPTER 14

Developing Business Deals Consistent With Your Core Values

Robin J. Harris

Since becoming the Ivy League Council of Presidents' second full-time executive director in 2009, Robin Harris has led the Ivy League to new heights, including negotiated a ground-breaking media rights agreement with ESPN; implemented the Ivy League Men's and Women's Basketball Tournaments; guided the league in the creation and development of the Ivy League Network (ILN); implemented a continuing, broad-based concussion research and prevention initiative; expanded and negotiated the Ivy League's television coverage agreements; fostered a long-term relationship with JMI Sports to introduce new leaguewide sponsorship deals; and focused the league's communication on core messaging points. The athletic and academic standing of the Ivy League on a national stage has soared under Harris' direction, with seven national champions in 2016 and 2017 alone and significant NCAA Tournament successes. Academically, the Ivy League has consistently led the nation in NCAA Graduation Success Rate (GSR) and Academic Progress Rate (APR) rankings. In 2016, *Sports Business Journal* selected Harris as a Game Changer, a national recognition of selected female sport executives.

Harris came to the Ivy League office after seven years at Ice Miller LLP, based in Indianapolis, where she served as senior counsel and cochair of the Collegiate Sports Practice and worked with the firm's college and university clients. Prior to Ice Miller, Harris worked nine years in increasingly responsible roles in the NCAA, ending her tenure at the NCAA National Office in 2002 as associate chief of staff for Division I. From 1993 to 1998, she was the NCAA's first director for the Committee on Infractions.

Harris is a graduate of the Duke University School of Law, where she

The author would like to thank the following individuals for their contributions to this chapter: Megan Murray for her research and for assistance with the initial drafts of this chapter while serving as an Ivy League summer intern, and Ivy League executive assistant, Amy Friedman, for her assistance in researching the use of core values in business.

served as an editor of the *Duke Law Journal.* Her student note, "Does the NCAA Play Fair? A Due Process Analysis of NCAA Enforcement Regulations" was published in the *Duke Law Journal.*

When I began my career in college sport, it was in response to the sage guidance that if you follow your passion, you will never work a day in your life. Now, almost a quarter of a century later, I have come to realize that it is even more important to ensure that your personal values match your employer's core values. I am fortunate to have found that connection at the Ivy League, where I have also come to fully appreciate the importance of the impact of values on decision making and the overall fabric of the enterprise.

While exploring sport career options in law school, I realized how much I appreciated the value and importance of an overall student-athlete experience that combines academic and athletic pursuits. My belief in the important connection between intercollegiate athletics and the educational experiences led me to choose a career in collegiate sport that has spanned more than two decades, including my tenure at the NCAA National Office and at a law firm cochairing the collegiate sport practice prior to my arrival at the Ivy League.

I have witnessed the rise in the commercialism of college sport while also noting that many remain unwavering in their commitment to amateurism and education as part of intercollegiate athletics. Skeptics about the amateurism of intercollegiate athletics abound in part because it is not enough to "talk the talk" and say you are committed to your core values; you must also "walk the walk." Your words must match your actions.

My experience at developing and negotiating a variety of business-related deals for the Ivy League has reinforced for me the importance of core values to an organization's revenue-producing activities. To advance and foster acceptance by key constituents, it is critical for an organization to match core values with its commercial approach and business dealings. During the development and negotiation of business deals, this includes focusing on core values throughout the entire process, knowing and communicating in advance the "nonnegotiables," compromising for the deal without compromising core values, and being able to explain the rationale for the organization's policies that are tied to the core values and that may limit the ability to negotiate on particular points.

As discussed in this chapter, keeping core values front and center results in business deals that fit within the culture of an organization, promote stability, and allow for growth and advancement that are acceptable to the constituencies.

Business deals, by nature, encompass a plethora of decision-making processes that vary with each organization. Successful deals ultimately share similar underlying principles and strategies. This chapter addresses one of the most important underlying principles: adherence to core values.

To enhance the likelihood of success, a business deal should align with an entity's core values and serve as the solidified foundation and "voice of reason" underlying each decision during the negotiations or deal-making process. Why are core values important when negotiating and developing business deals? They provide structure and direction for organizations that aspire to remain consistent with their most fundamental ideologies and help to ensure that stakeholders will accept, support, and embrace the ultimate decisions.

THE IVY LEAGUE: A GROUNDED APPROACH

The Ivy League follows a value-based approach to offer the ultimate collegiate experience for student-athletes who receive a world-class education while competing and succeeding at the highest level of intercollegiate athletics. The league's history and commitment to a grounded approach to sport dates back to as early as the 1800s, and several of the league's presidents were involved in the formation of the NCAA in 1906 when President Teddy Roosevelt assembled a group to address the safety of collegiate athletics. In 1954, to avoid the rising commercialization in college sport, eight college presidents officially founded the Ivy League, united by a set of core principles that have influenced decision making to this day. The league's core principles have evolved over time while remaining consistent with the founding principles. These shared core values united and continue to unite the eight Ivy League schools—a membership that has not changed—reflecting common objectives and approaches to intercollegiate athletics that apply across the most broad-based sport sponsorship in Division I athletics, with 33 conference sports and members averaging 35 sports per school.

In addition, the core values provide the foundation for the primary attributes of Ivy League athletics. To succinctly outline the main components of the Ivy League's core values, we produced a laminated card that serves as a readily available reference for key stakeholders. The key Ivy League messaging points that are based on core values are summarized in figure 14.1.

Firm commitment to these core values has been instrumental in the Ivy League's ability to develop and negotiate deals that enable the league to flourish and adapt to the modern state of collegiate athletics while remaining true to its underlying philosophy and principles. As discussed later, the Ivy League has successfully negotiated TV deals that have advanced the stature and visibility of the schools' athletics programs while also aligning with the league's core values. This grounded approach has led to buy-in by key stakeholders at member campuses.

The Ivy League's experience with the success of value-based deals applies to other sport organizations, including revenue-driven entities. Prior to the commencement of a business deal, an organization should develop or reaffirm core values. An article in the *Harvard Business Review* defines core values as "the deeply ingrained principles that guide all of a company's actions; they serve as its

GAME CHANGER

PAYING BACK A DEBT . . . WITH INTEREST

Richard A. Chaifetz

Dr. Richard A. Chaifetz shows that values can be translated into a legacy, and there is no limit on what form the legacy might take. Chaifetz is the founder, chairman, and chief executive officer of ComPsych Corporation, the world's largest provider of employee assistance programs. ComPsych provides services to more than 100 million individuals and 45,000 organizations, ranging from the Fortune 500 to smaller public and private companies and government entities throughout the United States and more than 160 countries. Dr. Chaifetz is also the founder and chairman of Chaifetz Group, a private advisory and investment firm. Dr. Chaifetz, a licensed neuropsychologist, is a magna cum laude graduate of Saint Louis University and received his PsyD from the Illinois School of Professional Psychology.

Courtesy of Saint Louis University. Photographer: Bill Barrett.

My high school education was at Eastern Military Academy in Cold Spring Harbor, New York, where I learned a lot about leadership, dealing with others, and keeping my commitments. I attained the rank of first lieutenant at the academy and because of my achievements, I was one of two cadets to receive an appointment to the U.S. Military Academy at West Point. I knew I did not want to make a career in the military so I declined the appointment, and after much prodding from the headmaster at the academy, I chose to attend Saint Louis University (SLU).

During the second semester of my freshman year at SLU, I received a call from the bursar's office telling me that my tuition had not been paid. My parents had been divorced for many years and my father, who I had limited contact with, had not paid the tuition as he had promised. I was going to have to leave school unless I worked out a special arrangement with the then president of the university, Father Paul Reinhart.

I immediately went to see Father Reinhart, who I had never met before and who certainly did not know me. I pled my case. I told him I was a serious student and was premed, and that school was very important to me as I had nothing else in my life. I also told him I believed I was going to be successful one day and I would pay the school back in a big way. After sitting silently for what seemed to be an enormous amount of time, he said "Rich, I believe in you . . . I trust you when you say you'll pay us back, and you can stay and pay the school back when you can."

Fast-forward many years. I had the good fortune to become financially successful through my business ventures, and I frequently told my wife about the commitment I had made to SLU. We had talked about it multiple times over the years, and I decided in the mid-2000s that it was time to do something to pay the school back and fulfill my commitment. Unfortunately, Father Reinhart, who I had made the promise to, had passed away a number of years earlier. Nevertheless, after much cajoling, as the school did not know much about me, the president and the head of development at the time agreed to have lunch with me. They had not known about my commitment made during my freshman year at SLU, only that I wanted to make a donation to the school. During the lunch, I shared my story about Father Reinhart and the commitment I had made.

As they explained the different projects going on at the school, they had no idea I wanted to do something with profound impact. When they finally got around to discussing the prospect of building a basketball arena on campus, my interest and passion were piqued.

In high school and college, sports were very important to me, particularly in college as I did not have any money. The sporting events at SLU, that is, the basketball, hockey, and soccer games, were frequently where I'd take dates for my typical Friday and Saturday night entertainment. The sporting events meant a lot to me and I know they meant a lot to other students. So, when the arena project came up, it didn't take me long to tell SLU I would be honored to take the naming rights. I donated $12 million to the project and Chaifetz Arena was born. In 2018, I donated an additional $15 million to name the Richard A. Chaifetz School of Business and the Chaifetz Center for Entrepreneurship.

THE IVY LEAGUE

#ONEIVY

The Ivy League offers the ultimate college experience for student-athletes to receive a world-class education while competing and succeeding at the highest level of intercollegiate athletics.

- The truest balance of academics and athletics in NCAA Division I

- Commitment to excellence on the field and in the classroom

- Most broad-based offering of conference-wide sports (33), averaging 35 varsity sports

- Common philosophy including academic standards and need-based financial aid

- A global alumni community and connection

- Forefront of student-athlete well-being, including concussion management, prevention and research

- Student-athletes enjoy a true collegiate experience

- Development of young people for current and future successes

Figure 14.1 A summary of the Ivy League's core values, as depicted on a laminated reference card distributed to key stakeholders.

cultural cornerstones" (Lencioni 2002, para. 10). It is imperative that core values reflect and focus on the company's image and main objectives. Hypothetically, if a company claims "customer service" as one of its core values and then does not prepare employees to handle challenging issues or complaints, an empty value has been established that might negatively impact the company and its reputation. Core values should be firmly entrenched in an entity's culture, should guide actions, and should never be compromised (Lencioni 2002). Core values should also be realistic, attainable, and consistent with the work the company and employees are truly performing.

In the most general sense, core values can be applied to every aspect of life and can be helpful in making both personal and business decisions. They serve as important "checkpoints" and should be consistently incorporated into how individuals and organizations make fundamental decisions. Businesses often face challenging and complex dilemmas when negotiating deals. Depending on an organization's core values, the ultimate objective may be to generate the most revenue, achieve the greatest market share, or improve a service or product. If an organization chooses a business deal that generates the most revenue to address a deficit but the terms of the deal (and the obligations of the organization) are inconsistent with the entity's core values, the deal and the organization may ultimately suffer. Relatedly, if one entity partners with another organization focused on different goals and values, the partnership is unlikely to achieve its potential. Conflicting core values create risks that could be avoided if further analysis is conducted early and throughout the negotiation process.

The number and size of business deals in the sport industry have grown exponentially over the past 20 years, often with staggering financial rewards. But, at what cost? Do these deals correlate to underlying core values (e.g., by using the revenue generated by certain sports—typically football and men's basketball—to support other "nonrevenue" or "Olympic" sports), or do they seem to shift the public's attention to the commercialization of Division I college sports? Aligning business deals with core values can help influence acceptance by key stakeholders.

CONTEMPORARY ISSUES

The remainder of this chapter provides three examples of contemporary issues in college sport (television negotiations, conference realignment, and corporate sponsorship deals) and discusses the importance of striking a balance between core values and "big business." The relevant principles and tensions that exist in college sport are applicable to other levels of sport, including international, professional, community, and regional sport organizations and activities.

USING SPORT TO EXPLAIN, ENGAGE, AND INSPIRE

Jon Chapman

Jon Chapman shows how his company, by staying true to its core values, has created programs and partnerships with sport organizations that extend well beyond the playing field. Chapman is the cofounder and president of EVERFI, Inc. Over the last 10 years, more than 16 million students have been certified in critical life skills across EVERFI's web-based learning platforms. Chapman currently runs EVERFI's global partnerships division, which works with major companies, organizations, and brands to bring community outreach programs into K-12 schools at no cost to students and teachers. He earned his MBA from the Robert H. Smith School of Business at the University of Maryland and his undergraduate degree from Bowdoin College. He resides in Annapolis, Maryland, with his wife Kirsten and their two children.

When you grow up in the Boston area, sport is often handed down as part of your family heritage. My family was no different. I cried when the Red Sox blew the '86 World Series. I pounded a basketball for countless hours pretending I was Larry Bird. And I cried again, this time tears of joy, when I witnessed the Patriots win their first Super Bowl in 2002. These collective experiences not only helped hone character traits that allowed me to reach many of my goals in life but also instilled within me a deep appreciation for the power of sport.

When my partners and I launched EVERFI at the beginning of the financial crisis in 2008, our core idea was a simple one: to teach financial literacy in a more interactive and engaging way using the latest technology. To do this, we turned to private-sector leaders and institutions, like banks and credit unions, to license and private-label our curriculum to get it into communities they cared about. We knew that a gamified learning experience using the latest technology offered a powerful way to convey these key concepts to students.

However, by 2011, we found an even more powerful way to teach financial literacy and other critical academic skills. Through a partnership with BBVA Compass, we decided to break our typical partnership model and do something new: create an NBA-branded financial education program and bring it into Texas schools with the help of the Dallas Mavericks, Houston Rockets, and San Antonio Spurs. We agreed not only to deliver our online product under these teams' brands but also to bring current and former players into classrooms.

Around the 2013 NBA All-Star Game, we held the first of these player events at a Houston elementary school. I'll never forget the way James Harden and Darryl Dawkins connected with the students who worked on the EVERFI course in the school's multimedia room. James and Darryl were pretty dialed in that day, asking the kids questions and providing encouragement. It was a special kind of connection that my team would help forge in hundreds of schools across the country over the next four years.

(continued)

360   *(continued)*

At the end of the day, the sport world is a relatively small one. Partners who do their job well stand to benefit from a tremendous network effect. Shortly after we entered our partnership with the NBA, we engaged the NHL about a STEM education course, which would become Future Goals, our first leaguewide program across all NHL markets in the United States and Canada. Future Goals quickly became the largest sport-supported school program in North America. Our work with the NHL attracted the attention of the NFL, with whom we launched a young adult healthy relationships program, Character Playbook. Most recently, we became Major League Baseball's official education partner with Summer Slugger, a program designed to combat summer learning loss for rising fifth-grade students. Individual sport heroes, like John Calipari, Allan Houston, and Jake Peavy, have also stepped up to sponsor courses in their communities.

All of our league and athlete partners recognize their unique platform to inform and inspire. Sport provides a common, engaging language to explain otherwise bland or abstract concepts. Protractors and polygons can't compete with the way a hockey puck brings to life the concept of angles. Whether or not a student is an avid sports fan, sport tells stories of teamwork, struggle, and triumph that are inherently relatable. And for this lifelong Boston sports fan turned technology entrepreneur, sport continues to inspire me and my EVERFI team to think creatively and imagine new possibilities in our space.

1. NEGOTIATING TELEVISION DEALS

One of the largest contemporary issues within the sport industry is the continuous battle for exposure on national television. How do smaller, less visible Division I collegiate sport programs compete for television exposure with the "Power Five" conferences and professional sports? How do these Division I conferences negotiate deals that provide exposure, make sense financially, and are acceptable to the conferences' member institutions? Relevant factors in evaluating the success of a deal include revenue generation, funding production costs, distribution (households) of the network, television windows (day and time), ratings, and inclusion of all conference schools while featuring the "best" games.

The Ivy League has successfully negotiated television deals for several sports with various networks, always consistent with the league's values. As noted earlier, the Ivy League is committed to providing student-athletes with an experience that allows for academic and athletic excellence. For example, the Ivy League would not agree to game times for television that require too much missed class time (e.g., Wednesday night football games) because that would be inconsistent with the Ivy League's core value that academics are a top priority. Instead, the Ivy League would negotiate to identify alternative television windows, perhaps with less exposure. Adjustments to "normal" Ivy League game days and times are sometimes considered (e.g., Sunday basketball, Friday night football), but those decisions always factor in the overall student-athlete experience and the league's core values.

For some conferences, exposure and revenue are the primary goals, which works when the final deal aligns with the conferences' priorities. Formulating business deals that are in sync with an entity's fundamental principles fosters trust and loyalty with constituent and target markets.

One of the most important factors when negotiating consistent with core values is transparency, including transparency with reference to core values. It is critical that constituent groups (e.g., employees, affiliates, potential partners in a business deal) be aware of the key core values and what is and is not acceptable.

In addition, it is important when negotiating consistent with core values to also understand the specific marketplace and business realities. Advance research and information gathering regarding typical practices within the relevant industry will aid the negotiation process. For example, early in the process, the Ivy League addresses available television windows and financial realities to assess whether a deal with a particular network is feasible. Often we engage expert consultants to gather information and assist with the negotiations. When partnering with these experts, we inform them of the relevant principles and core values. Being aware of how an organization's core values will match a potential partner's realities allows these experts to help the Ivy League make deals that are successful, value-based, and acceptable to the constituent groups.

2. CONFERENCE REALIGNMENTS

The relatively recent spell of collegiate conference membership realignments provides another example of the importance of core values. In the past 10 years, there have been changes in membership in almost 90 percent of Division I conferences. These changes resulted from institutional and conference goals focused initially on television markets and revenue (for the high-profile conferences) and then on survival and the need for members for the other conferences, with institutions looking for opportunities to "move up" to a more successful conference. Some conferences became stronger as a result of these realignments and some institutions found "better" homes. Which alliances are stable and which are unstable "marriages of convenience" of partners that do not share similar values remains unknown at this time. Ultimately, whether the alliances truly work will largely depend on whether there are conflicting core values and different approaches to handling collegiate athletics or whether there are common core values.

The logistics surrounding conference realignments are complex and in some ways unique, but there is a general lesson to be learned that can be utilized in various work environments across multiple industries where partnerships are necessary: the importance of trust and adherence to core values.

To aid the cultivation of trust in an athletics conference, it is important for members to have similar approaches to the relationship of athletics to the overall student-athlete educational experience, to possess similar views of key business concepts including media rights and scheduling alliances, and to share an overall commitment to the organization's core values. The Ivy League, for example, consists of eight schools that share common standards for rigorous academics and competitive Division I athletics. The Ivy League's membership has not changed. This stability and common philosophy builds trust that fosters an environment that allows time, energy, and resources to focus on the truly important issues that advance the collective good.

Trust based on core values is critical for successful conference relationships, and establishing a culture of trust is important in business deals and partnerships. As Howard Schultz, former Starbucks CEO and chairman, notes in his book, "In this ever-changing society, the most powerful and enduring brands are built from the heart. They are real and sustainable. Their foundations are stronger because they are built with the strength of the human spirit, not an ad campaign. The companies that are lasting are those that are authentic" (Schultz 1997, p. 248). The commonality of core values helps foster trust, authenticity, and stability in business relationships.

Organizations that have cultivated a climate of trust based on a commitment to core values are better positioned for collective success and advancement, as opposed to those where valuable time, energy, and resources are devoted to combating and resolving divisive issues and to defending against potential threats.

3. CORPORATE SPONSORSHIP DEALS

Corporate sponsorship deals have become an accepted and fundamental aspect of collegiate athletics. The revenue generated helps to support and fund many teams, including those that do not produce revenue. However, this commercial activity—with increasing dollar amounts—creates tension with the traditional philosophy of intercollegiate athletics and in particular the concept of amateurism. Collegiate athletics is intended to be a cocurricular aspect of the overall educational experience with student-athletes participating as amateurs.

There have been a number of major class-action lawsuits filed in the past decade challenging the NCAA's amateur model of collegiate athletics. These suits seem to be largely in response to the revenues generated by certain schools and conferences, as well as the increased compensation earned by their coaches, athletics directors, and conference commissioners. As the dollars associated with sponsorship and television deals have increased—exponentially for certain conferences and schools, particularly those in the "Power Five"—the media and the issues raised in various lawsuits are creating among the general public a more skeptical view of the amateur nature of collegiate athletics.

Why is there such scrutiny and concern about the revenue generated? Is there something fundamentally wrong with generating revenue through amateur sport? The revenue supports the overall operations of the athletics departments and benefits many student-athletes including those in the so-called nonrevenue or Olympic sports. In addition, the campuses at large benefit through the community-building nature of sport and the positive publicity attendant to successful programs.

Revenue generation by itself is not problematic. What is problematic is revenue generation that is inconsistent with an entity's core values. "While brands worldwide clamor for new opportunities to engage customers and consumers in meaningful ways, ensuring every expression is a discreet representation of your core values becomes paramount in today's shifting consumer landscape, and, this is ever more imperative when evaluating sponsorship allocation and relationships" (Mainwaring 2016, para. 1). Successful corporate sponsorship deals align an entity with a partner that is not in conflict with—and instead ideally matches—the organization's core values.

In fact, organizations should seek partners with similar core values and then explain to the relevant stakeholders how those values align. "Research says that 41.4 percent of influencers say that aligning with a brand's core values is the most important factor when partnering with a brand" (Phelon 2017, para. 10). Partnerships that genuinely embrace common values can also result in longer-term and more successful affiliation and acceptance by key constituents. "Mass advertising can help build brands, but authenticity is what makes them last. If people believe they share values with a company, they will stay loyal to the brand" (Schultz 1997, p. 248). Similarly, successful sponsorship deals in college athletics typically connect a brand strategy to messaging related to aspects of the collegiate athletics or educational experience or both.

These principles apply regardless of how strongly an entity prioritizes revenue generation. For example, an organization that does not emphasize revenue generation as a primary objective, and instead focuses on other mission-based principles, should be willing to pass on a deal—regardless of how lucrative it may be—that does not align with its core values. In contrast, an entity that is more focused on revenue generation as a fundamental goal—whether in a collegiate, professional, corporate, or other setting—must be prepared to explain how a deal is appropriate, worthwhile, and consistent with the organization's core values. Articulating the relationship of business deals to an organization's core values is fundamental to fostering trust and loyalty among stakeholders.

TOWARD A FULFILLING AND REWARDING CAREER

This chapter has illustrated through the use of three examples tied to collegiate athletics—negotiation of television deals, conference realignment, and corporate sponsorship deals—the importance of aligning an organization's core values with its business deals. Core values that fit within the culture of an organization and are well communicated lead to business deals that are more likely to be successful and accepted by key stakeholders. Genuine commitment to core values throughout the decision-making and negotiation process results in business arrangements that in turn promote stability and trust while allowing an organization to grow and evolve with the times.

DO WORK THAT FEEDS YOUR SOUL

Don Garber

Don Garber, author of chapter 9, imparts four pieces of advice for pursuing a career in sport—all of which hinge on articulating what is important to you personally and professionally, as Robin Harris advocates. Garber is MLS Commissioner and has overseen the league's tremendous growth and influence in its two decades of existence.

In looking back at more than three decades in professional sport, what is the most important advice I can offer to readers?

First and foremost, find something you really care about and then go out and doggedly pursue it. Because here's the truth: Life is a long time. I'm convinced that people cannot be truly happy in life unless they are doing work that really feeds their soul.

Fair compensation and a respectful work environment are extremely important. But trust me, they are not enough. Money, especially, is not everything. It's about what you do. It's about what you work for. It's about who you work with. And it's about whether you are inspired when you come to work every day and whether you're on the right path to do more and, hopefully, to grow in your career and as a citizen.

Aim to be fearless. It's a very complicated world out there. At times, there can be political turmoil or social media hysteria that could paralyze any of us. This doesn't mean you won't confront fear or doubt at times in your life. We all do—over a job, a decision, a relationship, or even the world. But do not let fear of failure overshadow your desire to succeed. I have always believed that we need to be at our best when things seem to be at their worst.

And always remember that integrity is our only true currency. There is a quote that I regularly revert to when I want to provide an important life lesson to young people: "Your true character is revealed by the clarity of your convictions, the choices you make, the promises you keep. So hold strongly to your principles and refuse to follow the currents of convenience. What you say and do defines who you are, and who you are . . . you are forever."

Used with permission of Don Garber.

From a career standpoint, it is important to know whether your employer's core values are truly reflected in its business operations (which will be explored further in chapter 23 by Deborah Yow), including the development and negotiation of business deals. Understanding how your organization's values influence expectations for your own work greatly enhances your ability to be successful. And, perhaps most important, matching your employer's core values to your own will in turn lead to an incredibly fulfilling and rewarding career.

References

Lencioni, P.M. 2002. "Make Your Values Mean Something." *Harvard Business Review,* July 2002. https://hbr.org/2002/07/make-your-values-mean-something.

Mainwaring, S. 2016. "The New Role of Sponsorship – Impact through Brand Collaboration and Values Alignment John Varvatos 13th Annual Stuart House Benefit." *Huffington Post,* April 27, 2016. www.huffingtonpost.com/simon-mainwaring/the-new-role-of-sponsorsh_b_9781008.html.

Phelon, P. 2017. "3 Reasons Why Kim Kardashian Won't Help Drive Your Business' Sales." *Forbes,* January 3, 2017. www.forbes.com/sites/promisephelon/#3d8f2d8b27a5.

Schultz, H. 1997. *Pour Your Heart Into It: How Starbucks Built a Company One Cup at a Time.* New York, NY: Hyperion. www.goodreads.com/work/quotes/90329-pour-your-heart-into-it-how-starbucks-built-a-company-one-cup-at-a-time.

CHAPTER 15

The Arc of the Deal

Donald Dell

Donald Dell is cofounder of the Association of Tennis Professionals and the founder of ProServ, a leading sport agency that has represented hundreds of star athletes across many sports, getting his start with some of the top tennis players in the 1970s and '80s, including Arthur Ashe, Stan Smith, Jimmy Connors, and Ivan Lendl. He is also a former captain of the U.S. Davis Cup tennis team, the founder of the Legg Mason Tennis Classic, and a television tennis commentator. He was elected to the International Tennis Hall of Fame in 2009, the same year he wrote *Never Make the First Offer (Except When You Should): Wisdom From a Master Dealmaker.* Dell was a three-time All-American tennis player at Yale University, reaching the NCAA singles final in 1959, played on two U.S. Davis Cup teams, and was captain of winning Cup teams in 1968 and 1969. He received his law degree from the University of Virginia and served as special assistant to Peace Corps founder Sargent Shriver in 1968 to 1969.

The second contract for any NBA player is often his chance to cash in on his early-career success. Such was the case with Chicago Bulls center Joakim Noah as the 2010 to 2011 season, his fourth as a pro, was about to get under way. Noah was my client, and I wanted to capitalize on his production and popularity to negotiate a new contract before his option year began. But there was a problem. A lockout or strike seemed imminent after the season ended in summer 2011. Bulls General Manager Gar Forman firmly said that he wasn't negotiating any contracts until any work stoppage was over. With Noah's permission, I laid it all on the line with Forman. "Gar," I told him, "I want to make it very clear. We don't have any leverage. You have it all. But understand that when the lockout is over and if we don't have a deal, he will be a free agent. I promise you that we won't be negotiating when his deal is over next year. We won't be coming back to Chicago." Forman said, "Wait a minute," and I interrupted him: "That's my only leverage. You either believe me or you don't. If you believe me, we make the deal now. If you don't, we're never making a deal because I'm not coming back. Tell that to Jerry [Bulls owner Jerry Reinsdorf]."

I trust that you see from that example how gaining leverage when you have none is one of several skills that will help you at various stages of a deal. It's not that leverage is overrated as an important factor in negotiations. It's the most important factor when you have it; it's just that more often than not you don't have it or don't have any way of knowing with any certainty that you do. If you don't accept that reality, you will struggle to reach your objectives.

NINE STEPS OF THE DEAL

In my book *Never Make the First Offer (Except When You Should): Wisdom From a Master Dealmaker,* I identify nine steps in seeing a deal through from start to finish. I also made the following statement in regard to a negotiation with Reebok pertaining to tennis star Andy Roddick's contract: "In my experience deals have a certain arc, and I could feel this one starting to fade away because of Tom (Shine's) silence" (p. 157). I won't go into the details of that story here, but for the purposes of this chapter, I want to expand on that idea of the arc of a deal. I will hit on just what I consider the most important of those nine steps, then provide insight into traits and skills that will make you better at negotiating, regardless of what stage of the deal you are at. My hope is that you will understand there is an organic process in deal making and a way to represent your client's interests more effectively by understanding that process.

I want to provide a few comments as a preface to the nine steps:

- Though I have garnered these experiences and my ideas about deal making through my long career as founder of ProServ, this chapter is not just for sport agents. It is for anyone who wants to negotiate more effectively and confidently. In or out of the sport industry, this skill encompasses many different types of roles and job titles.

- The steps are intended to be chronological, but only roughly so. Don't get hung up on each step always following neatly, one after the other. You will overthink rather than be in the moment, and that can be costly. A basic understanding of a deal's arc is a great foundation. As you gain experience, you will be able to adapt to the dynamic quality that is a staple of every negotiation. That can be scary . . . but it's also what makes it fun and challenging.

- For more details on the nine steps, for the full Roddick story (and for that matter, many other examples in my professional life), you can read my book. This chapter draws from it, but I also provide updated examples and additional ideas based on experiences I've had since *Never Make the First Offer* was published.

With those caveats out of the way, here are the nine steps of the deal that I identified in my book. This chapter will focus on steps 1, 3, 6, and 8 from this list:

1. Establish relationships; build trust.
2. Evaluate your opponent.
3. Use targeted knowledge.
4. Never make the first offer (except when you should).
5. Be creative.
6. Listen for what they need.
7. Keep it simple.
8. Listen for the moment of truth; be willing to walk away.
9. Shake hands.

PREPARATION

It would be appropriate to break up these nine steps into preparation (1-3), the deal itself (4-8), and closing (9). It's not by accident that two of the four essential items that I am highlighting come in the preparation stage: establishing relationships and using targeted knowledge. I think of the whole preparation stage as a triangle. The visioning is side one. A deal starts in your mind, as you envision what you want to accomplish with a particular product or company. A deal begins long before you go to the club or client for discussion. Ask yourself what the ideal deal would be. What do you want to do and what are you going after? You make plenty of notes ahead of time. That's when the deal originates, well before the first call. Understanding who you are doing business with is side two. If you know the person, or you know somebody who knows the person, that is a big help. Make phone calls to others to find out about your opponent. Is your competitor old or young? Uptight? Friendly? Competent? These questions may sound blunt, but just asking five or six questions of someone you trust who knows the person is time well spent—and yet another reminder of the value of being a trustworthy and responsible businessperson. It doesn't just serve you well in the immediate negotiation. It also ensures you are well connected and able to access information for your whole career.

The third side of the triangle is knowing how to conduct and use relevant research. You can expose your ignorance if you don't know the comparables, or "comps"—the relative value of your client, product, or service based on other recent activity for similar contracts. It is not much different from comps when buying real estate. Comps set the value of the market, and you need to understand where the value lies. In many ways, this information is so much easier to come by today than when sport business really started to take off in the 1970s and '80s. At that time, owners guarded the dollar amount and lengths of contracts as though they were state secrets; today, I can instantly find the basics of every player's contract. But access to information is only part of the equation. You must know what parts of the information are relevant to your needs. You have more data available than in the past, but so does the person you're making a deal with. It is up to you to do the legwork to make those data work for you and your client.

In Major League Baseball, agent Scott Boras has a reputation as a difficult negotiator with owners, looking to gain any edge he can to corner them and get every last dollar he can for his client. My take is that he consistently comes to the table armed with lots of numbers and points that illustrate patterns and reasons why his client deserves the amount they are asking for. He employs a large staff that compiles an enormous amount of research and analytics that he can use in a calculated way. His biggest strength is not some brusque demeanor, but rather doing serious preparation, having a handle on the comps, and knowing his stuff. He is no doubt tough, but as a competitive person myself, I will respect that as long as he is also fair.

LISTEN AND LEARN

Damn it, learn to listen!

I used that language for a reason. I wanted to make sure you were listening! Salespeople—and we all are salespeople at various points in our careers, even if we don't carry that title—often think they have to be in selling mode to get results. But really good salespeople know that when the negotiations get serious (see section on the moment of truth later in this chapter), it is time to listen. My book was titled *Never Make the First Offer (Except When You Should)*. It very easily could have been called *Listen and Learn,* because this piece of advice is so important to me.

The number one rule in selling is learning to listen. You learn only when you're listening. When you're talking, you know it all. You're talking about something you know . . . and you learn nothing. Listening is where you learn what the other party wants and needs, where the party wants to be headed. All of that can be discovered, blanks can be filled in, if you ask a few simple questions and then listen. I challenge you, the next time you are out in a public space, to strike up a conversation with a stranger. Test out your ability to ask questions to gain information. I was on a plane once when I heard a man speaking with a strong Southern accent. I asked him where he went to college. He said University of North Carolina. I told him I represented every Tar Heel basketball player who competed under Coach Dean Smith for 14 years. He was shocked and proud to talk more about UNC basketball. This was not a professional negotiation, but it was a reminder to me of the value of common interests. I gained a connection with him, and in a negotiation, that can lead to an advantage. Even when it wasn't a negotiation, I placed myself in the position of having an enjoyable conversation and, I hope, offering the same to another person.

GAME CHANGER
LISTEN AND RESPOND

Rich McKay

Rich McKay uses Mercedes-Benz Stadium as an example of the tangible results that come from listening, in this case to Atlanta Falcons fans. McKay is president and CEO of the Falcons, and he was general manager of the Tampa Bay Buccaneers when they won Super Bowl XXXVII. McKay is also chair of the influential NFL Competition Committee and played an instrumental role in negotiating the collective bargaining agreement between players and owners in 2011. Son of the late coaching legend John McKay, Rich earned his bachelor's degree from Princeton University and graduated from the Stetson University College of Law, and he was an attorney before entering the NFL. He and his wife Terrin have two sons, Hunter and John.

Atlanta Falcons owner Arthur Blank has founded each of his businesses on six core values: listen and respond, include everyone, give back to others, put people first, innovate continuously, and lead by example. In this piece I focus on *listen and respond*.

The value of *listen and respond* doesn't require a lot of thought or explanation; however, it does require exact execution. In other words, always ask the customer, always listen to the customer, and always respond to the customer. Too many times, as executives we think we have or know the answers to the questions we are asking, and that sense of bravado leads us to filter the answers that customers provide. *That filter is the problem.*

When we opened Mercedes-Benz Stadium in August 2017, we introduced something that had never been done in a professional sport stadium, fan-friendly pricing for all our concessions. Why did we do it? Because our fans asked us to. If you look at a fan survey for any professional league, you'll see that one of the top five complaints is the entire concession experience. It certainly was for us, and our fans were very quick to say their lack of satisfaction started with unreasonable and unacceptable pricing. Our pricing model was based on "market" as defined by concessionaires, in turn based upon a market of other stadiums and arenas where the pricing was likewise unreasonable and unacceptable.

In surveys, our fans told us that price, variety, quality, and speed of service were key issues they wanted fixed before we opened Mercedes-Benz Stadium. We listened to what they told us and tried to give them what they wanted. We added a lot more cooking capacity and 65 percent more points of sale than the Georgia Dome offered in order to ensure a better speed of service; we priced our food on a "street pricing" concept that would allow our customers to come into the building and be able to feed a family of four for less than $30.

As to quality and variety, we invited our fans to come to food tastings and tell us what they liked, what they didn't like, and how they would modify the choices we presented to them. One of the main reasons our food offerings have been so successful at Mercedes-Benz Stadium is the very process of allowing our customers to develop the food offerings themselves and not leaving it to us or the concessionaire.

We have seen tremendous success with our food and beverage program both in volume sold and in fan feedback. Hopefully, this will be a true disruptor to an industry that screams for disruption. The lesson learned: Listen to your customers, don't add your filter, respond to their input, and you will find success.

Something I like to say that is related to *listen and learn* is "Take the temperature in the room." Be observant and be curious when you are in a negotiation. What is your rival's body language? Are people getting tired? Irritated? Are they happy? I once went into a meeting with a new general manager in the league. My assistant peppered him with question after question. It made the new guy look bad, which was even worse for him because his owner was in the room with us. After lunch, when my assistant and I were alone, I let him know that I wasn't happy. "Well, that was brilliant," I said. "You just embarrassed the GM by showing how you know so much and how little he knows. Now go back and try to make a deal with him next month. You're going to have a really hard time."

BE PERSONAL

I don't want to sound like an old man cursing the modern world. I do believe there are plenty of reasons that rapidly changing technology is beneficial to our professional lives. But when it comes to deal making, I am a full-blooded Luddite. Negotiating is about building relationships, and you can't tell the temperature of the room in an email. You can't tell if you're being a pest, if you're selling too hard or too soft, or what your opponent's reaction is. All of that is visual.

Any deal that is worth doing, you have to do it on the phone, or better yet, in person. This is increasingly true as the stakes get higher. Technology gives us a false sense of intimacy, and this is a fatal flaw in business. The worst is to negotiate by email. It's too easy for either side to say, "We've decided to go another direction." What do you think the worst part of that decision is? It isn't failing to close the deal. It's that you don't know what it even means. You have no information that will help you correct the problem the next time. Use email or text for quick scheduling or logistical information: "I'll call you tomorrow at 4 o'clock," or "What's the best time to meet you?" or "I'll be in New York City next Thursday." But if you go further and try to negotiate through those electronic channels, you are asking for a failed deal and a colossal waste of your time and that of the others.

Connecting on a personal level with the people you do business with is to recognize the limitations of technology. Never take this realization for granted, even when reading body language and making "midgame" adjustments during a negotiation are unlikely to be necessary. Stan Smith was once the #1 ranked tennis player in the world, and his namesake tennis shoes are among the most iconic brands of sporting equipment ever conceived. He'd been with Adidas since 1972, and when the time came for negotiating another six-year deal some 40 years after that, I met with the Adidas Europe representative four times in person. I knew him and his company, and he knew Stan and me from the previous contract. There was no reason to expect any surprises, but I was not going to negotiate that deal over the phone. Stan and his product were too important to allow any misunderstandings.

Being personable is crucial for an often-overlooked aspect of business—being able to return to the bargaining table and make other deals. Ron Shapiro is a great

360

THE AGENT'S LIST

Bob Kain

Looking for a competitive edge, Bob Kain, author of chapter 5, turned the tables on chapter author Donald Dell. Kain headed IMG's tennis division and eventually had a client list that included Billie Jean King, John McEnroe, Bjorn Borg, Chris Evert, Venus and Serena Williams, Martina Navratilova, Pete Sampras, Rafael Nadal, Roger Federer, Monica Seles, Andre Agassi, Jennifer Capriati, and many more. Kain also engineered the purchase of the 27-acre Nick Bollettieri Tennis Academy and oversaw its growth to the 280-acre IMG Academies, the largest elite sport training academy in the world. He was a four-year letter winner in tennis at the University of Virginia before beginning a career in tennis management and event business with IMG. He told this story to Donald Dell's law students at the University of Virginia when Dell invited him to speak there.

When I was the young head of IMG's tennis business, we had no American clients and I was recruiting against Donald—CEO of ProServ and a former Davis Cup captain and player. Donald was king of tennis at the time. He managed Arthur Ashe, Stan Smith, Bob Lutz, Roscoe Tanner, and almost every great American player. In every recruiting battle he would tell the player and his parents he would manage the player himself. I kept hearing this over and over from these families. So I made up a long, skinny list of everyone ProServ was managing, about 30 players long. I figured Dell must have promised them all he would be their agent. The sheet looked like one of those grocery receipts—3 inches wide and 2 feet long. In my recruiting sales pitches, I started asking the player and parents if Dell had promised to manage the player personally. They always said yes. And then with great flourish I would pull the sheet from my sport coat and read this long list of names. I started signing some American players! In fact, I signed three great ones in the next year.

Postscript: Donald Dell confirmed this story to be true, and even added that Bob Kain showed the sheet of paper to the UVA students that day without telling the instructor in advance that he would do so. Donald said that Bob was a worthy competitor and an even greater friend through the years, and was an outstanding part of IMG's success.

---

agent. He wrote a book called *The Power of Nice: How to Negotiate so Everyone Wins—Especially You!* I get the book every year and give it to students in my law school classes at Virginia and Stanford. It sounds kind of corny, *the power of nice,* but his whole theory is based on a very simple and savvy business principle. You want to figure out something they want, they want to figure out something you want, and you make the deal based on that. As a result, you each get a little of what you want, and there will be later deals. There will be renewals.

THE MOMENT OF TRUTH

I mentioned the moment of truth early on. As you reflect on how my four main points—being prepared, listening, being personable, and being trustworthy—will permeate the nine stages for you, I want to highlight it.

There comes a time in every serious negotiation when you say, "Here's what I have to have if we're going to make this deal." If the other side believes you, you're going to make a deal, one way or the other. If they don't believe you, you're not going to make a deal. Not that one anyway. That's what I call the moment of truth. It could go either way, from you to the other side, or the other side to you. It generally comes late in the negotiation, after the nonessentials are covered, after both sides have passed the point where they are still confident they can extract significantly better terms, after a number of volleys back and forth making demands. Maybe I say that my client is not going to accept a three-year deal; he needs five. The team's representative says my owner isn't going to pay five years of cash; he needs two or three years deferred if we're going to get from three to five years. Both sides have laid out their cards at that point to make a final deal. The moment of truth, really, dictates how successful you are at closing. When you get where you want to be or at least very close to it, and you don't think you're going to get anything better or more, you have reached the moment of truth. You are willing to walk away at that point. Of course, your rival is also angling to get there too.

Sometimes, if you are not wed to a hard number or term and know that you want to keep the door open for a longer relationship with the other side, you can head off the moment of truth before you get there. It requires flexibility, and it feels counterintuitive to take this route in the ultracompetitive sport business world. But if you have done your preparation and are clear on your goals, it can be a useful strategy. In a recent negotiation, I told the general counsel for a shoe company, a man whom I know well, to take my offer to his principal. But I added that if the principal didn't like that number to please come back with another number. Don't just say you can't do the deal. You want to leave them in a position that they don't just dismiss the offer out of hand.

KEEP YOUR WORD

Being trustworthy and honest is about ethics and being a mensch and heeding the Golden Rule. It ensures that you can feel good about who you are and how you show up in your professional life. But I hope you have seen through this chapter and earlier ones that it is also good business and can get you significant results. In my nine steps of a deal, I close with *Shake hands*. That may seem very easy, but the meaning of the gesture is so much more. Say thanks a million, and sincerely say that you're glad we worked it out. Seal the deal. End on a high note. To me, it's simple. That's how finalizing a contract works. It's a done deal when you shake hands. It's a signal that you are good to your word. The guy who comes in and pounds the table and wants to win every deal—if there are

10 points, he has to win 9-1/2—he doesn't last long. The sport world is lucrative, but it's a small industry in terms of the number of people. If you lie or break your word to somebody, you're dead. People look at you differently. Word gets around.

We talked about Joakim Noah in the chapter opening, and I will return to him at the end with the result of our contract negotiation. But years before he was eligible for free agency, of course the Bulls first had to draft him. They were on the verge of doing just that with the ninth overall pick, but owner Jerry Reinsdorf was getting cold feet as the clock ticked down. I was sitting with Joakim's grandfather, Zachary Noah, who had come from Cameroon for the draft. "Oh my God, we meet here again," he said to me, smiling warmly. And, indeed we were. I represented Zachary's son (and Joakim's dad) Yannick Noah for 25 years when he was a star tennis player, and we had been on the same team for numerous negotiations before. The phone rang. It was Forman, then director of player personnel, and general manager John Paxson, who had been a ProServ client years earlier. Paxson asked if I would mind talking with Reinsdorf.

"Sure," I said, "but what about?"

Paxson said that Reinsdorf was having doubts about Noah.

"Don't be ridiculous," I said. "He's been telling me for months he would draft Noah."

I hung up and Jerry immediately called me. We had less than 10 minutes.

"Tell me about Noah," he says. "I don't really want to draft him."

"Why?"

"I don't like his ponytail."

"What?"

"I don't like the way he wears his hair and he has this stride, he's kind of cocky. He's just not my cup of tea. What do you think?"

"Jerry," I said, "I've known Joakim since he was 3 years old. This is a quality kid. He's a defensive player, not a real good shooter, he'll give you great effort in games and practice. He's a great passer and great runner. And his hair has nothing to do with it."

"Let me know one thing, give me your word, would you draft him?"

"Absolutely," I said, without hesitation.

A minute later, Noah became a Bull. He became a mainstay in the lineup for nearly a decade, winning the NBA Defensive Player of the Year Award in 2013 to 2014. I had 10 minutes to sell my client. And the only reason I got that was because Reinsdorf trusted me—someone who obviously was biased, wanting my client to go to the big-city team at as high of a pick as possible. Sometimes I'd sit with him before games and he'd say he was so glad I talked him into it. But I didn't talk him into it. Paxson and Forman, his player personnel experts,

Pat Rooney Jr.

Pat Rooney Jr. grew up in a family business that was very much in the public eye, which meant he understood the importance of reputation and responsibility long before he was making deals. Here, Rooney, a successful businessman and respected community leader in Palm Beach County, Florida, discusses lessons learned when one's grandfather owns the beloved Pittsburgh Steelers. Rooney is president of the Palm Beach Kennel Club and a consultant for Rooney's Beer Company, and was a representative in the Florida House (District 85) from 2010 to 2016. He was also a sport cohost on local ESPN 760 AM from 2003 to 2010. Rooney serves in many local roles, including director for the Autism Project of Palm Beach County; a founding board member for Potentia Academy in Greenacres; director and cochair for the not-for-

Patrick Rooney Jr., Patrick Rooney III, and Mean Joe Greene.

profit Rooney's Golf Foundation Inc., which raises money for local charities through various events held every year; and board member of Children's Healthcare Charity Inc. (The Honda Classic). Rooney graduated from Clemson University with a bachelor of arts in political science, earned his Juris Doctor at Villanova University School of Law, and his MBA from Lehigh University. Pat and his wife, Patti, have four children, Mary, Frannie, Patrick III, and Anthony.

Growing up related to somebody famous, even in a local sense, can be tough. Growing up related to somebody famous who owns a sports team, where wins and losses are front page news, can be excruciating (especially with the losses!).

My name is Pat Rooney Jr., and my grandfather Art founded the Pittsburgh Steelers football team in 1933. Luckily for me, born in 1964, the team was very successful during my formative preteen and adolescent years (1972-1980), winning the Super Bowl four times during that period. Not so much for my dad, Pat Rooney Sr., born in 1939 and having to endure many losing seasons during not just his preteen and adolescent period but also his young adult and adult life (1946-1971). During those 25 years the Steelers made exactly two (!) playoff appearances, promptly losing both, and had the worst record in pro football. My dad told me that the family generally attended games only in September and October for a couple of reasons. First, the team was usually not mathematically eliminated from the playoffs until November, and second, it usually didn't start snowing in Pittsburgh until then. I'd ask, Why did that matter? Because the owner's box at Pitt Stadium, where the Steelers played, was susceptible to thrown snowballs by the second half when the Steelers were normally hopelessly behind. He wasn't joking, either.

So yes, I was very lucky. Even growing up in Philadelphia where the Eagles soared, I was fortunate to be a small part of the team on the other side of the state. Most years my family would make the 5-hour drive west to catch at least a couple of games. It became a tradition to go for Thanksgiving; the team always seemed to play at home the Sunday after the holiday. This was really the only time all year that all 34 of my grandfather's grandchildren would get together. Besides ransacking my grandparents' house on Thanksgiving, it was always a treat to see if they could remember all of our names. (Although if you simply yelled out "Art" or "Dan" you had a 50/50 chance of being right).

Besides Turkey Day, the other games we got together for were the aforementioned Super Bowls. From freezing Tulane Stadium in 1974 to the picturesque Rose Bowl in 1979, the four big games all ended the same way, in wins! I can't begin to describe how special those years were, especially having since experienced being on the losing side of a couple of Super Bowls.

I'm in my early 50s now and my kids have luckily experienced winning a couple of Super Bowls themselves. But my dad and his brothers have divested most of their ownership interest in the team for estate planning purposes, and my grandfather has been gone for almost 30 years now. But what a magical 50-year ride.

I'd be remiss if I didn't mention one crucial element of my upbringing handed down from my grandfather to my father and then to me. That element was to never think of yourself as better than anyone else. You could think of yourself as "luckier" (because we were) but not better. In today's world of "branding" and "optics," my grandfather would have no clue, nor any desire to learn, what those words mean. Treat others as you would treat yourself. A simple mantra.

While neither my grandfather nor my father ever came right out and said we've built the Rooney name to mean something and to protect it, we certainly realized the responsibility of carrying ourselves a certain way in public, especially in Pittsburgh. I remember when my brother Joe, who attended nearby Indiana University of Pennsylvania, went out one evening in Oakland (the Pitt campus) and was observed having had too much to drink. Upon seeing my brother the next day for a Steelers game, my grandfather did not berate him for having a couple beers but rather for "big-shotting" it and using the Rooney name to get into some of the more popular drinking establishments. In other words Art was not concerned with public drunkenness as much as with one of us using the name in order to gain a privilege. That is a huge distinction that is still very evident in my family today. Don't worry about making a human mistake, but don't try to gain favor using the name. One is forgivable, the other isn't.

wanted Noah. I was just fortunate enough to be in position to be the last voice in his ear before a decision that turned out to be a good one. But I had that good fortune only because I had built up a trusting relationship with Reinsdorf over many years, including the nine years that ProServ worked with Bulls star Michael Jordan.

WINNING WITHOUT LEVERAGE

To start this chapter you read about Noah's free agent deal hanging in the balancer. Forman agreed to a five-year, $60 million contract in October 2010. When the 161-day lockout came the following July and ended in December 2011, every five-year contract in the league was cut back to four years. That gave him a full year, and he made a 20 percent premium on the deal. A few weeks after Noah signed, I got a call from the representative for Al Horford, Noah's former teammate and fellow two-time NCAA Champion at the University of Florida. The agent asked me to explain the terms to him, which I did, and when he contacted the Atlanta Hawks regarding Horford's contract, he said, "We'll take the Noah contract." There were only three deals made during that off-season (superstar Kevin Durant extending his contract with Oklahoma City was the other). All because when I threatened the Bulls nicely, they believed us. Sometimes that's the only way I can get them to negotiate—and I don't like losing when I reach the moment of truth.

References

Dell, D., and Boswell, J. 2009. *Never Make the First Offer (Except When You Should): Wisdom From a Master Dealmaker.* New York: Penguin.

Shapiro, R.M., and Jankowski, M.A. 2001. *The Power of Nice: How to Negotiate so Everyone Wins—Especially You!* Hoboken, N.J.: Wiley.

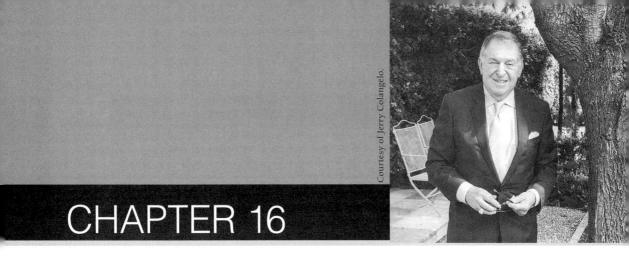

CHAPTER 16

Working Toward Consensus

Jerry Colangelo

Jerry Colangelo is former owner of the Phoenix Suns, Phoenix Mercury, Arizona Diamondbacks, the Continental Indoor Soccer League's Arizona Sandsharks, and the Arena Football League's Arizona Rattlers. He became the youngest general manager in professional sport in 1968 when he was hired as the expansion Suns' first general manager. He ultimately had the second-longest tenure running the same NBA franchise. Colangelo was named NBA Executive of the Year four times and was elected to the Naismith Basketball Hall of Fame in 2004. He was named director of USA Basketball in 2005. He is the national leadership director of the National Italian American Sports Hall of Fame and was also inducted into the Hall of Fame, located in the Colangelo Building in Chicago's Little Italy. Grand Canyon University named the Jerry Colangelo School of Business in his honor and in 2017 unveiled the Colangelo Museum to commemorate his accomplishments in sport business. Colangelo and his wife Joan have four children.

On New Year's Eve, 2004, I had surgery for prostate cancer. I chose that date to go under the knife rather than January because I wanted to begin 2005 with a clean slate. I was coming off a very traumatic year personally. I had sold my beloved Phoenix Suns and resigned as managing general partner of the Arizona Diamondbacks. On the plus side, I was inducted into the Basketball Hall of Fame. Shortly after my successful surgery, I got a call from NBA Commissioner David Stern. Keep in mind that 2004 had also been a traumatic year for the U.S. men's basketball team, which took the bronze medal at the Athens Olympic Games. Third place may not sound like a dismal showing, but we have a proud international tradition in a sport that was invented in the United States. And it was not the placing itself that was so disheartening. It was how the whole experience looked and felt both at home and abroad. Frankly, it was kind of embarrassing. David said to me, "Would you take over USA Basketball?" I've always been a person who is instinctive when it comes to big decisions, but even by my standards, I accepted pretty quickly.

"I'll do it, but I have a couple of conditions," I told him.

"What are they?" he said.

"One is full autonomy, where I pick the coaches and players," I replied.

The commissioner didn't blink. *"You got it. What is next?"*

"I don't want to hear about a budget," I quickly answered.

He yelled for a while on that one.

I said, calmly, *"Are you finished, David? It's still number two."*

He acquiesced, and after he did, I reassured him. "Don't worry about the budget. I'll sell the sponsorships. I'll create the revenue needed for what I want to do."

And that was the beginning of my journey with USA Basketball.

I've been blessed to embark on many journeys through the years. Really all of us have those opportunities, if we are paying attention—I like to tell students and young professionals, "You don't wait for your ship to come in; you swim out to it!" However you view it, there's no question I've had my share of journeys, and from the beginning, sport has been the ship I have most often swam out to meet. I always loved sport, and I quickly realized I liked sport business as well.

CONSENSUS-BUILDING
OPPORTUNITIES ARE EVERYWHERE

As I look back on my career, especially with the fledgling Chicago Bulls franchise and as the first general manager of the expansion Phoenix Suns back in the 1960s, it is entirely clear to me that consensus building is the most important skill I learned. Think about it. Every negotiation, whether complex or straightforward, with people you know intimately or with people you just met, no matter what the context or how ambitious or immediate your goal is, demands consensus. Without it, you are isolated . . . or will be when you need advice, resources, or a partner to move the ball forward. Opportunities to build consensus are everywhere to either leverage or ignore. I'm telling you, if you want to be a leader, you ignore these opportunities at your peril.

Consensus building to me is no more than two or more parties coming together to fulfill a shared goal. If this project involves people who are not part of the same organization or entity, it might seem very similar to a business negotiation or deal making. Consensus building and negotiating a deal can indeed be synonymous, but I would add this caveat: The shared goal of consensus building may not have an immediate tangible or monetary result; it may be simply laying or solidifying the groundwork for the future. If this project involves people within the same organization, then consensus building may seem time-consuming and even unnecessary. Why not look at the chain of command or the organizational structure chart, decide who is in charge, and follow that person's decision? And if you are at the top of the chart, hey, how much easier can that be? You decide, your subordinates enact!

I want to be very clear here. In either of these scenarios, external or internal, you will not achieve success, and you stand to lose a whole lot more, if you don't commit to incorporating a deep understanding of consensus into your organization from day one. Consensus building is about cooperation and support, about working as a team. Even if the goal at hand includes external individuals or organizations that are not part of your own staff, for the purposes of the project at hand, you all must work together as a team. Note that this definition does not claim consensus building is about fulfilling *your* personal goal. It is a *shared* goal, whether the parties are external or internal. And if the parties don't share that goal from the outset, then you have not built consensus. This is no small point. If you think of consensus building in these terms, then you don't bicker about who won and who lost later. You can't blame the other party for not shouldering their load when people are looking to pass the blame, and you don't take all the praise when people are looking to bestow praise. This combination of accepting your share of the responsibility and sharing the credit with others will serve you well if you want to be the best leader you can be. You succeed or fail together, and if you were committed to consensus building at the outset, you may come together again for a future project even if the first attempt was not a mutual success.

Here are two examples of cases in which I took a consensus-building approach to challenges my organizations faced, one external and one internal.

EXTERNAL: AMERICA WEST ARENA

When you are seeking consensus within an organization, it is a more intimate situation. You have more knowledge of the situation and subtext, access to the data and the culture, and likely more friendly faces to turn to. When you turn outside the organization, you enter less comfortable terrain. You must not lose sight of the fact that if you plan to reach the goal line, you must build consensus on a number of issues. Along with City of Phoenix leaders, I took a novel approach to public–private partnerships when the Suns organization worked with the city to develop America West Arena. In the late 1980s, the concept of a downtown arena had not yet taken hold in the pro sport landscape. Downtowns had been in decline and the country was going through a recession. But philosophically and financially, I strongly believed in the need for a downtown arena. Fortunately, so did Mayor Terry Goddard. And after two decades as general manager, I had just recently bought the team. With that consensus as a starting point, city and team set to work on a win-win proposition.

It required creativity and consensus, but by the time America West Arena opened in 1992, we had one of the first downtown pro sport venues. The city and team agreed to split the expected $70 million hard (construction) and soft (designs, architectural plans, and so on) fees, with any overage to be paid for by the Suns. As it turned out, the total cost was $110 million, and the team paid the $40 million difference. At every turn, we were partners. The city raised its share of the money through a hotel and rental car tax. The city had donated the site, but when the city ran short of the money needed to purchase the land, it asked the Suns for $500,000, which we contributed. When we decided to make the building larger than the original design, the Suns paid for those additional costs. We did something unique by bringing in Restaura, a restaurant concessionaire, to be part of the financing package—another bit of consensus building. It was an excellent model at the time. I describe in detail the arrangement in my book, *How You Play the Game*. "The upshot of this deal was that America West Arena was the first venue in the country financed not through collateral or hard cash, but with the promise of sufficient future revenues to pay for the cost of its construction. The deal wasn't based around bricks and mortar, but around the principals involved in the business" (Colangelo 1998, p. 91).

I also point out in my book that throughout pro sport, the word was that we got "more bang for our buck than any building constructed in a decade" (Colangelo 1998, p. 89). That makes me very proud, especially because as a result, it opened the door for many other teams in basketball and other pro sports to do the same.

INTERNAL: D-BACKS' SOPHOMORE SEASON

When we brought Major League Baseball to Phoenix in 1998, we did a great job of preselling our product. We got off to a robust financial start with 36,000 season tickets sold and strong media and sponsorship deals. On the field, we weren't as successful. As with most expansion teams, we struggled on the field in our debut season, finishing last at 65-97 in the National League West. As an organization, we had put together a five-year plan to develop our players through the farm system and to be ready to compete for championships within that time frame. Unfortunately, when we attempted to get renewals from our season-ticket holders for our sophomore season, we lost 25 percent of that base. As we researched what was happening, we discovered that with a losing team, people were rethinking the commitment of an 81-game purchase that a season ticket represented. Instead of investing in 81 games, multiple fans would go together and split games within a single season package.

That was an eye-opener to me, and it caused me to call a meeting of the Diamondbacks leadership group. This loss of income was enough of a hit that I acknowledged to my partners that we had a five-year plan but circumstances had changed. I was laying out a different, more urgent, plan. In order to protect the investment that we had already made in the stadium and the team, we needed to compete sooner. I outlined a four-year plan that would result in a solid eight-year payout. We sought established stars, most notably pitching greats Randy

Johnson in 1999 and Curt Schilling a year later. Immediately, we improved 35 games, to 100-62, winning the NL West, in 1999. By the time I left the D-Backs in 2004, we had won two more division titles and had become the fastest expansion team to win a World Series Championship in our fourth season.

Our new plan worked. New plans don't always work. Quite often, as die-hard sports fans know, an organization's five-year plan just bleeds into a new five-year plan. I give my partners and myself credit for recognizing the need to course correct as early as we did. *That* is why I give this as an example of successful consensus building. We worked together to agree on a direction. That consensus allowed us to prepare for the transactions that put us in position to win, and to be clear to our staff, coaches, players, and fans what our objective was. Of course, there were many more elements to our success, both from a performance standpoint and as a business. We revamped our ticket packages and ensured fans had a great experience at the ballpark. But any businessperson will tell you that without a good product, people will find other ways to spend their investment of time and money. We weren't willing to settle for putting a second-rate product on the field.

BE RELATIONAL!

Trust is essential to building consensus, as you saw in the America West Arena example. You want to believe that people trust you in your ability to make decisions, but the only way that takes place is if you show trust in them. The feeling, as they say, is mutual. People who are considered leaders very seldom make decisions in a vacuum, or at least they shouldn't. They either have mentors, colleagues, or staff that act as sounding boards, or they build consensus to confirm and solidify the position they are about to take. When there are decisions or plans to be made, you want to discuss them with people you trust. In effect, that is consensus building.

Trust is critical, but it doesn't happen overnight. So how can you start building trust, and also learn how to create consensus-building opportunities, when you are relatively new to the game? People are different in style and personality. There's no single best personality trait for building consensus, just as there is no single best way to interact with others, whether they agree or disagree with you. The best way to create partnerships is to focus on the skill of being relational. Looking at the arena example, trying to put that complex package in place was a good test for me. While I was familiar with my community and the sport and business of basketball, I was a newbie when it came to calling the shots as an NBA owner. I made that happen by raising $20 million and getting bank loans for another $24.5 million, all in six weeks, with really my sweat equity serving as collateral to my lenders. It was classic consensus building: "I was very fortunate to have been in the right time and place—and right frame of mind—to buy the franchise. I didn't have the wherewithal to do it myself, so I found others to join with me. All together, we made it work" (Colangelo 1998, pp. 237-238).

GAME CHANGER

"SIX WIN AND SIX LOSE"

Randy Vataha

Randy Vataha remembers what happened when the owners of the United States Football League failed to stay in consensus with their business plan. Vataha was a wide receiver at Stanford and played seven years in the NFL, 1971 to 1977. He served as player representative for the New England Patriots and was involved in negotiating several collective bargaining agreements with the NFL. Starting in 1977, his business career included being a founding co-owner, with George Matthews, of the USFL's Boston Breakers and serving as CEO of Bob Woolf Associates, a premier sport and entertainment agency. In 1993, Vataha cofounded Game Plan Special Services LLC, a boutique sport and entertainment investment bank, and he continues to serve as the company's president today.

I have had the incredible opportunity to experience team sport from just about every perspective. Since 1994, when Robert Caporale and I started Game Plan, we have had the good fortune to complete many record-breaking and landmark financial transactions for major professional sport franchises, such as the acquisition of the Boston Celtics, LA Dodgers, Golden State Warriors, and Sacramento Kings.

Over the years, several people have pointed out to me that I may be the only person in the United States to have played a major professional team sport and been a sport union representative, an agent for professional players and entertainers, a team owner, a team president, and a sport investment banker.

Given this background, I have come to realize there is one principle that is often misunderstood or completely ignored, especially by the press and parties looking to buy or invest in professional sports teams and leagues. This all revolves around the concept of how important winning on the field of play is to the success of teams, and more importantly, leagues. There must be a balance between the urge to win and understanding what it takes to be a successful owner. The following example illustrates my point; it's a math story problem and cautionary tale all rolled into one.

The United States Football League (USFL) was a start-up spring football league that began play in 1983. The last league meeting before the start of the first season was in New Orleans. All 12 ownership groups attended and we had an owners' dinner in the Rex Room at Antoine's, an iconic New Orleans restaurant. Early in the dinner, one of the owners clinked his glass for everyone's attention and the room went silent. The owner stood up and addressed John Bassett, owner of one of the other teams, the Tampa Bay Bandits. He asked John the following question: "John, you are the only owner in the room that has ever owned a professional sport team before. What do we all have to understand to have a successful league?" John had previously owned the Memphis Southmen in the World Football League that played in 1974 and 1975 as well as having prior ownership interests in other professional teams.

John was a charismatic, handsome, blond-haired businessman from a wealthy Canadian family who was also a former top Davis Cup tennis player. John thought about the question, then stood up and took a long drink from his double martini, paused, looked at every owner, and then asked the following question:

"Well, we have 12 teams, correct?"

All the owners answered, "Yes."

Bassett again, "Well, every week the league will play six games, right?"

Again the owners answered, "Yes."

Bassett once again, "Well then, *every week six teams are going to win and six teams are going to lose*." He then sat down.

The owners were bewildered and started talking to each other, and finally began laughing as if it was a joke. I do not think anyone took him seriously . . . but he was dead serious and turned out to be a prophet.

Here is why. When the USFL started, there was an unofficial player budget of $1.5 million per team, which totaled $18 million for the combined 12 teams. The league launched shortly after this dinner in the spring of 1983. Not one owner envisioned having a losing team. Every one of them was very successful in his business and highly confident he would field a winning team competing for the championship. However, the team of one of the USFL's wealthier owners, which played in a major indoor stadium that was also home to an NFL team, started the season losing four of their first five games and he was thoroughly embarrassed. So given that it was the NFL off-season, he went out and signed a number of NFL free agents and ran his payroll up to nearly $5 million. His team immediately started to win big. Other owners then started to follow suit and by the end of the year, the average team payroll was approaching $5 million per team. Consequently, the league had managed to increase its average payroll from $1.5 to $5 million. So at the launch of the USFL the total league was spending $18 million for its football product, and by the end of the year the league total was approaching $60 million, a whopping increase of $42 million. The initial football product of the USFL (before these exorbitant contracts were offered) was excellent, and attendance and TV ratings had exceeded expectations. However, the owners who were losing could not help themselves and all tried to buy a winning team.

So back to John Bassett. What he was trying to tell the owners in answering their question was, whether you spend $18 million on players or $60 million on players, *every week six teams are going to win and six teams are going to lose.* You can never change that math! The result of not understanding this and having owners overspending in an effort to all have winning teams doomed the USFL to financial failure. The league lasted two more seasons before suspending play and suing the NFL for antitrust violations. Though the league received some extra publicity in the first year from a few of its player signings, there was no need to increase the player payrolls in the very first year by 330 percent. There are many great lessons to learn from this example, but most importantly, new owners in professional sport leagues

(continued)

need to understand that the other owners are competitors on the field of play but, more importantly, they are your partners in the business and they all must act in the long-term best interests of their league. This realization that every week "six teams win and six teams lose"—no matter how much money you spend on players, coaches, general managers, and so on—is a cornerstone to understanding that building and maintaining a successful business in professional team sport cannot be based on every team winning.

John Bassett has since passed away, but I remember him often for his insight and wisdom. I feel certain that the USFL would be in business today had the USFL owners understood his simple premise: Six win and six lose no matter how much you spend.

Used with permission of Randy Vataha.

Each of us has pluses and minuses in our skillset, but I have always had the ability to be relational. I strongly believe that life is relational. If you have the ability to communicate and relate to people and understand all sides of an issue, you have a much better opportunity to make a deal and provide guidance for an organization's strategic decision making. My whole life has been some form of consensus building. When you're thrust into a leadership role, whenever that may be, you have the opportunity to build consensus. Most of my leadership experience was in sport, first as a participant who was captain of most teams I played for, getting players to buy in to the common goal. When I was just out of college, figuring out how I would support my family, I made a call to a man whose business card I had forgotten I even had. Soon I was part of Dick Klein's effort to bring professional basketball to Chicago. Generating enthusiasm for the new Chicago Bulls franchise was all about seeking consensus. We were looking for financial support, community support, and bringing the community together.

Being relational is more natural for some than others, but everyone can learn how to do it better. The following tips can help you.

KEEP YOUR MOUTH SHUT

Just days after we were awarded the franchise in Chicago, I hit the road and I was scouting the NAIA Tournament in Kansas City. We were the 10th NBA team, and back then half the teams didn't even scout. I got my credentials and went to press row. I didn't know anyone. Someone taps me on the shoulder and introduces himself. We watched eight games a day, three days in a row. Each night we went to the Italian Gardens restaurant. We would sit at a round table, and they all told stories over a drink and a steak. On the third night, one of those five guys, who turned out to be a Hall of Famer, New York Knicks coach Red Holzman, turns to me and says, "Hey kid, you're going to be OK in this league. You keep your mouth shut, because you don't know anything." I tell that story because I have always told young people to be a listener, a sponge. Be around people who have "been there, done that." Your time will come when you can pontificate. But pay your dues.

ONCE YOU MAKE YOUR DECISION, DELIVER

You are entitled to a period of due diligence. That's just good business. But once you say yes, you must be all in. Nothing ensures you will get more opportunities than giving it your all and excelling at the opportunity you are working on in the moment. When people in Phoenix wanted Major League Baseball, I was recruited because they believed I was the person who could deliver it. I thought to myself, hey, I'm being asked to do something here. I have been in the sport industry a long time. I know a lot of people in baseball. I need to come to a conclusion in my own mind whether or not it really makes sense. I discussed ownership with George Steinbrenner, Jerry Reinsdorf, Bud Selig, Donald Fehr, and others. I did my own reading, including the outstanding *Lords of the Realm: The* Real *History of Baseball,* by John Helyar, which served as a primer on the contentious collective bargaining issue that had cast a pall over the sport for years. At the end of the day, I decided baseball had turned a corner and was ready to blossom. I wanted to hear from a lot of people before I made my decision. When I said yes to my suitors, we were in consensus. My job was clear, and with tremendous support, I delivered.

YOU'RE NEVER ALONE, AND THAT'S A GOOD THING

Whoever said, "It's lonely at the top" was simply wrong with that glass half-empty attitude. Someone who embraces a relational mindset, that is, somebody who embraces consensus building, stands a much better chance of being the one who is at the top than someone who fears being the one whose butt is on the line. Look back at my example with the D-Backs. I was the one who would "fail" or "succeed," whatever that meant. But the process of determining if I wanted to take on the project is exactly what ensured I would succeed. I got buy-in. I increased my network of people invested in our success. I slowly built momentum. You're never alone, if you choose not to be. In sport business, capitalize on that reality; don't fear it.

CONSENSUS BUILDING IS NOT ONE SIZE FITS ALL

This may seem obvious, but it is important to explain what I mean. In the business world, you want to replicate when you can. If you understand business, you can transfer your knowledge and skills to many different business settings. Since I've run teams in so many different sports, people ask me all the time what the difference is among the various sports. My answer? The size of the ball. Sure, there are some nuances and differences with each sport, but from a business perspective, the work is by and large the same. However, when it comes to making decisions, you cannot expect there to be a clear-cut answer for each situation.

DOING THE UNPOPULAR

Senator George Mitchell

George Mitchell learned how to build consensus in stressful negotiations in sport and politics, including delving into Major League Baseball's performance-enhancing drugs issue. Senator Mitchell's long career in public service included several sport-centered probes, among them an investigation into the unethical behavior of members of the International Olympic Committee and of many members of National Olympic Committees in the bidding process for host cities in the Olympics, which was conducted prior to the 2002 Salt Lake City Games.

It still amazes me how much my name comes up in sporting circles since I am not and never have been much of an athlete. I played basketball for Bowdoin College in Brunswick, Maine, in the 1950s, but that is nothing compared to many others—especially the esteemed businesspeople and athletes in this book.

The reason any sports fans know me is mostly because of the 409 pages of the so-called Mitchell Report, which was released in December 2007 after more than a year of investigating the issue of performance-enhancing drug abuse in Major League Baseball. The big splash at that time was 89 players who were named because there was evidence that they used performance enhancers. Baseball's Steroid Era led to a lot of blame on all sides, from owners and players to the league office and media.

But as I look back on the lasting impact of that controversial report and the work my investigators did, I believe it shone a light on a dark period in the sport's history. The history of seeking performance enhancement in sport regardless of the rules goes back a long way. As long as human beings are involved, cheating in sport can no more be eliminated than crime can be eliminated from society. In this too-brief retrospective, let me share some of the positives that we would do well to remember as we continue to find ways to deal with rule breaking in sport.

■ Yes, MLB was slow to respond to the crisis as it developed. But when Commissioner Bud Selig did act, he did so vigorously. For that, Selig deserves credit. MLB remains the only pro sport in this country that has invited and authorized a fully independent investigation of drug use and finding programs to deal with it. Selig gave me complete independence. And when I made my report, Selig immediately adopted every single recommendation in my report that he could unilaterally adopt. For recommendations that required consent from the MLB Players Association, the two sides immediately entered negotiations and agreed to adopt most of the rest of our suggestions.

■ When we conducted the investigation, the players adamantly refused to cooperate in any way. Their association did its best to obstruct and prevent the investigation from being completed. I sent a letter to every player on a major league roster at the time, some 1,200 men, making the argument that a minority of players cheat by using performance-enhancing drugs, and that the principal victims of that are the majority of players who don't cheat. I made that argument based on listening to recently retired players who were no longer in the association and felt free to discuss the issue with me. In the intervening years, the players have come full circle and embraced that argument. They now support a rigorous testing program. That is a credit to them and gratifying to me.

■ I recommended a two-tier approach: strengthen the drug-testing program, with more tests that also were more random, *and* create a strong investigative arm that looked into abuse by players outside of testing and looked into evidence more vigorously. When the report was released, the media concentrated on the star players implicated in it, but the substance of the report was to both improve detection and reduce abuse. Before the report, MLB had little investigative capacity, meaning that, for all intents and purposes, there had to be evidence of use *in the form of a failed test* before any discipline would occur. Only after great public pressure, including congressional hearings, had the players and the league earlier agreed to even limited testing. But it was common knowledge then as well as now that tests aren't perfect. Strengthening the investigative arm had to be part of an effective long-term response to the problem.

Looking back more than a decade, we can see the benefits of adopting an independent investigation and giving that team the mandate of generating action-based ideas to implement. We can acknowledge that there was compromise on both sides. I believe my investigators proved the benefits of listening and providing leadership by making recommendations that were unpopular but forward-thinking to entrenched groups of people. I hope this work has made baseball, and sport generally, more transparent and aspirational.

Used with permission of George Mitchell.

You deal with facts when they are presented to you. You make decisions on what is in front of you. I don't think it's healthy to dwell on "what if?" Make your decision and move forward. That is why consensus building is so important. It provides you with an opportunity to process a variety of viewpoints. After your decision is made, whether it proved successful or not, you know that you made the decision with the best information available.

Despite my insistence on teamwork and multiple viewpoints, I would be negligent not to supply an example of when I forged ahead without asking for much feedback. You have to read situations to determine whether to lead from behind, or be more dictatorial, or when to enlist more help. A decade before the USA Basketball opportunity arose, I was in New York talking with David Stern. I stated clearly that we had a problem. I didn't like the way the pro game looked, and I felt we needed to make changes. Isolation basketball and muggings in the lane left the smaller players without a shot. Our guidelines for illegal defense were utterly baffling, for coaches, players, referees, officials, and the media.

David asked me to assemble a committee, and I did. Twelve top basketball minds met, and we made a number of significant changes that sped up the game and increased scoring. We allowed only 8 seconds instead of 10 to advance the ball past midcourt. We did away with arcane defensive guidelines, added lane violations on offense, cut back on the isolation game, and disallowed hand checking.

The normal procedure at that point would have been to go to the rules and competition committee, which had one representative from each team, and then go to all 30 coaches and ask for their thoughts on what we were considering. But knowing how some of them vote in their own interests and not the best interest of the game, I went before the committee and said, "Look guys, I used to chair this committee for a number of years, I know how the game is played. Here's what we're going to do. I'm just going to announce to you what we're doing. You don't have a vote. And here's why. . . ."

Next up were the coaches. There were three who were upset that they weren't consulted, all legends—Phil Jackson, Larry Brown, and Pat Riley. Another legend, Lenny Wilkins, was chair of the coaches group at that time. He spoke first: "Hey, you all know Jerry," Lenny said. "I just want to remind some of you who don't know the whole story, that most every benefit we have as an organization, you can thank Jerry because he always had our back." He then handed me the mic, and I took the same approach with the coaches. I told; I didn't ask.

Those rules changes have been widely applauded, and the quality and flow of NBA basketball is better than ever. We brought knowledgeable people together to determine what needed to be done. Then, when it came to executing the plan, we took a different route. In other words, consensus building was the answer on the front end, but not the back end. Depending on circumstances, consensus building takes many forms.

CONSENSUS BUILDING BUILDS ON ITSELF

The last point I want to make is about the long-term value of a commitment to consensus building in your professional philosophy and career. I left my Chicago home and a wonderful job with the young Bulls franchise to come out West and build a winner with the Suns. We won plenty, yet an NBA championship always eluded me. Look at all that transpired from that decision, though. Many experiences that I never could have dreamed of back in 1968 when I arrived in the Valley of the Sun: Arena football (where the Rattlers won two championships), WNBA basketball with the successful Phoenix Mercury, a real estate company, and of course, the Diamondbacks, who won a World Series Championship in just our fourth year, the quickest title in the illustrious history of MLB. I've been able to give back to the sport business world not just by chairing USA Basketball, but by lending my name and services to the Colangelo College of Business and as basketball program advisor at Grand Canyon University. These results would never have been possible without my ability to foster consensus. Maybe my greatest reward is being able to share my insights at an institution that shares

SUPPORT HELPED NEW GM LEARN ON THE JOB

Ann Meyers Drysdale

Ann Meyers Drysdale is a pioneer and one of the most decorated basketball players in history, but when she was a new general manager for the Phoenix Mercury she and her colleagues found consensus to make one of the franchise's biggest—and best—decisions. Meyers Drysdale is vice president and an award-winning broadcaster for the Phoenix Mercury and Phoenix Suns, following five seasons as Mercury GM, where she constructed the franchise's first two WNBA Championship teams in 2007 and 2009. She was VP in 2014 for their third title.

Meyers Drysdale was enshrined in the Naismith Basketball Hall of Fame (1993) and the inaugural Women's Basketball Hall of Fame class (1999) and was the first American woman inducted into the FIBA Hall of Fame (2007). She was the first high school player to make a U.S. national team (1974) and later was the first woman to receive a full

Courtesy of Barry Gossage.

athletic scholarship from UCLA, where she set 12 school records, led the Bruins to the 1978 national title, and was the first male or female to become a four-time Kodak All-American. She also competed in volleyball at UCLA and was part of a national championship track team (1975). As part of the first women's U.S. Olympic basketball team, Meyers Drysdale earned a silver medal at the 1976 Montreal Games.

The first player drafted in the Women's Professional Basketball League (1978) by the New Jersey Gems, Meyers Drysdale became Most Valuable Player and remains as the only female to sign a free-agent contract with an NBA team when she signed with the Indiana Pacers (1979). Her autobiography, *You Let Some Girl Beat You?*, was released in conjunction with the 40th anniversary of Title IX in the summer of 2012.

Meyers Drysdale has five sisters and five brothers, including brother Dave Meyers, who played basketball at UCLA. In 1986, she married former Los Angeles Dodgers Hall of Fame pitcher Don Drysdale. It was the first time a husband and wife were each members of their respective sports' halls of fame. The Southern California native and Drysdale, who passed away in 1993, have three children: sons Don Jr. (D.J.) and Darren, and daughter Drew.

I had been on the job as general manager of the Phoenix Mercury for only seven months when the 2007 WNBA Draft arrived. Despite having the lowest odds of every team in the draft lottery, we were fortunate enough to secure the first pick.

(continued)

That may seem like a dream scenario for a GM, but it also meant I felt a little bit of pressure. Fans, understandably, get excited about the first overall pick, and a team's decision makers want to make the best move for the franchise. Fortunately, I had the unwavering support of the rest of the team leadership. Before the draft, I had many discussions with Head Coach Paul Westhead about the possibility of trading away the top pick, and we were able to have buy-in from our top executives, including President and Chief Operating Officer Jay Parry, Director of Marketing Amber Cox, and Phoenix Suns President and Chief Operating Officer Rick Welts. I personally had to have confidence in myself to make the decision, but Westhead and I were in agreement that this was the best and quickest way to improve the Mercury. I had been a broadcaster for years before taking the GM position. I knew the players around the WNBA, and I knew the players coming out of the college ranks. All of my colleagues had a lot of experience to draw on too.

On draft day, we took Duke point guard Lindsey Harding with the #1 overall pick. Then, as planned, we traded Harding to Minnesota for Tangela Smith. Some fans didn't agree with the move, which is a reaction any GM gets accustomed to. Now, Smith was a five-time all-star at that point in her career, but I understood the concerns. Smith was 30 years old. The Mercury had not finished above fourth place in the West Conference since 1998. Some fans prefer to build around young talent. In this case, Coach Westhead and I believed Smith would be the missing piece in his system. We were confident that we had made a trade that would improve our team. It was a good feeling when we won our first WNBA title that summer and our second two years later, with Smith playing a vital role in those championships. In 2012, *SB Nation* called Smith-for-Harding the best trade in Mercury franchise history (Friday 2012).

I learned three things from that experience:

1. Take the shot. I had a long basketball career, but as a newcomer to the front office, taking the shot took on a new meaning. It meant being willing to do the unpopular.

2. Embrace the passion of your stakeholders. In this case, that meant our fans. Even if others disagree with you, if you and they have the same objective, then don't take criticism personally. Be glad that they are invested along with you in achieving success.

3. Most importantly, be grateful for the support you get. I made a lot of mistakes in my first few months as GM. We as management consistently communicated with each other and made decisions as a team, including what to do with our prized draft pick. Though we worked together to make the trade, as GM my name would be attached to the results, good or bad, and they had confidence I could handle that responsibility. When you get an opportunity, it means somebody believes in you. Keep that in mind when you doubt yourself, because I can tell you, you will occasionally doubt yourself. When I tried out for the Indiana Pacers—the first woman to ever try out for an NBA team— some people were resistant toward me. But many others believed in me and helped me. I have always had tremendous support, and I hope I never take that for granted. In a family with 11 children, and having raised a family of my own with my late husband Don Drysdale, that is a blessing indeed.

Used with permission of Ann Meyers Drysdale.

my Christian values as GCU does. That creates a legacy. See figure 16.1 to help you articulate where you want to go in your career.

WHAT HAPPENED WITH USA BASKETBALL

After agreeing to chair USA Basketball in early 2005, I set to work enacting a plan based on what I had seen and what I believed, namely that we had lost respect in the international basketball community and we needed to show respect to

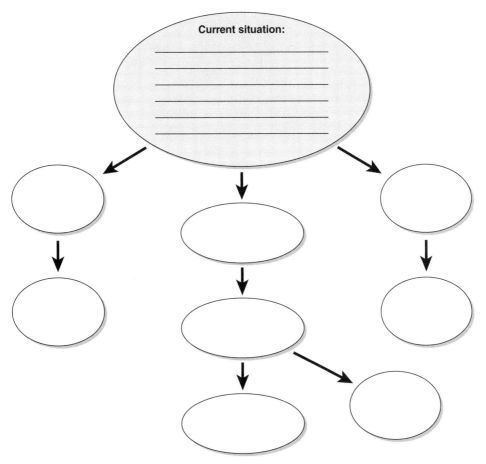

This brainstorming exercise is a fun way to ask yourself what you want to achieve. Start with your current situation in the large oval and then add new opportunities and spin-offs that might arise from that starting point. Create your own ovals as needed. Don't tie yourself down to anything you write here. For example, if I started with "GM of Suns" in the large oval back in the late 1960s, I never would have thought of "arena football" as another oval on the page. Don't write only what seems realistic. Dream a little. And ask yourself which directions are most appealing to you, then discuss with a trusted mentor or family member.

Current situation:

How can a consensus-building emphasis in your career help to make these possible career paths come true? In particular, consider how one oval leads directly to another oval.

Figure 16.1   Career brainstorming.

From R. Horrow, *The Sport Business Handbook* (Champaign, IL: Human Kinetics, 2020).

the rest of the world in order to get it back. I looked at some of the outstanding programs and what they had done, such as creating a national team roster of players that fit well together instead of an all-star roster. Philosophically, that made sense to me as a former coach, player, and executive.

I called a meeting in Chicago of all the former Olympic coaches going back to 1960 and a number of great Olympians, all the great names you could think of. We had about 40 people at an all-day meeting, and if you had been a basketball fly, that would have been the greatest room in your lifetime to be in. These were people who responded to me because of relationships we had nurtured through the years. They knew that ultimately the call would be mine in terms of selection. But they were there because they cared. I called on each of them and asked, "What did being an Olympian mean to you? Tell us about your experience. How do you read everything today? What do you think needs to be done?" Every one of them had a forum, and for them to share all of that was incredible to witness.

Then I put a list of coaches on the board and let them all talk to that subject. I followed that by doing the same with players, position by position. They knew I would make the final decisions, but my thinking was, who better to go to than guys who had done it, and experienced it, and had strong opinions? I cherished their opinions because I respected them. That's the ultimate in consensus building, in terms of turning around an entire program. With that inspiring beginning, we rebuilt the framework of respect that has, as of this writing, led to three Olympic gold medals and two golds and a bronze in the FIBA World Cup, plus a strong reputation in an increasingly competitive basketball universe.

References

Colangelo, J. 1998. *How You Play the Game: Lessons for Life From the Billion-Dollar Business of Sports.* AMACON.

Friday, S. 2012. "The Phoenix Mercury's Best Trade Ever: Tangela Smith for Lindsey Harding." *SB Nation,* August 22, 2012. www.swishappeal.com/2012/8/22/3259154/wnba-phoenix-mercurys-best-trade-tangela-smith.

Courtesy of Syracuse University.

CHAPTER 17

The Importance of Marketing in Deal Making

Rick Burton

Rick Burton is the David B. Falk Professor of Sport Management in Syracuse University's David B. Falk College of Sport and Human Dynamics. Previously, he served as executive director of the University of Oregon's Warsaw Sports Marketing Center, chief marketing officer for the U.S. Olympic Committee, and Commissioner of Australia's National Basketball League. He coauthors a regular column with Norm O'Reilly for *Sports Business Journal,* and their third book together, *20 Secrets to Success for NCAA Student-Athletes Who Won't Go Pro*, was published by Ohio University Press in 2018.

Because I was National Basketball League (the NBL) Commissioner from 2003 to 2007 before working as the chief marketing officer of the United States Olympic Committee for the 2008 Beijing Summer Olympic Games, I've seen my share of contract negotiations that led to different types of marketing.

Before those two postings, I was actually the advertising manager for Miller Lite Beer and then worked closely with the National Football League's then marketing arm, NFL Properties. Throughout my career journey, I watched closely the marketing initiatives of individuals and organizations I respected and admired. Given that scrutiny (something I couldn't help but do for the last 35 years), I wanted to present a few of them here because collectively I think they will inform readers about the importance of marketing in deal making.

The first on my list would involve NBA Commissioner Emeritus David Stern. I frequently tell students about David's insight in running a truly global league and his foresight in switching the marketing of the NBA from the teams in the league to the individuals who made the league great. He moved the emphasis in how the league and its TV partners promoted the game, from one of showcasing

Team A versus Team B (e.g., the Celtics versus the Lakers) to one of calling attention to a Larry Bird versus Magic Johnson matchup. Or a Michael Jordan versus Charles Barkley showdown.

The genius in David's strategic pivot, despite his intense obligation to work within network broadcast contracts and the nuances of the National Basketball Players Association (think collective bargaining agreements and revenue sharing), was understanding NBA fans were amazed by the individuals. And the marketing of those players was more important, on many levels, than advertising the NBA or discussing the business deals required to make the league work.

David has always been a stickler for details and I've never known anything to get by him. He has been a voracious reader not only of the news (across multiple industries) but also of the cultural tea leaves. He's always had a sense for where the NBA's fans were and where they wanted to go next. To me, an instinctual understanding of the NBA's fans, owners, players, and the media covering the games (the de facto free marketing of the NBA) is what made Stern one of the greatest league commissioners ever.

The next three people I so greatly admired (as I still do today) are Nike founder and Chairman Phil Knight, the aforementioned Michael Jordan (now owner of the Charlotte Hornets), and his then agent David Falk because there is no doubting those three combined to change the way athletes and an entire sport are seen.

I can write those words because I know a little about utilizing athletes to market and sell a brand.

SPORT MARKETING REVIEW: FROM LESS FILLING TO FLYING HIGH

As I mentioned, during the late 1980s I was lucky enough to work as the advertising manager for Miller Lite Beer. Lite had become hugely popular during the 1970s and '80s for leveraging football and baseball stars like Dick Butkus, Bubba Smith, Deacon Jones, Ray Nitschke, Brooks Robinson, Frank Robinson, Billy Martin, Bob Uecker, and Marv Throneberry.

Due to federal laws, athletes needed to be retired in order for Miller Lite to use them (active athletes couldn't, at the time, endorse alcoholic products). This legal hurdle meant we were always waiting to see who had stopped playing before we considered them for arguing about whether our product was "Less Filling" or "Tastes Great."

Those ads (created by the ad agency Backer & Spielvogel—and the best ones were finished long before I assumed the role as Lite's advertising manager)—were hugely loved. They were an early form of "Must See TV" not only because they were legitimately funny but because they were also amazingly adept at showcasing the brand's best attributes. The beer tasted great, and because it had a third fewer calories than Miller High Life, beer drinkers wouldn't get filled up.

But as the Lite Beer campaign reached the end of a remarkable run in the middle to late '80s, a shoe company, Nike, behind Phil Knight's instinctual brilliance, upped the ante considerably by featuring active athletes like tennis star John McEnroe, baseball–football cross-trainer Bo Jackson, and budding hoops legend Michael Jordan.

The greatest of those endorsers was Jordan, and I've often been asked to comment on Michael Jordan. Few would argue Jordan's complete domination of the game or his brilliance as a player. In fact, when he retired from the NBA the first time, I was quoted that week in *Time, Newsweek,* and *U.S. News & World Report* about Jordan's heroic legacy.

What was clear to just about everyone was that during his professional basketball career, Jordan's work with Nike was building the Air Jordan brand, a product line that still dominates at retail and is still seen on the feet of college athletes (think Jordan's alma mater the University of North Carolina or the University of Michigan) and many current professionals.

What I later learned from reading David Falk's book *The Bald Truth* (2009) provided some clarifying insight into an area I rarely see addressed. It is simple but reinforces concepts I always mention when lecturing at Syracuse University. The point is this: Be willing to go away from the crowd. To imagine and then perform the counterintuitive. To go small when others go big. To zig when they zag. And to see "marketing" as an army waiting to be unleashed.

Let me give you a fairly lengthy example. In the afterword of *The Bald Truth,* before Michael was even an NBA rookie for the Chicago Bulls, Falk discusses how Nike was getting ready to bring out Michael's first Air Jordan shoes. At the time (circa 1984), the designers wanted a shoe that was black (when almost every other basketball shoe was white). And they wanted a big red Swoosh.

Not cool. Ugly. Won't work.

That's what people were undoubtedly prepared to say.

What they forgot was who was actually wearing the shoes. Nike was about to create dynamic marketing via television advertising and print ads. And the marketing wasn't going to be hollow. Great advertising for a bad product is destructive. Great marketing with a solid product and a great endorser is always meaningful.

So much so that Nike generated $130 million in revenues with those Jordan sneakers. But then, when everyone else went to black and red, Nike and Jordan pivoted again. The Air Jordan II was white. Stark white. And collectively the messaging began suggesting, "Sorry, black and red aren't cool anymore. White is cool."

DEALS COME AND GO, BRANDS LIVE ON

You may well ask at this point how that story ties to the importance of marketing in deal making, and I will tell you that it's a pertinent question. So much has been written in the past about the "art of the deal," the importance of winning the negotiation, the concept of "Deal or No Deal" . . . but the "deal" is only a moment in time.

The marketing of the brand, the presentation of the product or the endorser, is what lives in the minds and lives of the consumer. The fan. The person spending the money to buy shoes, tickets, sweatshirts, miniature football helmets or miniature baseball helmets with ice cream in them. The fan doesn't see the deal, doesn't care about the agreement, and doesn't understand the terms of the contract.

Fans understand what they see. And they experience the dynamic in two places: on the court or field and in the various ways the parties market a combination of ideas.

Think of it this way: In the early 1980s, after Jordan finished playing for UNC, he had the good fortune to play in and dominate the 1984 Summer Olympic Games. At the same time, Nike and Knight wanted to sell lots of basketball sneakers to the millions of individuals who played the game. But so did Converse, New Balance, Pony, Puma, Adidas, and Reebok.

No one other than Jordan may have fully grasped how great he would become. As it was, few people now remember that Jordan wasn't even the first draft pick the year he became available. He was picked third.

DAVID FALK

David Falk knew Jordan would be very, very good. Certainly on the court, but his charisma and marketing upside held far greater promise than his shooting, rebounding, or defense. What Falk saw was Jordan's potential to reinvent the American ideal, if marketed correctly.

There had been greats in the American endorser pantheon before: Jack Armstrong (the All-American Boy), Chuck Taylor, Johnny Weissmuller (as Tarzan), Olympic pole vaulter Bob Richards (for Wheaties), and Mickey Mantle (for numerous products). All had been white. None of them played basketball. None of them offered the rare combination of what Falk called "style and substance."

Falk understood that Michael could be a global brand ambassador but he needed to be All-American first. He and Jordan steered away from thinking about global giants like Toyota or Nissan. They wanted to think more about McDonald's, Coca-Cola, and Chevrolet. But more important than those giants was the shoe Jordan would wear.

When a sport star tells a consumer to buy a car or a shirt, there are a few things we need to understand. First, the consumer may think the athlete is representing the car only for the endorsement money. Secondly, there is a chance the fan or consumer may believe the athlete knows nothing about cars and therefore isn't particularly credible. Customers may consider the car but they don't have an imminent, overpowering belief yet.

NIKE AND PHIL KNIGHT

With Jordan, a shoe endorsement would be very authentic. Playing for the Chicago Bulls, Jordan would wear *his* shoe every night. It would inform his jumping,

MODERN SPORT MARKETERS MUST VALUE THE EXPERIENCE

Chris Lencheski

Chris Lencheski explains how marketing is all about an emotional connection, whether selling shoes or developing partnerships in other areas. Lencheski is the global commercial partnerships director at MP & Silva and has authored industry-setting standards and practice guidelines followed by major entities from network and cable television groups to Fortune 500 companies. Chris served as vice chairman and CEO of IRG Sports & Entertainment—a TPG Specialty Lending Company, encompassing more than 1,150 motorsports, live entertainment, and corporate events annually. Prior to IRGSE, he was president of Comcast Spectacor's subsidiary Front Row Marketing and Analytics (FRMS). Lencheski was a multiple-team owner in the NASCAR Sprint and Nationwide Series, as well as owner of International Hockey League franchise the Quad City Mallards, affiliate of the NHL Philadelphia Flyers. Lencheski is a graduate of Syracuse University, where he is a four-term board member of the Falk College of Sports and Human Dynamics; an alumnus of Harvard Business School; and an adjunct professor at Columbia University.

I didn't get into sport per se, sport got into me . . . and at a very early age. Sport via the experiences that I had from playing, as well as being a fan, spanned from my early youth into my college years—then later in adulthood as a sport marketing professional. I was very blessed and truly fortunate to have had the ability early in my college days to foresee that the sports I played and viewed were changing, and the central nexus was the growing awareness on the part of companies that the experiences around these sports mattered. They mattered to many people, such as fans—fans who when serving as tribal supporters of their teams or dressed as their favorite athletes would act in a manner, if programmed correctly, that was very powerful commercially in support of their interests in their personal sport competition.

When I saw the forces of commerce and sport coming together, it was my opinion that moving into this line of work could be a most amazing ride. At 20 years in this business, I can look around as an architect and former sport agency owner of SKI & Company, one of the early and truly great agencies until its sale; as a team owner in NASCAR and minor league professional sport; as a CEO of a Comcast Spectacor sport company; and currently as a vice chairman and CEO of a publicly held

(continued)

MODERN SPORT MARKETERS MUST VALUE THE EXPERIENCE   *(continued)*

investment fund's holding company owning racing series and tracks. I feel blessed to receive calls from CEOs, leagues, and commissioners about strategy surrounding their respective lines of business in sport, which is a genuine privilege.

When I entered this business, there was no formal degree from any university, and the clear majority of sport executives were former professional players who had few to no specific educational paths to their roles; what they had was experience. There's that word again—experience. If the nexus was commerce and sport, then experience was the glue, and these experiences are what the modern-day sport marketers must evaluate to unlock value for their company's goals with sport as an instrument for economic change.

To understand *why* these experiences matter, go back in time and try to remember your very first trip as a child with your family or friends to a sport event—for illustration, a professional sporting event. Ask yourself if you remember what brand of car you were riding in to the game, what brand of sneakers you wore, what brand of shirt you wore, how much money your parents made, or what kind of neighborhood you lived in. I will assume with the benefit of life experience that you don't recollect most, if any, of that. But what you probably do remember is the way the *experience* of going made *you feel*! It made you feel love—love of the family or friends, the team, the game you were seeing. You likely remember the experience from door to turnstile to smells to tastes to sounds; a collection of these experiences makes a life. These experiences are authentic and evergreen in life, as they are refreshed with each passing year. These experiences matter much more to companies that market their product through commercial support of sport, and sport as an instrument for such allows a company to unlock emotive value for their brand or product. Sport, as a platform, is among the most powerful instruments in converting from "awareness" to "trial" and then to "adoption" of any one particular brand or service product.

We live in a skeptical, ever on-demand world, and so as sport professionals, we will be judged by the experience we gave, allowed, or provided. Those companies that tap into the "point of hatch" for those experiences will be the better for it; and I wish all of them the best of success as they chart a course of making experiences matter, whether this be as a player or marketer.

running, shooting, dunking, crossing over, and backpedaling and these shoes would never leave his feet. In one small way, the shoes were more important than the jersey or shorts because those things existed to market the Bulls, the NBA, and the league's official apparel supplier.

So consider this: Nike wanted to sell millions of shoes and Michael wanted to maximize his potential as an endorser. But pro sport careers are short, and no one can predict how long an athlete's knees or ankles will hold up. We also know players aren't robots or straw scarecrows to simply hang things on.

So Jordan's deal with Nike was key, but the marketing by Nike (and its ad agency Wieden+Kennedy) is what so influenced me (as a marketer) and set the stage for all of Michael's other future relationships. If Nike had gotten the marketing wrong with the one product that helped build Jordan's athletic success, they would greatly reduce his potential (and his credibility) with isotonic drinks, carbonated beverages, and anything else Jordan might consider endorsing.

That's why the Nike deal with Jordan was so legendary. Knight has talked about this before (his book *Shoe Dog* is brilliant, by the way) but, in short, Nike sped up the evolution of modern sport marketing by thinking not just about shoes but also about apparel (clothing lines) and other new products. Ultimately, Nike was willing to think long term and not associate Michael with the same shoe year in and year out. They understood that Jordan's products must evolve in the same way advertising changes every season.

Today, these aspects of strategy and vision sound logical and possibly even commonplace. But by 1986, as Michael Jordan came to dominate basketball, the importance of marketing in all of his agreements could not be overstated.

BRINGING STAR AND SHOE TOGETHER

So let's go back to the start of this example. Nike wants to sell shoes. Lots of them. And Jordan wants the right kind of relationship to serve as the foundation for his pro career. The big question is how does he get that first marketing arrangement right?

In Falk's book, he remembers saying to Nike executives, "If you sign Michael, then you need to know we are looking for something radically different than anything you've ever done in the past. We want him treated like a tennis player. We want him to have his own line of products, which would be promoted individually and apart from the team" (p. 54).

He also told them—and in my mind this was really bold at the time—that this negotiation was much more about what Nike was willing to spend promoting Michael's line of branded products than it was about what they were ultimately going to pay Michael. To paraphrase President John F. Kennedy's famous quote, it wasn't about what Michael could do for Nike but what Nike could do for Michael. This approach meant Falk was asserting this maxim: What Nike must do for Jordan in marketing was ultimately more important than its straight financial provision.

Now, don't get me wrong or think I'm undervaluing the financial aspects of a contract. Jordan certainly didn't. But the marketing commitment Jordan wanted was what tipped the scales. Falk and Jordan could easily place endorsement dollars from the various sneaker contenders in columns and easily determine the winner. But marketing plans and design intuition were far more intriguing and, for my money, far more important.

As most folks who have followed basketball, Nike, or popular advertising during the last 30 years probably know, Nike got the marketing right—starting with a video that finished with a branded logo reading, "Air Jordan. Basketball by Nike."

Sports marketing would never be the same.

More importantly, Nike showed they could successfully buck the conventional approach traditionally used at Converse, an aging brand already boasting play-

GAME CHANGER

THE FIRST SHOE DEAL CAME NATURALLY

Sonny Vaccaro

Sonny Vaccaro's visionary promotional innovations (beginning with the signing of Michael Jordan to his first major endorsement package) revolutionized the sport marketing genre with shoe contracts, team affiliations, and other groundbreaking promotional partnerships. In 30-plus years in the shoe industry, he brought his marketing and player development acumen to basketball programs at the world's three largest athletic shoe and apparel companies. Beginning in 1965, Vaccaro created several of the leading events in grassroots basketball. The Roundball Classic, America's original high school all-star game, was his first major event, begun as the Dapper Dan Roundball Classic in Pittsburgh. The most widely imitated event in prep basketball, this charitable game annually brought together the 22 most gifted high school all-stars in the country, and holds the all-time attendance record for a high school all-star event. From 1984 through 2006, the annual invitation-only camp, ABCD Camp, held each July was a must-be-there event that showcased the next wave of standout basketball players for scouts and college coaches. Sonny's Big Time Tournament in Las Vegas became the largest summer basketball tournament in the world, featuring more than 300 teams and 4,000 high school players. Vaccaro established the nonprofit organization Hoops That Help in 1990. Contributions have surpassed $4 million over the years for programs benefitting the homeless, AIDS education, Boys & Girls Clubs, and other charities.

In addition to helping produce the highly rated TV special, *A Comedy Salute to Michael Jordan*, Vaccaro continues to make media appearances because his frank and often controversial perspectives on student-athlete rights, regulatory hypocrisy, limitations on young athletes crossing over to professional status, and other hot-button issues have made him a widely sought-after guest on programs such as *60 Minutes*, HBO's *Real Sports* and *On the Record With Bob Costas, CBS Evening News*, PBS' *Frontline*, ABC's *Nightline* and *Good Morning America*, and ESPN's *Outside the Lines*. Vaccaro was featured in *Sole Man*, an ESPN original film for their *30 for 30* documentary series focusing on aspects of Vaccaro's life in basketball, sport marketing, and the landmark *O'Bannon v. NCAA* federal class action antitrust law suit. In the *O'Bannon v. NCAA* litigation, which has momentous implications for the future of collegiate athletics and athletes, Sonny served as a catalyst in a case brought to uphold the rights of players seeking to retain ownership of their images subsequent to their participation in collegiate athletics. In this game-changing case, Vaccaro served as an unpaid consultant by lead counsel Hausfeld LLP.

It started when I helped create the Dapper Dan Roundball Classic in my hometown of Pittsburgh, Pennsylvania. The first all-star game of its kind.

I marvel at the thought of how a kid from tiny Trafford, Pennsylvania, became arguably one of the most influential people in basketball. I rubbed elbows with some of the most influential coaches in the game and I grew as close as anyone to some of the biggest names to ever play the sport, from inner-city playgrounds to Hall of Famers.

The Dapper Dan paved the way toward an innovation that would completely transform basketball. Back then, there were no shoe deals. Coaches and schools paid for shoes and uniforms for their teams. It was 1977 and I was sitting across the table from Phil Knight at the Nike headquarters in Beaverton, Oregon, and I proposed that the company pay college coaches so their players would wear our shoes. In that moment of inspiration, I had innocently created the first-ever team shoe deal.

That idea led to another concept a few years later in 1983 that would transform Nike from a multimillion-dollar company to a multibillion-dollar shoe and apparel empire. That story too began with a spark of insight. Rob Strasser had the idea to create a signature shoe to build Nike's entire brand platform around. With total conviction, I said, you can pull that off only by giving the money to one guy—not the two or three top prospects they recommended. And for me there was only one player who had that level of athletic genius and charisma: Michael Jordan. With that decision, the first-ever individual player signature shoe deal was created.

I retired from the shoe business in 2007 having successfully created a system that rewarded coaches and athletes for wearing branded product. I have been credited as the father of sport marketing and other humbling titles, but I never set out to do something that had never been done before—the innovation came naturally based on inspiration and intuition.

In retirement, I have pushed for reform that would provide some means of compensation for the athletes to capitalize on their names and likenesses. Toward that end, I joined in a federal lawsuit with Ed O'Bannon, whom I knew very well as he rose through the basketball ranks in my elite events. A former national champion forward from UCLA, he had seen his number and likeness prominently featured in a video game, without consent or compensation long after he had graduated. Winning the O'Bannon case returned the rights of athletes to retain their name and likeness and to seek compensation for use in the future. This case was one of the most gratifying events in my life. The NCAA's decades of abuses related to use of athletes' personas had to be stopped somewhere.

Most recently in 2017, we learned of the adidas NCAA scandal; the main difference from past recruiting issues over the years is that this was the first in which offenders were being investigated by the federal government. There will continue to be scandals until the NCAA's "shamateurism" system is fixed and the athletes are rightly compensated.

My career achievements came from understanding the marketplace, speaking my mind, and seeking justice for the players whose athletic skills represent the single most valuable contribution to the game. I recommend that any young person who aspires to join the sport–entertainment world do the same and have the empathy and sensibilities to appreciate the sacrifices athletes have made to sustain the viability of these multibillion-dollar industries.

Game Changer: The First Shoe Deal Came Naturally, by Sonny Vaccaro. Used with permission.

ers like Magic Johnson, Julius Erving, Larry Bird, and others. Perhaps Converse thought Jordan would fit in as just another player in its stable.

Historians and fans are probably smiling at the thought of Jordan as "just another player."

Turns out Michael became a six-time world champion and arguably the greatest athlete-endorser ever. Not bad considering no one knows how much money Michael ever made from Nike. And not bad because few people in the sport world will ever forget his imprint on marketing.

Not surprisingly, Air Jordan became the greatest basketball shoes ever sold (far surpassing the old Chuck Taylor high tops) and Jordan became one of the most recognizable athletes in any sport, in any country. Let's not doubt that Michael's marketing prowess for Nike (and others; remember Gatorade's famous "Be Like Mike"?) really helped drive attendance for the Chicago Bulls and the NBA, while securing basketball's global appeal.

Michael Jordan and Bugs Bunny (*Space Jam*)? Impossible. Michael Jordan and Spike Lee as Mars Blackmon ("Money, it's gotta be the shoes")? Unimaginable. Michael Jordan, the greatest hoopster ever, switching to baseball? Stop.

Jordan's marketing visibility ultimately influenced every NBA contract and gave Jordan the financial foundation he needed to ultimately purchase the NBA's Charlotte Hornets.

THE CONSTANCY OF GOOD MARKETING

But what if, as you are reading this, you are saying, "Well, Rick, that was good for Jordan back in the 1980s when companies like Nike or Gatorade could create image trajectories for athletes they liked. Let's be honest, as we approach 2020, the media and marketing landscape is dramatically different. Companies like Amazon, Netflix, YouTube, Facebook, Twitter, and Snapchat didn't exist then. Isn't the marketing portion of deal making much different?"

My short answer, "no," may surprise you. The concept of marketing (what it means to "market" a product, good, service, or individual) is always evolving but also fairly constant. Pricing, placement, product, promotion, payment, populations, pushing, pulling, people, and power (*the heck with 5 Ps of marketing; here are 10 Ps*) are all levers an agent, player, employee, or CEO must consider.

If you are going to zig when they zag, you have to know the marketplace. If you are going to play small ball against a team of giants, you have to make your threes. You have to believe you can beat the favorite (shout out here to Malcolm Gladwell's wonderful book *David and Goliath*). If you are going to be counterintuitive, you have to really know what's going on.

Today, my Syracuse students know we start by looking at the individual athlete and assessing the marketplace as it really exists. I tell them we all exist in a global economy. A digital economy. A 24/7/365 economy. An instant economy.

Today's young people understand that technology is changing faster than most people can grasp what is happening. One of my favorite authors is Thomas Friedman and his brilliant book from 2016, *Thank You for Being Late*, where he discussed the realities of contemporary life and how our use of technology borders on all-consuming.

I know Friedman is right. When I'm attending NBA or NFL games, I look up to find the folks around me spending more time looking at their phones than they do the game. I know college players who care more about how many "followers" they have than how many points they scored. I know individuals who care more about getting a Tweet out first than wondering whether their Tweet is accurate.

Are those bad things? Maybe. But modern marketers must understand market dynamics in order to best represent any contract or agreement they are working on. The late Stephen Covey in *The 7 Habits of Highly Effective People* wrote about negotiations that are based on achieving "Win-Win," a naturally better option than "Lose-Win" or "Lose-Lose."

But let's add to the concept of "winning" the idea of comprehensively projecting far more than the deal on the table. There is more at stake than just the chips in the pot. Let's not play for the cash wagered but also for the table, chairs, and house.

If Nike's success with John McEnroe, Charles Barkley, Bo Jackson, Tiger Woods, or Michael Jordan teaches us anything, it might be that marketing successful individuals (who are capable of thriving in powerful partnerships) is best achieved when all parties take the long view. And take the marketing portion of the agreement really seriously.

The fact that Jordan became a hugely successful businessman long after his playing days were over is pretty impressive. And not just because Nike wanted to increase market share and annual earnings for their stakeholders. Rather, it was because the objectives of the brand and the endorser could be really leveraged in the same ways people think about annual compound interest.

LESSONS FROM AUSTRALIA

My final marketing hero comes from my time in Australia and involves that country's famous airline, Qantas. And I will use Qantas in this chapter to tell a story in which the brand didn't even get the "deal" but got the marketing right.

For the 2000 Summer Olympics in Sydney, numerous sponsors were pitched on serving as the official this or that for the Games. In the airline category, there were two considerations: Qantas and Ansett. For a variety of reasons, Ansett, the smaller of the two, won the coveted slot as the official airline of the Sydney Games. Qantas appears to have not been bothered. Despite losing the deal, they designed an ad campaign featuring a heartfelt Peter Allen song called "I Still Call Australia Home." In their commercials, they showed scenes of the Australian Girls Choir and National Boys Choir singing the heart-tugging tune in front of iconic Australian and global landmarks.

The ad campaign was so pervasive and so touching that foreigners and locals alike came to believe Qantas was the official airline sponsor for Australia's "Big Day Out." True, they outspent Ansett, but they used their loss of sponsorship

360

GLOBALIZATION OF THE SPORT AGENCY BUSINESS

Philip D.M. de Picciotto

Philip D.M. de Picciotto has been at the forefront of the sport and entertainment industry for 35 years, showing how globalization has permeated all aspects of the business. Over that time, Octagon has achieved a position of leadership in talent representation, property ownership, event management, and corporate marketing, and has been recognized for the breadth of its services, quality of its work product, global vision, and highly personalized approach. De Picciotto has been involved in many of the industry's most important initiatives, including the removal of tobacco sponsorship from professional tennis and the introduction of healthier drinks into New York City's public schools. He may be best known for building the brands and overseeing the careers of many of the world's most recognizable athletes

Courtesy of Octagon.

and celebrities, ranging from Super Bowl champions to Olympic gold medalists to royalty to network broadcasters.

Sport is a reflection of society, and nowhere is this more apparent than in the emergence of a truly connected, global sport landscape. As cultural and commercial interaction among world markets continues to accelerate, the globalization of sport has been one of the consistent pillars of competition, communication, and diplomacy.

As geopolitical barriers have disappeared, new regions are hosting events and supplying world-class athletes to leagues around the world. The fall of Communism and the opening of China have increased the number of super-wealthy business leaders with an appetite to play on a global stage, as well as a vastly expanded middle class of fans focused on consumerism. Added to this, the proliferation of media outlets has led to the need for endless amounts of content, which in turn has enhanced the need for agencies to navigate the complexities of reaching new and traditional audiences, fueling their emotions and interests, and enabling clients of all kinds to maximize their opportunities, if not just to survive.

On the brand side, international and global companies are looking to strengthen their presence in new or growing territories, or use assets in foreign markets to reach a TV audience back home. The rush of global brands to position themselves in China is one example of the former; early examples of the latter were Japanese brands sponsoring the Major League Baseball teams with Japanese stars on their rosters, and the signing of endorsement contracts by Chinese footwear brands with players on the NBA's Houston Rockets in order to capitalize on the TV interest in China generated by Yao Ming's superstar status.

Ownership of international properties has become commonplace. A growing number of American owners of NFL clubs now also own soccer clubs in Britain's Premier League, and Abu Dhabi United Group's ownership of Manchester City has led to follow-on acquisitions of stakes in major teams in Australia, Japan, Spain, Uruguay, and the United States. The professional tennis and golf tours are rooted in the global nature of their events, players, corporate sponsorships, and media rights.

The talent representation business is no longer a linear provision of employment (playing) negotiation services for an athlete, or the sale of a sponsorship to a corporate CEO who happens to be a fan of a particular athlete, team, or sport. Athletes now have a truly global platform on which to develop, train, and showcase their skills. Those at the high end have the opportunity to build their own brands, using social media and the conversation around sport to create value beyond the pitch.

The modern agency is the glue among all of the above, providing a broad range of services across platforms and territories that encompasses sophisticated strategic advice, marketing expertise, operational know-how, and the tactical implementation tools necessary to fulfill an unimaginably wide set of objectives in any sport or entertainment function in any part of the world. Data and research underpin every decision, and metrics provide measurement against objectives.

The win–lose mentality in sport has permeated the rest of society, and the gap between winning and losing is becoming increasingly consequential. Understanding how different cultures interact with sport is critical for good decision making, and the breadth of related expertise housed in the global agencies is an essential source of both value creation and risk management.

rights (which featured a significant cost) to make their marketing more compelling.

When I arrived in Sydney as the commissioner in 2003, I wanted to take a page out of the Stern–Jordan–Falk–Knight handbook. I wanted to celebrate the NBL's stars. But I quickly learned the American solution was not a good fit Down Under. Promoting the whole was more important than promoting the individual. The Aussies didn't fancy tall poppies.

A year later, when we signed Dutch electronics giant Philips as the league's naming rights partner (thus making it the Philips NBL), we figured out how to use all our teams and all of our players collectively. It was key to the deal and I'm happy to write we did some amazing marketing during those years, including staging a preseason tournament in Cairns (the gateway to the Great Barrier Reef and Australia's Heritage-listed rainforest), where we truly unified the look of our league and our relationship with Philips.

Hopefully, by now, you get my point. Great marketing loves the impossible, craves the dramatic opportunity, fires up the moment someone else says, "No. It can't be done. It won't work. It won't fly. They'll never go for that."

Great marketing has to be a part of every deal and when it's not there initially, it falls to someone to make sure it gets inserted. It must be imagined.

Great marketing builds and sustains great brands.

GREAT MARKETING SEES THE WHOLE COURT

Many people sell themselves or their products short. They fail to make the commitment to build a great identity. They don't want to get up early every day (with a competitive fire burning) to protect the image that consistently delivers on the promises and aspirations desired. I know that firsthand because I was fortunate enough to work with some of the most competitive humans I ever met during my time with the U.S. Olympic Committee.

Because of those experiences, I'd like to believe the best of the best never sign on to do poorly designed commercials. Those mega stars won't (or shouldn't) go for cheapened imagery. They shouldn't give in to concepts portraying them in any way other than who they are.

Big firms and amazing brands have undoubtedly waved crazy money at LeBron and Steph Curry, and the easiest thing in the world for those greats would be to take those dollars.

But the marketing done by the best of the best (Nike, McDonald's, Coca-Cola, Pepsi, Visa, Master Card, Lowe's, and so on) is what influences the trajectory an endorser gets. I won't say that good marketing is easy. Or that every athlete or agent gets it. But anyone who doesn't factor in the marketing and communications capacities of the brand involved should be avoided.

In a sense, every deal is a marketing agreement. Any time two parties bind themselves to an agreement, they create a new entity living and dying on the strength of the bond. Bad contracts don't imagine the future. Fast contracts for big dollars don't tend to work out or last because one party usually feels used.

Creators of great contracts, like great players, see the entire court, the stadium where the games are played, and, in rare cases such as the little movie Michael Jordan made for Warner Brothers, the entire galaxy.

References

Falk, D. 2009. *The Bald Truth*. New York: Gallery Books.

CHAPTER 18

Operating Successfully in the Public and Private Domains: The Birth of MAPS and the Rebirth of Oklahoma City

Ronald J. Norick

Born and raised in Oklahoma City, Ronald J. Norick was the city's mayor from 1987 to 1998. In 2008, he was inducted into the Oklahoma Hall of Fame. During Norick's 11 years in office, he and the Oklahoma City Chamber of Commerce conceived the original Metropolitan Area Projects Plan (MAPS), nine major Oklahoma City projects funded by a dedicated five-year, one-cent sales tax. MAPS is credited with leading Oklahoma City through a renaissance that made the city one of the most livable in the country. While in office, Norick also guided the city through the aftermath of the 1995 Oklahoma City bombing. Since leaving public office, he has remained an ardent supporter of MAPS and many community initiatives and organizations. He is currently chairman of the board of trustees at Oklahoma City University, the Oklahoma City Downtown TIF Review Committee, and the Oklahoma State Fair. Norick serves as vice chairman of the Oklahoma Industries Authority and the Alliance for Economic Development of Oklahoma City, Inc., and sits on the board of directors of the Oklahoma City Chamber of Commerce, BancFirst, and Merlon International. He and his wife, Kandy, have three children and seven grandchildren.

All that hard work and nothing to show for it. That's how we felt in October 1991 when United Airlines announced it had chosen to locate a large maintenance facility in Indianapolis instead of Oklahoma City. I had been mayor for four years, six months, and we had been working feverishly for over a year to win that prize. In February, the citizens had even passed a dedicated sales tax by a 72 percent margin, raising sales tax by one cent to pay for construction of the plant if United would come.

An unidentified source on the United site selection team said that Oklahoma City's proposal was "by far the best prepared, well organized, the most professional, the most responsive." So, why the hell didn't we win? Why had this happened?

As I asked these and other questions, I came to understand that United Chairman Stephen Wolf had decided he would rather be in a city where they had revitalized their downtown, brought in professional sport, and made quality of life a key factor. Oklahoma City was in the same position that Indianapolis had been in the 1970s—no vitality and no positive outlook. Our downtown was dying and we needed to do something. Indianapolis had done something about their city. Now, we needed to.

I thought if our citizens were willing to tax themselves to make their city look attractive to companies, then they ought to be willing to make themselves feel better about their own city. United was a bitter loss, but it was the best thing to happen to Oklahoma City. As with everything in life, time reveals these things. If we had been awarded United's maintenance facility, we would have wound up with an empty building and a bankrupt United Airlines like what Indianapolis had to eventually deal with. Our citizens would certainly have been upset with all that tax money raised and spent with nothing to show for it. But even more important, we would have had no MAPS program and no renovated and reenergized city the way we have today.

To appreciate how we turned a loss and made it a significant victory for a community, you first must understand the benefits of public–private partnerships.

BENEFITS OF PUBLIC–PRIVATE PARTNERSHIPS

When created in an effective and mutually beneficial manner, public–private partnerships allow the best of both the public and private sectors to blossom. They can fund large development projects that integrate needs of many stakeholders in a city, which in turn can lead to a communal feeling of unity as individuals and groups get to make use of the amenities. Such partnerships can also spread risk around, making the project more palatable for organizations that might otherwise be inclined to say no. All of this is true regardless of whether you develop a project at as grand a level as we did. It can be controversial and hard to sell public–private partnerships, but also very meaningful. Oklahoma City is now blessed with a world-class, vibrant downtown. But it was far from inevitable that we would get there.

MAPPING THE MAPS

So, how do you take a city with no downtown nightlife, few restaurants, and even fewer apartments and make it come alive? You go through an intensive and reflective process that includes three steps: (1) assessment, (2) choosing a course, and (3) generating consensus. I will guide you through that three-step process using the MAPS example throughout this chapter. I won't say that I saw the process in such distinct terms at that time, but I did know enough about the leadership required to get our work done. Recalling the process more completely in retrospect, and being able to explain it as a three-step process, will help you understand how to incorporate it into your decision making and your partnership building.

ASSESSMENT

Through the years, various projects had been kicked around in efforts to revive downtown Oklahoma City after the flight to the suburbs of the 1950s and '60s. But nothing had really ever gotten off the ground. One pressing need was our 30-year-old Triple A baseball stadium. All-Sports Stadium had been built at the State Fairgrounds in 1964, several miles from downtown. It no longer passed city codes or the newly passed Americans with Disabilities Act of 1990 requirements. So with this in mind, I started to piece together a plan during weekly talks with my city manager, Don Bown. Don had just been hired as city manager during the United process. We looked at an inventory of our publicly owned facilities. We had no money to deal with their problems and we couldn't take care of the properties.

You always need your civic leaders to guide you through any process like this, so I set up a small group of businessmen to get these discussions going. We had city officials such as City Manager Don Bown, Oklahoma County officials such as Commissioner Buck Buchanan and County Treasurer Joe B. Barnes. Chamber of Commerce officials such as bank president Ken Townsend and Kerr-McGee CEO Frank McPherson along with other businessmen such as Fred Jones Hall, president of Fred Jones Industries, Clay Bennett, chairman of Dorchester Capital, and Bill Johnstone of OKC Urban Renewal Authority were also involved in this process. This was our brainstorming group. One of the first things we decided as a group was to bring in a consultant to help us through the process. After several potential firms had been interviewed, Rick Horrow was chosen. Then we had to develop a list of what would be needed for the projects to be submitted to the citizens of Oklahoma City.

CHOOSING A COURSE

The group, along with consultant Rick Horrow, began looking at all the funding mechanisms from around the country that were being used by cities and states to fund projects. It was determined that because all the facilities were owned by the City of Oklahoma City, only city tax dollars could be used, eliminating the idea of a countywide tax that had previously been used by Oklahoma County to pay for the United Airlines facility had they come to Oklahoma City.

GAME CHANGER

HOW INDY USED SPORT TO BUILD CIVIC PRIDE

Greg Ballard

In the years before Oklahoma City's MAPS initiative, Indianapolis assessed its strategic situation and chose to use sport as an economic catalyst. Here, former Mayor Greg Ballard highlights why and how his hometown came to that decision. Ballard, a native of Indianapolis, served 23 years in the U.S. Marine Corps before becoming the city's 48th mayor. He is now a visiting fellow at the University of Indianapolis and was founder and chair of the Mayors Professional Sports Alliance for the United States Conference of Mayors.

Courtesy of Greg Ballard and Rob Banayote.

Before big sporting events became big sporting events, Indianapolis' reputation was mainly basketball. Our once-legendary high school state championship produced not only Oscar Robertson, but also state legend Bobby Plump, who still runs a restaurant in Indy named Plump's Last Shot. Bobby, now 80 years old and as feisty as ever, hit the actual last-second shot memorialized in the movie *Hoosiers*. Also, the Pacers were the dominant ABA franchise, and Bobby Knight was soon to follow. Other states had similar unique reputations, but in most cases, national interest was secondary to regional followings.

The ability of Indianapolis to host the biggest events with such precision didn't happen by accident. It was by design. Now, all those in the industry marvel at the relationship Indianapolis has with sport and the biggest events. The times in which this civic transformation occurred were much different than today. It happened mainly due to a civic sense of mission by so many who wanted to propel Indianapolis past the Indian-noplace and Naptown reputation. Businesses, nonprofits, foundations, and individuals would work together for the greater good. Some history helps.

In the '60s and '70s, what we now know as March Madness was just another national championship. The Super Bowl was a nice ending to the NFL season but Roman numerals weren't used at the beginning, and the game wasn't originally known as the Super Bowl. It was Joe Namath's lifestyle, pregame prediction, and subsequent win in Super Bowl III that got people more interested in the game. The Olympics caught our attention every four years, but the Olympic Trials held no interest for the general sports population. The Big Ten and the SEC had great football teams, but nobody cared outside of the Midwest and Southeast. The NBA

Finals were on tape delay late at night. Baseball was still the game for most, but it was local interest that mattered. For Indy, the Cubs, despite their foibles, held sway for many thanks to the reach of WGN. Nobody played soccer. ESPN did not exist.

Then in 1979, the Indiana Sports Corporation was formed, the first commission of its kind in the nation. The Sports Corp, as we call it, was one part of the broad civic mission by so many who wanted to propel Indianapolis into the national consciousness. The mission of the Sport Corps is "to create positive impact by hosting world-class sporting events that enhance vibrancy in the community, build civic pride, drive economic impact and media exposure, and encourage opportunities for youth" (https://indianapolis.bfg.org/nonprofits/indiana-sports-corp/statsheet). For most cities or states, they would focus on the words about hosting the events and driving economic growth; but in Indianapolis, what we take very seriously are the words about building civic pride and enhancing vibrancy in the community. As the former mayor of Indianapolis, I can personally attest that hosting a world-class sporting event is seen as an opportunity to enhance the city and it citizens. The phrase "It must be about more than the game" is the common sentiment. Super Bowl XLVI was but one example. Indianapolis involved breast cancer research, planting trees, helping the less fortunate, and so much more, all as part of the Super Bowl activity. There's a reason we had 13,000 people applying for the 8,000 volunteer spots.

Coincidently and fortunately, ESPN was founded in the same year as the Sports Corp. As the nation was figuring out ESPN and the oncoming proliferation of sport programming, Indianapolis began in earnest its quest to raise the presence of the city into the national spotlight, with sport as a catalyst. Indianapolis hosted the National Sports Festival in 1982 and then the Pan Am Games in 1987. It is accurate to say that with the success of the high-profile Pan Am Games, the people of Indianapolis realized that they could successfully compete with any city in the nation in hosting events. It gave the city confidence. Final Fours came, Olympic Trials happened (particularly swimming and diving and track and field), national governing bodies were courted to Indy, the Colts arrived, and the NCAA moved to Indianapolis.

The nation tuned in. Flo-Jo showed her stuff in Indy. Every major swimmer for the past few decades has passed through. Coach K won his national championships routinely in Indy. Gymnasts won championships and wowed the crowds. The Colts would draft a Tennessee quarterback who owned the city and the country with his artistry and humor, which led to the most fan-friendly, best-organized Super Bowl ever. The sought-after national reputation was achieved. The plan worked due to the foresight and selflessness of so many.

We capitalized on our greatest strength: smart, friendly, hard-working, civic-minded people who worked for the greater good. That's why we were successful. People. It's a good lesson for all.

Used with permission of Greg Ballard.

Next, the group looked at how long the tax should be collected to pay for the projects. It was determined through polling that the citizens would consider a five-year tax as temporary, but anything beyond that would look permanent. So the group decided to do a one-cent sales tax for five years, and put together those numbers for the projects.

With all the preparation work finished, I knew the next thing was to take it to the City Council for approval. That way, we could also set a ballot date. I also felt it was crucial that city leaders be unanimous. So working with them every step of the way and working to make every vote along the way a unanimous vote was important to me and the success of MAPS. We needed not only council input, but citizen input as well.

With all this in place we got to work. Ultimately, nine projects were selected with an estimated cost of $240 million. These projects were a new baseball stadium, a new arena, a new downtown library, a new canal, renovations of the 20-year-old convention center, renovations of the 1930s-era Civic Center, renovations at the State Fairgrounds, a new light rail trolley system, and a river project including a series of dams.

On October 13, 1993, I was excited that the City Council voted 9-0 for approval and a date was set for the citizens to vote 60 days out on December 14, 1993. It was a short time to sell a very big project to the citizens of Oklahoma City, so we hit the ground running.

GENERATING CONSENSUS

The Oklahoma City Chamber of Commerce raised money for the campaign to the tune of $365,000—a good amount in Oklahoma City in 1993. I wanted to be out front on this effort to let everyone know not only that I supported it, but also that I was excited about it. I knew I had to be the face of the project, the leader, and the spokesperson because they were looking to me.

Early on, I knew from polls conducted that there wasn't enough support for each individual project. Not a single one had 50 percent support, and only two projects came close: the river project and the library. But there was support for the entire package. It seemed to me that the folks in the arts community would not kill the sport projects if it also meant killing their projects. And the sports fans would not kill the arts facilities if it meant killing the sport projects. So the ballot was made to be one vote for all nine projects, yes or no. It would be either all up or all down.

In order to make this point, I felt the best approach would be to talk about the big picture of improving Oklahoma City as a whole, not only for us but for future generations. There would be no debt incurred because we would pay as we went. As the tax dollars came in, we would build the projects. That was key to the success of MAPS. So we just split up and went out to spread the word. I told everyone to make it an unwritten rule that if anywhere two or more people gathered to hear our pitch, we needed to make it. A wonderful architectural firm in Oklahoma City, Frankfurt Short Bruza, provided graphic renderings of the

STADIUMS ARE EASY TO BUILD—IT'S ONLY MONEY

Maher Maso

From left: Cowboys COO Stephen Jones, owner Jerry Jones, Maher Maso, and Frisco ISD Superintendent Dr. Jeremy Lyon break ground at The Star in Frisco, while Frisco students look on.

Like Ron Norick, Maher Maso worked successfully as mayor to use sport in public–private partnerships. Since 2017, Maso has proudly served as the CEO of the Prosper Economic Development Corporation. Maso also served as mayor of the City of Frisco, Texas, from 2008 to 2017, named by the U.S. Census Bureau as the fastest-growing city in the country in the last decade. Under Maso's administration, Frisco has received dozens of awards and attributions, including *Money Magazine*'s Best Places to Live list and Allstate's Safe & Secure Communities list. His initiatives in Frisco have resulted in the creation of more than 20,000 new jobs and positioned the city as a hub of first-class entertainment, sport, and sports medicine, including the home of the Dallas Cowboys. He has been interviewed by *Newsweek, The Economist, The Wall Street Journal, New York Times,* CNN, MSNBC, and others. Maso is a regular keynote speaker, including at the Dubai Sustainable Cities Conference and the Inc. 5000 Conference.

Look around Frisco, Texas, right now and it's hard to imagine that the city was mostly farmland not that long ago. In the 1990s, the only traffic signal was a blinking yellow light. There were three schools and a couple of restaurants to choose from.

Fast-forward to today and Frisco has one of the largest concentrations of destination dining, retail, and entertainment in the United States. Frisco Independent

(continued)

360 *(continued)*

School District has expanded a bit from those three schools; by 2018 the public school district is scheduled to operate 72 campuses. Explosive yet well-managed growth like this doesn't happen by accident. A community goes from rural to robust when visionary leadership seeks ways to differentiate and finds the right partners to "grow up" with.

While Frisco is known nationally as a leader in population and job growth, it's distinction as "Sports City, U.S.A" really defines the city's development success. Every professional sports team in the Dallas–Fort Worth area has a presence in Frisco: the Dallas Cowboys, FC Dallas, Dallas Stars, Texas Rangers' Double-A affiliate Frisco RoughRiders, and Dallas Mavericks' G League team Texas Legends. Yevgeny Marchenko and Valeri Liukin chose Frisco for the corporate headquarters of the World Olympic Gymnastics Academy (WOGA). Frisco is also home to publicly owned Fieldhouse USA, a 160,000-square-foot (1486 m^2) indoor basketball, volleyball, and soccer facility.

The Ford Center at The Star, Dr Pepper Arena, Dr Pepper Ballpark, and Toyota Stadium are all sport and event facilities owned by the City of Frisco and leased through a public–private partnership to the sport entities that manage and operate the properties. Communities that want to copy Frisco's public–private partnership model and focus strictly on the facilities are missing the most important factor. Building beautiful, state-of-the-art facilities can be a recipe for failure without the understanding that the people in those buildings are what fuel a successful sport and tourism economy.

The buildings are easy. It only takes money. Finding the right partner—one that is passionate and experienced with their sport or specialty—is the bigger challenge and the key. Partners like a Donnie Nelson of the Dallas Mavericks, Jerry Jones and his Dallas Cowboys organization, and Lamar Hunt, whose legacy continues through his sons Clark and Dan Hunt. Their passion and love of the sport make Frisco's facilities successful.

projects. The money raised by the Chamber paid for brochures to be produced for distribution.

The biggest event in the campaign happened in downtown Oklahoma City in front of the Myriad Convention Center. Citizens and businesspeople came together to support this rally. Hand-painted signs, balloons, and local business mascots made the scene a festive downtown celebration. News media including television stations, newspapers, and radio turned out to report this wonderful scene of support to Oklahoma City voters. The momentum was gathering, but I sensed it would be a close vote.

A NOTE ON PUBLIC OPINION

On December 14, 1993, the citizens of Oklahoma City voted to improve their community by passing MAPS, 54 percent supporting it to 46 percent not. You might say that's a landslide for a sales tax increase. Ten years later, a local poll asked how citizens voted on MAPS, and it showed that 76 percent said they voted for MAPS. The poll also showed that 89 percent of the people 10 years later had a favorable opinion of MAPS.

As we began work on the MAPS projects, I felt it was necessary that we keep the costs down to the estimates we originally gave the voters. It was a solemn promise we gave them and they trusted us to do what we said we would do. I also instinctively knew they wouldn't trust us again if we violated that promise.

EFFECTS OF EXTERNAL FORCES

A little over a year later, one of the most devastating criminal acts in America in that time period occurred when Timothy McVeigh detonated a truck filled with explosives in front of the Alfred P. Murrah Federal Building in downtown Oklahoma City, on April 19, 1995. We stood together as a community and faced this act of evil with unity and a desire that it would not define us as victims.

MAPS was delayed because of this, but it was also a part of rebuilding. As we worked to repair our downtown area, we also began building the ballpark. The baseball stadium was the first MAPS project completed. It came in below cost and on time. The citizens of Oklahoma City came out and saw this amazing structure and that it was done right and for the money set aside, within budget and with class. Opening night, the stadium opened to a full house, debt free.

Citizens enjoyed the projects as each one was completed. These came in succession: the canal, the Fairgrounds work, the Convention Center add-ons, the river project, and the Civic Center renovations. The 18,000-plus-seat arena was opened in June 2002. During its first year of operation it was ranked among the top 10 money grossing venues in the world by Pollstar.

Hurricane Katrina left New Orleans devastated August 29, 2005. Many were left homeless and were relocated around the country while the city was under repair and recovery. That also included the NBA team, the Hornets. The start of the NBA season was a little over two months away. Oklahoma City, Clay Bennett, and Mayor Mick Cornett stepped forward to offer help. The MAPS-funded and fully paid-for arena provided that new temporary home for the Hornets. For two seasons, the citizens of Oklahoma City adopted the team, and they and the NBA showed their love in return.

Two seasons after that, the owners of the Seattle Supersonics brought that NBA franchise to Oklahoma City to stay. This has changed the culture of our community and the state of Oklahoma. Consistent sellouts make the Oklahoma City Thunder one of the top franchises in the NBA.

THE AFTERMATH (OR THE CASCADING EFFECT OF PUBLIC–PRIVATE PARTNERSHIPS)

If I drive downtown today, I see a thriving, busy downtown. Not only where the MAPS projects were built, but in all areas, thanks to the goodwill and momentum that MAPS generated. MAPS for Kids became a noteworthy follow-up to the original MAPS (www.okc.gov/government/maps-3/maps-history), but other public–private projects emerged from MAPs that have enhanced OKC. The citizens of Oklahoma City voted a sales tax on themselves to pay for the $240 million MAPS project, and actually raised dedicated tax and interest added up to $350 million over that five-year period. But according to economic data compiled by the Oklahoma City Chamber of Commerce, our return on that public investment because of MAPS has been at least 10 times more than that original $350 million public investment. Hotels, restaurants, shops, and businesses line the downtown area where none existed in 1993. Since 1993, there have been 2,514 hotel rooms built in downtown Oklahoma City. Other areas are now thriving, including the original Bricktown warehouse district; Automobile Alley where early-day car dealers were located; Film Row where Hollywood film distribution centers once thrived, and so on. Apartments and condos spring up almost as quickly as our Land Run days saw homes and businesses spring up overnight. Since 1993, there have been 2,918 residential units built in downtown Oklahoma City, with 1,405 more to be completed by next year. Today, Oklahoma City is a far different city than it was 20 years ago, all because of a one-cent temporary sales tax initiated to make us feel better about ourselves. I'd say we feel pretty good right now.

CHAPTER 19

Mastering Licensing Strategies as Part of Your Brand

Joseph R. Castiglione Sr.

Since his arrival in 1998, Joe Castiglione has led a University of Oklahoma athletics department that has captured 18 national championships and 81 conference titles while setting records for grade point average and graduation rates. The 2016 to 2017 school year yielded four national championships, a school record that gave OU a nation-leading seven over the previous two years. In the spring semester of 2018, Sooner student-athletes then tacked on a 13th consecutive semester of a cumulative GPA at 3.00 or higher. Demonstrating his commitment to student-athlete development, $600 million worth of state-of-the-art facilities have been completed, with more in the planning stages. The nation's best athletics director in 2017, according to *Sports Illustrated,* and the 2018 U.S. Basketball Writers Katha Quinn Award winner for exceptional service to the media, Castiglione was named AD of the year in 2004 by the Bobby Dodd Charities Foundation and in 2009 by *Sports Business Journal.* He was also a finalist for *SBJ*'s award in 2016. Castiglione was named to the College Football Playoff Committee in January 2018. He previously served as chairman of the NCAA Division I Men's Basketball Committee and had a four-year term on the NCAA Baseball Committee, making him the first to ever serve on all three. Castiglione earned degrees from the University of Maryland and University of Oklahoma. In April 2007, he received the University of Maryland's Distinguished Alumnus Award. He held positions at the University of Miami, Rice University, and Georgetown University prior to a 17-year stint at the University of Missouri, serving the last 5 as director of athletics (inducted into the Missouri Sports Hall of Fame in 2015 and the Oklahoma Sports Hall of Fame in 2018).

For as long as the University of Oklahoma has fielded athletic teams, its team colors of crimson and cream have been an essential part of generating fan excitement about the Sooners. It was 1895 when the colors chosen by a committee were unveiled, and that same year Sooner fans began displaying those colors.

As college sports have grown to the level of popularity they enjoy today, so has the demand for team logos, apparel, and many other items representing universities and their teams. For more than a century, meeting the demand for school-related merchandise was left primarily to local or regional businesses. That business model has changed dramatically over the past few decades as schools have grasped the importance of branding and the licensing and marketing strategies that are key components of their brand.

It has been a dramatic paradigm shift for both collegiate and professional organizations in recent years. That change and the challenges that come with it concern not just marketing products but also, and most importantly for us here at the University of Oklahoma, communicating to the public the idea of who we are as an institution through our brand.

Core values, as discussed at length in chapters 9 and 14, are important to identify and embrace. At Oklahoma our core values are part of every decision we make involving the university, including serving as the basis of our brand in the marketplace. As athletics director, I want those values represented by our teams, coaches, personnel, and student-athletes. We also expect the same from our branding and marketing efforts. In order to accomplish that goal, we must begin with our message.

This point sounds so simple, and yet many organizations don't heed its importance. At its core, a licensing agreement is a branding decision. It must be taken as seriously as other income-generation strategies of an organization. I want to begin this chapter by emphasizing the significance of the organizational message when it comes to making licensing decisions. I use collegiate examples and terminology throughout the chapter, because that is the ocean I swim in. But these principles of licensing are relevant whether your sport organization is large or small, professional or amateur, well staffed or required to push forward on a shoestring.

THE SIGNIFICANCE OF THE MESSAGE

The first goal we have with regard to licensing is that it has to be part and parcel of our organization's brand. That doesn't begin with revenue or other benefits that accrue from merchandising, but with a core message about our institution that we want to impress upon the public, especially our stakeholders. Everything else flows from that message.

In order to impart that approach to others, let me talk broadly about messaging and branding, and then move on to how to implement the business and organizational models required to create successful licensing strategies based on that brand.

GAME CHANGER

GLOBAL SPORT INSTITUTE RESEARCHES ACROSS DISCIPLINES

Kenneth L. Shropshire

Kenneth L. Shropshire is CEO of the Global Sport Institute and the Adidas Distinguished Professor of Global Sport at Arizona State University. The institute is an example of how sport research can cut across campus lines and inform best practices. Shropshire closed out a 30-year career as an endowed full professor at the Wharton School of the University of Pennsylvania, where he was also director of the Wharton Sports Business Initiative, professor of Africana Studies, and academic director of Wharton's sport-focused executive education programs. He now holds the title of Wharton Endowed Professor Emeritus.

Courtesy of Shelley Marie Images.

As the sport industry has boomed as an economic engine over the past 50 years, it only stands to reason that academic study of it has grown as well. Research on sport was once considered a backwater activity. University faculty did impressive work on sport and sport business, but it has been a gradual evolution for some of that work to be held in the esteem that it is today.

It is important to me that solid research dedicated to improving outcomes gets shared with the sport industry. This is more important than ever today, considering the many roles that sport plays in our lives. If we take a multifaceted view of sport—many disciplines, many voices—then I believe we help create leaders who can think critically and act ethically, whether those leaders specialize in sport management, sport products, or health. When we do this, it makes the impact of the sport industry more positive, and ultimately makes the world a better place.

There are many research centers and institutes devoted to many aspects of sport that are doing great work around the world. The Global Sport Institute at Arizona State University is one of the most recent, and, I say this with humility, one of the most innovative. What we emphasize at the Global Sport Institute is a holistic approach in which we bridge the gap between research and best practices that our scholars study, so that our findings are shared with audiences that need them. Our partners are spread across the ASU campus, including the ASU Athletics Department, the Sandra Day O'Connor College of Law, the Walter Cronkite School of Journalism and Mass Communication, and the W.P. Carey School of Business.

(continued)

GAME CHANGER *(continued)*

In our online multimedia hub, GlobalSportMatters.com, launched in spring 2018, we tackle subjects ranging from proper hydration and stadium financing to the NFL's Rooney Rule and cricket scandals. Our goal is for readers to embrace the question, "Why should I care?" as they read thought-provoking, research-based articles. Improving the sport industry requires this rigorous effort across academic and practitioner settings.

Whether consulting or representing teams, leagues, and athletes, authoring books, or speaking and conducting research on the many economic and sociocultural issues that permeate sport, I have spent my entire life straddling academia and professional settings. I believe the Global Sport Institute is an opportunity to leverage meaningful academic work for better practices. Institute research can play a role in more just sporting practices and more equitable business practices. Each academic year, the Global Sport Institute awards seed funds of up to $20,000 to selected research projects. As the sport world continues to reach around the world and impact all of our lives, we are excited to become part of the growth over the next 50 years.

The people creating that message need to determine their own identity, their own vision, and the purpose behind their brand. There is a philosophy to that, but there is also a practical side: What do you want to convey that needs to be understood in any and all relationships you have with your marketing partners? This question is vital because they, as your representatives, are communicating the identity of your institution.

This is a process that requires diligence at every step. Instead of simply turning the job of licensing or manufacturing over to a business and reaping the financial benefits, it is for us an ongoing process, and one that is built on shared values. We think of these relationships as partnerships, not just business agreements. Therefore, we are actively engaged from beginning to end.

Once you have articulated your message as a foundation, then you can turn to branding that message, including the licensing of products. As I have written before in other forums, at OU the values expressed in our messaging and branding include respect, accountability for self and others, and a passion for comprehensive excellence, as well as a celebration of diversity and integrity in all of our affairs.

Our commitment to these values allows us to view everything we do through that prism. There are a variety of ways to attack the development of a licensing program, and the first is trying to create the purpose behind it all. What can an institution standardize and control and what is rightfully theirs as opposed to having outside entities take institutional names, marks, and colors to interpret for their own use?

That is reflected in how we approach branding and marketing, from the choice of vendors and products to controlling our mark, to concern over workers' rights, and ultimately to the satisfaction of the end customer.

My own philosophy in turning our ideals into working, successful branding and licensing models is based on the analogy of a three-legged stool (see figure 19.1). We concern ourselves with brand protection, management, and development.

DEVELOPING A LICENSING STRATEGY: SWEAT THE DETAILS

When we talk about brand development, we're talking about how we develop our brand with every single thing we do, and also how we take our brand to the marketplace through a licensing strategy.

That strategy of how we allow others to use our mark includes processes such as properly choosing our colors. While we can provide specific color matrices or other ways of describing or visually showing what our colors should look like, that doesn't always guarantee that it gets produced in the right way. It is up to us to be the curator of our brand and work with our partners in making sure those colors are our brand of crimson and cream.

For example, different materials accept paints or dyes differently, and they can alter the color of the end result from the color we want. Consequently, one shade of crimson is not another shade of crimson, or red or maroon, with a wide variety of shades and palettes in between.

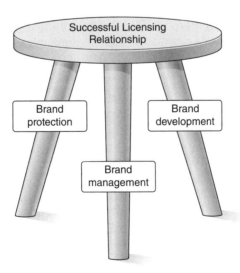

Figure 19.1   The three-legged stool of successful licensing of a brand.

So we carefully choose partners like those who manufacture apparel with our school colors because they are an extension of the mandate to curate our brand. In that endeavor we, and many universities and colleges, work with a licensing company to bring our products to market. In our case it is IMG College Licensing.

By virtue of the wide number of contacts that IMG College Licensing has, they can leverage the power of a large number of institutions in working with the type of manufacturing partners we desire to produce merchandise that benefits both our university and our fans.

A company like IMG College Licensing can also help us grow our brand nationally, as well as strengthen it regionally and on the local level. In fact, they have distribution systems throughout the world, so it makes the most sense for a school like Oklahoma that has supporters across the country and some around the world to have developed a national brand.

True, we have much more fan interest in our region of the country, so there we look to grow the number of items we offer and focus on product lines that certain regional retail outlets can carry. On the local level, the same is true as we also have a sensitivity to small businesses; they were the first ones to really understand the importance of developing brand merchandise for local college teams.

BRAND MANAGEMENT: CHOOSE YOUR PARTNERS WISELY

Brand management is also part of our institutional message, and this ties in to how we interact with our partners throughout the year.

For example, we are sensitive to issues such as the rights of workers who manufacture our licensed merchandise. Another area in which we have worked with our licensing partner is to build a more robust data analytics system in crafting strategies for the consumer.

Our approach is not one of just turning everything over to IMG College Licensing, giving them our marks, and then receiving our share of the royalty. We are very involved in many different aspects of the process of identifying suitable products and bringing them to market because we consider this a significant part of building our brand.

Getting approval for a new product line is one example. For instance, ideas for items that range from apparel to bumper stickers must be conducive to carrying a brand identity. That process involves a certain amount of exchange between the two parties on topics like what new products might be coming, how they would like to take it to market, what audience they are trying to reach, the price points, the look, and the quality of the item.

We certainly would not permit our logos, marks, and colors to be used on materials that we didn't think were of a certain quality of workmanship. In fact, we offer to be involved in product development. We also would not knowingly associate with any partner that didn't stress and uphold the highest in proper factory conditions and safety standards for their employees. We want to know how the manufacturers intend to create the product and what the connections are to get it to market.

This process also involves working with a wide variety of retailers. We want to know how, somewhere in that process, the product will be acquired, how it will be displayed, what the price point will be, and how items will be offered.

In order to take a product from idea to market we have an approval process that begins with seeking designs for the use of our marks. Once the manufacturers or vendors decide how that's going to be done they demonstrate it for us, whether it is artwork or sample products, for our review.

Then collectively we both may have ideas regarding new products and how those will ultimately be vetted and what we do to approve or decline. It's a behind-the-scenes process that is in place from concept to fruition. All of the different approvals need to be followed before anything goes into production.

I can't emphasize enough how important it is to have these intimate working partnerships in managing your brand. You need to know how your partners approach the relationship. For us, the licensee also needs to determine their own identity, their vision, and the purpose behind their brand. Certainly, the key aspect of their mission must be to understand that they are communicating a strong sense of the identity of our institution to the consumer.

This applies regardless of the size of a program or organization, because where sports are concerned, all kinds of opportunities are going to come your way. That doesn't necessarily mean that every opportunity is right for your brand. So before any significant decision is made, we have to take a variety of things into consideration regarding how it impacts us, our image, and our interactions with our key stakeholders, as well as how it might impact the rest of our other important business relationships.

Just to give a few examples: It is easy to get caught up in data and statistics, but if the decision isn't true to what your brand stands for, then any short-term gain will surely be met with long-term repercussions. Then there are times when we might decide a risk is worth taking, understanding deeply what that risk means. There are other times when we might forego a short-term gain in revenue because it doesn't meet our long-term goals or objectives. We've taken less from manufacturers because it better represented what we wanted in terms of what they were offering to our consumers, both current and future.

Now, there are some who try to get our business but the route to producing what we want is not the same as the route they present. We want people to continually be engaged in buying, wearing, displaying, and using Oklahoma-branded merchandise. We're not in for the quick dollar. We have to be able to address a wide variety of people, regardless of their income. So price points are important to us, as well as quality of the merchandise. We want people to be proud of wearing or displaying whatever branded merchandise they select, and we are conscious of the kind of enjoyment they get from it. We think of those kinds of things; we think of the end user before we make the final decision.

To sum up, our merchandising business partner has to first fit in terms of a relationship—just as with the teams and people in our athletic program—and then the financial incentives come into play.

For instance, we could have a really good business plan, but if the vendor is not good at meeting its own deadlines for production or delivery for access to the consumer at key points during the year, this directly affects our business. If partners fall short of delivery when people are most inclined to buy new merchandise, we will have angered the consumer. To me those aspects are all part of how we serve our key stakeholders. We have to have quality products in the marketplace when people are inclined to purchase them.

When you think in terms of supply-chain economics, that is particularly important to getting products to the marketplace, whether it's a traditional retail outlet or online. We are just as concerned about the fulfillment component and the happiness of the end user as we are about the quality of the item.

So, the brand management leg of that three-legged stool rests upon key elements like continuous partner interaction and shared values, supply-chain economics, quality and price points of the merchandise, and end user satisfaction.

BRAND PROTECTION: CHALLENGES IN THE DIGITAL AGE

The last leg of the stool is brand protection. The digital age has affected licensing and branding strategies just as much as it has other parts of our lives. It has been very beneficial in merchandising our brand but has also presented some unique challenges for our partners, and by extension, the university.

It has been mostly positive in terms of creating more opportunities for fans to purchase officially licensed products, but has been a challenge when it comes to brand protection. Websites like eBay are platforms that have given individuals an opportunity to sell a wide variety of products to a global consumer base.

Unfortunately, in a number of cases this includes the sale of unlicensed products. We frequently monitor these sites and enforce as best we can, but there is a great deal of entrepreneurial spirit flowing through the world and new items seem to develop almost daily.

A big influence has been the online social media industry, sites like Facebook and Pinterest, which provide a platform for counterfeiters to spread the word about their products much faster than ever before. What we've tried to do is meet it head-on, using the collective efforts of many in our position like our own peers across the country, to try and develop strategies to bring greater awareness to the issue.

On the flip side, the emergence of ecommerce has been a terrific area of growth for our brand and the industry as a whole. When talking about Oklahoma, we've seen a year-to-year increase that we estimate at near triple-digit growth in sales through the online channels of distribution.

HOW TO HANDLE THE COMPLEX MODERN WORLD OF COLLEGE ATHLETICS

Jack Swarbrick

Jack Swarbrick discusses how the role of modern college athletics directors (such as himself and Joe Castiglione) requires lots of multitasking, working with stakeholders on rights, and many other tasks. Swarbrick is director of athletics at Notre Dame University, from which he received his bachelor's in economics. He received his law degree from Stanford University and practiced law for 28 years at Baker & Daniels. He was the vice president of the team that successfully bid to host Super Bowl XLVI in 2012 in Indianapolis. Swarbrick and his wife, Kimberly, have four children.

College athletics today has got big issues to deal with in regard to the relationship between the student-athlete and the university—commercial rights, communications, and health and safety, just to name a few. Change is constant in our industry and it will continue to be. After conference realignment, we've lost some of the commonality that makes conferences strong. But in other matters I think it has helped. Sports are administered in a much safer and healthier way. Benefits extended to the student-athletes are better suited to their needs. Our fans are better served today than ever before. One aspect of the job that didn't exist 20 years ago is social media. I want our student-athletes to have freedom on social media. I do not want special rules for them; instead, we focus on educating them about the risks of bad digital behavior. I'm very comfortable with our students using their voice online in positive ways.

Even with college sport going through unprecedented change, we must find a way to produce improvements. As director of athletics at Notre Dame I have an unusual number of constituents, more so than a professional sport franchise. I have to communicate to faculty, students, parents, alumni, community members, coaches, administrators, the school president, and countless other stakeholders. There's no replica of that in professional sport. In contrast to virtually any other sport enterprise, we have 26 teams and 750 athletes, both male and female, and that is just at my one school! There are very different issues across sport and across very different student groups.

This is what creates one of the biggest challenges for me. Every day, I need to figure out what issues should be addressed (or ignored) and how best to do that; the answer is always changing. I best balance time and allocate resources by having systems that allow me to manage the individual sports effectively but also communicate across the sports effectively and remember the stakeholders involved.

Ecommerce is a big driver of sales for championship merchandise. We refer to these as hot-market opportunities. When one of our teams wins a championship, we know our fans will want to be part of that accomplishment, and purchasing licensed championship merchandise is one way for them to do so. Of course, those hot-market opportunities take weeks of advanced planning. When we anticipate that one of our teams has an opportunity to win a championship, the plans spring into motion. From developing a potential logo to commemorate the event to selecting which of our licensees will have the opportunity to create the product, it is quite an extensive process. All of the potential scenarios have to be taken into consideration, especially for an event like the College Football Playoff. Because it's such a quick turnaround from the semifinal game to the championship, designs for all outcomes must be approved well in advance to meet the product deadlines our licensees set. Ultimately, the thrill of victory makes all the advance work well worth it in our eyes.

It is our view that a big driver of this increase has been Amazon, as well as our online store partner, Fanatics. That is a company that is growing leaps and bounds and has been outstanding in creating greater access for the consumer and for fulfillment of their orders. The omni-channel approach is a growing trend among retailers that we are monitoring and is certainly important to the future growth of our licensing program.

There are a variety of licensing strategies that we employ to capitalize on various segments of our business, but our current standard royalty rate is 13 percent. However, it's not uncommon for us to negotiate high rates in exchange for product exclusivity or semiexclusivity over a variety of distribution channels as part of our strategic brand management. That percentage is calculated on the wholesale cost of goods produced with our trademark, not the retail cost. So the licensees that produce a wide variety of goods report their royalties to IMG College Licensing on a monthly basis. Then the calculations are processed and we are paid quarterly based on those amounts. Then there is a prenegotiated fee for utilizing IMG College Licensing services that is taken out of our total gross royalties. That fee pays for the services IMG College Licensing provides.

As far as numbers go, for fiscal year 2017 at Oklahoma we received $4.15 million in gross royalties. This is our seventh consecutive year to exceed $3.6 million, a number that is kind of an industry milestone. Not all collegiate institutions publish their annual royalty revenue but conservative estimates would rank us in the top 15 or top 20 nationally. During those years when we've had extraordinary team success or special anniversaries or something that is unique to a given year, in a good number of those years we finished in the top 10.

MAINTAINING OUR FANS' ENTHUSIASM AND LOYALTY

As an athletics director, I have to be concerned with many stakeholders. One group of course is our large fan base, which has only grown in terms of numbers and enthusiasm since 1895. No matter what challenges we face as a department, we owe it to the alumni and fans of the University of Oklahoma and its sport teams to match their devotion with the same high level of quality in merchandise bearing our brand.

Another group is the administrators at our university. There has been a sea of change in the world of collegiate branding, marketing, and licensing in the more than two decades since I became athletics director at Oklahoma. We have great support from our administration, but many in our position have had to work to bring a professional operation to their branding and marketing efforts. This also applies to sport businesses outside of academia.

When it comes to the academic world, it certainly is a more sophisticated operation overall, but getting to this point for many schools has required a steep learning curve for everyone involved. I remember that when we introduced just the *idea* of licensing merchandise, it was difficult for some officials to even understand the reason behind it. You could create compelling case statements for increasing revenue and that would get people's attention, of course. But the whole concept of an institution of higher learning getting involved in marketing was hard for some to envision.

Getting to the high-level marketing plans we employ today was sort of like eating an elephant; you can't eat it all at once, you have to eat it one bite at a time. And that first bite starts with a message about our institution that everyone can understand. Once the stakeholders in your organization are onboard with your message, you can begin to build your own three-legged stool. You can take your brand to business partners, and you have what it takes to build a successful brand and the marketing and licensing strategies that flow from it.

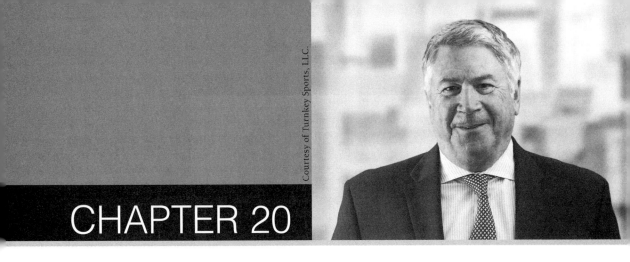

CHAPTER 20

Securing Strategic Sponsorships: The Sponsor's Perspective

Tony Ponturo

Tony Ponturo is a respected voice in sport media and marketing. Ponturo spent 26 years at Anheuser-Busch, the last 17 as CEO of Busch Media Group leading the in-house agency for all media sport and entertainment activity for all beer and theme park brands. He was annually ranked in the top 20 most powerful people in sport and ranked 14th among *Businessweek's* list of most prominent executives. Ponturo is a member of the Broadcasting and Cable Hall of Fame. Currently Ponturo serves as executive vice president–strategy for Turnkey Sports and Entertainment.

Most people consider the 1984 Summer Olympics in Los Angeles the first major modern-day sport sponsorship. It was the first major event that was managed privately. Peter Ueberroth, a successful travel executive, and his selected team won the bid for Los Angeles, managed the Games, and had to raise the sponsorship dollars that became essential resources to allow the Los Angeles Olympic Committee to run the games. There were no government dollars.

As background, the 1980 Summer Olympics in Moscow, Russia, had been boycotted by the United States; it was not clear that either Russia or China would participate in the 1984 Games. The Olympics had suffered in image and reputation. Plus there was global tension and conflict. In fact, Russia did boycott, but China decided to participate based on smart persuasion from Mr. Ueberroth.

In that environment, the LA Olympic Committee came to Anheuser-Busch and proposed an unprecedented $10 million sponsorship to be the exclusive beer sponsor. Keep in mind this was not the 50 percent market share company we later became, but the mid-20 percent market share company that was just thinking about a brand called Bud Light. Should we grab that opportunity? Although you the reader have the benefit of more than 30 years of observing experience, put yourself in my shoes and consider what you would have done in that situation.

What we considered in that situation were two core principles of strategic sponsorships that sponsors must address before they decide to make a huge buy. Before I share those, I want to clarify the two sides of the sponsorship negotiation.

THE LANDSCAPE OF SPONSORSHIPS

To understand sport sponsorship is extremely important, because today more than $60 billion are spent in this area, according to Statista. Most of these dollars are from public companies that have shareholders and a bottom-line accountability. Decisions have to be steeped in real business analytics and fully utilized execution in the marketplace and to the consumer.

OBJECTIVE OF SPORT SPONSORS: MAKING FRIENDS IS OUR BUSINESS

Early on at Anheuser-Busch, I was taught two very important objectives about our sponsorships in sport. First, our objective was not to be one of the largest sport sponsors in the industry, but to use these assets to sell beer and grow sales and market share. In 1982, when I was first hired at Anheuser-Busch as director of media, we had three beer brands and a 22 percent market share. When I left after 26 years, the last 17 years as vice president of Global Media and Sports and Entertainment Marketing, we had 50 brands of beer and a 50 percent market share. So, did sport sponsorships work to sell beer? You bet they did!

The second key point we learned at Anheuser-Busch was a saying that went back to Adolphus A. Busch: "Making friends is our business." What did it mean? We believed that teams, leagues, and broadcasters could do business with any beer company, and we wanted them to want to do business with Anheuser-Busch. In essence, sponsorships are partnerships in which both sides fulfill their respective business plans. As you've heard it said: a win-win.

A great example of partnership in sport sponsorship for me was at the 2006 World Series. This was the first year of the new Busch Stadium in St. Louis, Missouri. What made this first year in the stadium built just feet away from the old Busch Stadium so special was that the St. Louis Cardinals had made it to the World Series, in which they would play the Detroit Tigers.

One of the great traditions in St. Louis started when Anheuser-Busch owned the St. Louis Cardinals and the old Busch Stadium: The Budweiser Clydesdales ran around the field on the warning tracks before the first World Series home game in St. Louis. In the old days the great old ex-CEO of the company, Gussie Busch, would ride on top of the Clydesdale wagon waving this great big red cowboy hat. This tradition was loved by the citizens because Gussie had saved the Cardinals from leaving St. Louis in the 1950s by buying the team.

So now, let's jump to October 2006. I, of course, tell our CEO August A. Busch III that yes, the Clydesdales would run around the field again as tradition had expected. One key flaw. I had not yet talked to Major League Baseball or Fox, which was televising the game.

What's a person to do now, less than 24 hours before the first pitch?

What we learned was that continuing the tradition was not an issue. That was something I had anticipated. But Fox had already established their pregame broadcast set on the track that the Clydesdales would need to run on. TV cables and all the equipment were already set for the next evening's broadcast. That I hadn't anticipated.

So, we needed to go into action. My first call went to Tim Brosnan, who was executive VP of business operations at Major League Baseball. Anheuser-Busch was the official beer of the MLB and I had negotiated the deal directly with Tim.

I explained the situation. It was now 9 p.m. in St. Louis, 10 p.m. in New York. Tim was in New York, before he would fly to St. Louis the next morning.

He said, give me 10 minutes. He needed to call David Hill, CEO of Fox Sports, who was also a good partner and a friend as well.

As I waited, that felt like the longest 10 minutes of my life. No way could I call AAB III and state that the tradition was broken and we could not deliver the Budweiser Clydesdales before the game.

The call came in. Could you meet a representative from MLB and the Fox production people at 10 p.m. at the stadium? You bet I could, and off I ran to get into my car and drive downtown.

There I met everyone on the field, and with a great sense of partnership, they said, let's figure this out.

They figured they could somehow prop the TV broadcast cables up about 15 feet (4.6 m) so the Clydesdales could run under them and all would be happy. What made this partnership even more wonderful is that one of the Fox production people said, "Look at that great Budweiser sign in the outfield. We'll make sure we show that sign on your billboards during the game." What a sponsorship and what a partnership!

THE COMMERCIAL POWER OF SPORT FOR SPONSORS

Why sport? It arouses our emotions and has connectivity to us, the consumer, in today's busy world. We as consumers are bombarded with thousands of commercial messages every day. What is going to break through to us? As sports fans, we spend time with our team. We go to games, watch on TV, listen on the radio, and stream games on our devices. We follow our teams, players, and leagues on Twitter, Snapchat, and Instagram. We are connected to these games and these amazing athletes every minute . . . and with real passion.

The other element of passion and pride connected with sport is where we live. It's about pride in our city, our country. You have to go only so far as two major championship droughts that ended in 2016, with the NBA Champion

HAVING A PURPOSE GIVES YOU PERSEVERANCE

Jamey Rootes

Like Tony Ponturo being driven to achieve his goal during the 2006 World Series, Jamey Rootes knows that a sense of purpose is what allows sport leaders to accomplish great things even when it's hard. Rootes has been a leader with the Houston Texans since the team began operations in 2000 and currently serves as president of the club. Under Rootes' leadership, the Texans have earned numerous distinctions and maintained a reputation as an industry leader in many areas, including service, fan experience, and innovation. Rootes understands the importance of teamwork, and the Texans have been recognized as one of the top workplaces in Houston. In 2017, the Texans extended their home sellout streak to 16 consecutive seasons. As a result, the Texans have consistently been recognized as one of the most valuable professional sport franchises both in the NFL and globally.

Courtesy of the Houston Texans.

My career before sport comprised stints at IBM and Procter & Gamble with an MBA at Indiana University sandwiched in between. During these formative experiences I discovered the power of having a clear sense of purpose. This applies equally to people and organizations. Winning at anything typically requires tremendous perseverance. Having a strong "why" for a particular pursuit, a compelling purpose, is the fuel that allows you to carry on to victory despite obstacles.

When launching the Columbus Crew in Major League Soccer, our aim was to build a viable league for young American players to continue their careers past college and to put Columbus, Ohio, on the map as a major league sport town. Our sense of purpose kept us focused as we proved the numerous doubters wrong and finished our first season with an average attendance of 18,950. It pushed us forward as we failed twice to launch the first soccer-specific MLS stadium. In the end, we succeeded on our third try and started a trend that has helped the league become a mainstay in U.S. sport.

At the Houston Texans, our purpose is equally clear. We call it the *three imperatives*—win championships, create memorable experiences, and do great things for Houston. Our purpose inspires passionate efforts from our entire team and has helped the Texans become one of the most respected and most valuable franchises in pro sport. Purpose draws people in and it pulls them together in a manner that allows you to achieve extraordinary things. When your purpose is clear and compelling as an individual, it can change your life. When you harness this power of purpose with a group, it can change your world.

Cleveland Cavaliers and the World Series Champion Chicago Cubs. These brought tremendous pride to the citizens of these communities who had been starving for a winner. Nothing else in life can really elicit that element of enjoyment, camaraderie, and pride.

With all this passion, it makes much sense for a sponsor, an advertiser, to associate with and connect with the consumer. You want, in this example, Cavalier fans and Budweiser fans to be the same and share in the experience together. There are always the next Cavaliers or Cubs on the horizon. These championship droughts were extreme examples, but sport stories that capture a region's or a country's attention are everywhere. Underdogs, heartbreaking defeats, miraculous physical performances, comebacks from injuries or from a deficit on the court. Sponsors tap into all that, or at least they do if they are paying attention.

We understood this concept of community passion with the many sports teams we sponsored in the United States. At one time, we had a sponsorship participation in almost 90 percent of the teams across all the major sport leagues: NFL, MLB, NBA, NHL, MLS.

I feel this was one of the great strategies of our company: We went local. Such a big part of sport is following your team, as described earlier. If you build that foundation, then you can build the umbrella over those local assets with national TV sport broadcasts and impact the consumer with the "double punch."

What I hope you are picking up in this chapter is that in choosing a sponsor, you can never lose sight of your consumer. Your sponsorships have to have the elements and attributes you are trying to project to your customer base. Make sure you do the thorough work to understand your own company's brand. What are its attributes and value to the consumer? Now, align sport sponsorships that project those same traits. If the cost of the sponsorship does not enhance the value of your brand, then save your money. And lastly, you must activate the sponsorship—get the visibility of the asset as close to the consumer's touch as possible.

MAKING THE FIRST MOVE

One of the keys, in business in general and in achieving the right sport sponsorships, is to not wait for a team, broadcaster, or any other entity to come to you. To me, this falls under the old sport saying, "You have to meet the ball halfway."

There are many examples of that at Anheuser-Busch. After the 1996 Olympics in Atlanta, due to the great performance leading to the women's basketball USA Olympic gold medal win, the NBA decided to start the WNBA. Now 20 years into our history, we at Anheuser-Busch did not wait for the NBA to come to us. In fact, in those days Miller Lite was the official beer of the NBA, so why would they come to us first?

So what did we do? We put together as a sponsor our own proposal, with logic and rationale, and in fact became the official beer of the WNBA in its inaugural year. Also, we told the commissioner at the time, David Stern, not only that we

GAME CHANGER
PROTECTING GOLF'S IMAGE REQUIRED FACTS, PLAN

Joe Steranka

Joe Steranka built up his business by understanding how to connect potential sponsors with potential rights holders. The example he shares here shows how important it is to have a clear plan of action to get your message out to people. Steranka is a 40-year veteran of the sport industry, having worked for the NBA's Bullets and Cavaliers and the renowned athlete and event agency ProServ. His 25-year stint with the PGA of America culminated in his role as CEO from 2005 to 2012 in which he led the expansion of the Ryder Cup and PGA Championship and helped reintroduce golf to the Olympics. Today he is the chief global strategist for Steranka Sports + Strategy.

"Golf is bad."

Wow! I'd never heard that type of blunt criticism of our sport, but there it was in the pages of *The New York Times* in a January 22, 2006, column by Anne Kornblut connecting golf with the Jack Abramoff lobbying scandal. As a new CEO, with a degree in journalism and years of experience as a public relations professional, I knew just how damning those words could be.

What made it even more damaging was its coming on the heels of a legislative defeat during Christmas week of 2005. Congress passed the Gulf Opportunity Zone Act (GO Zone Act) legislation providing tax breaks for businesses in Gulf Coast and Atlantic seaboard states affected by damaging hurricanes. Specifically, the tax benefits were made available to owners of "qualified Gulf Opportunity Zone property." Unfortunately, the GO Zone Act excluded "any property used in connection with any private or commercial golf course [OR] country club . . ." (www.congress.gov/bill/109th-congress/house-bill/4440).

As the chief exec of the world's largest professional sport organization, the 27,000-member PGA of America, I knew firsthand that these issues would not have the same adverse impact on the professional game or the manufacturers of golf clubs, balls, and apparel. But it sure as heck would impact the small business golf courses that employed PGA Professionals. In contrast to their 600 wealthy counterparts that play on the PGA Tour and LPGA, these club professionals earn a median salary of $70,000 while working countless hours to make golf a better game. I accepted that the perspective of some in Congress and the *Times* reporter wasn't taking them into account; the question was how to change that point of view.

As an undergrad at the West Virginia University College of Media I'd learned how to build advocacy positions, even against daunting odds. This served me well in my first year as director of public relations for the NBA's Cleveland Cavaliers, who went through four head coaches and 29 roster players en route to a record of 15-67. But it was my time at ProServ listening in on contract negotiation sessions by uber-agent David Falk—the man behind the mega contracts of Michael Jordan and Patrick

Ewing—that demonstrated to me the value of cold, hard facts. I could almost see the pained expression of an NBA general manager on the other end of the phone as Falk indefatigably made his case again and again for a new record contract amount.

I knew I needed to have that same command of golf's economic statistics to help golf make its case to Congress and general-interest media. The data were there in the form of a study by SRI International, which reported golf's direct economic impact at more than $70 billion, larger than for newspaper publishing or the motion picture industry. Our 16,000 golf courses—each of them a small business—were the backbone for 2,000,000 jobs and more than $60 billion in wages. Oh, and contrary to the opinion of legislators and editors from big cities, the median round of golf in the country was only $28, making it affordable, healthy family entertainment.

Packaging and delivering this message now became the focus and I quickly found a number of allied professional organizations—the National Golf Course Owners Association, the Club Managers Association, and the Golf Course Superintendents Association—whose collective membership of 25,000 was also affected by this challenge to our business' relevance and honor. An alliance named We Are Golf was formed and equipped with professional messaging on the economic, human, and environmental benefits of golf. We came together for a first National Golf Day on Capitol Hill in 2008.

Today, under the auspices of the World Golf Foundation, National Golf Day is a fixture on the golf industry calendar, We Are Golf is more than a jingle, and a bipartisan group of congressmen and congresswomen meet under the banner of a Golf Caucus. The messages of jobs, $4+ billion in charitable impact, and 1.5 million acres of responsibly managed green space are too compelling to ignore. The view of golf has changed. Golf, my friend, is good.

---

wanted to be the sponsor of the WNBA but that as such we would prove to them we should also be the official beer of the NBA.

In time, we wrestled away the official beer from Miller Lite at the NBA, and Anheuser-Busch still enjoys that asset today. We took action, brought rationale to our sell. Why Anheuser-Busch? What would we do to execute this program? TV commercials promoting the association, sales materials in the marketplace, neons, pocket schedules, posters and displays in supermarkets and many other retail outlets.

ADDING VALUE—FOR YOU AND THE ASSET HOLDER

As a sponsor you want to sell your assets as a company and brand beyond just the dollars. How can you execute in the marketplace? How can you enhance the asset holder's brand and image?

As a sponsor, you become a partner. Both of you, asset holder and sponsor, should work together to maximize the association. In both cases 1 + 1 = 2, maybe even 3. If 1 + 1 = 1, then there is no reason to do the sponsorship. Bud Light + NBA has to create more value for both parties. The best case in a sponsor–rights holder partnership is when 1 + 1 = 3 (and keep that equation in mind when you read the next chapter by Stephen Jones!).

A great example of being able to create value for both sides is the Super Bowl. In 1988, we went to NBC, which had the Super Bowl in January 1989. We said we wanted to be the only beer in the telecast. We wanted to showcase Bud Bowl I. This was a concept that created a game within the game. Bud Bowl had Budweiser bottles playing Bud Light bottles in their own game. These were commercials inside the actual Super Bowl.

We went to NBC. No broadcaster had thought of selling just one beer in the Super Bowl telecast. Yes, it cost us 5 minutes of commercial time, but we owned the day and Anheuser-Busch enjoys this point of difference even today. We took the initiative. We created our own sponsorship and took this sponsorship to retail with displays in a big way.

At the end of the day, business is people dealing with people no matter what the business. Sometimes people try to make things too complicated, which hopefully this chapter does not do.

BRING YOUR "RATIONALE"

A big part of sport partnerships is the negotiations that take place between the sponsor and the rights holder, whether a team or league.

We were unique at Anheuser-Busch, because we negotiated our own sponsorships. We did not use a third-party agency, which frankly is the standard. We had a total of 150 media and sport marketing professionals that were all Anheuser-Busch employees. We were on a mission to build and grow our business but also to build partnerships with these professionals who were selling the sponsorships.

Our people had double-digit years with the company. To me, one of our great assets was the consistency of our people. We built trust with those selling the sponsorships. We had a clear reputation of being tough but fair.

We wanted rationale from those selling these sponsorships. It may or may not surprise you that many teams or leagues would say they wanted millions of dollars for their sponsorship but brought no rationale other than that they needed to maximize dollars to cover their costs.

We would argue that we could often come to terms with a partner on "out-of-pocket" dollars. But more importantly, we need to see value. We would bring back to them our value and rationale so we could negotiate with a foundation of facts, not emotion. Value in this context refers to whether the dollars you are spending on a sponsorship give you a return on investment—to move your business forward or to grow sales.

Sport sponsorships can fall into an emotional trap because most of us are fans. For example, you grew up as a New York Yankee fan and now you find yourself negotiating with the Yankees . . . wow! OK, get ahold of yourself and remind

ROLE REVERSAL: THINK ABOUT YOUR CHECK WRITER'S OBJECTIVES BEFORE YOU THINK ABOUT YOURS

Michael Whan

Michael Whan shares how important it is for all members of a rights-holding organization in sport to appreciate the importance of sponsors and to share that gratitude with them. Whan is commissioner of the Ladies Professional Golf Association, one of the longest-running and most successful women's sport organizations in the world. Whan assumed the leadership role on January 4, 2010, with an eye toward enhancing existing business relationships, growing the tournament schedule, increasing exposure for players, and maximizing the LPGA experience for fans. Whan continues to lead a resurgence of the LPGA on all fronts, embracing the global makeup of the tour and building on the "See Why It's Different Out Here" marketing campaign, which focuses on the unique and approachable personalities of the LPGA's players. His big-picture thinking, strong marketing skills, and bold risk taking have pushed the LPGA to historic levels across the board. Whan and his wife, Meg, have three children.

Most teams, leagues, and sports are run by people that spend almost all of their time thinking about the needs of their league, their athletes, and their fans. Conversely, they spend almost no time thinking about the needs (and business objectives) of the people who write checks to them. Without corporate check writers there would be no mega contracts, no huge TV deals, and no executive compensation packages.

Athletes and leagues tend to take sport sponsorship for granted. Leagues hire former coaches, athletes, and commissioners to grow their game, but once again, that misses the primary revenue source for growth—sponsorship.

At the LPGA, we believe in a culture of *role reversal*. Role reversal means we spend more time thinking about our check-writing partners than we spend thinking about tee boxes, shuttle buses, or camera angles. We know that if we deliver for our business partners and help them achieve *their* sponsorship goals, then raising purses, adding tournaments, and expanding TV coverage will be the result.

This is not a mindset of simply our staff members, but also our athletes. LPGA Tour players receive a "Partner Profile" card each week on tour (figure 20.1). That card shows them the four or five most important things the check writers want (and expect) from the LPGA that week. It also shares important information about why a sponsor is supporting the LPGA, important social media themes they should support, and tips on what they can incorporate in any interview that week. Lastly, it shares actual photos of the most important check writers who will be on-site that week, and provides mailing addresses so that players can send personalized thank-you notes to them.

This might feel a bit "old school" to some, but no company ever became successful by forgetting about the customer. In fact, most companies that lose focus on their actual check writers tend to go away over time. LPGA sponsors will tell you that the LPGA relationship is different from their sponsorships with other sports. That difference has resulted in a 50 percent increase in tournaments, a 70 percent increase in event purses, and 100+ percent increase in TV coverage the past five years. Sure, we want

(continued)

3 Things we need from you this week:

- **Go to the BBSI Pairings Party on Tuesday night at 6pm at Columbia Edgewater Country Club (on the Par-3 course)**
- **Tweet to congratulate Cambia on celebrating it's 100th year in business**
- **Tweet about enjoying the wonderful hospitality in Portland.**

Who's Writing the Check: Cambia Health Solutions

- Cambia Health Solutions is a Portland-based total health solutions company. It is the parent of a family of over 20 health-related companies. Its Regence brand of health insurance is the Blue Cross and/or Blue Shield licensee from Oregon, Washington, Utah, and Idaho. Most of the other companies are progressive new companies that assist employers, employees, and health care providers manage their health care system and wellness efforts.

Why They Sponsor the Event:

- To keep the LPGA in Portland because it is an important tradition for the city that has provided more than $18 million in charitable donations over 45 years.
- Business to business relationship opportunities via the pro-am and hospitality.
- The Portland Classic aligns with Cambia's mission to empower people to live healthier lives through exercise and wellness-related activities.

Title Sponsor Activities of Interest During Tournament Week:

- Tuesday night pairings party at the Fan Pavilion at Columbia Edgewater will feature an excellent dinner provided by Salty's restaurant, local wine and local craft beer. It is casual with live music. Player families are welcome.
- Wednesday Pro-Am awards party will be in the Optum Club on the 18th green and will be attended by the executives of our biggest three sponsors – Cambia, BBSI, and Optum. Please walk through after your round or practice.
- The driving range will feature four of the best food carts in Portland including LPGA player favorite Koi Fusion. In the same area there will be a beer garden featuring some of Portland's best craft beers.

Be Social:

#PortlandClassic
Facebook:
Cambia Portland Classic
Twitter:
@PortlandClassic
Instagram:
@LPGAPortlandClassic

Thank You Notes:

Mr. Mark Ganz President & CEO Cambia Health Solutions

Figure 20.1   Partner Profile card.

Partner Profile card © 2017 by LPGA. LPGA and the LPGA logo are registered trademarks of the Ladies Professional Golf Association. CAMBIA and the Cambia logo are registered trademarks of Cambia Health Solutions, Inc., or its affiliates.

to grow the LPGA, but to do it, we focus on our partners' business, not simply our own. Role reversal is the mindset that ensures the LPGA remains one of the most customer-centric businesses in the world.

Want to be a better league or better team? Remember that growth is not about you, but rather about those who find you!

Used with permission of Michael Whan.

yourself it's a business. You are representing your company. You need to get the right value for the dollars spent.

Today's consumers have the benefit of the incredible growth of technology: live streaming, social media, esports, and on and on. Following how new consumers spend their time on content is extremly important. In today's environment, media use is fleeting. No one has time, it seems, to spend 4 hours doing anything. That doesn't mean people are less interested in sport, but it does mean they can find multiple ways to feed that passion.

I was around when ESPN was introduced, and everyone questioned who would watch 24/7 sports. Later, there were skeptics about the Internet and social media. Needless to say, these became huge assets in terms of consumer communication and spending. The bottom line is that you must follow the consumer. An advertiser is not necessarily a fan. An advertiser is simply using sport as a vehicle toward growing the company's business.

1984 OLYMPICS: THE DECISION

Let's go back to 1984. We realized as a company that we wanted to build our business. We needed to build awareness, a strong image, and a point of difference and distinction versus our competition.

Anheuser-Busch used that platform to begin amazing growth over the next 25 years building on many sport sponsorships around the world.

What is so important and is the strategy I want most to leave you with is that sponsors should be willing to take risks—not uncalculated risks, but well thought-out risks for sponsorships that may be new but represent a vision for the future.

For us, we negotiated with properties like ESPN, Olympics, World Cup, WNBA, bull riding, beach volleyball, MLS, and yes, even NASCAR when it was considered a regional sport. Be a leader and not a follower by finding assets and building activation platforms with sport sponsorships that give your brands a point of difference versus their competitors.

For us, what better way, before the term "sport marketing" even existed, to be the only beer company sponsoring the LA Olympics in 1984? We felt it would be a huge event on U.S. soil and that Anheuser-Busch could activate this association to the full extent. We pulled the trigger to spend the $10 million and never looked back.

Even today, as I understand it, the USOC still shows a Bud Light TV commercial in which farmers in a field stop their work to clap as the Olympic torch goes by their farm. That was a time way before commercialization of the Olympic torch. In many ways this image created the vision.

Courtesy of Dallas Cowboys.

CHAPTER 21

Securing Strategic Sponsorships: The Rights Holder's Perspective

Stephen Jones

With 28 years of NFL experience, Stephen Jones has established himself as one of the brightest and most versatile executives in professional sport. Recognized as owner Jerry Jones' right-hand man, Stephen is the Dallas Cowboys' chief operating officer–executive vice president, as well as player personnel director and president of AT&T Stadium. His work involves managing the organization's 400-plus employees while also handling all of the club's salary cap and major player contract concerns. He is also active in the recruitment and management of all major events that come to AT&T Stadium and The Star in Frisco, Texas. Shortly after the turn of the century, Jones began spearheading the club's new stadium efforts, overseeing every element of the development and construction while also working closely with local leaders. Jones was directly responsible for the club's successful referendum campaign in the fall of 2004 that saw the City of Arlington agree to join forces with the Cowboys in building a new state-of-the-art stadium. The 100,000-plus seat stadium established the attendance record for an NFL regular-season game as 105,121 people witnessed the September 20, 2009, home opener, while the 108,713 who attended the NBA All-Star Game on February 14, 2010, became the largest crowd to witness a game in the history of the sport. Shortly after the new name for AT&T Stadium was announced, Jones took on the responsibilities of spearheading a partnership with the city of Frisco and the Frisco Independent School District to develop a new home for the Cowboys' world headquarters. The Star in Frisco opened its doors for operation in the summer of 2016.

The Jones family and the Dallas Cowboys organization are justifiably proud of The Star, our trendsetting, 91-acre complex off the Dallas North Tollway that opened in August 2016. In addition to housing our team's world headquarters and practice facility, we wanted to create something much more. We partnered with the Frisco Independent School District, the city of Frisco, and the Economic Development Committee for a mixed-use development that includes 250,000 square feet of specialty retail and restaurant space, two six-story office towers, and a 12,000-seat indoor stadium that we share with the local high school teams.

But our pride isn't just because the Cowboys brand—most identifiable by the ageless star on our football players' helmets—is stamped all over the place. It's because we were able to connect with top-tier partners such as Baylor Scott & White Health, Cowboys Fit, Ford, and Omni to add value to a development that, to be honest, could have been very successful even if we weren't in the heart of it. That may sound like a humble-brag, but I am serious about both parts of that assertion. We did add substantial value, but we also went into the deal very clear about who we wanted to work with in both the public and private sectors. When you start by putting together the world's most valuable sport franchise and one of the fastest-growing cities in the country on an undeniably dynamic piece of real estate, and then seek out quality commercial brands to hop on board, you create something that is better than the sum of its parts.

Creating something better than the sum of its parts is the goal when a rights holder partners with a sponsor. This chapter presents some reasons why we have been able to do that and suggests how you can develop strategies using that knowledge in your own organization.

JERRY JONES

$1 + 1 = 3$.

That is not fuzzy math on my part. Rather, that is the truth of what happens when two or more partners get together for the right reasons. There's something else contained in that truth. I assume it's not too difficult to comprehend the smart business mindset involved in that little formula. If you work together with a competent partner, it's not surprising that big ideas blossom. But look a little deeper, and you can see that there's great humility in that little formula as well. As strong as your brand is, you will falter if you overestimate what you can do alone. Even the Dallas Cowboys, the richest brand in sport, can't overcome a poor piece of property. Even the Cowboys, with a Hall of Fame owner and his dedicated family that has all hands on deck looking after the business, can't reach the full potential of The Star on our own.

I don't need to stick up for my father, Jerry Jones; he can do that just fine on his own. I suspect your perception of him fits nicely with the term *big ideas*, but maybe not so well with *humility*. I'm biased, of course. I've known him my whole life. Still, I can assure you that both of these fit him, and I believe both would fit many great entrepreneurs. His supposed bluster masks an uncanny ability to seek out and work with others' strengths—and certainly not dictate what the decision will be. This chapter highlights the Cowboys and our success at securing strategic sponsorships that benefit us as the rights holder as well as our partner sponsors. Not surprisingly, it draws on much of what I, my sister Charlotte, my brother Jerry Jr., and all Cowboys employees have learned from my dad. On a very basic level, that education consists of this: If you can master selling and you can show humility, you can be a successful businessperson.

MASTERING SELLING

The potential that can be unlocked by being able to sell, whether that means selling yourself, your idea, or your product, cannot be overestimated. This skill must be in the toolkit of anyone who wants to work in sport. Some people think "selling" is some sort of dirty word. They think selling is beneath them, and they fail to grasp that selling is at the heart of any business you will ever do and any relationships you will ever have. To me, such a mindset is arrogant. At the end of the day, the Dallas Cowboys are a sales organization. And if you wrote down all of Jerry Jones' assets, at the top of the list would be his extraordinary abilities as a salesman. His success correlates directly with that truth; it is no coincidence. He cut his teeth selling insurance for his dad, took proceeds from that, and off he went. My dad has always been able to find doors, open them, and, once inside, sell people.

Bill King said it well when he wrote about Jerry Jones for *SportBusiness Journal*'s Lifetime Achievement Award in the May 22, 2017, issue:

> [Selling] is a gift that has served Jones well, first in the insurance business and then in oil and gas, where he made his fortune, then football, where he risked it and then multiplied it. He says he came by it naturally, with a father who put on country music shows and amateur talent contests to attract customers to the family supermarket.
>
> By the time Jones bought the Cowboys, he had been around sports enough to understand the potential of its value in business. He knew what it meant to have the access to take a client to Augusta. He'd even seen the benefits in his own life. He recalled the way customers and other business associates in Arkansas lit up when he told stories from his days as a Razorback.
>
> If there was economic power to be had from any affinity for the Cowboys, the previous management had unlocked little of it. Jones went to work selling a business relationship with the Cowboys as something more than a sign at the stadium or a desk drawer filled with season tickets. . . .
>
> "Jerry Jones is one of the greatest salesmen, ever, in any business," said [Lamar] Hunt's son and current Chiefs Chairman Clark Hunt. "When he stands up in the room, I think a lot of us smile even before he begins speaking. We know what a great storyteller and orator he is. A lot of times his speeches go on for tens of minutes. But they are always entertaining and very persuasive."

Abraham D. Madkour, *SBJ* executive editor, wrote an editorial in that same issue, calling the "indefatigable" Jones' "uncanny salesmanship the best I've ever seen." He quoted a person from the Cowboys front office: "I have never caught Jerry in a moment where he is off, when he is not selling. He is always in that sales mode. He just loves it." That employee shared the example of Jones meeting with prospective season-ticket holders at an event. He "stood for four hours, offering his customary eye contact while learning first names and spending nearly 20 minutes with each fan. Onlookers were exhausted watching the man work the room and were equally astounded when afterward, he raved about the experience, saying, 'Now, that was some selling!'"

The list of innovations that Jerry Jones has brought to professional sport is long and profoundly influential. When an upstart network wanted to compete for NFL broadcast rights, he made sure they were heard while other owners brushed them aside. The ballooning media revenues that flowed into the league after Fox came on board benefitted all teams. When the NFL was a Coca-Cola league that centralized advertising through the NFL Trust, he struck a deal with Pepsi through his Texas Stadium Corporation. After much legal wrangling with the NFL, he prevailed and showed the way for other owners to follow suit and secure their own stadium sponsorship agreements. These are just two of his big ideas.

SHOWING HUMILITY

In the case of The Star, *we* had to sell *him*. More to the point, I had to convince him. The man who bought the Cowboys when they were bleeding money, the man who built the first $1 billion sport stadium—that opened during the Great Recession!—was very reluctant to invest in yet another risky, expensive, earth-shaking project. Had he been merely hardheaded about it, we would not have been able to accomplish it. But he was open to listening. That takes humility. I had been talking with Frisco Mayor Maher Maso (see chapter 18 sidebar) and City Manager George Purefoy, and I was struggling with how to approach my father about the deal. I knew he might not be up for another massive undertaking. Sure enough, he said, "Stephen, I'm 70 years old. I don't need a new practice facility. All they do is cost money. I just don't have an appetite to put 60 to 100 million dollars so that our players and workers have a little bit nicer place to work. This place isn't that bad. It's a nice place to come to work every day." I explained to him the numbers we were working with and he said, "Here's what we'll do: We need to have a return, business dollars, out of every dollar we spend out there. I'm not going to put 50 aside just because that's what it costs to build a practice facility. Every dollar we put in, we need a business dollar in return."

We were able to do just that. Obviously, the city gave us economic incentives, including $90 million to build the high school stadium because they saw value. Between sponsorships, our real estate business, and those incentives, we met his terms. Now he loves it out there and he is thrilled that we did it. But it was tough sledding early on to talk him into doing it.

To be clear, he was hardheaded. But in the most positive sense of the word. His directives and requirements were clear. He made sure we were convinced about what we said we wanted. When all was said and done, his suggestions required us to be more focused in our planning and even more conscientious about the partners we chose. In the end, it was one of the best deals we have ever done because he is a good listener and open-minded. And then he went on to put his magical touch on the project.

My brother Jerry Jr. was quoted as saying, "Everything we had been doing for 24 or 25 years that we had learned being with him, working as a family, was about how you could leverage the Cowboys and the brand to do great things. What all this is about is what he had taught us you could do." The writer followed up with this: "Make the Cowboys into something more by making more from something associated with the Cowboys. That's what Jones set out to do from the moment he bought the franchise in 1989" (King 2017).

Doesn't that sum up what any rights holder is after? What better way of stating how to work with partners to maximize a brand? Or put another way, 1 + 1 = 3.

CHOOSE PARTNERS WISELY—CUSTOMIZE

It may seem obvious, but you want to choose a sponsorship partner that is highly capable in its field and well versed in what you do in yours. This doesn't mean some cookie-cutter sales pitch that you trot out to every potential partner. It means you customize your sales pitch for the partner you think is best for a particular role. When we meet with a potential new partner, we don't start by explaining what we can provide. First, we ask what the sponsor would do with our brand. If you owned the Cowboys, I would bluntly ask, how would you use the Cowboys to sell your product? What do you see in us and how can we help you achieve it? This is common sense, because a lot of times there is no way I would necessarily know the business-to-customer initiatives of AT&T, Pepsi, Dr Pepper, or Bank of America. Why would I know the details of where they are in their journey in growing their business? What we want to do is customize a deal to scratch the itch, if you will, of a sponsor.

Many times, the most important consideration in a negotiation isn't the dollar amount or the length of the deal, which are the quantifiable numbers you read about in articles when a deal is consummated. Rather, it's the trust to pursue future deals that the first deal makes possible. It's the strengthening of your own brand when you are partnered with the absolute best organization for your brand. In the case of AT&T Stadium, we were willing to go without a naming-rights deal for four years in the middle of a recession in order to get our first choice. This also meant that for a $1.3 billion stadium, we would not have a naming-rights partner on the front end, which is useful in developing a finance package to help with the cost of building it. In this instance, we wanted AT&T from the outset and vigorously pursued them, trying to sell them on why it would be a great venue to put their name on. AT&T represents technology, communication,

GAME CHANGER

IN THE RIGHT PLACE AT THE RIGHT TIME

Dick Cass

Dick Cass, who has been president of the Baltimore Ravens since 2004, reminds us that the power of the brand is not enough to ensure all deals work out. No matter what property you represent, you have to do your homework, connect with people, and have some humility to generate results. Before joining the Ravens, Cass was a partner at Wilmer, Cutler & Pickering (now WilmerHale), a law firm in Washington, D.C. He is a graduate of Princeton University and Yale Law School.

One of the first lessons I learned when I became involved in the sport business is never to underestimate the importance of being in the right place at the right time.

I became involved in the NFL in the late 1980s through Jerry Jones. I was then a partner at Wilmer, Cutler & Pickering (now WilmerHale), a law firm in Washington, D.C. One of my law partners had represented Jerry in litigation in Arkansas, and Jerry wanted to meet someone at Wilmer who could represent him in acquiring an NFL team. I met Jerry, and the meeting went well. He called me several months later and asked me to come down to Dallas to represent him in acquiring the Dallas Cowboys. We completed the acquisition several months later, and I continued to represent Jerry and the Cowboys as an outside lawyer for the next 16 years until I left Wilmer to become president of the Baltimore Ravens in 2004. If I had not met Jerry, it is highly unlikely that I would have the job I have today.

I learned a lot while working with Jerry on Cowboys matters. One of the important lessons I learned is that there is no such thing as a sure thing in any business, including the business of an NFL franchise. Some might assume that if you bought the Dallas Cowboys based on a valuation of "only" $180 million, you would have smooth sailing for the next 25 years or so to reach a total valuation of more than $4 billion (which is what Forbes says the team is worth today). After all, when Jerry acquired the Cowboys in the late 1980s, the team was the most popular NFL franchise in the country and was commonly referred to as "America's Team." But the truth is that Jerry took an enormous financial risk in buying the Cowboys. The team was deep in debt and had a negative operating cash flow, a small season-ticket base, and a large number of unsold suites. In the late 1980s, the Dallas area was still recovering from distressed energy and real estate prices and failing financial institutions. The lucrative national TV contracts that the NFL now takes for granted were not there in the late 1980s, and the issue of player free agency was unresolved and looming. In reality, when Jerry bought the Dallas Cowboys, he was buying a turnaround situation. In the early days, there were surely times when he worried that he had made a terrible mistake in risking his entire fortune on the Dallas Cowboys. In the end, he achieved great success with the Cowboys. But that was no sure thing.

I have leaned heavily on Steve Bisciotti, the owner of the Baltimore Ravens, in trying to become an effective leader of the Ravens. Steve had learned a great deal about leadership from cofounding and building a large, successful, privately owned business before he became owner of the Ravens. While there are many lessons I have learned from him, two are worthy of mention, because these lessons are not ones you would generally expect from someone who has been as successful in business as Steve has. The first piece of advice he gave when he appointed me president of the Ravens was to make sure people at the team liked me. When Steve became the controlling owner of the Ravens, I was his only new hire. I was going to be leading a group of men and women who, in many cases, had been with the Ravens for years. He knew that Ravens personnel would have initial doubts about me and that to be successful I would have to be liked by my colleagues, which would ultimately lead to their respect.

Steve also emphasized to me the importance of humility in a leader. If you are arrogant and think you have all the answers, you will not listen to what your colleagues are saying and will inevitably make mistakes that could have been avoided.

I am frequently asked by young people how they could become involved in the sport business. Sure, it's a case of being in the right place at the right time, but I really draw on the experience of a number of young lawyers who worked with me at my old law firm and later left the firm and had success in the sport business, including these:

- Jay Bauman, who left the firm to join the legal department of the NBA and is now the NFL's senior vice president for legal and business affairs

- Sashi Brown, who left Wilmer to become assistant general counsel of the Jaguars and is now executive vice president of football operations for the Cleveland Browns

- Craig Masback, who left to become the executive director of USA Track and Field and is now a senior executive with Nike

- Alan Ostfield, who left Wilmer to take a job with the San Diego Padres and later became the president of the Detroit Pistons

- Alec Scheiner, who left the firm to become general counsel of the Dallas Cowboys and later became the president of the Cleveland Browns

These lawyers were all smart and talented, and they had the opportunity to apply their considerable skills in the sport world for two reasons. First, when they arrived at Wilmer, they were persistent and relentless in trying to do legal work in the sport world while at the firm. That experience, while not necessarily extensive, gave them an advantage in trying to work directly for a team or a sport league. Second, they were willing to take a risk by leaving a relatively "safe," well-paying job to take what was generally a lower-paying job that may or may not have led to something better—and to relocate to a city where they had few or no ties. In short, they were risk takers who were willing to take a risk to become directly involved in the sport business.

BE WILLING TO BLAZE YOUR OWN TRAIL— JUST DON'T FORGET TO BRING ALONG YOUR KEY STAKEHOLDERS

Larry Scott

Larry Scott has worked closely with his constituents to develop successful media and global marketing ventures as commissioner of the Pac-12 Conference. Throughout his career as a student-athlete, professional athlete, and sport executive, Scott has been a game changer: a bold, innovative leader with a vision for transformative change—from expansion and revitalization of the Pac-12 to equal prize money at Wimbledon. Prior to joining the Pac-12, Scott served as CEO of the Women's Tennis Association as well as COO of the Association of Tennis Professionals (ATP Tour). Commissioner Scott's firm belief that sport has the power to be a force for positive change has been the hallmark of his career.

Courtesy of Pac-12 Conference.

When leading an organization in an innovative new direction, there is always a little bit of table pounding and a lot of advocacy needed. You need to have the business case, but as much as the merits of your proposed strategic direction it's often the diplomatic efforts behind the scenes that get a proposed strategy over the line. As a leader of an organization it's important to remember the many interests in the mix. For example, at the Pac-12 Conference for which I am commissioner we've got big schools, small schools, urban schools, rural schools, public schools, private schools, strong football schools, strong basketball schools, strong women's gymnastics schools, and every variation in between. With a lot of different constituents, the art form is really about creating an exciting vision that everyone can buy into. Leading an entity like a collegiate conference, you need to lead by listening and collaborating with your members to achieve certain things collectively that would be impossible on their own.

A good example of this that I am particularly proud of is our Pac-12 Networks, the first and only collegiate media company owned by a conference. It started by achieving agreement and buy-in from our members to pool all their media rights in the center in lieu of licensing local individual school packages. In our case we asked all members to agree to share revenue equally, which was a critical factor to create a shared interest. Our universities aligned behind a vision that they would do better collectively with a cohesive package and shared interests. We knew that over time, technology would evolve and change so we knew a conference-owned network—the first of its kind—was an important piece of our comprehensive media strategy. We wanted to be master of our own destiny and control our own programming decisions, importantly to get exposure for sport and aspects of our universities that our broadcast partners ESPN and Fox would not provide. I feel good about that decision because now we are able to be at the cutting edge of direct-to-consumer, over-the-top programming and other emerging broadcast technologies.

Another example of being able to break new ground is our Pac-12 Global initiative. I was really impressed, when I started as the conference's commissioner, with the member universities' focus on globalization from an academic perspective. That led me down the path to develop a program in concert with our members to bring our college sporting events overseas, despite the fact that college sport is an inherently American pastime with almost solely a U.S. fan following. The key was to create a program that was first and foremost focused on the academic mission of our schools as embodied in their athletic programs, and the educational and cultural opportunities that sport can provide to student-athletes. Our initial approach was to focus on schools, like UCLA, for example, that are world-class brands, because that's what really resonates in other countries, and to major in a country of particular importance to our universities—in our case China. The experience is about showcasing Pac-12 college sport and the unique U.S. higher education model, and creating incredible opportunities for the student-athletes such as a day with the senior management of leading Chinese ecommerce company Alibaba. We combine the most prestigious academic institutions with the highest level of amateur athletics; that system doesn't exist anywhere else in the world.

As Pac-12 commissioner, I most enjoy when I can attend competitions and events at the campuses. I get a thrill out of being at our campuses because it keeps me thinking fresh and evolving my perspective on trends and developments. I really love that environment—being with young people who are challenging conventional norms and thinking about changing the world. And I get to interact with the student-athletes benefiting directly from the conference's initiatives.

America, everything you could want in a naming-rights partner. Other strong partners came to us with offers, but none seemed to make sense to us as the company whose name should be on the building. We were patient with AT&T and worked with them until, in 2013, the time was right to change Cowboys Stadium to AT&T Stadium. It has turned out great for them, I believe, and for our brand and our fans. We work with outstanding partners. You can see them throughout the stadium in Arlington and at The Star and all over north Texas. But in this case, patience and planning ensured we were doing what was best for our task of naming the building.

INVEST YOURSELF

No matter what your goal is in working with a specific sponsor, you improve your chances of success by making sure there is no doubt in their mind that you are totally committed to making the sponsorship work. We do this in a very literal way with some of our partners at The Star and also away from The Star in what we call sponsor-to-own projects. A good example is Papa John's. We structured the deal so that we have 50 percent ownership of the stores in north Texas, and then utilize the Cowboys brand to build their business. That motivates us to go above and beyond a typical sponsorship where we just license our marks. We put in our money, and Papa John's puts in its money. They get management fees, and we get matching sponsorship fees because that's what we each know how to do.

This arrangement is a quite literal extension of the question I mentioned earlier that I open conversations with: If you owned the Cowboys, how would you use the Cowboys to sell your product? In a humorous way, it also showcases my dad's salesmanship and humility again. If you are an NFL fan, you have seen the commercials and know exactly what I'm talking about: the "Hip-Hop Jerry, 5-Star Combo" advertising campaign in which he rapped and tried to dance. Someone asked him one time, "What would get into you to make you be willing to dance, breakdance like that?" Jerry said, "Because I own half the business, and if Papa John's thinks it's going to help sell pizzas, then I'm all in for it." My dad has always been willing to upset the apple cart, but he has also been willing to do crazy stuff if it is in the service of a partnership. Work with the Cowboys and we don't just lend you the star. The man is in the Pro Football Hall of Fame because he is consistently, relentlessly, all in.

This fully engaged approach emphasizing customization was rare in pro sport and especially the NFL when Jerry Jones pioneered it. It was unheard of for an owner to be so personally involved with the pitch to sponsors. But Cowboys sponsor revenue caught the attention of other teams. "Jones remembers addressing fellow owners at a meeting early on, explaining the tactics that were working so well for the franchise. 'We create relationships that are more than selling signs,' Jones told his colleagues. 'If that means being at the docks with them when the trucks come in, that's what we'll do.' After the presentation, Houston Oilers owner Bud Adams approached Jones. 'Jerry, I don't believe I understand 2 percent of what you just said,' Adams said, 'but I like your enthusiasm. I'm in'" (King 2017).

THE FUTURE OF THE STAR

These examples are just a few of the many that the Dallas Cowboys have successfully pursued by understanding the importance of customization, working with top-of-class partners and building trust with them, leveraging each other's strengths, and investing our organization in a personal and committed

THE JONES FAMILY: A FOOTBALL LEGACY

Stephen Jones

The close-knit Jones' are able to work effectively in striking business partnerships, but relationships within family still take precedence. Stephen Jones' experience as a major college football player and his years as one of the NFL's top executives were instrumental in his appointment to the NFL's Competition Committee. Beginning in 1989, Jones has played an integral role in the team's dramatic rise from a 1-15 record to becoming the NFL's Team of the Decade, with three Super Bowl titles in the 1990s.

When my dad, the legendary Jerry Jones, was inducted into the Pro Football Hall of Fame in August 2017, I realized during that magical time that it was not just one of the most rewarding moments of his life. It was one of my most rewarding moments too. He has always been effusive in his praise for his family and made sure that we all received credit when it was due. The Dallas Cowboys have always been a family affair, and he loves working with my mom, Gene, me, my brother Jerry Jr., and my sister, Charlotte Jones Anderson. Induction weekend couldn't have been done any better. I thought it was wonderful that Mom introduced him. She represented all of us so well, and she has always been the foundation of our family. The entire experience was a validation of Jerry's love of football, the NFL, and the Cowboys, and certainly of his family's involvement every step of the way.

I must confess, though, my son John Stephen quarterbacked Highland Park to a 5A State Championship in 2016, with all six playoff games at our facilities—three at the Ford Center at The Star in Frisco and three more at AT&T Stadium in Arlington. I told my dad that I thought I would trade the Cowboys' five Super Bowl titles for that one state title. He laughed at that. I really think he understood where I was coming from. When I played pee-wee, high school, and college football, he was at just about every game, just as he watched nearly every game my son has played in. He and Mom passed along the value of family and a love of football that will continue to be part of the Jones legacy. I'm pretty sure he enjoyed the state championship just as much as I did. Maybe, just maybe, he would have traded a Super Bowl title for it as well.

way. I encourage you to blend all of these traits and skills along with an open and creative mind and an appreciation for fiscal responsibility as you develop sponsorship opportunities for the entity you represent.

As the team with the star, we will always break the mold. It's been instilled throughout the Jones family and the Dallas Cowboys organization. The Star development is now a model being replicated elsewhere in the NFL. As the Omni Frisco Hotel opens for business, and medical staff that treated Tony Romo at Baylor Scott & White help other citizens rehabilitate, our 91 acres are still being constructed and occupied by other strong brands. We know that for all we have achieved, we are not done building, and we're also not done building relationships that are just as solid as this site. Indeed, if you don't build in both those areas, you will not find the most success you desire.

References

King, B. 2017. "The Lone Star: Jerry Jones. Continued Success with Cowboys Turns NFL Outlier into Sports Business Influencer." *SportsBusiness Journal*, May 22, 2017.

Part V

Mastering Leadership Skills

Part V is among the longest in the book. We know this is where you, the reader, want to be. Leadership is an aspirational concept, but as you will see from these six authors, it's not a mystical, elusive attribute that only some are born with. Even if you are born into a situation in which leadership is expected, hard work and an ability to be innovative and open-minded is essential if you are to maintain and improve upon what you have been trusted with. If, as with most of us, you don't inherit a successful property, you will be heartened by these chapters.

Paul Tagliabue introduces our deep dive into mastering leadership skills by presenting his approach on how to create a framework for leadership that was developed during his long career at the helm as commissioner of the National Football League. North Carolina State Athletics Director Deborah A. Yow links the establishment of a culture of integrity with a culture of excellence in her chapter on operationalizing an organization's philosophy and values. NCAA pioneer Judy Sweet, who has been called "the conscience of college sports," makes the business case for championing diversity, equality, and inclusion in the workplace. Kevin Warren, president of the Minnesota Vikings, uses a very personal life story to share leadership lessons learned the hard way—lessons that can be applied no matter your age, career stage, or job responsibilities. Don Shula, the NFL's all-time winningest coach, provides tips to cultivate a winning edge in sport and business. Bryan Trubey, head of the renowned HKS architectural firm, uses the context of sport facilities to show how sustaining excellence requires caring about the details and knowing your client—advice that is not limited to the building of acclaimed venues.

Leadership takes many forms; you needn't be in a position involving massive expectations or a title that fills up your whole business card to start thinking and behaving like a leader now. If you take seriously the idea of being a leader of self, then you are well on your way to being a leader of others. Of course, every chapter in this book would be appropriate to include in this part V on leadership. We believe that, to some degree, those earlier chapters all build to inform these chapters on leadership in which you, as leader, impact organizational decisions and have to look far beyond the next deal or a single aspect of the larger whole. This mix of being attentive to the everyday grind while keeping your eyes on the realities 10 years down the road is the essence of leadership. All 27 of our chapter authors, as well as the sidebar contributors, have experienced that reality. We hope you now have a better grasp of how to incorporate their lessons into your work.

Courtesy of Paul Tagliabue.

CHAPTER 22

Creating a Framework for Leadership

Paul Tagliabue

During Paul Tagliabue's 17-year tenure as commissioner of the National Football League, pro football grew to unparalleled heights. Tagliabue was elected to succeed Pete Rozelle on October 26, 1989, to become the seventh chief executive of the NFL. A few months later, the new commissioner set the tone for his administration. At the March 1990 owners meetings, Tagliabue and Broadcast Committee Chairman Art Modell announced a new four-year TV deal worth $3.6 billion, which at that time was the largest in television history. At that same meeting, Tagliabue announced the formation of a committee on expansion and realignment. The committee eventually recommended, and the clubs approved, the addition of two teams (the Jacksonville Jaguars and the Carolina Panthers), who began play in the 1995 season. In 1991, Tagliabue and the club owners launched the World League of American Football (now NFL Europe), which was the first sport league to operate on a weekly basis on two separate continents.

Labor peace was a hallmark of Tagliabue's stewardship. In 1993, the NFL and NFL Players Association officially signed a seven-year collective bargaining agreement that guaranteed more than $1 billion in pension, health, and postcareer benefits for current and retired players—the most extensive benefit plan in pro sport. It was the first of two successive long-term labor agreements with the players during Tagliabue's tenure.

Under Tagliabue, the NFL also addressed many other key priorities. During the Tagliabue era, the league supported the construction of some 20 new stadiums; created a leaguewide Internet network and the subscriber-based NFL TV Network; and secured the largest television contracts in entertainment history, totaling some $25 billion.

Before becoming the league's CEO, Tagliabue represented the NFL as an attorney at Covington & Burling, a Washington, D.C. law firm, and returned there after his stint with the NFL.

Before becoming NFL commissioner in 1989, I had worked with an exceptional leader, my predecessor Pete Rozelle, for 20 years. I knew that in the NFL there were leaders at many levels—league, teams, owners, coaches, players, and others. I also understood that, in a nutshell, my job was to lead the entire league, a unique collective enterprise. But knowing that you are expected to lead is a far cry from knowing how to lead. And leaders do come in many different shapes, sizes, and styles.

Leaders are both born and bred. Leaders are committed to making a difference, to being held accountable. Sometimes leaders create the conditions for making a difference. Sometimes those conditions come from events far beyond the control of the potential leaders. While leaders come from countless diverse backgrounds with different priorities and talents, they usually share many qualities in common: conviction, vision, selflessness, integrity, respect for other views, optimism, the will to excel, and staying power.

When examining the roots and traits of leaders, we can all be inspired by the lives of extraordinary figures of America's history, such as Abraham Lincoln and Martin Luther King Jr. Lincoln was confident in engaging with advisors who competed against him for the presidency, and he was able to pursue his goals not just with allies but with a team of rivals (Goodwin 2005). King too was a confident organizer, advocate, and orator with unrivaled persuasive powers. His oratory and style differed dramatically from Lincoln's but with comparable measures of clarity and determination in the pursuit of unprecedented goals (Carson 2001).

For careers in sport, it is also worth studying the backgrounds, leadership styles, and successes (and failures) of exceptional coaches. As the head coach of the Packers, Vince Lombardi epitomized the unbounded will to win and the power of preparation and passion (Maraniss 1999). As the 49ers' innovative head coach, Bill Walsh transformed the way football teams are coached and led—emphasizing skill, intelligence, planning, and execution and recognizing that teaching and communication are critical components of leadership (Walsh, Jamison, and Walsh 2010). And Tony Dungy, in leading the Buccaneers and Colts, emphasized that values "tell us and others what is important to us—as leaders, as an organization, and as individuals. They are the rudder that steers the ship" (Dungy 2010, p. 38).

Whether leaders are born or bred, their values and qualities are often shaped by their experiences as youngsters.

LEARNING ABOUT LEADERSHIP

I grew up in Jersey City, across the Hudson River from Manhattan, but a very long way from the Big Apple in terms of scale, entertainment, wealth, and international ties. Our neighborhoods were melting pots of mostly European ethnic and immigrant families, often defined by geography (such as the "Western Slopes") or by the boundaries of Catholic parishes (such as "St. Michaels Polish downtown"). Jersey City was a gritty industrial collection of activities, manufacturing, food processing, shipyards, rail and trucking, labor unions, and ethnic "social and athletic clubs." Many of these institutions were plagued by corruption, in politics, in government, in business and labor, in the travails of immigrants, and in sport.

But in sport there also were many extraordinary achievers. Before my own high school basketball years, our team was led by Tommy Heinsohn, later a star on the great Boston Celtics team featuring Bill Russell and coached by Red Auerbach. Heinsohn eventually coached the Celtics and was recognized in the NBA's Hall of Fame as both player and coach. I was thrilled when Heinsohn sought to recruit me to attend his alma mater, Holy Cross, but I chose Georgetown. In football, my high school produced many outstanding players, and one of my high school basketball teammates, Lou Cordileone, was the Giants' first-round pick in the NFL's 1961 draft, and then infamously traded to the 49ers for quarterback Y.A. Tittle.

So sports were a big part of the early lives of my three brothers and me, from the late 1940s through the early 1960s. In that era, the racial barriers of segregation were breached by the Dodgers' Jackie Robinson and others in baseball, by the Rams' Kenny Washington, Woody Strode, and others in pro football, and by Earl Lloyd of the Washington Capitals and the Knicks' Nat "Sweetwater" Clifton in the NBA. From those experiences, we all learned a lot about leadership, values, social change, prejudice, and opposition to change.

Other lessons from sport were eye-opening and widely discussed. Values were shaped by participating in sport, listening to coaches, parents, and older siblings; by just being around the games, the leagues, and other athletes; and by hearing and sharing the stories of sport experiences—good and bad. My parents often told us to "be a leader, not a follower." Don't follow your friends when you think they're doing stupid things; be sure you know it's OK before you do it.

In my case, all of these dictums were confirmed by the "point-shaving scandals" of the late '40s and early '50s involving some of the greatest players on college basketball's dominant teams—at the University of Kentucky, the City College of New York (CCNY), and Long Island University (LIU). Growing up in Jersey City, we talked a lot about how the players got "hooked," how they were pressured not just by bookies but by their peers, whether they "served time," and why they were banned from the NBA. In summer leagues, we even played against some of the banned players and listened to their regrets firsthand (Anderson 1998).

In this way, participation in sport—and these scandals or missteps by the players—became lessons for life and shaped our values: honesty, lead—don't follow, and be alert to threats to your values. At best, you became "street smart," skeptical of fast talkers with offers of money and assurances of secrecy, "No one will ever know." As long as you win, there's nothing wrong with "keeping the games close." So you learned to reject big promises and not be naïve.

In the early '60s, I relearned all of these lessons about peer pressure and the allure of "secrecy" after my Georgetown basketball team pulled a stunning upset of NYU in Madison Square Garden in 1961, and criminal indictments entered several years later revealed that the game had been "fixed" by bookies who had bribed vulnerable NYU players to "shave points."

These lessons were a solid foundation for my schooling. My high school in New Jersey often focused on workplace skills, not academics. So my efforts in academics actually enabled me to stand out and perhaps started to shape the way I saw myself. Offered a scholarship to attend Georgetown, a great school, and play basketball there, I seized it. At Georgetown, I developed confidence, because ultimately in 1962 I was team captain and class president. Now I was transitioning from adolescent to adult. In doing so, I began to understand what it was going to take to compete at the highest levels and keep pace with my peers.

After law school and a federal court clerkship, my understanding of the demands of leadership expanded dramatically when I worked in the Department of Defense (DOD), Office of the Secretary of Defense, on nuclear weapons policy matters involving the control of nuclear weapons and nuclear proliferation. This entailed intense study of very complex national security issues and collaboration with many units of the DOD and other U.S. agencies as well as with foreign governments.

A MENTAL FRAMEWORK FOR WORKING THROUGH AN ISSUE

From that time in the Pentagon, I've always had a mental framework that shaped how I saw issues and how I planned to address them. Here it is:

A Leadership Framework

1. *Identify your values*—the interests (public or private) that you are seeking to embrace or advance
2. *Articulate your vision*—the overall concept for the solutions you want
3. *Establish your goals*—the specific outcomes that must be produced or achieved
4. *Conduct an inventory*—the approaches or inputs (investments or managerial actions) you will need to achieve your goals
5. *Be innovative or creative*—the different, new, better (groundbreaking) approaches or inputs that can be deployed to get the job done (also what you can change or do differently)
6. *Execute*—the actual hard work that delivers the desired results

If you work through these six steps in analyzing an issue, you will probably find that you have the information needed to provide leadership.

Equally important, any aspiring leader has to engage on a personal level with partners, employees, customers, and others. If you say you're going to do X, then you have to do it. Your word actually has to mean something.

I'll give you an example from my time at the NFL. By 2005, I had been commissioner for 15 years, and Hurricane Katrina devastated New Orleans. This

BE NOT AFRAID OF GREATNESS

Frank Supovitz

As senior vice president of events for the National Football League from 2005 (near the end of Commissioner Tagliabue's tenure) until 2014, Frank Supovitz oversaw the meteoric growth of the NFL's showcase event, the Super Bowl, and the NFL Draft. For more than 25 years, Supovitz has led some of the world's most prestigious sport events. Supovitz was the group VP of events and entertainment for the NHL from 1992 to 2005, responsible for the All-Star Weekend and Stanley Cup, and developed the first NHL outdoor game in 2003 with the Edmonton Oilers. In 2014, Frank founded Fast Traffic Events & Entertainment, with offices in New York and Sydney, Australia, serving clients that have included the Indianapolis 500 and National Rugby League. He authored three books on event management and appeared in a cameo role as himself in Ivan Reitman's 2014 film *Draft Day*.

Courtesy David Drapkin.

For decades, the Super Bowl has been in a class all by itself. Not only does "Super Bowl" denote the pinnacle of achievement in football; it applies equally to the best of nearly every other experience. "The Super Bowl of . . ." often signifies attainment of the greatest level of importance, an activity that requires the most effort, focus, dedication, perseverance, or planning.

For Hall of Fame horse trainer Bob Baffert, the Pegasus World Cup Invitational was "our Super Bowl"—"our" referring to himself and Thoroughbred Arrogate in 2017. For the Massachusetts Audubon Society, their winter bird count competition is the Superbowl (sic) of birding. In 2014, CBS News referred to Comic-Con as the Super Bowl of conventions. And, for my accountant, his Super Bowl comes around every April 15th. Even some corners of the NFL think of the Super Bowl as their most important annual achievement, oddly, even if it isn't the Super Bowl. Browns left tackle Joe Thomas referenced the team's first and only win of the 2016 season this way on Christmas Eve. "You don't want to say it was our Super Bowl, but it really was," he told Cleveland's *Plain Dealer* (Cabot 2016). He didn't say it was a Christmas present. For me, I was blessed that for nearly a decade, my Super Bowl was the Super Bowl.

William Shakespeare, channeling Nostradamus in 1601, may have predicted the rise of the Super Bowl in his play *Twelfth Night* when he wrote "Be not afraid of greatness; some are born great, some achieve greatness, and some have greatness thrust upon them." That's because the Super Bowl was born neither great nor super. Frankly, it didn't want to be born at all. It was the dogged, tenacious persistence of

(continued)

BE NOT AFRAID OF GREATNESS   *(continued)*

an upstart American Football League filled with smart, maverick personalities like Bud Adams, Ralph Wilson, and Lamar Hunt, among others, that eventually forced the NFL's hand. Fighting for respect, these self-proclaimed charter members of The Foolish Club challenged the NFL's commissioner to an interleague championship game to demonstrate that they, too, could field teams that could play just as competitively, on the exact same 100 yards of grass.

The NFL had nothing to gain by agreeing to the match and ignored the invitation annually until they no longer could, and the first AFL–NFL World Championship Game—now called Super Bowl I—was born on January 15, 1967. At a $12.50 admission price, fans filled only 61,946 seats in the 90,000-seat Los Angeles Coliseum. The following year, the name Super Bowl was thrust upon the game, and soon greatness, too, was thrust upon it, but not without its skeptics. Cowboys' running back Duane Thomas mused to *Newsweek* before Super Bowl V that "if it's the ultimate game, how come they're playing it again next year?" (Barron 2017).

No one asks that question anymore. The Super Bowl is undeniably the greatest one-game event in the world. It is a phenomenon so ingrained in American culture that an entire nation will watch live coverage of a partial stadium blackout, captivated to such an extent that the viewership rating places the game among the top 10 most-watched television programs of all time. It is an entertainment and marketing behemoth that counterintuitively keeps viewers glued to their seats for the commercials, of all things—and that can generate even higher viewership levels than the game for the 12-minute concert that fits sometimes uncomfortably between halves. The greatness of the Super Bowl experience explained for many years why Super Bowl viewership remained consistently stratospheric even when the half-time score was so often lopsided that any hope of a comeback was beyond comprehension. That is, until Tom Brady came along and made even that so much the greater.

was not only a huge issue for the Saints but for every one of those flooded communities suddenly scrambling to survive.

I made it clear that I was personally responsible and that we couldn't allow the Saints or the league to abandon the people of that city. We needed to honor the community bond between football, meaning the NFL, and its fans.

It went back to a value set that my parents had always reinforced: "A friend in need is a friend indeed." That was why I felt the NFL needed to be the most proactive pro sport league in committing to have the Saints in New Orleans. We needed to ensure that everything the NFL could do was done . . . and done well.

I knew my values and those I wanted the league to reflect. My vision of the NFL's role in America meant that we needed to set immediate goals for supporting Louisiana to get back on its feet. The Superdome needed to be a focal point of the city's recovery efforts and in some cases the Superdome became one of the iconic images of that city. It wasn't easy, but we got creative and we executed.

In the years before Katrina, I had plenty of NFL on-the-job training about the demands of leadership. In 1982, an NFL strike caused the cancellation of seven games. And just after that in 1987 (just two years before I became commissioner), the league had briefly resorted to using "replacement" players. I can tell you, fans, broadcasters, and advertisers were not pleased. It was destroying the product.

Additionally, there was instability elsewhere in the league. Raiders' owner Al Davis was attempting to move the Oakland franchise to Los Angeles. In Baltimore, the Colts were planning to move to Indianapolis and there were legal challenges created by a new competitor—the USFL.

These challenges were in direct contrast to our storied past. We had enjoyed the great golden era of NFL football in the 1950s and 1960s with players like Johnny Unitas, Jim Brown, Gale Sayers, and Dick Butkus, and the 1970s had produced great dynasties with the Pittsburgh Steelers and Dallas Cowboys.

But the 1980s were a much different decade. The NFL had survived through those 10 years but as the decade ended after years of combat and warfare between the league and many others, the league needed to pick a new commissioner.

This was no longer the nostalgic NFL of the '50s or the "boom" NFL of the '70s. We had three networks covering our games and we had grown bigger than baseball. While our organization had been successful for the previous 30 years, our future hung in the balance. We recognized that we had big challenges but we also saw big opportunities. To take advantages of these opportunities called for new approaches.

One of my first challenges was to sit down with Gene Upshaw, the president of the NFL Players Association, to try to convince him that a new player employment system could be negotiated by his union—without litigation. Back then, there was an NFL owners' management council that had been responsible for labor negotiations. And those efforts had not gone well. So I went to the league's members and convinced them that the commissioner had to be in charge. We needed to create a new collective bargaining group that was coordinated with all other league activities and led by the commissioner.

That was the start of getting things done differently. I had a sense that Gene also felt things were changing and that he could articulate a new attitude to the league's players—specifically, that the league was not controlled by the same people who had "disrespected" the union in 1987. In the end, Gene and I developed a very strong relationship, built on mutual respect, and unlike what had happened in baseball (which had cancelled a World Series) and hockey (which had cancelled an entire season), we never had a work stoppage our entire time together.

But leading has its complexities. For one thing, leaders and their organizations must have what I call "a high tolerance for conflict." Organizations must recognize that hard choices and sharp differences of judgment are inevitable. This means that there must be room in innovative and successful organizations for serious evaluation of differing alternatives on key strategic matters, for conflicting data-driven analyses of strategies, and for well-developed clashes of perspective about choices.

As an example, in 1992, we were trying to establish a salary cap whereby we could get a minimum floor and a maximum ceiling. At the time, we had teams

ALL I KNOW ABOUT LEADERSHIP I LEARNED AS SENATE MAJORITY LEADER

Senator George Mitchell

Senator George Mitchell learned leadership lessons in the most high-pressure settings possible. He served as a U.S. district attorney, a U.S. district court judge, and a senator representing his home state of Maine, elected with 81 percent of the vote in 1988. He has held leadership positions with numerous companies (including the Boston Red Sox), higher education institutions, and bipartisan think tanks and global justice institutes. His diplomatic work in peace talks in Northern Ireland and the Middle East led to his being named Special Envoy for Middle East Peace in 2009 by President Barack Obama. He was awarded the Presidential Medal of Freedom and was nominated for the Nobel Peace Prize.

Courtesy of DLA Piper.

I've spent much of my life in charged political atmospheres, including as lawmaker, attorney, negotiator, diplomat, and special investigator. I was fortunate that relatively early in my career, I was chosen for a job that allowed me to develop leadership skills that would carry me through the rest of my life, both in and out of sport settings: senate majority leader.

Note that I didn't say it was the most rewarding job I've ever done. But it was the most instructive experience I've had in learning how to make progress in hostile, politicized environments. Had I not served as majority leader from 1989 to 1995, I'm sure I would not have been as effective in any of my later roles.

The position of majority leader is not mentioned in the U.S. Constitution or any statute. It developed as a custom in the mid-19th century when the Senate, without a specific presiding officer, found itself unable to function for lack of sufficient organization and scheduling. From that came the modern majority leader, elected by the senators who represent the majority party.

The job has a built-in conflict. A majority leader is elected by colleagues only from the individual's own party, but the responsibility is to manage the entire Senate. It takes some degree of experience and skill to effectively manage being responsible for the whole body as well as leader of your own party, and above all else to be responsible to the Senate as an institution and to the American people. The majority leader's job is complicated by the fact that a single senator has the power to stop the body from acting, at least for a period of time—and fewer than half of the senators can stop the body from acting at all. A large part of the majority leader's work is negotiating with senators from all over the country from both parties, to create a schedule that allows the Senate to undertake even the most basic business such as a budget and appropriations. Success as majority leader requires a high level of hands-on management and earning the trust of your colleagues.

Above all as majority leader, I learned patience. When you're dealing with 99 other senators—many of whom think they should be president, or at least majority leader—you must be a good listener. Senators like to talk; I know I sure did. When I became majority leader, I did a lot more listening, and found it to be productive because it allowed me to forge compromises that would satisfy both sides. It was time-consuming and difficult, but also incredibly valuable in teaching me to be a better leader and public servant.

I've held a lot of positions in my life since leaving the Senate. I served as U.S. Special Envoy to Northern Ireland, which led to the Good Friday peace agreement in Belfast in 1998. I developed a report in 2001 that provided recommendations for peace between Israel and Palestine, and later became Special Envoy for Middle East Peace. I led the investigation into performance-enhancing drugs in Major League Baseball (see chapter 16) that resulted in the Mitchell Report, and I chaired a commission that investigated the corruption surrounding the 2002 Salt Lake City Olympics. In all of those cases, as with many situations in business, sport, politics, and life, people come to the table with deeply entrenched positions. But in terms of complexity and dealing with people, nothing in my life compared to my six years as majority leader. Without that experience I couldn't have honed the skills that allowed me to take on the rewarding roles that followed.

My most rewarding role? That is a program in which each year I give out one scholarship to a graduate of each of Maine's 130 public high schools. Many of these students otherwise wouldn't be able to go to college, as they are chosen based on financial need, academic record and promise, and community and public service spirit. Sixty percent of them are the first in their families to go to college. I've also given the commencement address at every high school in Maine, public or private. My main goal, though mathematically a likely unattainable one, is to ensure that every single child in Maine who has the talent, desire, and willingness to work can get a college education. I've met some of the world's most influential people and I've worked in tense situations, but an educational legacy in my home state is what will always keep me going.

Used with permission of George Mitchell.

---

at both ends of the spending spectrum who objected to floors and ceilings. As examples, there were high spenders like the Redskins and 49ers and low spenders like the Steelers, Raiders, and Dolphins. We needed to find a solution such that one group's player costs would come down and the other group's would come up.

There were a lot of candid conversations that I led, and I was always forcing the respective parties to focus on the long term. I needed to deal head-on with conflict. That's true in all businesses, but holding on to those values is surprisingly complex when there is a shifting continuum of organizational politics, entrenched positions, environmental factors, and daily or hourly commentary from experts and interested parties.

NFL LESSONS

Having reflected on my years as commissioner, I've identified what I call NFL lessons, and my simple summary looks like this:

NFL Lessons: Anticipate and Innovate

1. Make sure that core values are clear and that strategic goals are clearly defined.
2. Anticipate the future, not just the big opportunities but also the glacial changes and the big risks.
3. Stay focused on strategic goals while recognizing that execution is critical; operate with a sense of urgency.
4. Cultivate and reward innovation—if it ain't broke, fix it anyway.
5. Don't sacrifice long-term interests for short-term gain.
6. Strive for consensus but recognize that choices and decisions must sometimes be made without it.
7. Lead with entrepreneurial executives who balance teamwork and individual responsibility.
8. Have a high tolerance for conflict—it can't be avoided, and it can be both a key organizational attribute and pressure for innovation.

Among these lessons, the one I have often prioritized is the second, which calls for leaders to anticipate the future and to recognize that some changes move slowly while others are lightning fast. For many older readers, the decision to add an NFL game on Monday night was revolutionary. Today, that decision might seem slow next to decisions that must embrace social media platforms like Twitter, Instagram, Facebook, Google, Netflix, and even a retailer like Amazon.

Another imperative is to assume that the unexpected will be far more dramatic than anyone can project. I could note many examples here (such as Hurricane Katrina), but my tenure as commissioner will often be defined by our leadership choices and actions after the terrorist attacks of September 11, 2001.

THE 9/11 DECISION

On that day, commercial airliners were converted into intercontinental missiles that destroyed civilian centers in New York City (the World Trade Center), central Pennsylvania, and Washington, D.C. (the Pentagon), transforming our nation. In an interview with Larry Weisman of *USA Today*, I told him, "This was probably the most emotional year in sport because of the attack and the impact it had and continues to have. The loss of life was enormous." As Weisman noted,

GAME CHANGER

DEFY EXPECTATIONS . . . PROVE YOURSELF

Bryan R. Sperber

Like Commissioner Tagliabue, Bryan R. Sperber emphasized anticipating the future when he set out to improve expectations for what NASCAR could deliver in Phoenix. Sperber has been involved in the motorsport industry since 1990. He has held key executive positions with International Speedway Corporation and has served as president of Watkins Glen International in New York and chairman of Auto Club Speedway in Los Angeles. He was president of ISM Raceway (Phoenix Raceway) from 2002 to 2018. Sperber also serves on the executive boards of the Fiesta Bowl and YPO Gold Arizona and as president of the West Coast Stock Car Hall of Fame

Hip-hop star Lupe Fiasco has a lyric that in essence says if you are great, then life's a stage . . . prove it. I think when it comes to sport that's very true on many levels.

We've all been subjected to the hype of the press releases regarding the latest trend or development in sport with each communication touting how great, impactful, or innovative this or that will be. But, really, the question is always: Will whatever it is truly deliver?

There is plenty of skepticism to go around these days because of the sheer volume of communications we all receive across so many different types of platforms. That certainly raises the bar for all of us in the entertainment and sport industry. The late NASCAR CEO Bill France used to say "either we are moving ahead or we are falling behind. Nothing stays the same."

I carried with me that thought when I was appointed president of Phoenix Raceway back in 2002. While NASCAR was certainly on the rise in those days, there were plenty of challenges and to some degree, built-in bias. I remember my first communications director not even being allowed into the offices of a network affiliate. There were other indignities too that we had to suffer as some in our market viewed Phoenix Raceway and NASCAR through a lens of prejudice. In some corners, we were thought to be unsophisticated rubes and certainly not ready to be on the main stage in a market the size of Phoenix.

While this was disappointing and discouraging to our staff, I really viewed it as a positive. We had an opportunity to win over the media and others in our market by delivering at the highest level.

I think of it as the "Law of the Unexpected." When the audience believes that we are unrefined, blow them away by being incredibly professional, innovative, and thoughtful.

Once we embarked on this effort to strive to exceed the preset expectations, we started unlocking all sorts of opportunities. Suddenly those media companies and sponsors that had lukewarm interest in us turned and started approaching us about projects. We were able to craft incredibly powerful relationships that, even today, still are in place.

(continued)

GAME CHANGER   *(continued)*

All of this really came full circle for me in January of 2017 when our board of directors approved a $178 million rebuild of Phoenix Raceway. It was another opportunity to show who we really were and to exceed expectations. Since that announcement, we have partnered with a leading technology company to rename the venue ISM Raceway. And through that relationship, along with the complete redesign of the bricks and mortar, we created a one-of-a-kind 360-degree sport and entertainment venue. We developed an amazing facility that also has a rich and robust digital entertainment environment.

As Mr. France said, nothing stays the same. In our case we are speeding ahead and looking to create a truly innovative experience—even if no one expected it from us.

that "frontal assault altered people, perceptions, roles and responsibilities [with] games initially dismissed as unnecessary to the American psyche, even as a stunned population looked to sport leaders for guidance, comfort and a sense of when normalcy might return (Weisman 2002)."

No book or degree can adequately prepare any leader for responding to situations in which lives are lost. Occasions such as Pearl Harbor, President Kennedy's assassination, epic storms, and tragic events such as 9/11 may well occur during any leader's tenure. I did not anticipate the need for the league to be at the center of a traumatic nightmare such as the 9/11 attacks. Nor did I anticipate the need to lead in framing the responses to such horrific actions. Events like 9/11 can bring out the best in people, but that recognition must start at the top.

Across the nation, opinions were sharply divided over whether organized sport should continue to play without interruption. Vocal factions argued that the postponing of sport events—such as NFL games—would be "letting the terrorists win," signaling a lack of resolve to respond promptly with adequate retaliatory force. Others contended that while certain states and communities might need to focus on their extraordinary losses, others should "carry on" with sport events to be presented with symbols of unity, grief, patriotism, and the will to sacrifice.

With inspiration from one of America's great patriots, Thomas Paine, I concluded—in a message to the NFL clubs—that the 9/11 attacks "try our hearts and souls" and that they will do so "not just for now but for years, lifetimes, generations." As a nation and as individuals, I said, "we will respond in many ways on many fronts. . . . We will carry on—not move on and forget—but carry on. . . . We will not play games this weekend."

By coincidence, I had worked on counterterrorism in the 1960s at the Pentagon and probably understood far more than others what was really at stake. My experience helped me understand that America needed a time of mourning and reflection to deal with its collective trauma.

I could also certainly see that our employees in New York needed reassuring and time to find their inner strength. I learned again that leaders must communicate their humanity when colleagues need reassurance in order to survive and be resilient.

I was honored to be entrusted with an enterprise as special as the NFL for 17 years. My leadership values and service came from simple concepts that most students and entry-level managers can learn. We all bring different strengths to each situation, but integrity and a singleness of purpose are essential for personal and organizational success.

References

Anderson, D. 1998. "College Basketball: When Sherman White Threw It All Away." *New York Times,* March 22, 1998.

Barron, D. 2017. "Duane Thomas: His Own Man." *Houston Chronicle,* February 5, 2017. www.houstonchronicle.com/sports/texans/article/Duane-Thomas-His-own-man-10894868.php.

Cabot, M.K. 2016. "Cleveland Browns overcome with emotion after beating Chargers: 'It was like our Super Bowl.'" *Plain Dealer,* December 24, 2016. www.cleveland.com/browns/index.ssf/2016/12/cleveland_browns_emotions_come.html.

Carson, C., ed. 2001. *The Autobiography of Martin Luther King, Jr.* New York: Warner Books.

Dungy, T. 2010. *The Mentor Leader: Secrets to Building People and Teams That Win Consistently.* Carol Stream, IL: Tyndale House.

Goodwin, D.K. 2005. *Team of Rivals: The Political Genius of Abraham Lincoln.* New York: Simon & Schuster.

Maraniss, D. 1999. *When Pride Still Mattered: A Life of Vince Lombardi.* New York: Simon & Schuster.

Walsh, B., Jamison, S., and Walsh, C. 2010. *The Score Takes Care of Itself: My Philosophy of Leadership.* New York: Portfolio.

Weisman, L. 2002, "Tagliabue lets guard down." *USA Today,* January 10, 2002.

NC STATE UNIVERSITY

CHAPTER 23

Operationalizing Philosophy and Values While Building a Culture of Integrity and Excellence

Deborah A. Yow

Deborah A. Yow is director of athletics at North Carolina State University, where she has served in that capacity since 2010. She previously held the same position at the University of Maryland (1994-2010) and Saint Louis University (1990-1994). Prior to her numerous administrative roles, she was the head women's basketball coach at the University of Kentucky, Oral Roberts University, and the University of Florida. She has served as president of the Division IA Athletic Directors Association (now the Lead1 Association), and also as president of the National Association of Collegiate Directors of Athletics and as a member of the NCAA Management Council and the National Football Foundation board of directors. She has coauthored and contributed to numerous articles and books. She has spoken at numerous prestigious conferences and venues, including Harvard Law School.

Both Street & Smith's *SportsBusiness Journal* and the *Chronicle of Higher Education* have cited Yow as one of the 20 most influential people in college athletics. She earlier served as the chair of the Atlantic Coast Conference Television Committee, which is charged with overseeing the league's TV contracts and other related media issues. She is married to Dr. William W. Bowden.

By way of introduction, I have been fortunate to serve as the first female athletic director in the Atlantic Coast Conference, as well as serving as the longest-tenured AD in the modern era at the University of Maryland. I was privileged to work in College Park for 16 years from 1994 to 2010. It was an exciting era in which

The author would like to acknowledge the assistance of Joshua Dalton and Dr. William Bowden for their editorial assistance in the preparation of this chapter.

Maryland won 20 national championships and set numerous new student-athlete academic achievement levels.

However, for this chapter on leadership, let's consider another important kind of "ERA," one that I have relied on to guide my leadership actions in the humbling world of the National Collegiate Athletic Association (NCAA).

My ERA looks like this:

- Establish the culture.
- Reinforce the culture.
- Act with integrity when the culture is threatened.

For many readers, a reliance on 14 simple words might seem too simplistic or limiting, but I present those letters and the chart shown here (see figure 23.1)

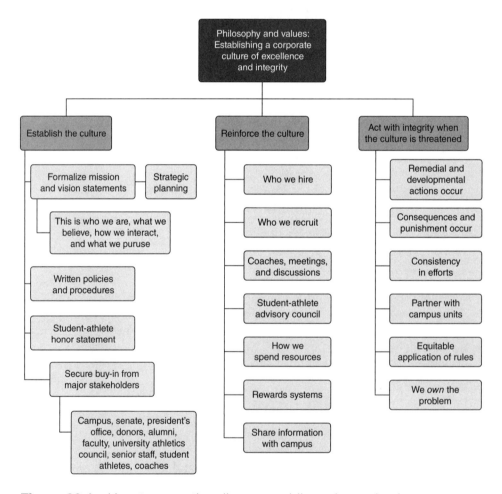

Figure 23.1 How to operationalize your philosophy and values.

Courtesy of Deborah A. Yow.

with great intentionality. When we convene monthly head coach meetings at North Carolina State University (where I have been blessed to serve as director of athletics since 2010, back in my home state) and discuss ERA, I know that a number of our newer coaches' eyes are going to glaze over. They might not want to believe that it is possible for someone's values and philosophies to enable and influence department-wide excellence.

I had the opportunity to be a collegiate athlete as well as a head coach at the University of Kentucky, Oral Roberts University, and the University of Florida. And if there's one thing I know about coaches, it is that they love winning. In fact, for most of them, winning the next game becomes a consuming priority.

So when we start talking in staff or head coach meetings about how to establish and reinforce a culture of excellence, some folks do not automatically see how culture can be a determinant for winning. They will acknowledge that successful teams have an enabling culture. But to be completely candid, their eyes and body language have already told me they don't want a philosophy lesson. They want to get back to their field, court, or arena to prepare for their next competition.

In our minds, philosophies are nice for administrators, but not for helping a shooting guard come off a pick and make the shot. I happen to disagree. Culture, established at the top from the get-go, influences everything we do and how we do it.

I grew up in a small town in North Carolina in the 1960s and my sisters, Kay and Susan, and I were pretty competitive. Actually, we were fiercely competitive in everything we did. We played hard, always wanted to win, and looking back, I'd say we understood the concept of hard work and the value of competition.

"Meat on the bone" is an expression referring to the essence of a thing. So whether it is our coaches who are thinking about their next practice, or members of our senior staff who aspire to become athletic directors, they want to know how establishing a culture is going to help them win games or secure that first athletic director position.

I zero in on this principle: Each individual must decide in advance who she aspires to be and how she is going to conduct herself as a professional. College athletics, much like life, forces all of us into high-pressure situations. In fact, I don't know a coach or an administrator who isn't continually preparing for those situations in which the clock is winding down, the team is losing (or winning), and a lot of significant expectations are staring that coach or AD in the face.

Are all who are involved familiar with their role for this last play? Have we worked on what we want to do in this situation? Pressure is, of course, something of our own making, but the scoreboard and the clock make it very real.

Interestingly enough, I think that the culture we set in preseason and that we uphold throughout the season does play a major role in winning and losing. Hall of Fame legend John Wooden was known to teach his players the proper way to tie their shoes. My late sister Kay Yow, who won conference championships and gold medals as a successful coach with the U.S. national team and the U.S. women's basketball Olympic team (and is also in the Naismith Basketball Hall of Fame for her collegiate success), was committed to establishing a prevailing team culture.

Let's examine the three key components of creating a culture of excellence.

ESTABLISH THE CULTURE

The *E* in the ERA acronym is what all leaders must initiate from day 1 of their tenure. The minute they are announced as the CEO, CMO, CFO, AD, head coach, or any other position of responsibility, the clock is running. They have a window of opportunity to enhance and shape the culture.

In my world, the focus is on winning championships, both conference and national, as well as graduating our student-athletes. The athletic director and head coach must lead in establishing the culture (how we do things), because people are watching closely from the moment the new athletic director or head coach is announced and the message boards start lighting up.

As soon as someone hears that so-and-so has been hired or will be taking charge, everyone in the organization wants to know how the appointee "rolls." And they immediately wonder:

- What's this person like?
- What changes are going to be made?
- Is anyone's job in jeopardy?
- Will we lose any resources that are important to our success?
- Is this person qualified and known as an efficient and effective administrator?
- What progress was made at this individual's last place of service? Was there any success?
- How quickly will the staff and coaches get called together for a first meeting to discuss this individual's vision for our department?

There are perhaps 20 other questions that folks ask themselves and then their coworkers, but all of them are about the issue of culture and what style the new leader is going to implement. It actually starts a second wave of questions such as these:

- Does this person play by the rules?
- Is this person committed to winning?
- Will we have resources to match the expectations?
- How soon will the current culture begin to change?

Leaders understand that these questions are being asked because in most cases, leaders were once employees and have experienced leadership change at some point in their career. Surprisingly, some leaders do not analyze the existing culture as compared to the one they plan to implement. Instead, they emphasize

GAME CHANGER

EQUAL PAY IS A BETTER BUSINESS MODEL

Butch Buchholz

Butch Buchholz tried to establish a culture where equal pay for men's and women's tennis tournaments was expected. Buchholz followed a career in which he was inducted into the International Tennis Hall of Fame by becoming executive director of the Association of Tennis Professionals and commissioner of World Team Tennis. He was ranked one of the world's top amateur players in the pre-Open era, and played for the U.S. Davis Cup squad. As a pro he won the 1962 U.S. Pro Championship. In 1992, Buchholz teamed up with Arthur Ashe to found the Good Life Mentoring program to benefit children in the greater Miami area.

I haven't always succeeded. Not in life, not on the tennis court. In all honesty, I initially failed at something that ultimately became one of my greatest successes.

Pushing for and ultimately achieving equal pay for men and women in major tennis tournaments was not an easy task. Back when I was the executive director of the ATP in the early 1980s, I had the goal of building the International Players Championships. I first got the ball rolling with the ATP and WTA owning an event together and the WTA refused to sign on to the event if there was not equal prize money. These two organizations were the first to have a combined-sex event in professional tennis other than the Grand Slams, so getting everyone from these two organizations on board to split the prize money 50/50 was not an easy task.

From the very onset, there was a ton of resistance from male players who said it wasn't fair that women were being paid the same as they. The men argued that their matches were five sets while the women played three and that they'd had more marquee names over time, so they wanted more money. But at the ATP, when we looked at it over time, we realized that there had been numerous times when women were stronger in the sport than their male counterparts. Nonetheless, getting the players to agree was still challenging. John McEnroe refused to play. Ivan Lendl played but was very upset about the whole deal. That first tournament was a rocky start, and there were moments when we simply could not arrange for equal pay. But I kept fighting for equality.

Pulling off this tournament was the first step in the right direction because it put a lot of pressure on the U.S. Open to have equal prize money. Despite other majors not having it, our first ATP–WTA tournament with equal pay was an American event. From an outside perspective, equal pay has always made sense to me because it provides a much better business model. Sponsors have shown their willingness to pay more for a tournament including both men and women, and combined events have always garnered a lot more attention.

Initially, it was very discouraging to see John McEnroe and other top 10 players not play in the International Players Championships. I felt that all of my efforts were

(continued)

for nothing. But if you asked John McEnroe now about that first tournament, he would say that he was wrong. Equal pay in tennis was such a new idea that it was controversial. To see how far the sport has come for both men and women today is nothing short of amazing. The International Players Championships had a rough start, but today you now have eight combined-sex Masters Series events and four Grand Slams with equal prize money as well. It took a while, but it works for our fans, for our sponsors, and for television.

problem solving on day 1 and believe that working long hours will cause the rank and file to see and embrace a strong work ethic.

There's nothing wrong with trying to make good first impressions. That is important for any leader. But establishing the culture should be the *first step*. Leaders generally want those who are privately asking questions to be reassured in a timely way.

In figure 23.1, you can see the game plan for establishing the culture. There will be a formalization of the mission and vision statements, with ensuing strategic steps. We will comprehensively review and modify, as needed, written policies and procedures. We will also secure "buy-in" from the major stakeholders I will collaborate with, including the university president, major donors, media partners, and sponsors, as well as from the senior staff and head coaches.

REINFORCING THE CULTURE

This leads us to the R of ERA, which is *reinforcing the culture*. And while this may sound similar to establishing the culture, the reinforcement shapes and buttresses our future. It determines whom we hire, whom and how we recruit, how we spend our finite resources, how we protect and enhance our physical assets, how we reward individuals for performance, and how we communicate with our many internal and external constituencies.

Astute thinkers usually acknowledge that there is little we can do about the past but there is a great deal of work to be done when it comes to influencing and molding the future. That's why *reinforcing the culture* sits in the middle of our three platforms. It is central to the acronym and the core of our beliefs.

It also sets up our next component.

ACT WITH INTEGRITY

The *A* in ERA is the action. The meat on the bone. *Act with integrity* when the culture is threatened. This component is where we live our beliefs. This is where we observe and deal with our choices. This is the place where we can measure our results and our consistency. This is the place where leaders must make decisions about compensatory actions or the consequences of choices made by others.

Make no mistake, NCAA student-athletes are often held to a higher standard than their collegiate peers. But so are coaches and so am I. As an athletic director (and one of the few female athletic directors in the Power Five conferences), I am observed under a different microscope.

In figure 23.1, you will note the last box, the one in the lower right, that says "We own the problem." And, in fact, as an organization, we do. But I am ultimately responsible for acting with integrity when there is an issue that threatens our culture. I will take responsibility for that problem if I have failed to establish and reinforce a culture of compliance and one that is always seeking to put the health, well-being, and accomplishments of our student-athletes first.

In a book like this, authors can sometimes make leadership sound easy or possibly something that can be extracted from a textbook and implemented with ease. I caution you against believing that. This book is valuable, and all of the chapter authors have provided words of wisdom drawn from their careers.

But a book such as this one works only when we implement the best messages and find ways to incorporate them (or articulate them) in our individual situations. If you are reading this book but are unlikely to ever lead an NCAA athletic department, then language about coaches or student-athletes may seem marginally useful.

But I suspect that every enterprise operates with a guiding sense of philosophy and values. To that end, I think that all readers of this book should logically be able to look at the leaders around them and perceive the value set of that entity. We read daily about organizations that cheated and got caught. We hear constantly about individuals failing to provide sound leadership and falling from grace. It is painful to read those narratives because I sense that values-based people know how to act with integrity. They know right from wrong.

Certainly, I should not speak as an ethics professor. But I will say this: The person who will someday follow me at North Carolina State University will sense from the first day in the office what our prevailing culture is all about and how those cultural standards have shaped the outcomes of our various athletic teams and our department as a whole.

And those coaches and administrators who sat through meetings with my talking about adhering closely to our values and reinforcing our established behavior will no doubt look for sound cultural direction from the new leader. But they will not be uncertain about the culture that has existed up to that point.

I'll end here, but as I often do when I'm giving presentations, let me leave you with a few key points that might help bring to life some of what we've covered here.

LEBRON'S VALUE IS CHASING EXCELLENCE ON AND OFF THE COURT

Frederick R. Nance

Deborah Yow pairs integrity and excellence as twin pillars for an organization to strive for. Here, Frederick R. Nance expresses those two objectives in the person of his most famous client. Nance is the global managing partner of Squire Patton Boggs (U.S.) LLP, a highly regarded legal and business counselor, a nationally recognized sport and entertainment law practitioner, and a leader in his global law firm. In 2006, Nance was one of five finalists for the position of NFL Commissioner, and he subsequently served for three years as general counsel to the Cleveland Browns. He has represented athletes and entertainers in a wide variety of endeavors, including, notably, having served as business counsel to NBA star LeBron James from the very beginning of James' professional career.

Courtesy of Squire Patton Boggs.

When you represent LeBron James, as I do, it is more than just representing a player—you are representing a global icon. With nearly 40 million followers on both his Instagram account and his Twitter account, when you look at the on-court accomplishments with the MVPs, the all-star nominations, the playoff records, and the NBA Championships—and when you take a look at his international business portfolio—you quickly realize that LeBron James is not just a great basketball player. He is a dominant professional athlete and a unique multinational conglomerate.

No other athlete in the world provides the comprehensive package that LeBron does. While his on-court accomplishments are obvious and undeniable, his increasingly well-known business interests are indicative of a new level of athlete that the world has not seen before. As his lawyer, I am neither a business partner nor a life counselor. But from time to time I do have the occasion to observe his dealings and share my viewpoint. In that context, I have been able to observe the tremendous growth and evolution of the LeBron James brand. When you layer on that the very humble circumstances from which he came as a kid from Akron, Ohio, the dizzying heights to which he has now ascended are all the more remarkable.

The way he handles himself on social media is also special to observe. He instinctively knows what interests people and, more importantly, what inspires them. He accepts the tremendous responsibility that comes with the power and platform of his celebrity and he aspires to articulate and live up to inspirational values because the world is watching.

With all of the focus on his acumen as both an athlete and a businessman, one facet of LeBron's signature accomplishments that is often overlooked is his work as a philanthropist. His foundation does some incredible work that has already had a dramatic impact on the lives of many hundreds of Akron school kids. In partnership with the University of Akron, LeBron's foundation has established the mechanism to allow his students to get full-ride scholarships to college. In addition, he has now secured the approval to open his new "I Promise School" under the auspices of the Akron public schools. From crushing record after record in the NBA, to his innovative global business platform including already succeeding in the entertainment industry, and unparalleled philanthropy at such a young age, LeBron clearly is, as I sometimes have the privilege of telling him, "lightning in a bottle." And in many respects, he's just getting started!

KEY POINTS

1. No issue is more important than establishing a *culture* of sound and compliant behaviors and high-quality outcomes for student-athletes, coaches, and administrators.

2. Philosophy and values must be manifested via *specific actions* and *outcomes*.

3. Focus on the causes of negative incidents. Negative and destabilizing outcomes are usually symptoms of larger concerns.

    Example 1: Multiple student-athlete criminal issues for an NCAA school are a symptom. A cause could be poor character evaluation in the recruiting process.

    Example 2: Costs for intercollegiate athletics have risen sharply and are a symptom. The causes could be related to a values shift in our country related to winning and losing (coaches' compensation and facility enhancement) or the value of women having an intercollegiate sport opportunity (Title IX).

4. Symbolism matters: Documents and statements that reflect and espouse our values and establish our culture are where we should begin.

5. Missteps are magnified via public reports, at times impacting negatively the public perception of intercollegiate athletics. This will not change.

6. It is our responsibility to share our perspectives and intent, with specific actions to support those perspectives, for example, a strategic plan or roadmap to develop a culture of integrity and excellence.

7. In summary, ERA means establishing a culture of excellence, reinforcing the culture of excellence, and acting with integrity when the culture is threatened.

PROCESS, PEOPLE, PLAN, AND CAREFUL EXECUTION

Nick Sakiewicz

Nick Sakiewicz explains the systematic way to create organizational success, just as Deborah Yow insists on consistency in all systems to create a culture of integrity and excellence. Sakiewicz was a founding executive of Major League Soccer and the founder of the Philadelphia Union franchise within it. He developed two MLS stadium deals. He was chosen in 2016 as commissioner of the National Lacrosse League, where he is responsible for helping grow another emerging sport in the United States and Canada. A former professional soccer player, Sakiewicz has built an extensive career in sport marketing, management, and real estate development.

When I took over the New York–New Jersey area franchise of Major League Soccer known as the MetroStars in 2000, the owner asked me to accomplish two important goals. First, after four seasons of abysmal performance on the field and poor business results, he wanted to fix his team on and off the field. This was something I was very familiar with and had successfully done several times before in my career. I had a refined formula and it worked: Hire good people, create a plan, inspire them thoughtfully, and follow the plan strategically. Process. People. Plan. Careful execution. These were the pillars of my success.

The second challenge was to get a soccer-specific stadium built in a good location somewhere in the New York metropolitan area. I had never done that before. At the time, I could only relate the project to large-scale real estate development. I'd never done that either. But, I figured, how hard could it be? I never turn down big challenges like reviving companies from the abyss and starting new ventures from scratch. I had no idea building a soccer stadium with public money would be such a monumental challenge.

Most first-timers underestimate their task. With a combination of a super-competitive nature, a "can't take no for an answer" personality, and naïveté, I set out on a five-year journey that taught me how vital learning and respecting the *process* is in acquiring public money and approval for sporting venues. I also learned how important it is to carefully stick to that process when attempting to get deals to the finish line in public–private finance projects.

The lessons learned and the stories created over the next five years can all be described as "stuff even the best fictional novelist couldn't make up." Through economic meltdowns, political scandals, terrorist attacks, and a number of unscrupulous New Jersey politicians either transitioning out midstream or trying to kill the project, it was the process I discovered that ultimately prevailed, and, on September 15, 2006, I broke ground on what is today Red Bull Arena. What took me five years to accomplish in the New York market I was again able to achieve in two years in Philadelphia, and with better financial results.

Even though each project is different and there is no specific template to follow, there is a unique process associated with acquiring public buy-in and potentially funding.

The biggest challenges I experienced during the course of both of my soccer stadium projects were the unforeseen events you have no control over. In 2001, the technology meltdown hit Wall Street, and later that year the world was forever changed when two planes flew into the World Trade Center towers on September 11. In Philadelphia, 30 days after we broke ground, the worst recession in U.S. history hit the capital markets, and every bucket of money I pieced together to fund the Philadelphia Union's soccer stadium was looking to cancel, which would have collapsed the project, and MLS' 16th team may have never been launched. The lessons I learned during both these projects and what ultimately brought them both to a successful conclusion were these: (1) Surround yourself with capable people; (2) stick to the original plan; (3) use a careful and well-thought-out communication strategy; and (4) build strong political relationships with key stakeholders of the project.

Used with permission of Nick Sakiewicz.

I have attempted to keep my messaging short but practical. I want everyone associated with North Carolina State University athletics to know our mission as an academic institution; our vision for athletic excellence; and the importance we place on the health, well-being, and continuous development of our student-athletes.

In collegiate athletics, our most important stakeholder is our students. Similarly, if I were leading a company in the corporate sector, I would view my employees, not our customers, as my most important constituents. Why? Because that group of individuals will essentially determine the viability of the company—what we sell, how we sell it, and whether we win market share and profitability.

Other leaders have suggested that businesses operate so as to maximize financial benefit within social parameters. But in higher education, including intercollegiate athletics, we operate to maximize societal benefits within finite financial resources.

Said another way, in the world of collegiate athletics, before we can sell a ticket, a service, an experience, or an outcome, we need to make sure that the *culture* of our department sits on the bedrock of sound purpose and ethical operating principles.

CHAPTER 24

Championing Equity, Diversity, and Inclusion in the Workplace

Judy Sweet

Judy Sweet's professional career has included significant leadership roles and several firsts. *SportsBusiness Journal* said, "Sweet has developed a reputation as the conscience of college sport through her work as a tireless defender of Title IX and other diversity issues" (Lombardo 2012, para. 5). She was the first woman to serve as NCAA membership president. When selected in 1975 to be athletics director at University of California at San Diego, she was one of the first women nationally to direct a combined men's and women's athletics program. She was cofounder of the Alliance of Women Coaches and president of NACWAA (now Women Leaders in College Sports), and she served on more than 20 NCAA committees, including the Minority Opportunities and Interests Committee and Committee on Women's Athletics. Judy was the first designated Senior Woman Administrator at the NCAA when she was appointed senior vice president for championships and education services.

Early in my career at University of California at San Diego, where I became one of the first women athletics directors in the country to direct both men's and women's programs, I would often be asked if I were living out a childhood dream. When I was elected the first female membership president of the NCAA, I was asked that same question. I would have liked to answer yes, but the reality was that never in my wildest dreams could I have anticipated serving in those positions. As a child, I didn't see anybody that looked like me in athletics administrative roles, and I saw very few women in a leadership role of any kind. There was an even greater void for girls and women of color.

I played sports all my life, but never had an opportunity to represent my high school or university on a team because organized competition for girls and women was almost nonexistent at schools. Before Title IX, girls may have had sport opportunities through a recreation program with occasional play days or sport days, but no interscholastic or intercollegiate competition. I had to create my own sport opportunities with the boys in the neighborhood and through local recreation programs.

Career choices for women were also very limited, so I can fully appreciate the difference Title IX has made for girls and women through the years. I would like to think that today's student-athletes—young girls, young people of color—see people like themselves and can have those wild dreams about being in positions of leadership within the sport community or other professions that have traditionally been dominated by white men. The numbers are still woefully low, but there has been some progress in diverse hiring of women and people of color in administration as athletics directors and conference commissioners, although there has never been a woman commissioner of a Power Five conference. And unfortunately, women coaches are losing ground as the percentage of women coaches coaching women's teams dropped from 90 percent in 1972 to about 40 percent in 2017. The percentage of women of color in administration and coaching is disturbingly small. In addition, very few women are head coaches of men's teams, so considering the total pool of coaching opportunities in 2017, women held less than 20 percent of those positions. Increasing the numbers for underrepresented populations requires a commitment to seeking a diverse pool of candidates, not as tokens but as serious candidates.

In the best of circumstances, we wouldn't need a federal law in place, as we have had in the United States since 1972 with Title IX, to be committed as a society to equity, diversity, and inclusion. I can't speak for all diverse populations about the biases they experience and what would fully constitute inclusion for each of them, whether in society at large or in the world of sport. But I can speak to the importance and value of equity, diversity, and inclusion in society at large and in the world of sport. I have shared with you from personal experience the debilitating impact of not being able to fathom a dream. You could define diversity in many ways and plan for it and measure it in many more ways. This analysis is important work, but at its heart, diversity is recognizing that strength is derived from diverse experiences and viewpoints that result in new ideas and new approaches, and that all people are respected and invited to bring their experiences and viewpoints to the table.

When an organization fails to do that, it suffers from missed opportunities and resorting to the same limited mindset. It goes without saying that the world is constantly evolving, challenging us in new ways. Sadly, some people try to hold back the tides of change. It is counterproductive and damaging. To be sure, there is value in having people who understand an organizational culture and work their way up inside an organization. But if those people don't consider problems, solutions, opinions, and innovations in new ways that come from outside the traditional organization, continuity and institutional memory are not benefits; they're hindrances. Ensuring that equity, diversity, and inclusion are prioritized throughout an organization is imperative to keep that from happening.

You will notice my theme throughout this chapter—your business is better if you embrace, encourage, and prioritize equity, diversity, and inclusion. I am not advocating this emphasis as just a moral good, a social service that makes us a more compassionate and thriving species. It is much more. I happen to believe that with all my heart, and I've spent much of my life fighting to promote equity, diversity, and inclusion. In divided times, this is no small assertion, and it is worthy of being made. In addition, I want to highlight the business imperative for greater equity, diversity, and inclusion. If you want to succeed in the sport industry and aren't convinced diversity is an important issue, I hope you will be open to reading my chapter and learning from my experience. If you already believe that equity, diversity, and inclusion are integral to achieving success in the sport industry, I hope my words will reinforce your beliefs and help you better advocate for those causes.

There are three points I want to make before getting deeper into this chapter:

1. My life has been spent in intercollegiate sport for almost five decades, so you can expect that I will be using examples from my experience. But the assertions made here, the issues at play, and the suggestions offered are just as relevant to pro or other elite-level sport and youth and recreational sport as they are to college. The pathways to providing awareness and solutions may simply be different.

2. There are an infinite number of minority groups that any organization must be aware of. We immediately consider sociocultural labels related to race, gender, ethnicity, sexual orientation, religion, country of origin, or immigration status. These are important categories, because people are persecuted, ignored, or marginalized when they are members of minority groups within these categories. But there are other categories in which minority status is a missed opportunity when diversity is not emphasized: economic status and political affiliation, for example. As you read, consider the breadth of minority groups and the reasons why a commitment to equity, diversity, and inclusion can unlock new directions for your organization.

3. In our society, we commonly think of diversity in binary terms when real life is anything but. Delving into those social and biological debates is beyond the scope of this chapter and irrelevant to my thesis, which is that opening your doors to a diverse set of people—whether employees, business partners, customers, or any other stakeholder you can imagine— leads to a more robust, creative, productive, and flexible workplace, from the executive suite to the many people who keep your organization open for business every day.

IT STARTS AT THE TOP

As with so many initiatives in corporate culture, a commitment to developing a diverse and inclusive environment starts at the top of a sport organization. There should be a statement on the website from the CEO on the importance of equity, diversity, and inclusion and the organization's commitment to such. This is important from a strategic and managerial perspective in getting results, but just as important is the message it sends to participants and fans. Athletes should be able to see people in leadership positions who look like them and ensure that they feel they are being represented and are understood. In my positions at both UCSD and the NCAA, it was important to me to have a diverse staff, and I encouraged open discussions with diversity of thoughts and perspectives. I truly believe that both organizations benefitted as a result.

The paying customers should know that they are thought of as more than just a wallet. An honest commitment to diversity sends these messages. In educational settings, Title IX provides legal authority based on gender equity, and there are other nondiscrimination laws that must be followed as well. But by and large, the success of the laws is dependent on organizational commitment and not the courts. Equity, diversity, and inclusion must be enacted by leaders who choose to do so and can catalyze support from throughout their organization and among colleagues and competitors. One of my mantras has always been "watch, listen, learn . . . and then lead." It's important to watch and listen to others, learn all you can from their thoughts and experiences, and then move forward as a leader with an open mind and inclusive actions.

In the late 1980s, I was a member of the NCAA Council, a 44-member leadership body with representatives from all divisions including university presidents, faculty representatives, and athletics administrators. One of our discussions was how we could better address some of the challenges and lack of opportunities that women and racial minorities were facing in intercollegiate athletics. As a result, we recommended and ultimately voted to have a committee on women's athletics (CWA) and a committee on minority opportunities and interests (MOIC). To this day, both committees are actively engaged in addressing gender and race issues and have made important recommendations with resulting progress.

When the minority opportunities and interests committee was formed, my colleague NCAA officers and I knew it was important that we as officers of the larger organization be members of that committee even though we weren't a racial minority. We felt that our involvement showed our sincere commitment and sent a powerful message from NCAA leadership that we were determined to improve circumstances and opportunities for minorities. By the same token, it is important to have men contributing to women-centered committees and organizations. Advocates don't always have to look like each other. This guards against the formed committees or groups becoming isolated or lacking the diversity to make it as strong as it can be. But it also keeps the majority leadership from taking a hands-off approach. The onus is not placed squarely on the

MORE SPORTS = MORE LEADERSHIP DEVELOPMENT OPPORTUNITIES

Ray Anderson

While national trends lean toward downsizing athletics departments and eliminating non-revenue-generating sporting programs, Ray Anderson has made his mission clear to add more sport opportunities at Arizona State University, where he was named vice president for university athletics and athletics director in 2014. Anderson was named by *Forbes Magazine* in February 2016 as one of the 25 Most Influential Minorities in Sports, noting that he had "helped position the Sun Devils as one of the most innovative brands in college sports" (Belzer 2016). Anderson is a board member of the National Football Foundation's College Football Hall of Fame, a member of the NCAA Football Oversight Committee, chair of the Ad Hoc NCAA Competition Committee, and most recently a member of the Green Sports Alliance. Anderson was also one of a group of minority ADs to meet with NCAA leaders to encourage creation of a collegiate version of the Rooney Rule to encourage diversity and inclusion in the hiring of athletics leadership. Anderson previously served as executive vice president of football operations for the NFL and as executive vice president and chief administrative officer of the Atlanta Falcons. He cofounded a sport law practice and was a sport agent after earning his JD from Harvard Law School and earning letters in football and baseball while getting his BA in political science from Stanford.

Courtesy of Arizona State University Athletics.

I spent several interesting years in the NFL league office. I also spent time as an executive vice president of the Atlanta Falcons, as a player and coach agent, and as a young attorney in a law office. I loved all that work, and I still have friends spread across those organizations. But with all due respect to all of them, I love what I am now doing in the college ranks. In the pros, we discuss bargaining agreements and how to make the combine more interesting. At Arizona State University, my staff and I are in the leadership development business. We want to create and innovate new opportunities for our young athletes, no matter what their profession becomes.

I was the beneficiary of a varsity athletic experience. It gave me lessons in time management, life skills, and responsibilities that helped propel me to my childhood goal of going to law school. Now, I want to provide an athletic experience to as many Sun Devils as I can. We had 22 varsity sports when I arrived at ASU. Since then, we have added others, including men's ice hockey, women's triathlon, women's lacrosse, and men's tennis. Our goal is to add more—in a smart way—because that means more of those opportunities.

(continued)

I take seriously that responsibility, and that is why "smart" is the operative word in that last sentence. It doesn't do our school or our student-athletes any good if we can't sustain a varsity sport over the long run. We do our homework to be able to make the case to financially support a proposed sport. If we don't believe we can reasonably sustain the operations of a program for 15 years with upfront dollars, whether through pledges, sponsorships, or other funding sources, we won't move forward with a proposal. And we achieve that through articulating the vision to our stakeholders. People want to be involved with a cause they can believe in. This takes a lot of work, but it is why I like the college athletics experience. It is passionate, and it is very much a people business that gives you an opportunity to make a big impact in individuals' lives.

No matter where you work, in or out of sport, whether pro, college, or anywhere else, I guarantee that you won't find success as a leader if you go it alone. A dictator is destined for failure. You are going to be only as good as the people you hire.

underrepresented group with a potentially condescending mandate to come back to us with some ideas and then we'll talk. Rather, responsibility is shared. The NCAA didn't just add something structurally. The goal was to set up that structural addition for success so that the whole organization and its many arms of outreach were improved.

The NCAA encourages athletic departments to have diverse staffs and administrative teams. Even though there is a provision by the NCAA for institutions to identify the highest-ranking woman in their athletics department as Senior Woman Administrator (SWA), with that woman having opportunities to serve on NCAA governing committees, there are still departments that do not yet have a woman administrator identified. And too often, where there is a designated SWA, that individual is not given meaningful high-level responsibilities or included in the decision-making process. This is not true inclusion and diminishes the female voice.

BE WILLING, AND PATIENT ENOUGH, TO EDUCATE

I have been speaking about issues of social justice and equal representation for women and minorities for almost 50 years. During that whole time, I have done my best to check my judgment at the door, to try to understand differing viewpoints and share my perspective. If people disagree with me about the value of diversity, if they think Title IX is causing men's programs to get dropped, if they think that women or people of color are unable to handle certain roles, then I see it as an opportunity to share my point of view with them and hopefully expand their thinking. Although we all have some biases, including unconscious biases, I feel confident that my research and experience provide me with a perspective that reasonable people will listen to and learn from. That's what I ask from people with whom I debate these issues, and it's what you need to ask from others as well.

Research dramatically shows how important diversity is. I like the approach of Todd Pittinsky, professor of technology and society at Stony Brook University. He goes beyond the numbers and finds that a commitment to diversity in the workplace is nuanced. Among the benefits: Countries with more social cohesion experience greater economic growth over the long haul; tolerant attitudes toward groups other than one's own lead to more open communication, better mentoring, and greater commitment to work, as well as the ability to generate ideas through discourse and debate (Dishman 2016).

When I speak with groups, I acknowledge that it is easy for people to see differences in gender and color, but I ask them to really think about how they would feel if they were a member of a group that is on the outside looking in. If you're a male, how would you feel having the experiences that a female has? Putting that in the athletics context, would male athletes be willing to accept the opportunities and support provided to women athletes and coaches, and vice versa?

What biases might LGBTQ individuals be subjected to, and if you're straight, how would that make you feel? I continue with this line of questioning, moving to differences like these: if people who had blue eyes were treated less fairly than people with brown eyes, or those with blond hair were treated less inclusively than those with brown hair, or right-handed people had fewer opportunities than left-handed people. Would each group be willing to accept the circumstances of the other group? It opens people's eyes to look at things differently than they might otherwise, walk in someone else's shoes, and expand their thinking on equity, diversity, and inclusion.

When I became assistant athletics director at UCSD shortly after Title IX became law, my responsibilities included budget preparation and oversight. As a result, I quickly identified the disparity in how men's teams had been funded compared to women's teams. Women's teams had only local competition while the men traveled throughout the state. The men's basketball budget was 10 times that of the women's. I immediately developed a formula that addressed equitable treatment for all men's and women's teams in funding, scheduling, and practice times. When some of the men's coaches questioned the changes, I asked them how they would feel if they were the team receiving less support than others. That expanded their thinking, especially if they had daughters.

I've heard from many women that they are not given access to their department's budget. That gives them pause on why, and whether something is being hidden. Some of this information may be found through the Equity in Athletics Disclosure Act (EADA), which provides public information on institutions' spending and staffing. Understanding budgets is critical to understanding departmental philosophy and priorities. While there may be justification for differences, transparency allows for increased understanding and an opportunity

GAME CHANGER

MAKING A DIFFERENCE IS A KICK

Rolf Benirschke

Rolf Benirschke found that sport gave him a platform to educate the public on an issue he cared about. Benirschke is CEO of Legacy Health Strategies, a patient engagement company, and founder of the Grateful Patient Project. As a former NFL placekicker, his 10-year career was nearly derailed during his third season by a life-threatening battle with ulcerative colitis and ostomy surgery. After a miraculous comeback, he returned to play seven more seasons with the San Diego Chargers and earned numerous honors, including Walter Payton NFL Man of the Year, NFL Comeback Player of the Year, and All-Pro, and became the 20th player inducted into the Chargers Hall of Fame. Following his NFL career, Rolf has dedicated his life to supporting patients and is now a respected leader

Courtesy of Rolf Benirschke.

and speaker in the health care industry. He is married and the father of four children, including three with special needs. He is also the author of three books, including his autobiography, *Alive & Kicking*.

My father was a medical school professor and researcher, and I watched him always doing something "important" that was making a difference . . . and I wanted to do the same. So being drafted into the NFL by the San Diego Chargers as their place-kicker in 1977 was a bit of a detour for me, and a bit of a disappointment for him.

My third season was cut short when I collapsed on a cross-country team flight while battling ulcerative colitis. After undergoing two emergency surgeries six days apart, waking up with two ostomy bags attached to my side, and being 65 pounds (29 kg) below my playing weight, my life hung in the balance for six weeks in the intensive care unit. Miraculously, I survived and was able to return to play seven more seasons. I was humbled by several honors, including the Walter Payton NFL Man of the Year, NFL Comeback Player of the Year, and the opportunity to play in the Pro Bowl.

Because of the visibility of the NFL, my story garnered a considerable amount of media attention and I began receiving hundreds and hundreds of letters from patients all over the country who were struggling with ulcerative colitis or facing ostomy surgery. They were all looking to me for one thing—hope. They wanted to know that they could overcome their illness, just as I had, and could look forward to a healthy and happy life.

I quickly realized that I had been given a unique platform to make a difference, to shed light on a little-talked-about illness and surgery, and to be able to encourage other patients and their families. I embraced my newfound role as a grateful patient by speaking, creating a program called Great Comebacks, and by writing my biography, *Alive & Kicking,* and *Great Comebacks from Ostomy Surgery* and *Embracing Life.*

Through my experiences, I was afforded the opportunity to connect with thousands of patients and realized there was a tremendous opportunity to bridge the relationship between the pharmaceutical–medical device industries and the patients they serve. So I founded Legacy Health Strategies, a patient engagement agency, and launched the Grateful Patient Project, designed to harness the collective voice of grateful patients and channel it for good. And today, as a national patient advocate I speak to audiences around the country and work with legislators to promote legislation that encourages life-saving research and innovation and ensures that patients are heard and protected.

to address disparities that might exist. Our goal should be to treat our male and female student-athletes equitably, as we would our sons and daughters, sisters and brothers.

Title IX also covers sexual harassment and assault. Many such bad behaviors have surfaced in recent times although they have been going on for years. I ask you to think about how you would feel if you were a victim, fearing retaliation if you spoke up, or no one listened to you when you did. It's critical that you have a process in place to prevent abuse and to respond proactively.

OVERCOMING HIRING BIASES

I realized early on that hiring biases, specifically unconscious or hidden biases, were partly responsible for not having a more diverse workplace. After all, you must get your foot in the door of an organization if you are going to contribute your ideas to it. I am not a certified diversity trainer, but I do consult with and present to organizations and their search committees about how hiring biases influence outcomes in negative ways. My goal is not to be critical, but to increase awareness and improve actions since these biases may be restricting an organization's ability to maximize productivity.

We need to be sure that our hiring practices encourage a diverse pool of applicants and our interview process and interview questions are free of bias. As an example, you can block off names from resumes so that assumptions about names and gender are removed from consideration. If an organization commits itself to being open-minded and objective at the outset of an employee's tenure, a more diverse staff is likely, and the message expressed to employees is a positive one regarding your commitment to equity, diversity, and inclusion. Employers and employees must be held accountable for creating an environment that is welcoming, respectful, and free of bias. This expectation should be included in job descriptions and performance reviews.

I distinctly remember in the early 1990s having a discussion with the NCAA Council on what kind of progress had been made with respect to Title IX on college campuses. Some people on the council asserted that we had made great progress and we were exactly where we should be with respect to gender equity. Several of us knew that wasn't the case and advocated for a gender equity survey to get actual data from schools. Results of the survey—some 20 years after Title IX was enacted—showed that we were far from achieving equity. There were large gaps in participation opportunities, scholarships, operating budgets, recruiting, and so on. Even though enrollment at colleges in many instances was close to a 50-50 split between men and women, opportunities for women in sport were much fewer (about 30 percent) and support was very disparate.

Women were receiving 30 percent of scholarship funds, 23 percent of operating budgets, and 17 percent of recruiting funds. Despite a federal law that was 20 years old, the numbers showed the lack of real commitment to supporting female athletes equitably. That research led to the creation of an NCAA Gender Equity Task Force. Based on new initiatives advanced by the task force, by the late 1990s women's participation had increased to 43 percent, and the other areas saw increases as well, though still not achieving equity. Unfortunately, progress slowed after the turn of the century and there has been little change since 2002. Today, participation is still only at 43 percent, even though women's enrollment at universities is often greater than 50 percent. My point is that we saw steady growth for about 10 years after the task force recommendations and resulting NCAA legislation, but now we have stalled out. This is true even though one of the three prongs that an athletic program can use to show compliance under Title IX is to have athletic participation that is proportionate with the campus gender enrollment.

This same lack of opportunities has occurred with athletics directors and coaching positions where women and people of color are disproportionately represented. We need to continually advocate for more diverse hiring pools that include women and people of color. We know there are many women and people of color who are strong leaders and are well prepared to fill leadership positions as head coaches and athletics directors. Those people hiring must actively seek out individuals from underrepresented populations to ensure diversity in hiring pools. That is why the Alliance of Women Coaches (now called We Coach), a program that I helped found after the launch of the NCAA Women Coaches Academy in 2003, and the Women Leaders in College Sports (formerly NCAWAA) for administrators exist. They receive financial support from the NCAA for education programs to provide professional development, mentoring, and networking that are beneficial to participants as they chart their career paths. See table 24.1 for research compiled by The Institute for Diversity

TABLE 24.1 Racial and Gender Report Card: Major Sport Hiring Practices Through the Years

The Institute for Diversity and Ethics in Sport at the University of Central Florida has provided an annual report card for more than two decades. It has become the definitive assessment of diversity in hiring practices in professional and major college sport. The information in this table shows a snapshot of the past decade.

League	'04	'06/'07	'08	'09	'10	'11	'12	'13	'14	'15	'16	'17
NBA	A/B	A/B−	A+/B	A+	A/A−	A+/A−	A+/A−	A+/B+	A+/B+	A+/B+	A+/B	A/B
Overall	B+	B+	A−	A	A	A	A	A	A	A	A	A−
NFL[a]	B/D+	B+/-	B+/-	A−/C B+/A−	A/C	A/C	A/C+	A/C	A/C−	A/C+	A/C+	A/C
Overall	C	—	—	B	B	B	B	B	B	B	B	B
MLB	B+/C	B+/C+	A−/C+	A/B	A/B	A/B−	A/C+	A/C+	A/C+	A/CC+	A C/C+	B+ C+/B−
Overall	C+	B	B	B+	B+	B+	B	BB+	BB+	B	B	C+B−
MLS	C+/B	A/D+	A/C+	A/B	A/B	A/C+	B+/A−	B+/B B	B+/C+	B+/B	B+/B	B+/C+
Overall	B−	C+B−	B+	B+	B+	B	B+	B+	B	B	B+	C+B−
WNBA	A/A	A/A	A+/A+	A+/A+	A/A+	A+/A	A+/A+	A+/A+	A+/A+	A+/A+	A+/A	A+/A
Overall	A	A	A+	A+	A+	A	A+	A+	A+	A+	A+	A
NCAA college	B−/B+	B−/B	C+/B	C+/B	B/B	B/B	B/B	—	C+/C−	B/C+	C+/C	C+/C+
Overall	B	B	C+	C+	B	B	B	—	C	B	C+	C+

Race is on the left and gender is on the right in each cell. The combined overall grade for the year is underneath.

[a]In 2006 and 2008, the NFL office did not participate in the study so information on gender could not be confirmed. Thus, no gender or overall score was calculated.

Data from The Institute for Diversity and Ethics in Sport (TIDES), https://www.tidesport.org/racial-gender-report-card.

and Ethics in Sport at the University of Central Florida. Richard Lapchick began these annual reports many years ago, and they remain a useful tool for seeing the results of hiring practices across the major sport leagues in North America.

SOCIALIZATION: CHANGING ATTITUDES FROM THE BOTTOM UP

At the start of this chapter, I said that change starts from the people in executive positions who decide to make diversity an imperative within the organization. That is true. But we also must recognize the socialization and the history of underrepresentation that can keep minorities from even applying for positions in the first place. Perhaps you've heard the statistic that men apply for a job when they meet only 60 percent of the qualifications, but women apply only if they meet 100 percent of them. This finding came from a Hewlett Packard internal report and has never been validated in a research setting.

While Tara Sophia Mohr questioned the assumption behind the statistic—that women need to have more faith in themselves—and discovered men have many of the same doubts, her survey of more than 1,000 men and women revealed another socialization factor that could affect women's ambition. Fifteen percent of women indicated that the top reason they didn't apply was that "I was following the guidelines about who should apply." Only 8 percent of men gave this as their top answer. The message that girls and women should follow the rules can create a barrier in pursuing a job that men may be less burdened by.

The same study also found that men were less concerned about going for the position and failing than women were (Mohr 2014). Other anecdotal research suggests that women in athletics are reluctant to apply for leadership positions if they don't meet all the listed qualifications while men apply if they meet 20 percent. The Alliance of Women Coaches and Women Leaders in College Sports help participants recognize those self-limiting decisions and act against the false stories women tell themselves to keep from following their dreams.

> "What I really believe is, we start telling little girls not to lead at very young ages, and we start telling little boys to lead at very young ages, and that's a mistake," said Facebook Chief Operating Officer Sheryl Sandberg, a long-time proponent of closing the gender pay gap. "I believe everyone has inside them the ability to lead, and we should let people choose that, not based on gender, but on who they are and who they want to be." (O'Connor 2017, para. 4)

LEARNING TO DREAM

When I reflect on my career, I focus on the proactive path I followed. While there were many challenges and hurdles to overcome, I never imagined the career opportunities I have enjoyed and am so grateful for them. When I became athletics director, I enrolled in an MBA program to strengthen my business skills. I

360

ALI CENTER SUPPORTS ATHLETES' PUSH FOR CHANGE

Eli Wolff

Eli Wolff shares about the social justice and civil rights work of the Muhammad Ali Center. Wolff is the director of the Power of Sport Lab, a platform to fuel and magnify innovation, inclusion, and social change through sport. Projects of the Power of Sport Lab include Disability in Sport, the Olympism Project, and Athletes for Human Rights. Wolff is also the cofounder of the Sport and Society initiative at Brown University.

Some of the work that I am proudest of in my career is with the Muhammad Ali Center in Louisville, Kentucky. The tagline for the Ali Center is "Be Great, Do Great Things," a phrase that I truly stand behind. Athletes have so much power, and they can elect to use it in a transformative way in their communities and throughout society. Ali showed the world just how to use one's voice as a vehicle for change. He inspired me to focus my work on social justice and social change. The Ali Center has more significance than just as a museum; it is a gathering place to celebrate the power of sport, opportunity, and Ali's legacy.

When I was 2 years old, I had a stroke that forever changed the course of my life. Historically, people with disabilities have been treated and looked at differently by others. For so long, people with disabilities who wanted to play sports were looked at as being on the sidelines. The words "retard" and "gimpy" were tossed around as though they held no weight; they do. But at a young age I discovered the power of sport and what it can do. Not only did I pursue a career as an Olympic athlete, ultimately participating in the 1996 and 2004 Paralympic Games as part of the U.S. Paralympic Soccer Team, I have since dedicated my life's work to advancing opportunities in sport for people of all abilities, and to advocating for equality, diversity, and inclusion in sport for all.

Many athletes currently working on social change are isolated, without a sense of community, so that is a big part of what the Ali Center is trying to change. The Ali Center wants athletes to know that they are not alone in their push for change. The spectrum of work that athletes embark on varies—from policy reform, education, and outreach, to forming new community organizations—but just as Ali showed us, the outcomes are always tangible and can make a real difference on a grassroots level. Everyone needs to realize just how much power and influence sport has. Not only can it give one a purpose, but it can also ultimately inspire one to go out and make a difference in someone else's life.

believe in the power of preparation, hard work, taking risks, showing initiative, and receiving support from others. It's important to distinguish yourself from other candidates with your accomplishments, skills, and values. Watch, listen, learn . . . then lead. I have often said that my being the first female AD to oversee both men's and women's programs was a matter of timing, but that the most important thing was that I wouldn't be the last. All who have been a pioneer for their minority group understand how important that responsibility is.

In the early years of women's athletics under the Association of Intercollegiate Athletics for Women (AIAW), women were athletics directors for women's athletics programs. When the NCAA began sponsoring women's championships in 1981, many men's and women's athletics programs were merged, and in almost every situation the men's director became the director for the merged department. There were many well-qualified women prepared for and capable of leading a merged department, but they weren't given the opportunity. Since that time there has been modest progress in the hiring of women to lead combined programs, with that number hovering around 20 percent but less than 10 percent in Division I. Some of the early leaders in the AIAW and role models for women in athletics were Christine Grant (University of Iowa), Charlotte West (Southern Illinois University), and Donna Lopiano (University of Texas and Women's Sports Foundation). These women, along with others, were strong spokespersons for equity and integrity in college athletics.

Courtesy of NCAA.

Judy Sweet was the first woman to serve as NCAA membership president.

A small number of women now lead Division I BCS programs, including Sandy Barbour at Penn State, Heather Lyke at Pitt, Desiree Reed-Francois at UNLV, Debbie Yow at North Carolina State, and Jen Cohen at Washington. In 2017, Carla Williams was appointed director of athletics at the University of Virginia, the first African American woman to lead a Division I Power Five department. As Carla rightfully stated in the press conference announcing her appointment, "Dreams do not know categories. Dreams do not know genders or colors." And recently, Vicki Chun was selected as the first woman to lead the program at Yale.

We have a long way to go in achieving a truly equal society, and I am not so naïve that I don't see the challenges that threaten my goal of having a lasting commitment to equity, diversity, and inclusion. However, I also see a different world than when I grew up. I see progress alongside disappointments, and any person who strives to take on a leadership role must be able to accept that those are constant twins on the journey, whether it's diversity, deal making, or strategic planning. I hope you see from this chapter that I maintain that a commitment to equity, diversity, and inclusion must be a core competency of any good leader, just as important as critical thinking, crisis management, and team building.

I see a world where more girls than ever are participating in sport, an African American man became president of the United States, and grades on gender and race report cards of sport leagues are improving in some cases. I see a blockbuster film about a woman superhero, and the woman director's dignified response when another acclaimed director, a man, minimized the movie's popular reviews. When James Cameron called Wonder Woman "an objectified icon," and said "it's just male Hollywood doing the same old thing," *Wonder Woman* director Patty Jenkins didn't denigrate him. She graciously accepted his positive words on a prior film of hers, and merely responded in a tweet: "I believe women can and should be EVERYTHING just like male lead characters should be. There is no right and wrong kind of powerful woman. And the massive female audience who made the film a hit it is, can surely choose and judge their own icons of progress" (Mumford, 2017). Sounds like a great way to view our future. If we have motivated, ambitious people from all different backgrounds and experiences feeling confident, empowered, and supported, who knows how much we can dream and turn those dreams into reality?

References

Belzer, J. 2016. "The Most Influential Minorities in Sports." *Forbes*. February 24, 2016. www.forbes.com/sites/jasonbelzer/2016/02/24/the-most-influential-minorities-in-sports/#42795f452e7b.

Dishman, L. 2016. "How to Make a Better Business Case for Diversity." *Fast Company*, April 14, 2016. www.fastcompany.com/3058909/how-to-make-a-better-business-case-for-diversity.

Lombardo, J. 2012. "Champions: Judy Sweet, Collegiate Trailblazer," *SportsBusiness Journal*, March 26, 2012. www.sportsbusinessdaily.com/Journal/Issues/2012/03/26/Champions/Sweet.aspx.

Mohr, S.T. 2014. "Why Women Don't Apply for Jobs Unless They're 100% Qualified." *Harvard Business Review,* August 25, 2014. https://hbr.org/2014/08/why-women-dont-apply-for-jobs-unless-theyre-100-qualified. www.tidesport.org/reports.html.

Mumford, G. 2017. "Patty Jenkins Hits Back at James Cameron: 'He Doesn't Understand Wonder Woman'." *The Guardian,* August 25, 2017. www.theguardian.com/film/2017/aug/25/patty-jenkins-hits-back-at-james-cameron-criticism-of-wonder-woman.

O'Connor, L. 2017. "Sheryl Sandberg Says We Have A Problem 'Telling Little Girls Not To Lead.'" *Huffington Post,* July 30, 2017. www.huffingtonpost.com/entry/sheryl-sandberg-equal-pay_us_597e5fdfe4b02a8434b72ebf?utm_medium=email&utm_campaign=__TheMorningEmail__073117&utm_content=__TheMorningEmail__073117+CID_00245b0ca364ce074083049d7df48934&utm_source=Email%20marketing%20software&utm_term=thinks%20theres%20a%20big%20problem&ncid=newsltushpmgnews__TheMorningEmail__073117.

CHAPTER 25

Leadership Lessons Learned the Hard Way

Kevin Warren

Kevin Warren is chief operating officer of the Minnesota Vikings and the highest-ranking African American executive working on the business side for an NFL team. In 2015, Warren became the first African American chief operating officer of an NFL team. He received his first exposure to sport law after receiving his law degree from Notre Dame and working on NCAA violation cases for various universities at the law firm of Bond, Schoeneck & King. Warren later established his own sports and entertainment agency. Once hired by the St. Louis Rams, he took on a front office position as vice president of player programs and football legal counsel and later as vice president of football administration. After a stint with the Detroit Lions as senior vice president of business operations and general counsel, Warren joined the Vikings in 2005 after working with the current ownership group during the acquisition of the team. He was instrumental in the construction of U.S. Bank Stadium, which hosted Super Bowl LII, as well as internal restructuring of organizational management and serving on influential NFL committees such as emergency planning and workplace diversity. Warren is active in Twin Cities civic life, serving on boards that represent youth, education, and health issues, and creating numerous grant and scholarship programs with his wife Greta. They have a daughter, Peri, and a son, Powers. The Vikings COO played on the University of Pennsylvania's 1981 to 1982 Ivy League championship basketball team before finishing up his successful collegiate basketball career and his bachelor's degree at Grand Canyon University. Warren, who grew up in Tempe, Arizona, received his MBA from his hometown Arizona State University and his law degree from the University of Notre Dame School of Law.

The chapter opener photo features Kevin Warren (upper left) with wife Greta (lower left), son Powers (upper right), and daughter Peri.

On a beautiful and clear warm summer day in Tempe, Arizona, at the age of 12, I learned an incredibly painful, physically powerful, but valuable lesson. This, along with many other lessons, was conveyed to me by my maternal grandmother, Ramona Padilla Mosley, affectionately known by everyone as "Big Mama." All the people who heard me talk about Big Mama's many life lessons always had a perplexed look on their face if they were fortunate enough to actually have met her. Why? Because Big Mama was at best 5 feet 2 inches (about 1.6 m), 100 pounds (about 45 kg) soaking wet, and had attended formal school in Mexico only to the fourth grade. But believe me when I say that woman was what in today's world we call an influencer. The life lessons provided by Big Mama were always carefully spooned out the way a loving parent feeds a young infant the warm cereal needed to survive. Big Mama made it her life lesson to feed her grandchildren necessary life nutrients—if we were willing to listen and learn.

Great teachers are those individuals who both show and tell you about life, which is what Big Mama did. Leadership is a term we hear a lot about these days in the business world, in both research and practice. In this book, you hear from leaders who own teams, run massive organizations, and bring creative new ideas into being. These are great resources, but leaders are all around us, if we choose to seek them out. It is important to explore what it means and what we expect of our leaders and of ourselves if we choose or are thrust into a leadership role. Leaders must be great teachers.

What made Big Mama such a great teacher, an incredible inspiration, and someone who I deeply loved and admired, was simple: The woman was willing to do the work. Period. How many people who you work with could you say the same about? Could you say it about yourself? She attended school only to the fourth grade, she dropped out of school to work to help support the family, she spoke broken English because she was born and raised in Guadalajara, Jalisco, Mexico, she was a maid in Fort Huachuca, Arizona at the army base where she met my grandfather. She became a maid in Phoenix, Arizona; she never had a driver's license, never drove a car, never flew on a plane, took only public transportation, was never late for an appointment, and lived in the hardscrabble housing projects on 19th Avenue and Buckeye Road (which is where I would spend weekends with her). She raised two children: Uncle Freddie (an army veteran who abused alcohol), my mother Margaret (truly a saint), and countless grandchildren.

In retrospect, I believe Big Mama was addicted to cigarettes and also a recovering alcoholic who created "her own" Alcoholics Anonymous 12 Step Plan and made up her mind that she needed to survive and prosper to provide her young grandchildren like me the hope, desire, grit, strength, moxie, and perseverance to fulfill our God-given abilities. Big Mama smoked only a single Camel nonfilter cigarette a day, yes, only one. She also limited the number of Miller High Life beers she would drink. She would allow us to "taste" beer (if we so desired). She cursed like a sailor, but she said her rosary every morning, said her prayers on her knees every night, and attended Mass regularly. She never hid

GAME CHANGER

OPPORTUNITY KNOCKS WHEN YOU OPEN YOUR MOUTH

Stan Kasten

Stan Kasten, like Big Mama, has never been afraid to speak his mind—a trait that allowed him to embark on a lifetime at the upper levels of Major League Baseball. Kasten is president and part owner of the Los Angeles Dodgers, as he joined Magic Johnson, Peter Guber, and Mark Walter of Guggenheim Partners for a $2.15 billion winning bid for the historic franchise in 2012. Kasten is also former president of the Atlanta Braves, Washington Nationals, Atlanta Falcons, Atlanta Hawks, and Atlanta Thrashers. He became the youngest general manager in the NBA when at age 27 he held that role for the Hawks. In 1986 and 1987, he became the only person to win back-to-back NBA Executive of the Year awards. He is a graduate of New York University and Columbia Law School.

I had no idea when I was crossing the country attending baseball games, taking a break after finishing law school and two bar exams, that I would initiate a conversation with Ted Turner at Busch Stadium in St. Louis that would change the trajectory of my life.

But that's what happened. I recognized the Atlanta Braves owner that night. I don't know if anybody else did. After the game, I just walked up to him and started chatting. We kind of hit it off and he invited me to Atlanta. Within two years, at age 27, I was the youngest general manager in NBA history for Turner's Atlanta Hawks.

Here's what you need to know about that encounter:

- Opportunities often present themselves when you least expect it. Often. Don't give them away. Good luck doesn't get enough positive press. It's around us all the time.

- I had no plan when I opened my mouth. It was unpredictable. However, I suspect I had done enough thinking to be confident enough that it was the right thing to do in that circumstance. I tell students sometimes that they could walk out of the room we're in right now and bump into somebody in the hall who could change their life. That could absolutely happen. Are you ready?

That anecdote is fun to tell, and sure, it was exciting to me when it happened. But even at the time I knew that if I didn't perform, I would be the youngest ex-GM ever. It is an understatement to say I took an unorthodox path to becoming an NBA GM. My first work with the Hawks was when I got pulled over for some daily work for the interim GM soon after Turner bought the Hawks. Not only was I an attorney with the Braves and Turner Broadcasting System, I hadn't been a player or a coach and didn't have my own network of contacts throughout the league or colleges. I knew I would have to outwork people and be as prepared as I possibly could when making decisions.

(continued)

In 1986 and 1987, I was still the youngest GM in the league, and I became the first (and still only) person named NBA Executive of the Year in back-to-back seasons. That was an award voted on by my peers, which was incredibly meaningful to me. That told me I was doing something right. In 1986, I added the title of team president for the Braves and Hawks.

Since then, I have been team president of the Washington Nationals and now the Los Angeles Dodgers. My career and my success have been in building teams. At each stop I have led a thrilling life, because I get the challenge of competing against more than two dozen gifted front offices that are trying to beat our brains out every night. Having said that, LA is the most fun and most important job I have had. From the day we bought the team, we articulated to fans three prongs in our strategy: (1) We would build our product for long-term and short-term success (the Dodgers can't go through a prolonged rebuilding period); (2) customer relationships would be prioritized (as shown in renovating our gem of a ballpark, Dodger Stadium, so that it retained its familiarity while providing a 21st-century fan experience); and (3) we would develop strong community relations, which includes the Dodger Dream Field program that has built 50 youth ballfields throughout Southern California. All successful companies and teams must ensure that customers believe in their brand. If they do, they will stay with you through ups and down. With the Dodgers, we have enthusiastically resuscitated a historic and iconic brand. For someone in my line of work, that is a rare opportunity—and as you know, I am very familiar with the topic of opportunities.

Used with permission of Stan Kasten.

her weaknesses—a trait that too few leaders are willing to acknowledge for fear of looking fallible, uncertain, and vulnerable. Instead, she used her vices, if you wish to call them that, to teach us about life. She was truly a rare person, very similar to my wife Greta, who has opened her heart and soul to me, to teach me the true essence of love, loyalty, and honesty and that human beings are truly imperfect but still very special.

As I grew older, I began to realize that Big Mama was the perfect human being to actually deliver painful and valuable lessons because her entire life had been based upon pain and perseverance. Many people provide "paid advice" (psychologists and lawyers). Many other people provide "free advice" (family and friends). A handful of people provide "authentic advice" (Big Mama), which is advice gained from pain and trauma. Big Mama was tough but she had a beautiful spirit. Very similarly, a larva becomes a beautiful butterfly only after it endures trauma during the process of leaving the cocoon.

SIX LESSONS FROM BIG MAMA

I have so many stories about Big Mama and the many lessons she taught me that I have grouped them into six categories. That said, I will focus only on the first

Big Mama.

of these six here. All six are valuable for anyone to heed, but the first one is an especially good reminder to sport business professionals and students who want the path to open wide for them when they have a good idea or an ambition they want realized. She would teach these lessons to me and many others while she cooked in the kitchen, while we ate dinner, while we did our chores, while we walked to the local market, or while we were on the local bus.

One day I plan to write an entire book on the lessons of Big Mama; we will save that for another day. But let me share with you the six categories of life lessons that I have created to help articulate to me what to make of Big Mama's stories:

1. Life is not fair.
2. Formal education is critical.
3. Be a maniacal worker.
4. Give more than you take.
5. Be humble.
6. Love God.

A LIFE-CHANGING EVENT

On that sunny Arizona summer day when I was 12, circumstances set in motion for me the opportunity to really heed these lessons firsthand. If I had not already been paying attention to Big Mama before that day, I certainly was shortly afterward. The trajectory of my life changed forever when I was riding my bike to go play basketball with friends at the local high school. I lived four blocks away from the high school and had made this simple, safe ride on my bike literally

Pete LaCock

Pete LaCock saw the value of hard work as a child through his father's show biz world and later as he embarked on life as a professional athlete. LaCock played nine seasons in the major leagues plus one more year in Japan. He was drafted in the first round by the Chicago Cubs in the 1970 draft and was with the Kansas City Royals during three division titles and one American League pennant. He served several stints as a hitting coach for teams in the United States and Canada. LaCock, the son of singer and game-show host Peter Marshall and nephew of actress Joanne Dru, has stayed active in Cubs alumni events since retirement.

Sport and entertainment. Take it from me, somebody who met Sammy Davis Jr. and Joey Bishop at my house when I was a kid and then got to play alongside Ferguson Jenkins and Billy Williams, the two are inextricably intertwined.

Whether it has to do with Rat Pack stars or Major League Baseball Hall of Famers, our society's desire for entertainment drives a massive economic enterprise. I played nine years in the major leagues, including five with the Chicago Cubs. My father, Ralph Pierre LaCock—better known as *The Hollywood Squares* game-show host Peter Marshall—was an immensely talented singer and actor who knew most everyone in post–World War II show biz.

It sounds corny to say it, but in both spheres, hard work separates you from the pack. It is tempting to credit natural talent for the home runs we watch sail out of the park or the soaring melodies our favorite singers corral with their voices. Of course innate talent is part of it, but the will to work and the joy in doing it gets you much closer to your goals than you might ever know.

My dad started singing in New York nightclubs when he was 12 years old. His father died young, so my dad had real motivation to push himself and become a success. He found something he loved and rode it as long as he could. Even into his 90s, he continues singing and hosting a radio show. That's a pretty nice ride.

I played only briefly with Ernie Banks, but his infectious love of the game is a story told many times by now. I cherished the chance to observe Banks, Jenkins, and Williams play baseball with great joy and respect. Such a winning attitude helped expand the Cubs' brand—not that we were calling it that back then—even when we were not accumulating wins the way the team does now.

There are significant differences. I believe the entertainment business is based much more on who you know, whereas in baseball and sport, everything is tied up in your numbers. If your statistics, whether traditional or sabermetric, don't add up, you won't be playing very long.

The money was microscopic back then compared to what it is now. But I will never complain about that. I was fortunate to observe top performers at the peak of their game, on stage or on the diamond. As part of the Cubs family today, I join World Series–winning manager Joe Maddon's annual golf tournament for his hometown of Hazelton, Pennsylvania.

In what area of life do you find joy in putting in the hard work to be a success? The sport and entertainment industries are wide open for you to seize the opportunity.

hundreds of times. You know the type of kid: After finishing my required daily chores and homework during the school year, I was outside playing sports, riding my bike, or riding my bike on the way to play sports. Why would this day be any different? I woke up early, took a shower, brushed my teeth, got dressed, had breakfast, completed my chores, and told my sister-in-law, who happened to be at our house, where I was going. Both my mom and dad had left the house early in the morning for their respective jobs as a school teacher and an administrator.

What made this ride smooth and easy was that it required me to take only side streets and no busy streets. As I slowed down to turn into the high school entrance, out of the sky I heard a loud screeching noise—clearly created by the tires on a car traveling way too fast for our neighborhood. I thought to myself, in that split second, how strange it sounded. No sooner had that brief thought left my mind than I felt metal hitting my bike. All of a sudden, I was airborne for more than 30 feet. As I got older, I recognized the symbolism that 30 feet is 10 yards—exactly the distance to get a first down in football. Every time I walk on a football field or watch a football game, I recognize how far 30 feet or 10 yards actually is and how fortunate I am that God chose to spare my life by allowing me to land on a simple patch of grass to cushion my fall. A few feet in any other direction and my parents would have been writing my obituary and lowering me into the ground before my life really started. I should have died that day, but God made it clear to me that I needed to truly understand that *Life is not fair.*

My accident resulted in many days lying flat on my back in the hospital in traction and many more days in a body cast, trying to drink water and eat food

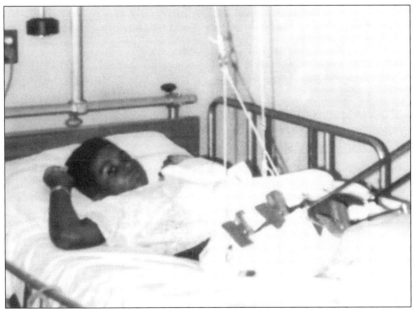

Courtesy of Kevin Warren.

Kevin Warren, age 12, recovering after his accident.

without choking. Still to this day, I cannot drink from a straw because the plastic straw touching my lips brings back too many painful memories of my accident and subsequent recovery. Having to go to the bathroom in a bedpan for days upon days, months upon months, and not being allowed to take a bath or shower was awful. *Life is not fair.*

The weight gain, the inability to walk, doctors telling me my sports career was over before it began, nightmares, and depression were very traumatic. That said, that accident softened my heart and subsequently taught me about perseverance, hope, positive energy, faith, and grit. It provided me with a "can-do" attitude and a resolve to make the most of every second, of every minute, of every hour, and of every day. It taught me that although life is not fair, life is a gift that should not be taken for granted. It also taught me always to look for opportunities to help another person who may be smiling but is truly in pain.

What does this story have to do with business and especially the business of sport? Everything! I have been blessed to have an incredible personal and professional life. I have met some truly amazing people. I have touched the lives of so many people, and so many people have touched my life in return. I have been married for nearly 27 years to an incredible woman who makes me better on a daily basis and has blessed us with two phenomenal children. I do not take lightly that in 2018, I entered my 20th NFL season, being part of winning Super Bowl XXXIV with the St. Louis Rams, being voted into my college athletic hall of fame, being heavily involved in assisting the Wilf family during their purchase of the Minnesota Vikings, and being the first African American to become a chief operating officer in the NFL (and unfortunately still the only one). Similarly, being on the deal team that figured out a way to create a public–private partnership that was the catalyst for building U.S. Bank Stadium for $1.1 billion, which to this day is the largest construction project in the history of the state of Minnesota. Similarly, negotiating various major naming rights and founding partner agreements. Also empowering women in the workplace, hosting Super Bowl LII, being part of the deal team to build Twin Cities Orthopedics Performance Center, a "next-generation" development that will incorporate our new world headquarters. While I was in the middle of every single one of these business deals, I would think back to those weekends spent in the projects with Big Mama when she would tell me in her Spanglish (combination of Spanish and English), "Kevin, you are special, you will make history but you will have to endure many tough days, you will face pain, you must be tough as nails, and you must learn that *life is not fair.*"

To that end, God spared my life on that warm summer day and gave me a second chance to become a corporate mountain climber and to create a path for many people who will come behind me. So many times in the corporate business world, people sitting across elegant conference tables, drinking sparkling water, writing with expensive pens in expensive leather binders, wearing expensive clothes and shoes talking about deals that are in the millions or billions of dollars fail to realize that business deals involve people and people have feelings. Incredible success can be created in the business world by putting others first and doing the right thing.

360

PROBLEM SOLVERS VERSUS PROBLEM CREATORS . . . CHOOSE WISELY

Pat Gallagher

Pat Gallagher recognizes that the best employees—the problem solvers—realize that life is not fair and find solutions anyway. Gallagher has spent more than four decades in management in the sport and entertainment industry and is best known for his key roles with the San Francisco Giants and the Super Bowl 50 Host Committee. He is the coauthor of *Big Game Bigger Impact*.

When you work in this business for a long time, you learn about the qualities and ingredients that are necessary for success and also the humility that comes with the best-laid plans that don't work out. Many of you who are reading this have spent years in the business in some capacity. To those of you who aspire to get into this business, I'm thinking mostly about you as I write this.

I always appreciated the veteran elder statesmen and stateswomen who were kind and patient enough to share their wisdom and experience with a young kid just finding his way. Their stories and advice meant more to me than any of them will ever know.

I was fortunate to be managed by a few great leaders and a few not so great. I've directly managed a few hundred people and indirectly several thousand in over four decades. Here is a simple general observation about people I've learned over the years that I hope those of you just starting in the business will find of value.

I believe that there are really only two kinds of people: the ones who *solve problems* and the ones who *create more problems* than they solve. We've all seen them, gone to school with them, or worked with them. Both types can be highly educated, intelligent, and attractive and say all of the right things. But the ones you must seek to have on your team are the ones who are devoted to the mission and focus on *problem solving* above everything else. These are the ones you can rely on no matter what.

Problem solvers have the ability to be a part of a team or to lead a team, depending upon the situation. They are calm under pressure, can always be counted on—particularly during the tough times that every company, team, or event will invariably go through—and will bring a positive, can-do attitude to work every day. They step up not only during the good times, but especially during the challenging ones. And in my experience, they usually are also people who are the most fun to be around.

The *problem creators* can look attractive on paper, but for whatever reason, they tend to focus on the negative first—or worse—are dishonest or betray the trust of the team. They get tangled up in interpersonal issues, give excuses on why they fell behind on deadlines or deliverables, or come to work with an unproductive attitude and a sense of entitlement. They can be a cancer on an entire organization, and for everyone's sake, should be avoided at all costs. In a mission-driven organization,

(continued)

360   *(continued)*

most of them eventually get discovered and shown the door, but usually they don't understand why because they are too busy deflecting what was their responsibility.

Try to hire or be regarded as the former and avoid being or associating with the latter. As a manager, the trick is ferreting out which one is which soon enough to limit the damage the problem creators can cause and mobilize the problem solvers to let them do what they do best. You won't always get it right, but as a manager, you owe it to everyone else on the team to sharpen your antennae to make the right call. As a manager, if you don't figure out who the problem creators are quickly enough and cut them from the pack before they sabotage the show, you may get shown the door and you probably will deserve it.

Used with permission of Pat Gallagher.

FINAL WORDS TO HEED

In business, always remember that life is not fair and always strive to treat the woman or man on the other side of the table with honor, respect, love, and decorum. Refuse to put the financial terms of a deal first; money will always show up when you do what is right from a business standpoint. You will exceed your wildest dreams and leave a positive legacy that will last for as long as the earth is round. Thank you, Big Mama, for pouring your experiences into me, and also thank you to the woman who hit me with her car—they both changed my life for the best, in vastly different ways. I clearly realize life is not fair but it is life, which means we have an opportunity to make the world better each and every day. Go make phenomenal business deals. Conquer your dreams and desires. Godspeed.

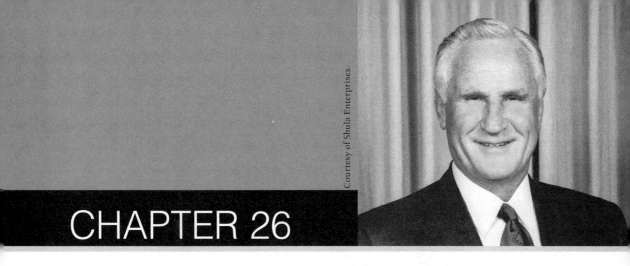

Courtesy of Shula Enterprises.

CHAPTER 26

Cultivating a Winning Edge

Don Shula

On July 26, 1997, Coach Don Shula capped an illustrious career when he was inducted into the Pro Football Hall of Fame in Canton, Ohio, in his first year of eligibility. Shula's unanimous election to the hall was the ultimate honor in a career full of record-setting accomplishments. Shula's record as head coach of the Dolphins (1970-1995) and before that as head coach of the Baltimore Colts (1963-1969) is unmatched in NFL history. In 1995, he concluded his 33rd season as an NFL head coach and his 26th season as head coach of the Dolphins. He is the winningest coach in NFL history with a career record of 347-173-6 (.665), including a regular-season mark of 328-156-6 (.676). Shula won Super Bowl titles in 1972 and 1973, one of only five coaches in NFL history to win consecutive Super Bowls. His 1972 team went 17-0, recording the only undefeated season in NFL annals. He has appeared in more Super Bowls (six) than any other coach and is one of only two coaches to reach the Super Bowl three straight seasons (1971-1973).

Along with his football responsibilities, Shula always has given considerable time, plus financial and emotional support, to many area charities. The Don Shula Foundation was established in 1992 and was formed primarily to assist in breast cancer research. Moffitt Cancer Center's Don & Erika Wallace Comprehensive Breast Program has been a recipient of funds from that foundation since 2003. In 2014, The Shula Fund at Moffitt Cancer Center was established. Shula also has been active in the American Cancer Society, March of Dimes, American Red Cross, the United Way, and Catholic Charities. Because of his success on the football field and his long-time civic and charitable service, Coach Don Shula was honored on February 3, 2010, as the first recipient of the Moffitt Board of Advisors Philanthropy & Leadership Award in a ceremony attended by nearly 400 guests in Miami Beach. In addition, he has received countless prestigious awards recognizing his contributions, including the 1993 *Sports Illustrated*'s Sportsman of the Year Award, the 1994 Horatio Alger Award, the Bert Bell Award, the Lombardi Award, and

the Pete Rozelle Award. In 1995, along with Ken Blanchard, he coauthored *Everyone's a Coach,* a highly acclaimed book that outlines the
application of their managerial philosophies for business and personal
success. Shula personifies those business principles himself, serving
as a partner in two highly successful enterprises, Shula Enterprises Inc.,
along with Don Shula's Steak Houses LLLP. Coach Shula and his wife
Mary Anne reside in Miami and continue to be very active in charitable
and community affairs. They were married on October 15, 1993, and
their family together now includes eight children, 16 grandchildren, and
two great-grandchildren.

The Graham family dated back to the founding of our community, Miami Lakes. Their son, Bob, had been a U.S. senator and Florida governor. Their other son Phil was publisher of the *Washington Post.* It is a wonderful and influential family that people don't easily say no to. They asked me many times during the 1980s to license my name for their restaurant, Legends. I repeatedly declined. What did I know about the restaurant business? My first wife, Dorothy, was insistent that I start to consider postcoaching interests. The Grahams said they would rebrand around our 1972 perfect season. As my son Dave, a former NFL coach and player and now a coach at Dartmouth, told the *Miami Herald* in 2015, "Probably the biggest hitch, the part that slowed [my dad] down, is you realized that you can only lose your reputation once. He wasn't going to be running it and had put a lot of faith in the Grahams and their ability to be able to run this facility in a way that would represent his name and the reputation that went along with it in a positive way" (Morrisey 2015, para. 11). Dave said it well. I always worked hard on the details, and I always obsessively prepared. If I am not committed to excellence, I don't want to waste my time on an endeavor. Fortunately, my family and friends understood how important my reputation was to me, and they developed the restaurant's theme accordingly.

As I look back on the success of the dining establishments that bear my name, I wonder why I was so reluctant to enter into that business. After all, the theme of excellence, of winning, surrounded me in both coaching and the restaurant industry. Success in one field quite literally made the other possible. I am proud that my name is directly linked to aspirational words like those. I was right to not give away my reputation without serious thought, but I was simply shortsighted to not see the synergy of success, whatever the endeavor. The core principles are the same. When you cultivate a winning edge, you choose to sacrifice and persistently push to meet your goals. In both areas, I was consistent in my approach.

In *Everyone's a Coach: Five Business Secrets for High-Performance Coaching,* business guru Ken Blanchard and I provide five secrets of success: Be Conviction-driven, practice Overlearning, be Audible-ready, have Consistency, and be Honesty-based . . . put together that equals COACH. I hope that the two Cs in the acronym are clear on their face: To be conviction-driven means you don't compromise your beliefs (as has been reinforced throughout this book, in the personal SWOT analysis exercise in chapter 1, in Robin Harris', Don Garber's, and Deborah Yow's chapters, among others). To be consistent is to respond predictably to performance—train, prepare, and focus intensely to get the results you want. As for the other three letters, overlearning means to practice until you are as close to perfect as you can be. Audible-ready refers to knowing when you need to change and take the steps necessary to effectively do so. Honesty-based means that you exude trustworthiness—you do what you say you're going to do. For a leader, this last point is essential if you are going to get others to buy into your vision. Knowing these five skills and traits is a good place to begin this chapter. They permeate all the points I will share.

DELIBERATE PRACTICE

I am fortunate to be known as the winningest coach of all time in the NFL, and I'm especially proud of how consistently my teams won, as evidenced by my teams' winning percentage and success in making the playoffs. In talking about cultivating a winning edge, these hard numbers express in very clear terms the concept of winning. I don't want to diminish how important I saw my stated task of winning football games. To win often, and be fiercely competitive and honorable in the process, was my job and my passion. Yet, as a coach, I knew that wins were the result of an immense amount of work; enjoying that work was where I generated a will toward excellence, not solely the desire to accumulate wins, or for that matter other drivers such as wealth (which also can be measured in hard numbers) that are so important to some.

The term *deliberate practice* has gotten a lot of attention in the past decade or two. It should, because it can be differentiated from the concept of hours logged or simply practice. Deliberate practice is as important on a football field or a weight room as it is to a board room or an office. You have to know what you want to accomplish, then point yourself and your team in the right direction. Some people keep that light on until midnight and then get up at the crack of dawn, yet they don't accomplish anything. Others don't look as though they're working hard, but they are working on the important tasks and training that move them forward in their pursuit of a goal. Pinpoint what it takes to be successful and undertake the work that applies to your own situation. Deliberate practice often gets paired with the idea that you have to spend 10,000 hours at an activity to master it. I have never cared to figure out why 10,000 is the magic number. I know it takes a lot of sacrifice to succeed, and there are no shortcuts to doing that. But I would caution about clocking in and out of your chosen pursuit just to meet that mark. Better to commit yourself to working on the most effective strategies to reach a high level of achievement. I suspect if you love what you are doing, you eventually will reach 10,000 hours. But you won't care, because you'll be too busy enjoying the journey, seeing improvements, and finding new avenues that continually make your passion interesting.

GAME CHANGER

FROM ATHENS TO LA TO PHOENIX: KEEP CHASING YOUR DREAMS

Derrick Hall

Derrick Hall cultivated a winning edge to turn what could have been a crushing defeat at a crucial moment in his budding career as a sport executive into a victory. Hall, Arizona Diamondbacks president and CEO, has turned the D-backs into a model franchise within the sport industry and throughout the business world during his 14 seasons at the helm of the club. Hall focuses the organization's efforts in five areas he has called the "Circle of Success"—fan experience, performance, community, culture, and financial efficiency—each of which has seen tremendous success during his tenure. He has positioned the D-backs as one of the largest philanthropic entities, surpassing $55 million in charitable giving since 1998, including more than $6 million in 2017. He has created a corporate culture that led Yahoo! to deem the club "the best workplace in sports."

Courtesy of Arizona Diamondbacks.

So many of us dream of having a career in sport but lack the knowledge or clarity to chart a path to get there. I was certainly in that boat as I graduated from college, desperately searching for an entry point. I had no contacts in the industry and was merely chasing a dream.

I moved to Las Vegas and was working three odd jobs to make ends meet while blindly sending resumes out by the dozens, nearly all of which went unanswered. I was beyond frustrated until my father called me one day and told me to quickly turn on ESPN. The network was featuring Ohio University and its master's program in sport management. In the segment, I learned that one student was selected each year from there to intern with the Dodgers—this was energizing, as that was my favorite team growing up in Los Angeles.

I applied for the program and was selected as a finalist and invited to travel to Athens, Ohio, for some intense and stressful interviews. I was convinced afterward that I had impressed the panel and had done enough to earn admission. After traveling back home and sharing the experience with my wife, we decided to pack up our apartment and make plans to move east for this opportunity. A week or so later, with moving boxes full and taped, I received my letter from the university. In a shocking turn of events, I was notified of my rejection.

This provided greater motivation for me, as I was now determined to do it on my own. So I flew to Miami for the annual Winter Meetings and registered to be a part of a career search. A few days into it, I realized that I was not going to land a meaningful job, nor were the other 300 hopefuls who were just as eager as I was. Dejected, I left the banquet hall and found myself in the lobby of the hotel where I spotted a sign that displayed the hotel's events that day. One that immediately jumped out was "Ohio University Sports Administration Alumni Reception, 7:00, Suite 601." And I quickly thought, "That's a party I'm going to crash."

I went to the suite, saw the program's director in the back of the room, cornered him, asked if he remembered me, and chewed his ear for an hour on why I should have been selected. He finally cut me off, asked me to come back, and try again the next year. I followed his advice, successfully joined the program, earned the internship with the Dodgers, and eventually became a senior vice president in Los Angeles before coming to Arizona, where I have thoroughly enjoyed my career as president and CEO.

The moral of my story is to keep chasing your dreams. Do not let anyone tell you that you cannot achieve something you desperately want. Shoot for the stars and work in an industry you crave involvement in, because if you truly love what you are doing, you will never work a day in your life!

Coaches are notorious for being obsessed with making even incremental progress at all times and taking care of the details to help make that occur. I'm certainly guilty. Anybody, coach or not, can take this too far, and that is not healthy. But what is often forgotten in this situation is that when you pay attention to the details, you are constantly looking to improve systems and reviewing and practicing what needs to be done. This can be an opportunity to create a more efficient unit that doesn't have to work extra-long hours to get the desired results. Of course, this is a constant balancing act, but understand that taking details seriously is not about micromanaging or forcing everybody to work more hours at the job. Taking details seriously is the effort that creates a winning culture more quickly; leaders of an organization play a vital role in making that a reality. I made this point in *Everyone's a Coach*:

> Someone has said that a river without banks is a puddle. When I apply that saying to human interactions, it reminds me of the job of a coach. Like those riverbanks, a good coach provides the direction and concentration for performers' energies, helping channel all their efforts toward a single desired outcome. Without that critical influence, the best achievements of the most talented performers can lack the momentum and

drive that make a group of individuals into champions. In my work with the Miami Dolphins over the years, one single vision of perfection has motivated all of my coaching—that's winning every football game. Without exception, every coaching strategy I've adopted has been aimed at that one target. A broad target that's easy to achieve leads to the "puddle" of mediocrity. Keeping that specific focus before the team and concentrating the efforts within narrowly defined limits are my tasks as the coach of this football team. (p. 28)

PAST ISN'T PROLOGUE, BUT IT SURE HELPS

There are coaches and executives in and out of sport who have a reputation for developing winners. When you enter a situation, whether it's a winning organization or one that is looking to find an edge that has been lacking, you cannot simply apply the same patch—or sledgehammer—that worked at your previous job. Each situation is different, and you must be flexible in assessing what will work best for the present one. Your past experiences and training can be valuable tools and a knowledge base with regard to the decisions that you need to make now. But never let a past success or failure lead you down the false path of believing you will get the same result this time around if you take the same action. In your own mind, you've got to sort out and make sure you're doing something that is within the possibility of success.

Learn from the past, but don't live there. Make sure that you take the lessons you've learned and utilize them for your future success. I always tried to learn along the way; the lessons from the past allowed me to take on the challenges of the future.

Notably, the Dolphins were 3-10-1 the year before I came to Miami, and the first thing I had to do was change the culture from losing to winning. In order to do that, you have to win every day, every hour, and every minute; never settle for failure; and be positive in everything that you do. Thus, the practices that led to success were taught.

You see, most teams had a curfew and a bed check on away games; I was just a little more clever. I issued a curfew, but rather than bed checks I gave the elevator operator a football and told him to have every player that he saw after 10 p.m. sign it. I also told him to not mention where he got the football, but that I wanted to see the football in the morning. The big reason for the team's turnaround was eliminating the errors that led to failure by maintaining rules and regulations that put us in a position to win.

My belief has always been that every situation and the principal people involved are different. (Even if some of the people are the same, they may be in a different position or mindset than the last time you worked with them.) The most important part of being a decision maker is to get as much information as you can, then make your decision based in the present. You learn from past experiences, but you can't let past experience make future decisions for you. This is hard advice to heed when you are in a difficult moment. It becomes a crutch to rely on the past rather than take ownership of the decisions ahead. Whether you use 1 percent or 100 percent of the past experience in influencing a given decision, know that the research was not a waste. It all went into putting you and your organization in the best possible position.

USE YOUR RESOURCES

Part of using the past to inform the present is drawing upon your mentors and your experiences with other leaders. I was fortunate to play two seasons under Paul Brown while I was with the Cleveland Browns. In 1958, I began my coaching career as a defensive backs coach with University of Virginia. I moved to the same position at the University of Kentucky the next year. This was an incredible opportunity for me. The coach there was Blanton Collier, and there was a winning culture already established there. Collier was a Paul Brown disciple to the core, and that year helped establish the foundation of my learning process. It became important in developing my coaching philosophy. I don't know if Collier ever played a down of high-level football, but he was a great teacher. Brown always said that instruction consisted of four steps: listening, writing, reviewing, and then practicing. I believe in those, and Collier was diligent in those first three. I can't say he learned through practice himself, but he was smart and able to observe what other people needed to do in order to be successful on the field.

It is imperative to investigate what other successful people in your area of interest do. How do they carry themselves? How do they go about making decisions? What did they find helped them reach their level of success? You can find this out through reading articles and books such as this one, listening to podcasts, and watching presentations from these thought leaders. Never shy away from accepting an opportunity to ask them questions in person, through your network of contacts, or at conferences and events. Learn from others what they think it takes to be successful; then, as with past experiences, incorporate what you find most helpful into formulating what you believe. Who is your mentor? Who would you like to be your mentor? Seek that person out.

BRUTAL HONESTY

In *Everyone's a Coach,* I list my five coaching beliefs:

1. Keep winning and losing in perspective.
2. Lead by example.
3. Go for respect over popularity.
4. Value character as well as ability.
5. Work hard but enjoy what you do (p. 29).

You have to own #3 if you are willing to be brutally honest in your ongoing assessments of yourself, your organization, and your team members. If you are committed to building a winning and successful culture, you can't tolerate all of those elements not being in alignment. This does not always make you popular,

THE LESSONS OF COMPETITIVENESS

Bob Griese

Bob Griese quarterbacked some of Don Shula's greatest teams. He also shared his coach's competitive fire that helped fuel the Dolphins' winning culture. Griese led the offense in three consecutive Super Bowl appearances, two of them victories, following an All-American career at Purdue University. He was inducted into the College Football Hall of Fame and the Pro Football Hall of Fame, and he later worked as a commentator for college football games on ABC and ESPN.

I learned early in life to maximize benefit from unexpected events. While studying at Purdue University, I didn't have any aspirations about playing professional football; I just wanted to do the best I could in all areas to open doors for myself. I put in all-around hard work and the doors indeed opened themselves—I had a couple of good football years, I finished second in the Heisman voting to Steve Spurrier, and we won the Rose Bowl. After those somewhat unexpected events I was drafted first by the NFL's Miami Dolphins.

The spring prior to the 1972 perfect season, Coach Don Shula petitioned owner Joe Robbie saying we needed somebody who could play as a backup. Robbie agreed and followed through (reflecting one of his great traits) by signing league veteran Earl Morrall. I ended up getting hurt in the fifth game. Earl was not a good practice player, so a lot of our teammates were concerned when he had to go in. Somewhat unexpectedly, Earl led the team to win 11 games. When I was healthy from my dislocated ankle, I came back to play in the AFC Championship game and then also in the Super Bowl, which we won, capping off the NFL's only undefeated season. There would have been no perfect season without Earl Morrall.

Aside from maximizing the unexpected, an important lesson from my life is the power of competitiveness. I was very competitive in the athletic environment and also in the classroom. I remember back in grade school, the teacher would stand everyone up in the back of the room and we'd have a spelling contest; if you spelled the word wrong you had to sit down. I made sure to do whatever I had to do to be the last person standing.

Yes, competitiveness can create greatness; but that doesn't always mean doing it alone. For example, in the Super Bowl of our undefeated season, I threw only 10 or so passes. Coach Shula let me call the plays in the huddle, so if I wanted to be the MVP of the Super Bowl I could have thrown 25 or 30 passes to get my stats up, but that's not what we needed to do to win. My competitiveness pushed me to play to our strengths, which were Larry Csonka, Mercury Morris, our offensive line, and not necessarily my passing. Strive for greatness and be competitive, but it's important to understand how that takes form.

when you alert someone that his performance is subpar and may require putting a new person in his place. Or when your team is happy with simply being "good enough." I always want anything I am in charge of and has my name on it to be done with excellence, whether in football or my restaurant. I never wanted to lose a game because of mental errors or committing a costly penalty. We were often the least-penalized team in the league. There is a film clip of our great running back Larry Csonka talking about me after a game that we had won but hadn't played well. I knew that if we had continued to make those kinds of mistakes we wouldn't win in the future. Csonka is quoted as saying, "Hey, I thought when you won a game the coach was happy. But Shula wasn't. He was obsessed" (850 Business Magazine, para. 5). If you are brutally honest with yourself and explore the reasons why a decision or action didn't work, you will develop great confidence in your abilities. In turn, your team will have faith in what you want done. You won't repeat mistakes. These are the ingredients for cultivating a winning edge.

Leaders identify what it takes to be a winner and are, first, honest with themselves about whether they are doing that. This requires self-introspection and a willingness to admit your own mistakes and find other ways. This requires honesty and objectivity.

Some of us can be honest but harsh toward ourselves but unwilling to be either toward the team members we are leading. There is no single right way to deal with people. The sooner you accept that, the better. You can't judge people by what their colleague or predecessor does or did. Judge all of your charges on their own respective merits, be clear about your expectations, and determine how best to motivate them. You want to always feel as if you're getting the most out of your ability and your organization's potential. Don't be the one who looks back and has all the excuses when your way doesn't work. Brutally honest assessments guard against that tendency. So does #1 on my list. I want to win more than anybody I know, but I also keep Ws in perspective. If you're honest and true to yourself about your skill level, about your preparation level, about your goal, then you are more likely to see winning not as conquering another but getting the most out of what you bring to competition. You keep the bigger picture in mind, don't dwell on mistakes, and rise above things. That mindset will get you through some difficult times when perhaps winning is not happening as often as expected. If you are tasked with turning around a struggling organization, don't forget that.

TURNING AROUND A STRUGGLING ORGANIZATION

People ask me if it is more difficult to turn around a losing situation or to maintain a program once you have had some success. Clear intention and careful planning go into both, so I don't want to compare them. The process and considerations

HOW ORLANDO USED SPORT TO GET OUT OF A RUT

Mayor Buddy Dyer

Sometimes, an organization—or a city—doesn't have to be at rock bottom to consciously make a change toward better results. Orlando Mayor Buddy Dyer saw sport as a way to infuse life into an already vibrant and popular city. Dyer previously represented Orlando in the Florida Senate for 10 years, including 3 when he was the Senate Democratic leader. Dyer and wife Karen have two sons.

In 2003, I was elected mayor of Orlando, the biggest city in a Central Florida region known as the world's premier vacation destination.

While the tourist-facing side of our city was booming, the other half—the part where people lived, worked, played, learned, and raised families—needed help.

It wasn't that our community was suffering. We had thousands of new residents clamoring to move here year after year, the foundations of emerging industries outside of the tourism realm, and the kind of superior quality of life that comes when your city has more than 300 days of sunshine annually.

It was more as though our city was . . . stuck in a rut. Orlando was a relatively small city on the cusp of becoming a much bigger one, with all of the opportunities and challenges that come along with that kind of evolution.

Our downtown's population of residents, along with its number of retail and restaurant establishments, was in steady decline. How could we breathe life back into our center city and make it a more powerful economic and cultural hub for our region?

Greater Orlando was home to (or within a short drive of) the best higher education institutions in the state, yet year after year we watched our young people grow up, go to college, and then move elsewhere to pursue their dreams. What could we do to keep our homegrown talent here and attract the young people, quality employers, and residents of the future that would improve and diversify our economy and advance our quality of life?

Part of the answer was found in the most unlikely of places: sport and entertainment.

I had campaigned on a plan to revitalize Downtown Orlando and build a long-sought-after world-class performing arts center. Both of these, we believed, would be key to our overall economic strategy.

At the same time, the Orlando Magic was looking for a new arena and seriously considering leaving. A few blocks away, the once-great Florida Citrus Bowl stadium was decaying. These antiquated buildings were the reason major events had been bypassing Orlando for years. Yet public polls showed little support for spending public money on venues. Residents did like the idea of building a performing arts center, but any kind of a real plan to make it happen had struggled to gain traction.

An idea began to take shape. Sport and entertainment could complement our already world-leading tourism industry. Sport and entertainment venues would provide places for our residents to make memories with one another and strengthen the connections that our residents felt with their city. And, sport and entertainment could help attract and retain the young people who would be essential to Orlando's future.

We believed that if we focused on one venue at a time, competing interests would get territorial and oppose that venue. Faced with that polarized reality, we had an inkling of an idea. To bring these game-changing buildings into reality, we needed these different constituencies and jurisdictions to work together, to make compromises, and to develop a shared plan and vision. If we lumped all three venues together *and made them indivisible*, then the multiple constituencies would have to work together.

Before we could build buildings, we had to build partnerships. Lots of them.

It didn't happen overnight. And, it certainly didn't happen by accident. But, slowly and deliberately, our community rallied around a collective, regional vision of using sport and entertainment "venues" as the building blocks for a reinvention of Orlando.

We got stakeholders from across Central Florida to buy into our vision, and with each new partner our vision got bolder and more focused. We fought to help our partners think beyond decades-old partisan or jurisdictional challenges that had hampered projects like these before. A huge step was convincing the powerful tourism industry to allow a small portion of our Tourist Development Tax to be used to build these facilities.

Of course, nothing ever goes exactly as planned. In the middle of our effort, Orlando, and all of America, faced a recession that slowed our progress. But we endured. We worked through more challenges and stops and starts than I can possibly list.

In 2010, the first part of our vision became reality. The Amway Center (the new state-of-the-art basketball arena) opened. It was the first of a $1.1 billion trio of projects that would redefine our city. In 2014, the renovation of the Citrus Bowl was completed. And, later that year, our world-class performing arts center opened its doors.

A funny thing happened on the way to the completion of the venues. The venues themselves, and the relationships it took to make them reality, created momentum and a kind of "playbook" to accomplish other big-idea projects. We were able to secure a major league soccer team along with a privately funded soccer-specific stadium. We executed a plan to launch a downtown campus for the University of Central Florida that would be the educational centerpiece of a larger downtown neighborhood dedicated to innovation and technology called the "Creative Village." And, plans began to take shape for a full-scale sport and entertainment district, complete with a hotel, conference center, shopping and dining options, and event space.

If you just happened to be in Orlando in March of 2017, you would have seen the results of more than a decade of hard work and partnership on full display: NCAA Tournament games, one of the first home matches for Orlando City Soccer in its new stadium, the NFL's Pro Bowl, and WWE's WrestleMania at Camping World Stadium, some of the best concerts and plays imaginable—a true, unique sport and entertainment ecosystem.

Looking back, it took a special community to pull something like this off. I'm not sure I knew just how special Orlando was when our sport and entertainment idea was just that, an idea. But, looking forward, we know that our special mix of partnership, continuity of leadership, and resolve can turn just about any idea our community comes up with into reality.

The best part to this story is, we're not done yet. Not even close.

that I'm describing in this chapter are required in both situations, but I did want to make a comment about turning around a struggling organization.

When I arrived in Miami in 1970, the Dolphins had never achieved a winning season in their short history. In my first year as head coach, we went 10-4 and made the playoffs. The following season, we lost the Super Bowl. The season after that? Perfection. There were some good players when I arrived, but they didn't know how to win. I created an elaborate schedule when I took over, explaining that this is how we're going to do things. It shocked them at first. "They didn't know what hit them. They were walking around complaining, bitching and moaning about everything. And then we won. (After that) they bought into it, knowing that hard work equals success" (*850 Business Magazine*, para. 10).

EMBRACING THE SIDELINE

Shula's Steak House was not equivalent to my taking over the Dolphins. Legends was already doing well. However, the Grahams did an outstanding job in changing the restaurant, and the results were immediate. "He probably doesn't know this," Dave continued in that *Miami Herald* interview, "but the way that the decisions were made as to design and menu and style of service, what type of a steakhouse would we be—always came down to: What atmosphere would Coach Shula be comfortable in? And that says a lot about him. He's always wanted to do things in a first-class way, but not pretentiously, not over the top" (para. 12). I finally said yes, and our first Shula's Steak House opened in 1989. Sales increased fourfold in year 1. Dorothy was able to see that happen before she passed away in 1991 from breast cancer.

In the introduction to *Everyone's a Coach,* I write, "In the end, whether it's sports or business, winning and losing doesn't depend on trick plays or using new systems each week. The information your competition has is not that different from yours. So what are you going to use to win? It comes down to a matter of motivating people to work hard and prepare to play as a team. That's what really counts. In a word, it's coaching" (p. 12).

I add in that introduction that passion and enthusiasm are what drive all real success, and I can't give you that, in a book or otherwise. Neither can anyone else. If you have a desire to win and not quit at what you love, you're on the right track. If you want to build a team that feels the same, I hope this chapter has provided some insights on gaining that winning edge.

I believe there is nothing quite like game day. There's so much to think about, and intense emotions, with split seconds to make decisions that have major consequences for the outcome. Sometimes we hear that the sideline is for those people who are unable or unwilling to get into the game. I disagree. I say the sideline is not a place for the faint of heart (*850 Business Magazine*). If you are in charge, you monitor and cajole and assess and inspire and strategize all the time from the sideline or from the board room or over the phone. You have to want that responsibility and be willing to take all that comes with it—the pressure and the inevitable mistakes—and rise above it with a brutal honesty about yourself and what you are willing to do to accomplish what you want.

References

850 Business Magazine. 2010. "A Conversation with Don Shula." February 2010. www.850businessmagazine.com/February-2010/A-Conversation-with-Don-Shula/.

Blanchard, K., and Shula, D. 1995. *Everyone's a Coach: Five Business Secrets for High-Performance Coaching.* Grand Rapids, MI: Zondervan.

Morrisey, S. 2015. "The Winning Touch: Shula's Steak House Marks 25 Years in Business." *Miami Herald.* January 4, 2015. www.miamiherald.com/news/business/biz-monday/article5408922.html.

CHAPTER 27

Sustaining Excellence: From Stadiums to Stewardship

Bryan Trubey

Bryan Trubey is a principal with the global design firm HKS, responsible for all sport and entertainment projects. He is also a member of the firm's executive committee. Recognized as one of the 20 Most Influential People in Sports Facility Design, Architecture, and Development by *SportsBusiness Journal,* Bryan has worked with many of the giants of sport, including the Dallas Cowboys, Los Angeles Dodgers, Indianapolis Colts, Los Angeles Rams, Atlanta Braves, Milwaukee Brewers, Chicago White Sox, Texas Rangers, NBA Mavericks, and NHL Stars.

Bryan's most notable projects are regarded as the first to effectively integrate the sport environment with entertainment, creating timely, memorable spaces. This, combined with his focus on new ways to increase revenues, has resulted in his projects being considered the latest in innovative, experience-driven, and profitable sport destinations. He is a fellow of the American Institute of Architects (FAIA) as well as a member of the Texas Society of Architects and the Dallas chapter of the AIA.

Creating a great sport venue is more than designing a beautiful stadium. It's about generating excitement, building community, and developing a memorable experience. The most innovative stadiums in the world do all of these things and more. They are iconic symbols of their cities that bring people together for a common purpose. They also create value for their investors, owners, and communities.

The reason my firm, HKS, is continually selected to design premier sport venues is our innovative, value-driven approach. We delve into the DNA of the team, the town, and the culture and match the knowledge we gain with years of creating facilities that maximize return on investment in dollars and experience. We combine market research, brand analysis, programming flexibility, and architectural creativity to create a high-revenue venue that provides an emotional experience for users and visitors.

This process has been developed and refined since the early days of my career. I began my career with HKS in 1992. Since then, I've been fortunate enough to have had a hand in creating some of the most recognizable stadiums of the last 25 years. Projects like the Indianapolis Colts' Lucas Oil Stadium, the Dallas Cowboys' AT&T Stadium, the Minnesota Vikings' U.S. Bank Stadium, and the future home of the Rams in Los Angeles are arguably the most influential among them.

Before joining HKS, I worked in Hong Kong. At that time, in the late 1980s, Hong Kong was still a part of the United Kingdom, and the atmosphere encouraged a mindset of experimentation. There was nothing that you couldn't do, nothing that you couldn't accomplish. It was an incredibly exciting time and I immersed myself in the culture. Hong Kong Stadium was my expression of that period and place. That connection of culture and place has become the focus of my practice and work as an architect.

The reason we work to evolve the design of this building type is to increase the quality of the experience for the fans. With premium seating, clubs, retail spaces, and activated entertainment zones, we offer new ways for fans to support their teams while simultaneously providing owners and investors with new revenue streams.

DAWN OF MULTIUSE STADIUMS

Our creative focus to develop the new generation of multiuse facilities has inspired the next wave of design innovations that reinvent and improve this building type. AT&T Stadium has set the standard for this new generation of stadiums by earning more than half of its revenue from sources other than football. This new design strategy expands the usage of the facilities and provides a better return on investment for owners, operators, and taxpayers.

Every stadium we create is unique to its place and time. We research the location, the climate, the culture of a city before we ever put pen to paper because we believe this sort of major financial investment should result in something special. These places become iconic symbols of the city. Whether you are driving by them or flying over them or looking at them on TV, you know where you are just by looking. They do have some things in common—unparalleled access to the action on the field, be it an NFL game, a soccer match, or a concert, plus an enhanced fan experience provided through different types of seating environments that appeal to different types of fans, plus an array of amenities and state-of-the-art technology. We also make sure our designs are energy efficient with a minimal environmental impact.

Courtesy of Cowboys Stadium, LP.

AT&T Stadium.

COMBINING STRENGTHS TO CREATE
A FORCE FOR CHANGE

When we started the sport and entertainment group in 1992, HKS was already working on the ballpark in Arlington. As the architect of record, we were responsible for the technical construction drawings, but not the design. HKS excelled at documentation and delivery. I saw this as an incredible opportunity to merge my talents with the firm's technical prowess.

At the time, Dallas was one of the largest cities in the country yet saddled with a sport infrastructure that was one of the least-developed or redeveloped. I believed that if we could build premier buildings here, we could export our services nationally and internationally in the future. This is a competitive business. Our goal is to be the best at what we do. When we entered the sport business sector, we needed to make a bold step to differentiate ourselves from our competitors.

Of course, a successful stadium isn't achieved in a vacuum. It is the result of a major team effort between the city, the owners, the design and delivery team, and the community. During my first projects at HKS, I was introduced to John Hutchings, one of the five key leaders of our group today. John is a technical and management genius. With his help and the support of the rest of our team, we've developed our methodology by bringing design, culture, and business thinking together. By studying these closely, we developed the form and combination of our projects in a unique way and unlocked hidden value.

Extensive market research is key to what we do. We employ anthropologists, brand experts, and others to understand the unique attributes of the place and the people. We also examine what fans consider important about their experience. For example, at Miller Park in Milwaukee, which opened in 2001, we aimed to simulate major market revenues in a middle market. Through research, we learned that fans watching baseball avoided sitting farther back, regardless of what kind of accommodations you could offer. We moved suites and other premium seats closer to the field, farther down than had previously been done, to offer spectators the same views combined with a unique environment that could accommodate larger groups. It was a good compromise that helped us win the national competition for the project.

We have evolved this building type over the past 25 years. To achieve this, we formed a team of people whose varied perspectives and talents provided a combination of technical and creative know-how that enables unprecedented innovation. Our team has expertise in concepting, designing, and delivering exceptional sport and entertainment venues. But, the most rewarding part of our job is being in the stadium and seeing how the fans and the teams react to what we accomplished together.

CONVINCING THE CLIENT TO BUY INTO INNOVATION

Building a $1 billion stadium is a daunting task. We have to consider every aspect of the design and make sure it works for the city, the owners, the teams, and the fans. We see our role as a trusted advisor to our clients. Nothing moves forward without our clients investing in our ideas. We must demonstrate that the unprecedented aspects of our designs are worth the investment.

One of the things we discuss in our initial meetings with the owners is that we believe we can increase valuation of their franchise dramatically. We demonstrate how our design research and branding strategy has increased the value of our past clients' franchises and facilities. In this business, moving from number 27 in the NFL to number 10 or 11 is a difference of billions of dollars. We make it clear that we are offering far more than a design solution. We are offering a business solution in harmony with the owners' vision for their franchise.

In Minneapolis, we deconstructed the city's stadium program to explain to the client how we could add value. The first part of putting the program back together was convincing the client that a retractable roof wasn't the right investment for the project. Our experience has proven that there are certain operational constraints of retractable roofs that relate to climate. The strong wind conditions in the Twin Cities and heavy snowfall overlap with the football season. These factors minimize the utility of a retractable roof. One of the big struggles with the previous stadium, the Metrodome, was removing snow from the roof. In fact, heavy snow caused the Metrodome roof to collapse in 2010.

To find a better solution, we looked to our in-house research group to develop a strategy responsive to the history, the culture, and the climate. What we came up with through this process was a structure with a single ridgeline and a steeply

Kevin Demoff

Kevin Demoff is enthusiastic thinking about the innovative possibilities of the Los Angeles Rams' new stadium. Demoff is in his ninth year as chief operating officer and executive vice president of football operations with the Rams. In this capacity, Demoff serves as the team's top front office executive and liaison to owner and chairman, Stan Kroenke, on all organizational matters. After serving on the working group that helped Kroenke return the Rams—Los Angeles' original professional sport team—home to LA, Demoff is now playing a significant role in delivering on Kroenke's vision to design and construct the 298-acre sport and entertainment district in Inglewood that will serve as the future home of the Rams.

As a Los Angeles native I am particularly proud to have spearheaded our franchise's return. The Rams were in LA for 49 years before leaving. I think coming back was the right decision at the right time for our franchise. To be welcomed back by the people of LA, to see the response in 2017 from the fans—I don't think anyone will ever feel good about leaving a market, but we are very excited about the return to Los Angeles.

It's amazes me what Hollywood Park can become. We have hopes for a transcendent stadium and a surrounding sport entertainment district both designed to harness the power of connecting with the fan. Now, with the Chargers joining as cotenants we have an iconic two-team stadium at the heart of a terrific market. In Los Angeles, tides lift all boats. There are two professional teams from every major sport league and two major university programs; there's the beach, there's Hollywood, you have diverse demographics, and so on. These conditions make everyone better; for us it's about learning. We are in an environment where we can learn from all those potential competitors, which makes us smarter and better in what we're doing. I try to spend as much time as I can outside of sport to get new ideas. The most innovative ideas our staff comes up with originate from other leagues, other sports, or other industries. It's important to think of our job as being in the content business, technology sector, and hospitality industry, and then bring those industries' best practices back to sport.

I think for us to come back and be successful in Los Angeles we have to have strong brand equity locally and worldwide. We want to be a global brand; that's one of the reasons we played in London and why we are planning to play in Mexico and in China. There is an on-field component needed to truly become an iconic brand, but we can supplement that with things within our control: engaging fans, creating a world-class in-game experience, providing diverse programming, giving back to the community, and so on.

In this business you have to wear many hats, but the best leaders are able to compartmentalize skills, and for me that manifests as being the best teammate I can be. If I can be a great teammate for every member in our organization, then the better teammates we all can be as a staff, as an organization, as a real estate organization, as a content provider, and more. This maximizes the success we are going to have.

Courtesy of Corey Gaffer. © 2016

U.S. Bank Stadium.

pitched roof. It's a very simple response to buildings that have been built in northern climates for thousands of years. We also covered the entire sun-facing south side of the roof with ethylene tetrafluoroethylene (ETFE), a clear material that has been revolutionary in building design.

ETFE offers the advantage of bringing the outdoors inside without having to incorporate a retractable roof. Combining this material with the single ridgeline solved the major challenges of snow removal while creating the unique look of the building. We also added five of the world's tallest pivoting doors that can be opened to allow ventilation without compromising the utility of the stadium. The result is a stadium that feels current and relevant in keeping with the culture of Minnesota and the Vikings' franchise. It's a striking design that has become an icon for the city viewed by millions in person and on television. This quality of investment should result in a globally recognizable brand expression.

SPURRING THE EVOLUTION OF AN INDUSTRY

Building a premier stadium a few decades ago meant building a building that was very similar to existing facilities with a few branding aspects that reflected the

GAME CHANGER
CREATING A COMMUNITY GATHERING PLACE: U.S. BANK STADIUM

Trip Boswell

Trip Boswell explains how U.S. Bank Stadium was the result of many discussions with the client, the Minnesota Vikings. Boswell is an associate principal at HKS, where he works with top-level corporate clients on innovative and experiential revenue generation for sport facilities.

Creating a branded environment is more than just applying a team's logo and colors to the walls of a stadium. It's imbuing the whole environment with the spirit of the team and the place. We have a team of cultural anthropologists at HKS who have proven invaluable in helping us understand local cultures and communities.

U.S. Bank Stadium is a prime example of this thinking. In this new stadium, we wanted to tell more than just the story of the Vikings. We wanted to embrace all the distinct cultures that mingle in Minneapolis. The building has clear roots in Scandinavian culture, but it also has features that relate to the large Hmong population that immigrated to the area from China.

Minnesotans are passionate about the outdoors, so we worked with the local park system to make sure the stadium wouldn't just be inwardly focused. The five massive doors that open to the plaza welcome visitors but also serve to blur the line between the indoor and outdoor "rooms."

The multipurpose U.S. Bank Stadium is a perfect example of commercial and cultural convergence. It was designed to accommodate a variety of events in the bowl, in the amenity area, and on the public plaza, thus expanding its use beyond sport to private and public events.

Used with permission of Trip Boswell.

franchise. The areas around these buildings were often neglected by the developers and design firms involved. Today, HKS is often responsible not only for the stadium, but also for creating a master plan for the whole surrounding district that will encourage additional development that extends the life of the project.

When designing the new stadium for the Vikings, the key was to build a stadium that would be the exact opposite of the previous facility, the Metrodome. The old stadium was built without regard to the surrounding area and it caused that part of town to languish, even though it's directly adjacent to the downtown core of Minneapolis.

For the new Vikings stadium, one of our key points was that for a billion-dollar stadium, we believe you should get $4 to $6 billion in adjacent real estate activity and development. That number comes from our understanding of increasing real estate values over time. To deliver on this, we focused equally on what we call the outdoor room and the indoor room. We designed an immense, three-block-long plaza in front of the building. It creates this incredible gathering place in conjunction with the stadium. The synergy between the two becomes far greater than either would possess individually—essentially creating a beachfront for real estate development. Within a year of completion, there is already more than $2.5 billion in economic activity around the new stadium.

It has become crucial to the efficacy of modern stadiums to design them with a host of capabilities that maximize their impact and profitability. For HKS, that strategy began with AT&T Stadium. It was a radical idea at the time, and it has made the Cowboys' stadium one of the best entertainment venues on the planet.

We took that principle a step further with the Vikings stadium. The Metro-dome had been hosting high school and college baseball events for years, and it was very important to the community in Minneapolis that the tradition continue. This wasn't the first NFL stadium to accommodate a baseball diamond, but existing designs lacked optimal seating, required lengthy breakdown and setup periods that limited scheduling, or both. We solved this challenge by designing a large section of retractable seating. This design element improved the stadium's practical use for multiple purposes while also improving the quality of the experience for the fans.

Designing iconic NFL stadiums is something we are proud of. But we are equally proud of the many collegiate, high school, soccer, and spring training facilities we have designed. When we designed the Salt River Fields at Talking Stick, it became not only the first MLB spring training complex to be built on Native American land, but also the first Leadership in Energy and Environmental Design (LEED)-certified facility of its type.

The Estadio Corona in Torreon, Mexico, represents another major accomplishment. On top of being Mexico's premier, multipurpose stadium, it includes an education center open to the local community. It set a new standard for other international stadiums in safety, comfort, and amenities.

Our interest is not limited to U.S.-based opportunities. We are working with owners, teams, and municipal governments all over the world. From Canada to Mexico, Europe to Asia to the Middle East, we are pursuing opportunities that will dramatically change the way people experience sport.

LEADING AN INDUSTRY

Ours is a culture of continuous improvement. We learn from every new assignment and adapt what we have learned and what we know works. Our position as one of the most influential architecture and design firms in the world comes with a heightened sense of responsibility to make a positive impact on the clients and communities we serve.

We are working to incorporate sustainable measures that mitigate and minimize the environmental impact of our monumental structures, both in construction and in operation. One of the largest contributors to the carbon footprints of these facilities is the manufacturing and transport of the materials from which they are built. With Salt River Fields, we looked at how we could minimize the impact of this process. We were fortunate that our client put an emphasis on environmental stewardship. The spring training complex for the Arizona Diamondbacks and Colorado Rockies was constructed with raw materials harvested from the land of the Salt River Pima–Maricopa Indian Community. By using indigenous materials located within a short distance of the site, we minimized the environmental impact and created an aesthetic that complemented the natural environment.

By employing passive heating and cooling techniques in the design of our stadiums, we can also reduce the amount of energy they consume. A common challenge for typical dome-shaped roofs in colder climates is the density and weight of the roof needed to compensate for the higher wind and snow loads. By designing a single ridge in the roof of the Vikings' facility, we created a large loft where heat pools together and melts the snow. This, combined with the use of ETFE, helped reduce snow accumulation, allowing us to save costs and material on the construction of the roof and supporting structure. We also redistributed that heat at a lower energy cost than it would otherwise require to heat the building. On the flip side of that, we used passive cooling on a monumental scale in our design of the Corps Physical Training Facility at the Virginia Military Institute.

We are focused on pioneering new ways to attract fans to live games in an era when they can have a phenomenal experience at home with modern entertainment systems. Jerry Jones has been an early adopter of many of our innovations, and he's been one of our key clients in addressing the competition of broadcast sporting events. The center-hung video board at AT&T Stadium has been a game-changing experience. This screen technology combined with the live game creates an experience that can't be replicated at home and offers fresh appeal to fans.

These innovations are more than an effort to stay one step ahead of the competition. They are firmly rooted in the belief in corporate responsibility, for the benefit of fans, owners, and the environment. The means are every bit as important as the ends for HKS, and we've proved that responsibility and success are not mutually exclusive.

FLOURISHING WITH THE COMMUNITY

The process of delivering a monumental building can span many years from initial planning to opening day. Staying focused throughout that period requires a perseverance that comes from a deep commitment and passion for what these buildings represent. As a team, we put a large value on the impact of our designs. With that, there is a moral commitment to doing the right thing.

OBSERVATIONS FROM YEARS WORKING IN "THE FUN BUSINESS"

Pat Gallagher

Pat Gallagher is no architect, but he knows that many aspects of a sport facility come together to create community and a purpose for people to come out to an event. Gallagher has spent more than four decades in what he calls "the fun business," and is best known for his key roles with the San Francisco Giants and the Super Bowl 50 Host Committee.

I've spent my entire career in some form of entertainment. From my first job in high school as an hourly show host at Sea World in San Diego, through many years as the marketing–idea guy for the San Francisco Giants, to my role in helping secure and deliver the milestone 50th Super Bowl for the San Francisco Bay Area, I reflect on my working life in what I like to call "the fun business."

■ Nobody ever paid to see me do what I do, but I made a life being paid to help create what others pay to see. I'm a lucky guy.

■ The live event business is like an iceberg. The audience sees just the show on the tiny tip above the waterline, but not the years of planning or massive numbers of talented people who work enormous hours below the surface. I made my living working inside the iceberg, as one of many pulling the strings behind the scenes to make it all happen. Whether it's in the theme parks, stadiums, theaters, or concert venues, putting on the "show" is so much more than what you see in front of you as the audience.

■ Anything presented live has drama. Will the team win or lose? Will anybody get hurt or worse? If your show is important enough, a legion of experts who make their living predicting what will happen will be on hand to dissect and chronicle every brilliant move or pratfall as it is revealed. If it's not important enough, nobody will bother to talk about it, which means nobody cares, which is not good.

■ In a live show, nobody knows exactly what will happen until it actually happens, and that's the irresistible beauty of it all.

■ During my years with the Giants, I liked to joke that the main difference between working for a bad baseball team and a bad show is that when you realize the show is bad and people stop coming to see it, at least you can pull the plug and shut it down. In baseball, no matter how badly your team plays, you have to finish out the season. As a marketing guy, if the team you are trying to sell is bad, you hope the extent of the badness won't be revealed until late in the season, after most of the tickets have been sold. But, thankfully, after the season ends you get to start over. Unless things get *really bad* and you get fired. Getting fired is not the end of the world. For some, it's just the beginning.

■ Sometimes all of the stars line up at exactly the right time and you get to be part of a championship organization. For every champion there are scores of others who, despite their best efforts, fall by the wayside during the chase and wind up looking up at the champs. You get to have your time, and then it is someone else's time. Nobody can be the champions or the best every year.

I wish you well in whatever part of the fun business you aspire to become involved in.

Used with permission of Pat Gallagher.

We have a firmly rooted commitment to the relationships we create between our clients and their patrons. It's about providing a community gathering place offering remarkable new experiences that create lifelong memories for the people who use them. It's about providing new value for the investors, owners, and the communities involved. An anthropological and a savvy business focus enable us to create buildings that will not only last, but flourish in the communities they engage.

I've spent half of my life focusing on these values in design. What I've learned is that there is value in this approach for nearly any project in any industry. Whether as a fan, a player, or an owner, participating in sport and entertainment is about being part of a community and creating something larger than life. There are no ceilings to the value we can add by looking to culture for inspiration.

EPILOGUE

Rick Horrow

I ended my first book, *When the Game Is on the Line,* with a list of 10 items that I dubbed the Horrow Principles. "No matter where I travel or what enterprise I undertake, I rely heavily on certain principles devised from trial, error, necessity, inspiration, and desperation. The following have served me well, and can be a guide for any kind of deal-making" (Horrow and Bloom 2003, p. 192).

What I realize now, some 15 years later, is that those principles align with many of the same points that other leaders in the sport business espouse in their contributions here. My journey is as unique as that of each of the 100-plus other people whom you have just met and learned from in this book, just as yours is. Those journeys should be celebrated for their uniqueness, but we also shouldn't lose sight of the commonalities found within them. It is validating to me when I see that people I respect are acknowledging similar priorities and discoveries.

I certainly hope you gained useful information and inspiring ideas to apply in your work from the time you spent in the large conference room I described in the preface. *You* get to decide what is valuable and worth adding to your toolbox and your personal philosophy and SWOT analysis. But I would like to share some of my takeaways, and share where they intersect with the principles I identified. By doing this, I am attempting a form of inductive reasoning at the conclusion of our time together. I would argue that the approach is similar to what Bernie Swain, Washington Speakers Bureau cofounder, does in *What Made Me Who I Am,* and Tim Ferriss does in his bestseller *Tribe of Mentors: Short Life Advice from the Best in the World.* That is, seek out the high achievers you know and be curious about what goes on in their heads. This doesn't provide a neat and tidy ending—inductive reasoning rarely does—but it may help you to structure some of your thoughts. It did for me.

These were the principles I identified back then:

1. Look at imagination as reality.
2. Always do things a certain way. Unless you don't.
3. Get up off the canvas.
4. Bring strangers, even enemies, to the table.

NASCAR WHIZ KID LEARNS THE TWO Rs EARLY IN HIS CAREER

Michael Nichols II

Michael Nichols II, known as the "NASCAR Whiz Kid" in racing circles, has learned at a young age not to be afraid to get off the sidelines. Nichols II served as a *Sports Illustrated* Kid Reporter for the 2017 to 2018 school year. During that time, he was able to cover Tom Coughlin's Jay Fund golf outing, the one-year anniversary of the opening of the United States Tennis Association National Campus, the 2018 NFL Pro Bowl, and numerous NASCAR events. In his young career, he has already cohosted Daytona 500 Media Day with the Orlando Fox TV affiliate, presented a Snapchat takeover of Daytona International Speedway, and is now serving as a contributor to NASCAR's Acceleration Nation, the official NASCAR digital experience for kids. When he is not at the track, Michael resides in Ormond Beach, Florida—the town just north of Daytona Beach—with his mom, dad, and younger sister, ZZ.

The NASCAR Whiz Kid with Dale Earnhardt Jr.

Courtesy of Michael Nichols.

The idea of following some of the most iconic names in the history of the sport business is admittedly intimidating—especially when I'm asked to comment on what the sport industry will look like over the next 50 years. After all, what could a 12-year-old kid offer to a discussion that these accomplished leaders with a lifetime of experience and proven success have not already said?

While I certainly don't pretend to be able to project the future direction of the sport business any more than these icons, perhaps my inclusion in this book will serve as a helpful lesson for others, and a reminder for myself of what I will need to do to be successful over the next 50 years of my career.

In the spring of 2017, I was fortunate enough to be selected to serve as one of 15 *Sports Illustrated* Kid Reporters nationwide for a one-year assignment writing for the SIKids.com website. My primary passion has always been NASCAR (I'm known at the track as the "NASCAR Whiz Kid"), but this opportunity allowed me to branch out and cover other sporting events such as the NFL's Pro Bowl. That is where I introduced myself to this book's editor, Mr. Horrow.

I did not know him. My dad pointed him out in the press box that day and encouraged me to introduce myself. I went back to my chair, put back on the black blazer that accompanies my signature checkered flag bow tie, and made my way over to say hello. Mr. Horrow was very gracious and asked me what I was doing at the Pro Bowl. When I told him I was covering the event for *Sports Illustrated Kids,* he soon afterward told me about this book, and then immediately offered me the chance to contribute with my thoughts on the future of the sport industry. It happened so fast, I really didn't know if he was kidding! But here I am, and maybe appropriately, this one incident illustrates the two words that have served me well in my two years in the sport industry that I believe will serve anyone for the next 50 years: *reputation* and *relationships.*

Whatever sporting event I'm attending, I make sure to dress up in my bow tie and present a professional image. Because I am surrounded by adults, it helps create the first impression that I belong and am not just a kid who has wandered into a place he's not supposed to be. When asked, I am able to produce a business card with my likeness that shows I belong. I make a point of behaving so as to make sure that I am not in the way of the "true professional," and am there as a valued contributor. This is where I have built my reputation. Small interactions like those with Mr. Horrow have formed relationships that hopefully become friendships to last a lifetime. Introducing myself to sport industry executives and treating everyone I meet with respect has produced countless opportunities and a lifetime of memories already at a young age. My biggest challenge now is to make sure to continually maintain the relationships and reputation that I have built in just two years to serve me in my career, whatever it may be, for the next 50 years.

5. Finesse the powerful ego.
6. Follow the seven-minute rule.
7. Get off the sidelines.
8. Find the positive in the negative.
9. Ratchet, ratchet, ratchet.
10. Don't let criticism get you down.

Among the recurring themes I identified in these pages were these:

1. Have a vision of the end result, even if you don't know how you will get there. It's necessary for yourself when obstacles arise, and for others you will need to buy into or support any challenge worth striving for. We saw this repeatedly, with Tom Ricketts and Don Shula changing the cultures in their organizations; Bob Kain and IMG creating new events, products, and markets; or a wonderful anecdote from Tony Ponturo about reintroducing the Budweiser Clydesdales to the World Series.

2. Be flexible. This is critical if you are to achieve your goals (see #1). It's also a necessary complement to the single-minded drive that visionaries must have. Jerry Colangelo, Gary Bettman, Peter Moore, and Donald Dell all expressed this in various ways, balancing a cool head to find solutions in red-hot situations.

3. Be willing to make mistakes. If you think you will be the first person not to make any, you are sorely mistaken. If you think you can be a success without making them, you are also mistaken. Ask Oliver Luck and Larry Lucchino. Sometimes a presumed failure can become arguably your greatest success. Ask Butch Buchholz.

4. Look for win-win results. The media and society focus on the present at the expense of the legacy building that true leaders and entrepreneurs want to achieve. Your career and your organization are more important than immediate bragging rights. The power of a win-win mentality can lead to greatness, as Donald Dell, Lyn St. James, Rick Burton, Ron Norick, Stephen Jones, and others recognized.

5. Have a sense of humor. It gets you through your mistakes (see #3) and it helps keep your work in proper perspective. Plenty of serious businesspeople in these pages, including Andy Dolich, Derrick Hall, Bob Kain, and Donald Dell, also found ways to laugh at themselves and the craziness of life.

6. Be in forward motion. Action begets action, and you can't know with certainty how it will all eventually play out. You see this constantly in this book. MVP Index cofounders Shawn Spieth and Kyle Nelson acted on a technological need. Ted and Zach Leonsis leap into new ventures as a market is building for a product, and Mark Lazarus makes sure media coverage is keeping up with audience needs. Look at Jerry Colangelo's progression in the Valley—a place that initially appealed to him mostly because of the weather. He made it his home, a place he cared for greatly, and he made it better. Some objectives didn't occur for decades, and some things that he created he didn't even know he wanted. But first, he had to move.

7. Tap into passion, both your own and that of the stakeholders—especially fans—that support your organization. Passion is intensely personal. It's a terribly overused term. But it is inextricably linked with sport, no matter what level you are talking about. If you didn't see the passion emanating from these pages, you weren't paying attention. Checking into his level of passion is what Jack Nicklaus asks himself before he takes on any venture. It's why Stephen M. Ross overpaid for the Dolphins, and why the Jones family so relentlessly pushes the Cowboys brand. It's why Joseph R. Castiglione Sr. is meticulous in choosing partners to work with who can meet the passion of his Sooner fans. We all know of examples where unbridled passion got people into trouble, but passion coupled with sound business sense is an equation for success.

8. Create your breaks. You can always find reasons why something can't be done, or why you aren't in a position to contribute, or why you should push a decision or initiative down the road. Judy Sweet pushed for break-throughs when many chose to ignore the importance of creating a more diverse sport world. Tom Ricketts didn't wait until the Cubs were for sale before putting himself in a position to buy them. Donald Dell didn't let a lack of leverage keep his client from getting the best contract he could.

9. Embrace the importance of selling. Whether selling yourself or your product, this skill permeates any business strategy. Another way of saying this might be to use your available leverage. Situations vary widely, so you can't rely on always having leverage. But you can rely on the knowledge that you can sell whatever you have to sell, with integrity and confidence. Jack Nicklaus' chapter punctuated that point, and I hope you internal-ized the importance of identifying your values, from the personal SWOT analysis exercise in chapter 1 to chapters by Robin Harris, Don Garber, Paul Tagliabue, Deborah A. Yow, and Bryan Trubey.

10. Learn to listen. To your mentors, to your fans, to your employees, and notably, your critics. You won't always take their advice, as Kevin Warren did with his grandmother, but respect their experiences. That may seem obvious, especially as you just read this book's nearly 400 pages so you could listen to what established leaders had to say. But forget it at your peril, or else you may fail in your role to help your successors or become arrogant and isolated. Practically every chapter in this book acknowledges the value of listening.

There are nuances between the two lists, but it's not too difficult to create a one-word bridge for each of the corresponding numbers of the two lists:

1. Vision
2. Flexibility
3. Resilience
4. Collaboration
5. Perspective
6. Urgency
7. Passion
8. Preparation
9. Selling
10. Listening

Marketing experts would have a field day trying to pull these 10 words together into a coherent framework, but I'm going to simplify it (see figure E.1). Consider a word that ties these impact words together. Throughout the book, you heard

360

A PRODUCER'S PERSPECTIVE

Tanner Simkins

Tanner Simkins has discovered lessons during his work as a producer with the editor that sound similar to the advice of contributors to this book. Simkins is founder and CEO of Complete SET Agency, a full-service sport entertainment firm that works with multinational brands, athlete entertainers, and accredited investors. Simkins holds degrees from the University of Miami and Columbia University.

I have worked with Rick Horrow almost daily for the past three years. This manifests itself in many different ways: business development, digital strategy, content creation, and so on. But it is in my role as producer in that digital content mix that I have learned the most. I am a believer in what I call the law of proximity, *be around those who do what you want to do best*. During my time working with Rick, I have been present for each of his marquee interviews: C-suites of global companies, team owners, and league commissioners, unicorn movers and shakers, and the most tenured leaders in sport and business. Naturally, with 350+ interviews under our belt together, my *proximity* to the most sought-after business heavyweights has taught me invaluable lessons I will carry with me during my career. Here are some common threads:

- Prepare to make sacrifices.
- Be thoroughly prepared.
- Respect the past but continue to innovate.
- Defy expectations.
- Let the passion flow.
- Embrace diversity.

If you keep positioning yourself in the same room with the best in the industry, sooner or later you are going to get a chance to show what you can do. It's crucial that when that time comes you are able act on what you learned. Actively listening to business front runners is half the effort; you have to employ the inside advice you soaked up. That will put you on your own path to success.

---

repeatedly about the power, the capital, the passion, the strategizing, and the resources tied up in a brand, and the relevant verbs associated with the term: launching, building, rebranding, rehabilitating. We even devoted a part of the book to building your branding skill sets. As the sport industry was about to explode in the 1970s, branding was primarily a business school concept. Marketers, public relations agencies, corporations, consultants, those folks were

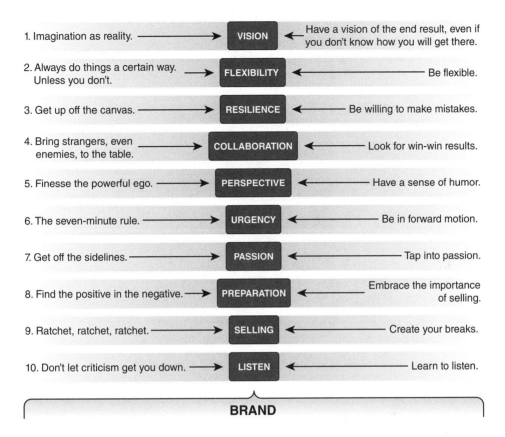

Figure E.1   Ten takeaways.

starting to get it. But outside of a few individuals, the sport industry really wasn't yet thinking strategically about brands to any large degree. The term was barely used then. That, to put it mildly, is no longer true.

Brands permeate the sport industry, and you must be aware of what they represent if you want to build up your business. Sport is particularly relevant in that regard, but business in general in the modern world requires it. Everybody now has a brand: athletes, leagues, conferences, teams. People now are much clearer about how important it is to sell and be consistent with the principles espoused in a brand. To endure, you must appreciate that reality. That is why brands are emphasized so much more today. Branding can easily be overlooked as merely another business buzzword, but when properly understood, branding is far greater than that. The term has reached outsized importance over the past half century for good reason. Look again at that list of 10 words and see if you agree with me that *brands* and *branding* are the terms that tie them together. Maybe we can say that what we've learned more than anything is that the trillion-dollar business of sport, while more creative, diverse, and entrepreneurial than ever, depends on the same principles for success as anything else. It just took 50 years for us to find that out.

I hope this list of principles is an enduring takeaway from this book. The list informs not just the sport business, and business and deal making more generally, but also success and the creation of a meaningful life. I am reminded of bestselling author Earl Nightingale's brilliant and enduring definition of success—"the progressive realization of a worthy goal or ideal" (Nightingale 2013, p. 6)—and Pat Williams' not too shabby definition of his own that he advocated in chapter 7—"When your greatest talent intersects with your strongest passion." All I would add is that both of these quotes suggest the critical impact of working hard and embracing the necessarily fluid process that is part of any goal worth pursuing. The takeaways are where your 100-plus mentors must leave you behind; if you desire success, putting them into action is your job now.

References

Ferriss, T. 2017. *Tribe of Mentors: Short Life Advice from the Best in the World.* New York: Houghton Mifflin Harcourt.

Horrow, R., and Bloom, L. 2003. *When the Game Is on the Line.* New York: Da Capo Press.

Nightingale, E. 2013. *The Strangest Secret.* San Francisco: Rough Draft Printing.

Swain, B. 2016. *What Made Me Who I Am.* Brentwood, TN: Post Hill Press.

Index

About the Editors

Rick Horrow

Rick Horrow, JD, is a leading expert in the business of sport and has orchestrated over 100 deals worth more than $20 billion. The CEO of Horrow Sports Ventures (HSV), he has served as a sport business analyst for Fox Sports, Bloomberg TV, *Bloomberg Businessweek*, Reuters, NBC, National Public Broadcasting, and the BBC. As the leading commentator on sport business and as a well-connected entrepreneur, he has access to many of the top names in sport, including commissioners, owners, general managers, coaches, and athletes. His clients have included some of the biggest organizations and companies in the world of sport and business: NFL, NHL, MLB, NASCAR, PGA, Great White Shark Enterprises, Cisco Systems, Golden Bear International, Enterprise Rent-A-Car, LPGA, and MLS. He has also been managing editor of sports business for the U.S. Library of Congress. Horrow is nicknamed the Sports Professor, thanks to his time spent as a visiting expert on sport law at Harvard Law School, where he earned his degree.

Rick Burton, MBA, is the David B. Falk Endowed Professor of Sport Management in the David B. Falk College of Sport and Human Dynamics at Syracuse University. Prior to his appointment at Syracuse in 2009, he served as the chief marketing officer for the U.S. Olympic Committee at the 2008 Beijing Summer Olympics. He has also previously served as the commissioner of the National Basketball League, which played in Australia, New Zealand, and Singapore. From 1995 to 2003, Burton led the University of Oregon's Warsaw Sports Marketing Center to international prominence. He has written for the *New York Times*, *Wall Street Journal*, *SportsBusiness Journal*, *Sports Illustrated*, *Sport Business International*, *Stadia*, and *Ad Age*. He has had numerous research manuscripts published in academic journals and has authored two books on sport business and marketing.

Photo by Andrew Burton.

Myles Schrag, MS, is a former acquisitions and developmental editor at Human Kinetics, responsible for its sport management book list for 13 years. He is a cofounder of Soulstice Publishing and the author of four books. His freelance credits include *Sports Illustrated*, *Publishers Weekly*, *Runner's World Online*, and *Trail Runner*. He earned an MS in kinesiology from University of Illinois at Urbana-Champaign. He lives in Flagstaff, Arizona.

© Human Kinetics

All photos courtesy of Rick Horrow.